W9-BCA-831

CCNP SWITCH 642-813

Official Certification Guide

David Hucaby, CCIE No. 4594

Cisco Press

800 East 96th Street

Indianapolis, IN 46240

CCNP SWITCH 642-813 Official Certification Guide

David Hucaby, CCIE No. 4594

Copyright© 2010 Pearson Education, Inc.

Published by
Cisco Press
800 East 96th Street
Indianapolis, IN 46240 USA

Printed in the United States of America

Seventh Printing: September 2012

Library of Congress Cataloging-in-Publication Data:

Hucaby, Dave.

  CCNP SWITCH 642-813 official certification guide / David Hucaby.

    p. cm.

  ISBN-13: 978-1-58720-243-8

  ISBN-10: 1-58720-243-3

  1. Virtual LANs—Examinations—Study guides. 2. Telecommunications engineers—Certification. 3. Cisco Systems, Inc.—Examinations—Study guides. I. Title.

  TK5103.8.H8327 2010

  004.6076—dc22

                                 2009050384

Warning and Disclaimer

This book is designed to provide information about the CCNP SWITCH Exam (Exam 642-813) for the CCNP Routing and Switching certification. Every effort has been made to make this book as complete and as accurate as possible, but no warranty or fitness is implied.

The information is provided on an "as is" basis. The authors, Cisco Press, and Cisco Systems, Inc. shall have neither liability nor responsibility to any person or entity with respect to any loss or damages arising from the information contained in this book or from the use of the discs or programs that may accompany it.

The opinions expressed in this book belong to the author and are not necessarily those of Cisco Systems, Inc.

Trademark Acknowledgments

All terms mentioned in this book that are known to be trademarks or service marks have been appropriately capitalized. Cisco Press or Cisco Systems, Inc., cannot attest to the accuracy of this information. Use of a term in this book should not be regarded as affecting the validity of any trademark or service mark.

Corporate and Government Sales

The publisher offers excellent discounts on this book when ordered in quantity for bulk purchases or special sales, which may include electronic versions and/or custom covers and content particular to your business, training goals, marketing focus, and branding interests. For more information, please contact: **U.S. Corporate and Government Sales**   1-800-382-3419   corpsales@pearsontechgroup.com

For sales outside the United States please contact: **International Sales**   international@pearsoned.com

Feedback Information

At Cisco Press, our goal is to create in-depth technical books of the highest quality and value. Each book is crafted with care and precision, undergoing rigorous development that involves the unique expertise of members from the professional technical community.

Readers' feedback is a natural continuation of this process. If you have any comments regarding how we could improve the quality of this book, or otherwise alter it to better suit your needs, you can contact us through email at feedback@ciscopress.com. Please make sure to include the book title and ISBN in your message.

We greatly appreciate your assistance.

Publisher: Paul Boger

Associate Publisher: Dave Dusthimer

Executive Editor: Brett Bartow

Managing Editor: Patrick Kanouse

Development Editor: Andrew Cupp

Senior Project Editor: Tonya Simpson

Editorial Assistant: Vanessa Evans

Book Designer: Louisa Adair

Composition: Mark Shirar

Indexer: Tim Wright

Business Operation Manager, Cisco Press: Anand Sundaram

Manager Global Certification: Erik Ullanderson

Copy Editor: Keith Cline

Technical Editors: Geoff Tagg and Sean Wilkins

Proofreader: Apostrophe Editing Services

About the Author

David Hucaby, CCIE No. 4594, is a lead network engineer for the University of Kentucky, where he works with healthcare networks based on the Cisco Catalyst, ASA, FWSM, and VPN product lines. David has a Bachelor of Science degree and Master of Science degree in electrical engineering from the University of Kentucky. He is the author of several Cisco Press titles, including *Cisco ASA, PIX, and FWSM Firewall Handbook*, Second Edition; *Cisco Firewall Video Mentor*; and *Cisco LAN Switching Video Mentor*.

David lives in Kentucky with his wife, Marci, and two daughters.

About the Technical Reviewers

Geoff Tagg runs a small U.K. networking company and has worked in the networking industry for nearly 30 years. Before that, he had 15 years of experience with systems programming and management on a wide variety of installations. Geoff has clients ranging from small local businesses to large multinationals and has combined implementation with training for most of his working life. Geoff's main specialties are routing, switching, and networked storage. He lives in Oxford, England, with his wife, Christine, and family, and is a visiting professor at nearby Oxford Brookes University.

Sean Wilkins is an accomplished networking consultant and has been in the field of IT since the mid-1990s, working with companies such as Cisco, Lucent, Verizon, and AT&T and several other private companies. Sean currently holds certifications with Cisco (CCNP/CCDP), Microsoft (MCSE), and CompTIA (A+ and Network+). He also has a Master of Science degree in information technology with a focus in network architecture and design, a Master's certificate in network security, a Bachelor of Science degree in computer networking, and an Associate of Applied Science degree in computer information systems. In addition to working as a consultant, Sean spends a lot of his time as a technical writer and editor for various companies.

Dedications

As always, this book is dedicated to the most important people in my life: my wife, Marci, and my two daughters, Lauren and Kara. Their love, encouragement, and support carry me along. I'm so grateful to God, who gives endurance and encouragement (Romans 15:5), and who has allowed me to work on projects like this.

Acknowledgments

It has been my great pleasure to work on another Cisco Press project. I enjoy the networking field very much, and technical writing even more. And more than that, I'm thankful for the joy and inner peace that Jesus Christ gives, making everything more abundant.

Technical writing may be hard work, but I'm finding that it's also quite fun because I'm working with very good friends. Brett Bartow, Drew Cupp, and Patrick Kanouse have given their usual expertise to this project, and they are appreciated.

I am very grateful for the insight, suggestions, and helpful comments that Geoff Tagg and Sean Wilkins contributed. Each one offered a different perspective, which helped make this a more well-rounded book and me a more educated author.

Contents at a Glance

On This Book's CD:

Contents

Command Syntax Conventions

The conventions used to present command syntax in this book are the same conventions used in the IOS Command Reference. The Command Reference describes these conventions as follows:

- **Boldface** indicates commands and keywords that are entered literally as shown. In actual configuration examples and output (not general command syntax), boldface indicates commands that are manually input by the user (such as a show command).

- *Italic* indicates arguments for which you supply actual values.

- Vertical bars (|) separate alternative, mutually exclusive elements.

- Square brackets ([ ]) indicate an optional element.

- Braces ({ }) indicate a required choice.

- Braces within brackets ([{ }]) indicate a required choice within an optional element.

Foreword

CCNP SWITCH 642-813 Official Certification Guide is an excellent self-study resource for the CCNP SWITCH exam. Passing this exam is a crucial step to attaining the valued CCNP Routing and Switching certification.

Gaining certification in Cisco technology is key to the continuing educational development of today's networking professional. Through certification programs, Cisco validates the skills and expertise required to effectively manage the modern enterprise network.

Cisco Press Certification Guides and preparation materials offer exceptional—and flexible—access to the knowledge and information required to stay current in your field of expertise or to gain new skills. Whether used as a supplement to more traditional training or as a primary source of learning, these materials offer users the information and knowledge validation required to gain new understanding and proficiencies.

Developed in conjunction with the Cisco certifications and training team, Cisco Press books are the only self-study books authorized by Cisco and offer students a series of exam practice tools and resource materials to help ensure that learners fully grasp the concepts and information presented.

Additional authorized Cisco instructor-led courses, e-learning, labs, and simulations are available exclusively from Cisco Learning Solutions Partners worldwide. To learn more, visit http://www.cisco.com/go/training.

I hope that you find these materials to be an enriching and useful part of your exam preparation.

Erik Ullanderson
Manager, Global Certifications
Learning@Cisco
January 2010

Introduction: Overview of Certification and How to Succeed

Professional certifications have been an important part of the computing industry for many years and will continue to become more important. Many reasons exist for these certifications, but the most popularly cited reason is that of credibility. All other considerations held equal, the certified employee/consultant/job candidate is considered more valuable than one who is not.

Objectives and Methods

The most important and somewhat obvious objective of this book is to help you pass the Cisco CCNP SWITCH exam (Exam 642-813). In fact, if the primary objective of this book were different, the book's title would be misleading; however, the methods used in this book to help you pass the SWITCH exam are designed to also make you much more knowledgeable about how to do your job. Although this book and the accompanying CD have many exam preparation tasks and example test questions, the method in which they are used is not to simply make you memorize as many questions and answers as you possibly can.

The methodology of this book helps you discover the exam topics about which you need more review, fully understand and remember exam topic details, and prove to yourself that you have retained your knowledge of those topics. So this book helps you pass not by memorization, but by helping you truly learn and understand the topics. The SWITCH exam is just one of the foundation topics in the CCNP Routing and Switching certification, and the knowledge contained within is vitally important to consider yourself a truly skilled routing and switching engineer or specialist. This book would do you a disservice if it did not attempt to help you learn the material. To that end, the book can help you pass the SWITCH exam by using the following methods:

- Covering all the exam topics and helping you discover which exam topics you have not mastered

- Providing explanations and information to fill in your knowledge gaps

- Supplying exam preparation tasks and example networks with diagrams and sample configurations that all enhance your ability to recall and deduce the answers to test questions

- Providing practice exercises on the exam topics and the testing process through test questions on the CD

Who Should Read This Book?

This book is not designed to be a general networking topics book, although it can be used for that purpose. This book is intended to tremendously increase your chances of passing the Cisco SWITCH exam. Although other objectives can be achieved from using this book, the book is written with one goal in mind: to help you pass the exam.

The SWITCH exam is primarily based on the content of the Cisco SWITCH course. You should have either taken the course, read through the SWITCH coursebook or this book, or have a couple of years of LAN switching experience.

Cisco Certifications and Exams

Cisco offers four levels of routing and switching certification, each with an increasing level of proficiency: Entry, Associate, Professional, and Expert. These are commonly known by their acronyms CCENT (Cisco Certified Entry Networking Technician), CCNA (Cisco Certified Network Associate), CCNP (Cisco Certified Network Professional), and CCIE (Cisco Certified Internetworking Expert). There are others, too, but this book focuses on the certifications for enterprise networks.

For the CCNP Routing and Switching certification, you must pass exams on a series of CCNP topics, including the SWITCH, ROUTE, and TSHOOT exams. For most exams, Cisco does not publish the scores needed for passing. You need to take the exam to find that out for yourself.

To see the most current requirements for the CCNP Routing and Switching certification, go to Cisco.com and click Training and Events. There you can find out other exam details such as exam topics and how to register for an exam.

The strategy you use to prepare for the SWITCH exam might be slightly different from strategies used by other readers, mainly based on the skills, knowledge, and experience you already have obtained. For instance, if you have attended the SWITCH course, you might take a different approach than someone who learned switching through on-the-job training. Regardless of the strategy you use or the background you have, this book is designed to help you get to the point where you can pass the exam with the least amount of time required.

How This Book Is Organized

Although this book can be read cover to cover, it is designed to be flexible and allow you to easily move between chapters and sections of chapters to cover only the material that you need more work with. The chapters can be covered in any order, although some chapters are related and build upon each other. If you do intend to read them all, the order in the book is an excellent sequence to use.

Each core chapter covers a subset of the topics on the CCNP SWITCH exam. The chapters are organized into parts, covering the following topics:

Part I: New CCNP Exam Approaches

- **Chapter 1, "The Planning Tasks of the CCNP Exams"**—This chapter explains the roles of a networking professional in the context of the Cisco Lifecycle Model, where network tasks form a cycle over time. The CCNP SWITCH exam covers real-world or practical skills that are necessary as a network is designed, planned, implemented, verified, and tuned.

Part II: Building a Campus Network

- **Chapter 2, "Switch Operation"**—This chapter covers Layer 2 and multilayer switch operation, how various content-addressable memory (CAM) and ternary content-addressable memory (TCAM) tables are used to make switching decisions, and how to monitor these tables to aid in troubleshooting.

- **Chapter 3, "Switch Port Configuration"**—This chapter covers basic Ethernet concepts, how to use scalable Ethernet, how to connect switch and devices together, and how to verify switch port operation to aid in troubleshooting.

- **Chapter 4, "VLANs and Trunks"**—This chapter covers basic VLAN concepts, how to transport multiple VLANs over single links, how to configure VLAN trunks, and how to verify VLAN and trunk operation.

- **Chapter 5, "VLAN Trunking Protocol"**—This chapter covers VLAN management using VTP, VTP configuration, traffic management through VTP pruning, and how to verify VTP operation.

- **Chapter 6, "Aggregating Switch Links"**—This chapter covers switch port aggregation with EtherChannel, EtherChannel negotiation protocols, EtherChannel configuration, and how to verify EtherChannel operation.

- **Chapter 7, "Traditional Spanning Tree Protocol"**—This chapter covers IEEE 802.1D Spanning Tree Protocol (STP) and gives an overview of the other STP types that might be running on a switch.

- **Chapter 8, "Spanning-Tree Configuration"**—This chapter covers the STP root bridge, how to customize the STP topology, how to tune STP convergence, redundant link convergence, and how to verify STP operation.

- **Chapter 9, "Protecting the Spanning Tree Protocol Topology"**—This chapter covers protecting the STP topology using Root Guard, BPDU Guard, and Loop Guard, and also how to use BPDU filtering and how to verify that these STP protection mechanisms are functioning properly.

- **Chapter 10, "Advanced Spanning Tree Protocol"**—This chapter covers Rapid Spanning Tree Protocol (RSTP) for Rapid PVST+ and Multiple Spanning Tree (MST) Protocol.

- **Chapter 11, "Multilayer Switching"**—This chapter covers interVLAN routing, multilayer switching with Cisco Express Forwarding (CEF), and how to verify that multilayer switching is functioning properly.

Part III: Designing Campus Networks

- **Chapter 12, "Enterprise Campus Network Design"**—This chapter covers different campus network models, hierarchical network design, and how to design, size, and scale a campus network using a modular approach.

- **Chapter 13, "Layer 3 High Availability"**—This chapter covers providing redundant router or gateway addresses on Catalyst switches and verifying that redundancy is functioning properly.

Part IV: Campus Network Services

- **Chapter 14, "IP Telephony"**—This chapter covers how a Catalyst switch can provide power to operate a Cisco IP Phone, how voice traffic can be carried over the links between an IP Phone and a Catalyst switch, QoS for voice traffic, and how to verify that IP Telephony features are functioning properly.

- **Chapter 15, "Integrating Wireless LANs"**—This chapter covers different approaches to integrating autonomous and lightweight wireless access points into a switched campus network.

Part V: Securing Switched Networks

- **Chapter 16, "Securing Switch Access"**—This chapter covers switch authentication, authorization, and accounting (AAA); port security using MAC addresses; port-based security using IEEE 802.1x; DHCP snooping; and dynamic ARP inspection.

- **Chapter 17, "Securing with VLANs"**—This chapter covers how to control traffic within a VLAN using access lists, implementing private VLANs, and monitoring traffic on switch ports for security reasons.

Part VI: Final Exam Preparation

- **Chapter 18, "Final Preparation"**—This chapter explains how to use the practice exam CD to enhance your study, along with a basic study plan.

There is also an appendix that has answers to the "Do I Know This Already" quizzes and an appendix that tells you how to find any updates should there be changes to the exam.

Each chapter in the book uses several features to help you make the best use of your time in that chapter. The features are as follows:

- **Assessment**—Each chapter begins with a "Do I Know This Already?" quiz that helps you determine the amount of time you need to spend studying each topic of the chapter. If you intend to read the entire chapter, you can save the quiz for later use. Questions are all multiple choice, to give a quick assessment of your knowledge.

- **Foundation Topics**—This is the core section of each chapter that explains the protocols, concepts, and configuration for the topics in the chapter.

- **Exam Preparation Tasks**—At the end of each chapter, this section collects key topics, references to memory table exercises to be completed as memorization practice, key terms to define, and a command reference that summarizes relevant commands presented in the chapter.

Finally, there is a CD-based practice exam. The companion CD contains a practice CCNP SWITCH exam containing a bank of test questions to reinforce your understanding of the book's concepts. This is the best tool for helping you prepare for the actual test-taking process.

The CD also contains the Memory Table exercises and answer keys that come up at the end of each chapter.

How to Use This Book for Study

Retention and recall are the two features of human memory most closely related to performance on tests. This exam-preparation guide focuses on increasing both retention and recall of the topics on the exam. The other human characteristic involved in successfully passing the exam is intelligence; this book does not address that issue!

This book is designed with features to help you increase retention and recall. It does this in the following ways:

- By providing succinct and complete methods of helping you decide what you recall easily and what you do not recall at all.

- By giving references to the exact passages in the book that review those concepts you most need to recall, so you can quickly be reminded about a fact or concept. Repeating information that connects to another concept helps retention, and describing the same concept in several ways throughout a chapter increases the number of connectors to the same pieces of information.

- Finally, accompanying this book is a CD that has exam-like questions. These are useful for you to practice taking the exam and to get accustomed to the time restrictions imposed during the exam.

When taking the "Do I Know This Already?" assessment quizzes in each chapter, make sure that you treat yourself and your knowledge fairly. If you come across a question that makes you guess at an answer, mark it wrong immediately. This forces you to read through the part of the chapter that relates to that question and forces you to learn it more thoroughly.

If you find that you do well on the assessment quizzes, it still might be wise to quickly skim through each chapter to find sections or topics that do not readily come to mind. Look for the Key Topics icons. Sometimes even reading through the detailed table of contents will reveal topics that are unfamiliar or unclear. If that happens to you, mark those chapters or topics and spend time working through those parts of the book.

CCNP SWITCH Exam Topics

Carefully consider the exam topics Cisco has posted on its website as you study, particularly for clues to how deeply you should know each topic. Beyond that, you cannot go wrong by developing a broader knowledge of the subject matter. You can do that by reading and studying the topics presented in this book. Remember that it is in your best interest to become proficient in each of the CCNP subjects. When it is time to use what you have learned, being well rounded counts more than being well tested.

Table I-1 shows the official exam topics for the SWITCH exam, as posted on Cisco.com. Note that Cisco has occasionally changed exam topics without changing the exam number, so do not be alarmed if small changes in the exam topics occur over time. When in doubt, go to Cisco.com and click Training and Events.

Table I-1—CCNP SWITCH Exam Topics

Exam Topic	Part of This Book Where Exam Topic Is Covered
Implement VLAN-based solution, given a network design and a set of requirements	
Determine network resources needed for implementing VLAN-based solution on a network.	Part II, "Building a Campus Network" Chapters 2–10
Create a VLAN-based implementation plan.	
Create a VLAN-based verification plan.	
Configure switch-to-switch connectivity for the VLAN-based solution.	
Configure loop prevention for the VLAN-based solution.	
Configure access ports for the VLAN-based solution.	
Verify the VLAN-based solution was implemented properly using **show** and **debug** commands.	
Document results of VLAN implementation and verification	
Implement a security extension of a Layer 2 solution, given a network design and a set of requirements	
Determine network resources needed for implementing a security solution.	Part V, "Securing Switched Networks" Chapters 16–17
Create a implementation plan for the security solution.	
Create a verification plan for the security solution.	
Configure port security features.	
Configure general switch security features.	
Configure private VLANs.	
Configure VACL and PACL.	
Verify the security solution was implemented properly using **show** and **debug** commands.	
Document results of security implementation and verification.	

Table I-1—CCNP SWITCH Exam Topics

Exam Topic	Part of This Book Where Exam Topic Is Covered
Implement switch-based Layer 3 services, given a network design and a set of requirements	
Determine network resources needed for implementing a switch-based Layer 3 solution. Create an implementation plan for the switch-based Layer 3 solution. Create a verification plan for the switch-based Layer 3 solution. Configure routing interfaces. Configure Layer 3 security. Verify the switch-based Layer 3 solution was implemented properly using **show** and **debug** commands. Document results of switch-based Layer 3 implementation and verification.	Part II, "Building a Campus Network" Chapter 11
Prepare infrastructure to support advanced services	
Implement a wireless extension of a Layer 2 solution. Implement a VoIP support solution. Implement video support solution.	Part IV, "Campus Network Services" Chapters 14–15
Implement high availability, given a network design and a set of requirements	
Determine network resources needed for implementing high availability on a network. Create a high availability implementation plan. Create a high availability verification plan. Implement first-hop redundancy protocols. Implement switch supervisor redundancy. Verify high-availability solution was implemented properly using **show** and **debug** commands. Document results of high-availability implementation and verification.	Part III, "Designing Campus Networks" Chapters 12–13

For More Information

If you have any comments about the book, you can submit those via the Ciscopress.com website. Just go to the website, select Contact Us, and type in your message. Cisco might make changes that affect the CCNP Routing and Switching certification from time to time. You should always check Cisco.com for the latest details. Also, you can look to http://www.ciscopress.com/title/ 1587202433, where we publish any information pertinent to how you might use this book differently in light of future changes from Cisco. For example, if Cisco decides to remove a major topic from the exam, it might post that on its website; Cisco Press will make an effort to list that information as well via an online updates appendix.

Part I: New CCNP Exam Approaches

This chapter illuminates some of the hands-on and practical skills that have become increasingly tested on the CCNP SWITCH exam. As you work through the chapter, notice how planning and design functions are integral to a network professional's job.

CHAPTER 1

The Planning Tasks
of the CCNP Exams

Perspectives on CCNP Exam Topics Related to Planning

Cisco introduced the Cisco Certified Networking Professional (CCNP) certification back in 1998. Since then, Cisco has revised the exams and related courses on several occasions. Each major revision adjusted the scope of topics by expanding and adding some topics while shrinking or removing other topics. At the same time, the depth of coverage has changed over time, too, with the depth of coverage for each topic either becoming deeper or shallower.

The most current version of CCNP, corresponding with the 642-813 exam about which this book is written, narrows the breadth of topics included in CCNP compared to the previous version of CCNP. Cisco removed several sizable topics from CCNP, such as quality of service (QoS), wireless LANs (WLAN), and many security topics. In other words, the new CCNP squarely focuses on routing and switching.

Although the smaller number of CCNP topics might seem to make CCNP easier, two other factors compensate so that it is still a challenging, difficult, and therefore respected certification. First, the exams appear to require a higher level of mastery for most topics, making a clear distinction between the knowledge learned in CCNA and the advanced coverage in CCNP. Second, that mastery is more than just technical knowledge—it requires the ability to plan the implementation and verification of a network engineering project.

Many CCNP SWITCH exam topics list the word *plan*, collectively meaning that the CCNP candidate must approach problems in the same manner as a network engineer in a medium- to large-sized business. For example, you might find the following skills in such a workplace environment:

- The ability to analyze a network design document and extrapolate that design into the complete detailed implementation plan, including completed configurations for each router and switch

- The ability to analyze a design document and discover the missing items—questions that must be answered before a detailed implementation plan (including configurations) can be completed

- The ability to perform a peer review on another engineer's implementation plan, to discover weaknesses and omissions in the planned configurations, and to update the implementation plan

- The ability to build a verification plan that lists the specific **show** commands and command options that list key pieces of information—information that directly either confirms or denies whether each planned feature has been implemented correctly

- The ability to write a verification plan that can be understood and used by a less-experienced worker, allowing that worker to implement the change and to verify the changes worked, off-shift, when you are not on-site

- The ability to perform a peer review on another engineer's verification plan, to discover which key design features are not verified by that plan, and to discover inaccuracies in the plan

This chapter discusses the whole area of implementation and verification planning for the CCNP SWITCH exam, and it covers how you should prepare for these exam topics. By considering the ideas in this chapter first, you should have the right perspectives to know how to use the tools that help you add the planning skills and perspectives needed for the exam.

CCNP Switch Exam Topics That Do Not Require the CLI

Cisco lists a set of exam topics for each CCNP exam. These exam topics follow a general type of phrasing, typically starting with an action word that defines what action or skill you must do for the exam. (Unfortunately, this style seldom gives much insight into the breadth or depth of coverage of a given topic.)

For example, consider the basic topic of Layer 2 VLANs. Table 1-1 lists the topics or skills related to VLANs as found in the CCNP SWITCH exam blueprint.

Table 1-1   *CCNP SWITCH Exam Topics Related to VLAN*

Implement VLAN-based solution, given a network design and a set of requirements.
Determine network resources needed for implementing a VLAN-based solution on a network.
Create a VLAN-based implementation plan.
Create a VLAN-based verification plan.
Configure switch-to-switch connectivity for the VLAN-based solution.
Configure loop prevention for the VLAN-based solution.
Configure access ports for the VLAN-based solution.
Verify the VLAN-based solution was implemented properly using **show** and **debug** commands.
Document results of VLAN implementation and verification.

The four gray-highlighted exam topics focus on tasks that you can complete by using the commands available from the command-line interface (CLI). Specifically, you need to be able to create a VLAN, connect the VLAN from switch to switch, configure the Spanning Tree Protocol to prevent Layer 2 loops over the VLAN, and configure switch ports to use the VLAN where end users are connected. After those things are accomplished, you need to be able to use the CLI to verify that your configurations are correct working properly. The technical information you will need to study about configuring and using VLANs is presented in Chapter 4, "VLANs and Trunks."

Notice that the other nonshaded topics begin with words such as *determine*, *create*, and *document*. These represent the "bigger picture" skills necessary to plan and carry out a successful implementation. Although these topics may require knowledge of Catalyst IOS commands, these tasks do not require any hands-on activities from the CLI. Instead, when doing these tasks in real life, you would more likely be using a word processor rather than a terminal emulator.

Planning Exam Topics

After a first glance through the CCNP SWITCH exam topics (listed in the "Introduction"), you might think that the new CCNP certification has been changed significantly—and you therefore need to significantly change how you prepare for CCNP. However, by focusing on the following aspects of your study, you should be well prepared for the CCNP exams in general and the CCNP SWITCH exam in particular:

- As with any other Cisco career certification exam, understand the concepts and the configuration commands.

- As with any other Cisco career certification exam, master the verification tasks and troubleshooting (**show** and **debug**) commands.

- *Unlike* most other Cisco career certification exams, spend some time thinking about the concepts, configuration, and verification tasks as if you were writing or reviewing a network design document, a network project implementation plan, or a verification plan.

In this list, the first two tasks are what most people normally do when preparing for a Cisco exam. The third item represents the new type of preparation task, in which you simply think about the same concepts, commands, and features, but from a planning perspective.

Why is Cisco adding more career-oriented tasks into the CCNP exams? Because, over time, a networking professional may be called upon to deal with every aspect of a network. Tasks related to switch configuration tend to be snapshots in time, where some feature or function is needed right now. If a longer time period is examined, the same network professional must deal with many other networking aspects—such as planning for configuration commands, collaborating with other network professionals, and verifying work.

Cisco uses the prepare, plan, design, implement, operate, optimize (PPDIOO) network lifecycle approach to describe the life of a network over time. Figure 1-1 shows how the lifecycle is broken down into six phases, denoted by the letters in the PPDIOO acronym. Generally, after a network has gone from the prepare phase all the way through the operate phase, it is functional and begins supporting business activities. Some time later, some new features or new policies may need to be introduced, or the network might need to scale to support new growth. At that point, the organization needs to prepare for the new additions, and the lifecycle starts all over.

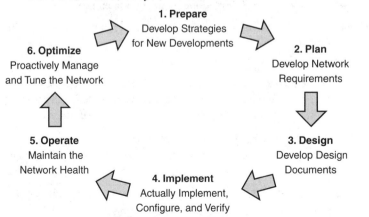

Figure 1-1 *The Cisco PPDIOO Network Lifecycle*

Relating the Exam Topics to a Typical Network Engineer's Job

The need to plan, and the need to document those plans, increases as the size of the organization increases. Even if only one person at a company cares about the router and switch infrastructure, that engineer probably does not want to be writing configurations at 2 a.m. Sunday morning when the change window begins. In addition, the company probably does not want to rely on one engineer's knowledge of its network, especially if that engineer becomes unavailable (for example, if the engineer leaves the company or takes any time off).

When the staff grows to three or four people, particularly when some of those people work different shifts, the need to document the design, implementation, and verification/operational procedures becomes more important. That team of people probably needs to agree on a common vision or design, and it needs to be based on collaboration and teamwork, with some oversight from peers.

For perspective, this section examines a medium- to large-sized company, along with some of the planning tasks done in the real world—the same kinds of tasks listed as part of the CCNP SWITCH exam topics.

A Fictitious Company and Networking Staff

Think about a company (perhaps the one where you already work) and its structure or organization. If the company is small or based in one location, the network might be rather small and have a modest number of users. The company might have a server room or a small data center.

If the company is large, it might be spread over many geographic locations, with many different campuses and remote sites. The data center might be located in one large space, or it may be distributed across several redundant locations. The company might have an enterprisewide IP telephony deployment, video over IP, network security devices, a growing teleworker community, multiple Internet connections, and several network connections to partner companies.

Regardless of the size of the company, the IT needs are basically the same. Consider the various roles in the network and the type of work done by the people in those roles:

- Help desk personnel may perform diagnosis of network health, taking a general problem statement from a customer down to a specific issue (for example, that a user's device is not responsive or reachable).

- Operations staff may be the second level of support for problems, both reacting to calls from the help desk and monitoring the network proactively. The operations staff also often implements changes on behalf of the engineering team during off-shift hours.

- The network engineering team may be the third level of support for problems, but they typically focus on project work, including the detailed planning for new configurations to support new sites, new network features, and new sites in the network.

- The network designers may actually log in to the network devices much less than the operations and engineering teams, instead focusing on gathering requirements from internal and external customers, translating those requirements into a network design, and even doing proof-of-concept testing—but leaving the details of how to deploy the design for all required sites to the network engineering team.

Of course, the number of individuals in each of these roles varies across different organizations. In a small organization, maybe only a single network designer and single network engineer are required, with perhaps two or three people as network operations specialists—not enough for 24×7 coverage with a specialist, but close. The help desk position may simply require most people to have the same networking skill set, depending on the size of the shop. On the other end of the scale, in the largest companies, the staff might consist of several departments of network engineers.

In any event, someone has to perform each of the functions to properly support the organization. Your job as a network professional or network engineer is to work independently, while providing plans, documentation, and verification to other IT professionals.

The Design Step

Next, consider the basic work flow when a new network project happens, new sites are added, or any noticeable change occurs. The network designer first develops the requirements and creates a plan. That plan typically lists the following:

- Project requirements
- Sites affected
- Sample configurations
- Traffic analysis
- Results from proof-of-concept testing
- Dependencies and assumptions
- Business requirements, financials, management commitments

Many other items might also be included.

The network designer often uses a peer review process to refine and confirm the design. The designer cannot simply work in a vacuum, define the design, and then toss the design document to network engineering to be deployed. In smaller shops, a peer review may simply be two or three people standing around a dry erase board discussing the project. In larger shops, the design peer review probably requires a thorough written document be distributed before the meeting, with attendance from network engineering, operations, and the help desk, and with formal sign-off required.

Implementation Planning Step

The next step in the life of the project occurs when a network engineer takes the approved design document from the design team and begins planning the implementation of the project. To do this task, the network engineer must interpret the example and general cases described in the design document, and develop a very specific implementation plan that lists all significant tasks and actions by each group and on each device. The design document, for instance, may show example cases of typical branch offices, a typical district (medium sized) site, and so on. The network engineer must then determine what must be done on every device to implement the project and must document those details in an implementation plan.

For example, a company might plan to deploy IP telephony across a campus network. The design document might list the following basic requirements:

■ Specific switch models with Power over Ethernet (PoE) at each remote office

■ The convention of placing all phones at a site in one VLAN/subnet, and all PCs in a second VLAN/subnet

■ VLAN trunking between the access layer switches and the distribution switches

■ A particular Catalyst IOS software version and feature set

■ High availability features designed to provide maximum uptime for telephone calls

■ QoS policies that give voice traffic premium treatment over other types of traffic

After a thorough review of the design, the network engineer then develops an implementation plan that includes items such as the following:

■ A list of all campus locations, with notations of which require a switch hardware upgrade (for PoE support) and which do not

■ Total numbers of switches to be ordered, prices, and delivery schedules

■ A table that lists the specific VLANs and subnet numbers used at each location for the phone and PC VLANs and subnets

■ The IP address ranges from each subnet that needs to be added to the DHCP servers configurations for dynamic address assignment

■ A list of the switches that require a Catalyst IOS software upgrade

■ Annotated sample configurations for typical access layer switches, including VLAN trunking, high availability, and QoS configuration commands

The preceding list represents the types of items that would be documented in the implementation plan for this project. The list is certainly not exhaustive but represents a smattering of what might end up in such a plan.

The implementation plan probably has many informal reviews as the network engineer works through the plan. In addition, larger shops often conduct a peer review when the plan is more fully developed, with network designers, operations, and fellow network engineers typically included in the review.

Verification Planning Step

The design step tells us "this is what we want to accomplish," whereas the implementation planning step tells us "this is exactly what we will do, and when, to accomplish this design." The verification plan explains how to verify or confirm that the implementation plan actually worked.

The verification plan is used with the actual implementation of the changes in the network. More often that not, the operations staff follows the implementation plan, or more specific instructions for each individual change window, taking the appropriate actions. The engineer who implements the changes then uses the verification plan to determine whether the changes met the requirements.

The most important part of the verification plan, at least as far as the CCNP exam is concerned, is to identify the commands that confirm a correct and functioning implementation. For example, suppose IP telephony is being implemented. The following list describes some of the actions that might be listed in the verification plan:

- After copy/pasting or entering the configuration changes in a switch, use the **show interfaces status** command to confirm connected devices and their speed and duplex modes.

- Use the **show cdp neighbor** command to verify active Cisco IP Phone identities.

- Use the **show mac-address-table dynamic interface** command to verify the MAC addresses of Cisco IP Phones and connected PCs.

- Observe the IP Phone display to confirm that the phone has obtained an IP address and has downloaded its firmware.

- Make test calls from IP Phones.

The important part of the verification plan lists the specific commands to be used (and at what point in the implementation process) and what output is expected. In practice, this plan should also include output samples, spelling out what should be seen when correct and what output would alert the operations staff that the change did not work correctly.

Documenting Implementation Results

After a set of changes is attempted or implemented during a change window, some documentation must be changed based on the results. Any deviation from the implementation plan should also be recorded for future reference.

Summary of the Role of Network Engineers

The CCNP certification focuses on skills required to do the job of a network engineer as generally described in this chapter. By interpreting the CCNP SWITCH exam topics, a CCNP network engineer

- *Does not* create the design document

- *Does* participate in design peer reviews, finding oversights, asking further questions that impact the eventual implementation, and confirming the portions of the design that appear complete and valid

- *Does* plan and document the specific configurations for each device, documenting those configurations in the implementation plan so that others can add the configuration to various devices

- *Does* participate in peer reviews of the implementation plans written by fellow network engineers, finding omissions, caveats, and problems.

- *Does* create the verification plan that others use to verify that the changes worked as planned when implemented off-shift

- *Does* perform peer reviews of other engineers' verification plans

- *Does* verify that the changes worked as planned when implemented

Now that you know a bit more about the role of a network engineer, the following section brings the discussion back to the best ways to prepare for the CCNP SWITCH exam.

How to Prepare for the Planning Topics on the Exam

Can you create a networking implementation plan for each technology area on a CCNP exam? Can you create a verification plan for those same technologies? According to the CCNP exam blueprint, these skills are now tested on the CCNP exams. These tasks normally involve large amounts of time devoted to project planning and documentation—things that are not practical during a timed Cisco exam.

Even though the exam might not ask you to literally create a plan, you do need the skills to perform those same tasks. The new CCNP SWITCH course doesn't have much content directly related to planning, other than some common-sense advice. In the past, the CCNP exams were limited to the scope of the corresponding course. With the new exams, such as 642-813, this isn't necessarily the case.

To come up with an implementation plan, you must begin with some goals or objectives. These are generally based on the following things:

- **Business requirements**—What does the business need out of the network? What policies must be met?

- **Business constraints**—How much will the planned solution (hardware and labor) cost?

- **Technical requirements**—Which switch features should be leveraged? How should the switch configurations be carried out? What limitations are there?

As network professionals, we might or might not have a role in identifying these requirements, but we do have a role in carrying out the work. Usually, our work follows this sequence:

Step 1.   **Plan** the network architecture and every switch feature that will be used. This can be done as a detailed project plan or as something sketched on a napkin over lunch. The idea is to know what needs to be done beforehand.

Step 2.   **Implement** the plan with switches, cables, protocols, and features. The CCNP exams have traditionally focused on implementing things.

Step 3.   **Verify** that the implementation works and meets the objectives of the plan.

Now hold that up against the new 642-813 exam blueprint. There are several broad categories where you can find the words "implement" and "verify"—always with the words "create...a plan," as in the following examples:

Create a VLAN-based implementation plan
Create a VLAN-based verification plan
Create an implementation plan for the Security solution
Create a verification plan for the Security solution
Create an implementation plan for the Switch-based Layer 3 solution
Create a verification plan for the Switch-based Layer 3 solution
Create a High Availability implementation plan
Create a High Availability verification plan

So how would you "create a plan" on a Cisco exam? You might get multiple-choice questions that ask for a best approach to a problem. More likely, you might get one of those complex scenario questions. You know—the ones where you have to read a lengthy explanation in one window, squint at the network diagram in another window, and interact with some switches in some other windows, all on one small screen.

The key here is with the scenario description. It's nothing more than a huge word problem that lays out things like business requirements, business constraints, and a list of goals to reach. Even the network diagram becomes a part of the project definition. As you read through the scenario and look over the diagram, you have to **create an implementation plan** in your mind.

The scenarios don't give you a sequence of things to do; instead, they present a bunch of things to accomplish. You must figure out what specific features you'll need, what steps you'll need to configure for each feature, which switch you'll have to visit to type in configuration commands, and so on.

Even as you work through a scenario on the exam, you should spend time **creating a verification plan** so you can test and make sure each feature you have configured actually works as it should. Otherwise, whatever you typed into the switch emulators might not be correct and might not earn you valuable points.

Why did Cisco move toward such broad strokes on the exam blueprint? One possibility is to test your knowledge of the many Cisco IOS features and which ones can be used to accomplish something. For example, the exam blueprint covers the following types of plans:

■ VLAN-based plans
■ Security plans
■ Switch-based Layer 3 plans
■ High Availability plans

Those don't say much about specific switch features, commands, or protocols. Instead, you should think of each one as a big toolbox; you need to know which tools are in each toolbox so you can formulate a plan of attack on any given situation. As the old saying goes, not every problem needs a hammer.

Here is a sample scenario that should help you get a feel for this process. Suppose an exam question has a scenario text as follows, and a network diagram as shown in Figure 1-2:

> A company has a network as shown in the network diagram. Switches A and B form the core, while C and D act as distribution switches. Switches A through D are already configured with working links and routing protocols.
>
> Switch E is added into the access layer. It is connected to switches C and D by two uplinks each. Each pair of uplinks should be joined together as a single logical link using a standards-based approach.
>
> Switch E needs to support two distinct groups of users in the Accounting and Engineering departments, to be placed on VLAN 10 and 20, respectively. Each VLAN needs to have a highly available gateway address in the distribution layer, using the .1 address in the appropriate subnet. The network should be configured such that the Accounting users normally pass over the link between switches C and E, while Engineering users pass over the link between D and E.

Do not change the routing configuration on switches A, B, C, or D, other than to advertise the new Accounting and Engineering subnets. Make sure that all uplinks are functioning and that users in the Accounting and Engineering subnets can ping the 192.168.199.10 server located in the data center.

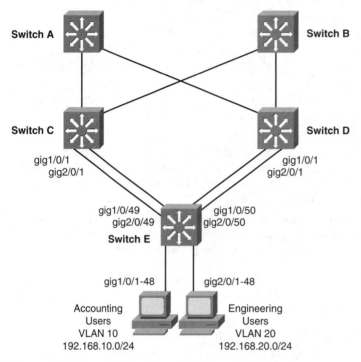

Figure 1-2 *Sample Exam Scenario Network Diagram*

Whew! That scenario covers plenty of ground, and it's really just one question on the exam! Notice that the scenario didn't really specify any switch features or protocols to be used. Instead, you have to put on your thinking cap and develop an implementation plan—fast! Remember that the exam clock is ticking. Your plan should include the following things:

■   **Create VLANs**—VLAN 10 for Accounting and VLAN 20 for Engineering

■   **VLAN extent**—The VLANs should exist on Switch E, where the users live, and also on C and D, where the gateways and routing protocols live.

■   **EtherChannels**—Bundle one pair of uplinks between C and E and another pair between D and E. For a standards-based EtherChannel, use LACP.

■   **Trunks**—VLANs 10 and 20 will need to be carried between Switches C and E and between D and E.

■   **Layer 3 interfaces**—You'll need an interface vlan10 and an interface vlan20 to provide Layer 3 connectivity for the user subnets. Those will be configured on Switches C and D.

■   **HSRP**—To get highly available gateways on both VLANs 10 and 20, you'll need to configure two different HSRP groups.

- **HSRP load balancing**—The two user groups need to normally pass over different up-links. You'll need to tune the HSRP priorities so that the gateways are split across the two distribution switches.

- **Routing**—You will need to add the new subnets into the **network** commands for the preconfigured routing protocols on switches C and D.

The scenario also mentions some things to test and verify. Your mental verification plan can include things like the following:

Function to Verify	Example Commands	Verify on Switch
VLAN creation	**show vlan**	C, D, E
Working Ether-Channels toward Switches C and D	**show etherchannel summary**	C, D, E
VLAN trunking	**show interfaces** *type/num* **trunk**	C, D, E
Layer 3 interfaces	**show interfaces vlan10** **show interfaces vlan20** -OR- **show ip interface brief**	C, D
HSRP configuration and load balancing	**show standby brief**	C, D
Routing	**show ip route**	C, D
List	**ping 192.168.199.10 source vlan10** **ping 192.168.199.10 source vlan20**	C or D

To test whether the server is reachable from each user subnet, a regular, simple ping won't do. Instead, it's better to use extended pings so that the source address can be set to the Layer 3 interface that sits on each user subnet.

This book contains several tools to help you prepare for the planning topics and exam scenarios. At the end of each chapter, an "Exam Preparation Tasks" section presents a reminder of key topics covered in the chapter. The key topics can help you locate major features and functions that can be used to plan a switch configuration project.

After you have read through a chapter, you can continue to gain benefit from it by skimming for the Key Topic icons. Each chapter also presents the commands needed to configure a switch feature in the order in which they should be entered. Knowing this sequence of operation should help you understand the sequence of the implementation planning tasks.

Finally, each chapter ends with a command reference section in which configuration and verification commands are summarized in a table format. The left side of the table lists the task to be performed, while the right side shows the command syntax. Don't worry about memorizing the exact or complete command syntax, though. Instead, concentrate on the task and the basic command keywords.

Cisco Published SWITCH Exam Topics Covered in This Part

Implement a VLAN based solution, given a network design and a set of requirements:

- Determine network resources needed for implementing a VLAN-based solution on a network

- Create a VLAN-based implementation plan

- Create a VLAN-based verification plan

- Configure switch-to-switch connectivity for the VLAN-based solution

- Configure loop prevention for the VLAN-based solution

- Configure Access Ports for the VLAN-based solution

- Verify the VLAN-based solution was implemented properly using **show** and **debug** commands

- Document results of VLAN implementation and verification

Implement switch-based Layer 3 services, given a network design and a set of requirements:

- Determine network resources needed for implementing a switch-based Layer 3 solution

- Create an implementation plan for the switch-based Layer 3 solution

- Create a verification plan for the switch-based Layer 3 solution

- Configure routing interfaces

- Configure Layer 3 security

- Verify the switch-based Layer 3 solution was implemented properly using **show** and **debug** commands

- Document results of switch-based Layer 3 implementation and verification

(Always check Cisco.com for the latest posted exam topics.)

Part II: Building a Campus Network

This chapter covers the following topics that you need to master for the CCNP SWITCH exam:

Layer 2 Switch Operation—This section describes the functionality of a switch that forwards Ethernet frames.

Multilayer Switch Operation—This section describes the mechanisms that forward packets at OSI Layers 3 and 4.

Tables Used in Switching—This section explains how tables of information and computation are used to make switching decisions. Coverage focuses on the content-addressable memory table involved in Layer 2 forwarding, and the ternary content-addressable memory used in packet-handling decisions at Layers 2 through 4.

Monitoring Switching Tables—This section reviews the Catalyst commands that you can use to monitor the switching tables and memory. These commands can be useful when troubleshooting or tracing the sources of data or problems in a switched network.

CHAPTER 2

Switch Operation

To have a good understanding of the many features that you can configure on a Catalyst switch, you first should understand the fundamentals of the switching function.

This chapter serves as a primer, describing how an Ethernet switch works. It presents Layer 2 forwarding, along with the hardware functions that make forwarding possible. Multilayer switching is also explained. A considerable portion of the chapter deals with the memory architecture that performs switching at Layers 3 and 4 both flexibly and efficiently. This chapter also provides a brief overview of useful switching table management commands.

"Do I Know This Already?" Quiz

The "Do I Know This Already?" quiz allows you to assess whether you should read this entire chapter thoroughly or jump to the "Exam Preparation Tasks" section. If you are in doubt based on your answers to these questions or your own assessment of your knowledge of the topics, read the entire chapter. Table 2-1 outlines the major headings in this chapter and the "Do I Know This Already?" quiz questions that go with them. You can find the answers in Appendix A, "Answers to the 'Do I Know This Already?' Quizzes."

Table 2-1 *"Do I Know This Already?" Foundation Topics Section-to-Question Mapping*

Foundation Topics Section	Questions Covered in This Section
Layer 2 Switch Operation	1–5
Multilayer Switch Operation	6–9
Switching Tables	10–11
Troubleshooting Switching Tables	12

1. Which of the following devices performs transparent bridging?

    a. Ethernet hub

    b. Layer 2 switch

    c. Layer 3 switch

    d. Router

2. When a PC is connected to a Layer 2 switch port, how far does the collision domain spread?

    a. No collision domain exists.

    b. One switch port.

    c. One VLAN.

    d. All ports on the switch.

3. What information is used to forward frames in a Layer 2 switch?

    a. Source MAC address

    b. Destination MAC address

    c. Source switch port

    d. IP addresses

4. What does a switch do if a MAC address cannot be found in the CAM table?

    a. The frame is forwarded to the default port.

    b. The switch generates an ARP request for the address.

    c. The switch floods the frame out all ports (except the receiving port).

    d. The switch drops the frame.

5. In the Catalyst 6500, frames can be filtered with access lists for security and QoS purposes. This filtering occurs according to which of the following?

    a. Before a CAM table lookup

    b. After a CAM table lookup

    c. Simultaneously with a CAM table lookup

    d. According to how the access lists are configured

6. Access list contents can be merged into which of the following?

    a. CAM table

    b. TCAM table

    c. FIB table

    d. ARP table

7. Multilayer switches using CEF are based on which of these techniques?

    a. Route caching

    b. Netflow switching

    c. Topology-based switching

    d. Demand-based switching

8. Which answer describes multilayer switching with CEF?

    a. The first packet is routed and then the flow is cached.

    b. The switch supervisor CPU forwards each packet.

    c. The switching hardware learns station addresses and builds a routing database.

    d. A single database of routing information is built for the switching hardware.

9. In a switch, frames are placed in which buffer after forwarding decisions are made?

    a. Ingress queues

    b. Egress queues

    c. CAM table

    d. TCAM

10. What size are the mask and pattern fields in a TCAM entry?

    a. 64 bits

    b. 128 bits

    c. 134 bits

    d. 168 bits

11. Access list rules are compiled as TCAM entries. When a packet is matched against an access list, in what order are the TCAM entries evaluated?

    a. Sequentially in the order of the original access list.

    b. Numerically by the access list number.

    c. Alphabetically by the access list name.

    d. All entries are evaluated in parallel.

12. Which Catalyst IOS command can you use to display the addresses in the CAM table?

    a. show cam

    b. show mac address-table

    c. show mac

    d. show cam address-table

Foundation Topics

Layer 2 Switch Operation

Consider a simple network that is built around many hosts that all share the same available bandwidth. This is known as a shared media network and was used in early legacy LANs made up of Ethernet hubs. The carrier sense multiple access collision detect (CSMA/CD) scheme determines when a device can transmit data on the shared LAN.

When more than one host tries to talk at one time, a collision occurs, and everyone must back off and wait to talk again. This forces every host to operate in half-duplex mode, by either talking *or* listening at any given time. In addition, when one host sends a frame, all connected hosts hear it. When one host generates a frame with errors, everyone hears that, too. This type of LAN is a *collision domain* because all device transmissions are susceptible to collisions.

An Ethernet switch operates at OSI Layer 2, making decisions about forwarding frames based on the destination MAC addresses found within the frames. This means that the Ethernet media is no longer shared among connected devices. Instead, at its most basic level, an Ethernet switch provides isolation between connected hosts in several ways:

- The collision domain's scope is severely limited. On each switch port, the collision domain consists of the switch port itself and the devices directly connected to that port—either a single host or, if a shared-media hub is connected, the set of hosts connected to the hub.

- Host connections can operate in full-duplex mode because there is no contention on the media. Hosts can talk *and* listen at the same time.

- Bandwidth is no longer shared. Instead, each switch port offers dedicated bandwidth across a switching fabric to another switch port. (These frame forwarding paths change dynamically.)

- Errors in frames are not propagated. Each frame received on a switch port is checked for errors. Good frames are regenerated when they are forwarded or transmitted. This is known as *store-and-forward* switching technology: Packets are received, stored for inspection, and then forwarded.

- You can limit broadcast traffic to a volume threshold.

- Other types of intelligent filtering or forwarding become possible.

Transparent Bridging

A Layer 2 switch is basically a multiport transparent bridge, where each switch port is its own Ethernet LAN segment, isolated from the others. Frame forwarding is based completely on the MAC addresses contained in each frame, such that the switch will not forward a frame unless it knows the destination's location. (When the switch does not know where the destination is, it makes some safe assumptions.) Figure 2-1 shows the progression from a two-port to a multiport transparent bridge, and then to a Layer 2 switch.

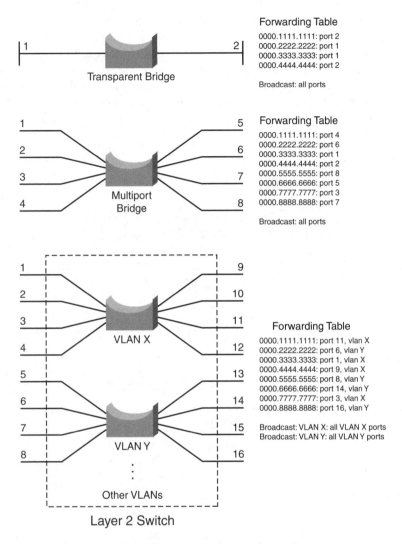

Figure 2-1 *A Comparison of Transparent Bridges and Switches*

The entire process of forwarding Ethernet frames then becomes figuring out what MAC addresses connect to which switch ports. A switch either must be told explicitly where hosts are located or must learn this information for itself. You can configure MAC address locations through a switch's command-line interface, but this quickly gets out of control when there are many stations on the network or when stations move around.

To dynamically learn about station locations, a switch listens to incoming frames and keeps a table of address information. As a frame is received on a switch port, the switch inspects the source MAC address. If that address is not in the address table already, the MAC address, switch port, and virtual LAN (VLAN) on which it arrived are recorded in the table. Learning the address locations of the incoming packets is easy and straightforward.

Incoming frames also include the destination MAC address. Again, the switch looks up this address in the address table, hoping to find the switch port and VLAN where the destination address is attached. If it is found, the frame can be forwarded out that switch port. If the address is not found in the table, the switch must take more drastic action— the frame is forwarded in a "best effort" fashion by *flooding* it out all switch ports assigned to the source VLAN. This is known as *unknown unicast flooding*, with the unicast destination location unknown. Figure 2-2 illustrates this process, using only a single VLAN for simplification.

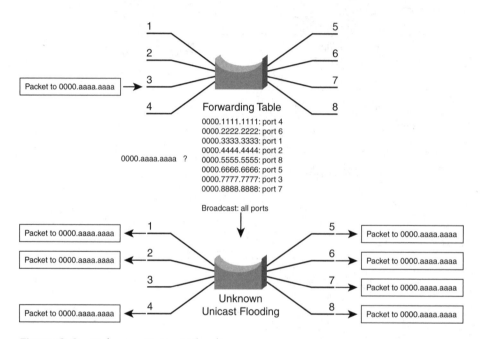

Figure 2-2   *Unknown Unicast Flooding*

A switch constantly listens to incoming frames on each of its ports, learning source MAC addresses. However, be aware that the learning process is allowed only when the Spanning Tree Protocol (STP) algorithm has decided that a port is stable for normal use. STP is concerned only with maintaining a loop-free network, where frames will not be forwarded recursively. If a loop formed, a flooded frame could follow the looped path, where it would be flooded again and again.

In a similar manner, frames containing a broadcast or multicast destination address also are flooded. These destination addresses are not unknown—the switch knows them well. They are destined for multiple locations, so they must be flooded by definition. In the case of multicast addresses, flooding is performed by default.

Follow That Frame!

You should have a basic understanding of the operations that a frame undergoes as it passes through a Layer 2 switch. This helps you get a firm grasp on how to configure the switch for complex functions. Figure 2-3 shows a typical Layer 2 Catalyst switch and the decision processes that take place to forward each frame.

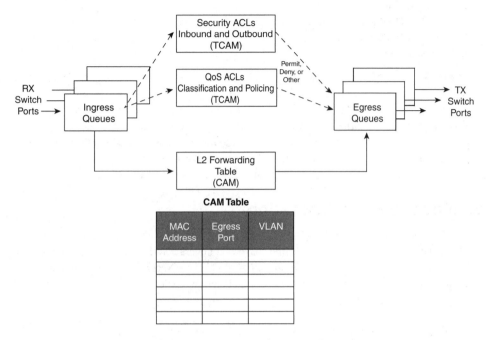

Figure 2-3 *Operations Within a Layer 2 Catalyst Switch*

When a frame arrives at a switch port, it is placed into one of the port's ingress queues. The queues each can contain frames to be forwarded, with each queue having a different priority or service level. The switch port then can be fine-tuned so that important frames get processed and forwarded before less-important frames. This can prevent time-critical data from being "lost in the shuffle" during a flurry of incoming traffic.

As the ingress queues are serviced and a frame is pulled off, the switch must figure out not only *where* to forward the frame, but also *whether* it should be forwarded and *how*. Three fundamental decisions must be made: one concerned with finding the egress switch port, and two concerned with forwarding policies. All these decisions are made *simultaneously* by independent portions of switching hardware and can be described as follows:

- **L2 forwarding table**—The frame's destination MAC address is used as an index, or key, into the content-addressable memory (CAM), or address, table. If the address is found, the egress switch port and the appropriate VLAN ID are read from the table. (If the address is not found, the frame is marked for flooding so that it is forwarded out every switch port in the VLAN.)

- **Security ACLs**—Access control lists (ACL) can be used to identify frames according to their MAC addresses, protocol types (for non-IP frames), IP addresses, protocols, and Layer 4 port numbers. The ternary content-addressable memory (TCAM) contains ACLs in a compiled form so that a decision can be made on whether to forward a frame in a single table lookup.

■ **QoS ACLs**—Other ACLs can classify incoming frames according to quality of service (QoS) parameters, to police or control the rate of traffic flows, and to mark QoS parameters in outbound frames. The TCAM also is used to make these decisions in a single table lookup.

The CAM and TCAM tables are discussed in greater detail in the "Content-Addressable Memory" and "Ternary Content-Addressable Memory" sections, later in this chapter. After the CAM and TCAM table lookups have occurred, the frame is placed into the appropriate egress queue on the appropriate outbound switch port. The egress queue is determined by QoS values either contained in the frame or passed along with the frame. Like the ingress queues, the egress queues are serviced according to importance or time criticality; frames are sent out without being delayed by other outbound traffic.

Multilayer Switch Operation

Catalyst switches, such as the 3750 (with the appropriate Cisco IOS Software image), 4500, and 6500, can also forward frames based on Layers 3 and 4 information contained in packets. This is known as *multilayer switching (MLS)*. Naturally, Layer 2 switching is performed at the same time because even the higher-layer encapsulations still are contained in Ethernet frames.

Types of Multilayer Switching

Catalyst switches have supported two basic generations or types of MLS: route caching (first-generation MLS) and topology-based (second-generation MLS). This section presents an overview of both, although only the second generation is supported in the Cisco IOS Software–based switch families, such as the Catalyst 3750, 4500, and 6500. You should understand the two types and the differences between them:

■ **Route caching**—The first generation of MLS, requiring a route processor (RP) and a switch engine (SE). The RP must process a traffic flow's first packet to determine the destination. The SE listens to the first packet and to the resulting destination, and sets up a "shortcut" entry in its MLS cache. The SE forwards subsequent packets in the same traffic flow based on shortcut entries in its cache.

This type of MLS also is known by the names *Netflow LAN switching*, *flow-based* or *demand-based switching*, and *"route once, switch many."* Even if this isn't used to forward packets in Cisco IOS–based Catalyst switches, the technique generates traffic flow information and statistics.

Key Topic

■ **Topology-based**—The second generation of MLS, utilizing specialized hardware. Layer 3 routing information builds and prepopulates a single database of the entire network topology. This database, an efficient table lookup in hardware, is consulted so that packets can be forwarded at high rates. The longest match found in the database is used as the correct Layer 3 destination. As the routing topology changes over time, the database contained in the hardware can be updated dynamically with no performance penalty.

This type of MLS is known as *Cisco Express Forwarding (CEF)*. A routing process running on the switch downloads the current routing table database into the *Forwarding Information Base (FIB)* area of hardware. CEF is discussed in greater detail in Chapter 11, "Multilayer Switching."

Follow That Packet!

The path that a Layer 3 packet follows through a multilayer switch is similar to that of a Layer 2 switch. Obviously, some means of making a Layer 3 forwarding decision must be added. Beyond that, several, sometimes unexpected, things can happen to packets as they are forwarded. Figure 2-4 shows a typical multilayer switch and the decision processes that must occur. Packets arriving on a switch port are placed in the appropriate ingress queue, just as in a Layer 2 switch.

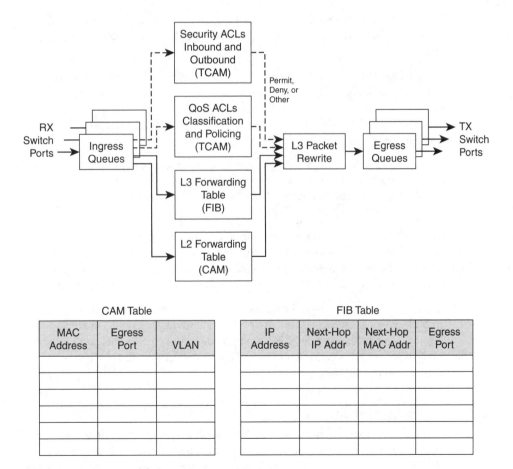

Figure 2-4 *Operations Within a Multilayer Catalyst Switch*

Each packet is pulled off an ingress queue and inspected for both Layer 2 and Layer 3 destination addresses. Now, the decision of *where* to forward the packet is based on two address tables, whereas the decision of *how* to forward the packet still is based on access list

results. As in Layer 2 switching, all these multilayer decisions are performed simultaneously in hardware:

- **L2 forwarding table**—The destination MAC address is used as an index to the CAM table. If the frame contains a Layer 3 packet to be forwarded, the destination MAC address is that of a Layer 3 port on the switch. In this case, the CAM table results are used only to decide that the frame should be processed at Layer 3.

- **L3 forwarding table**—The FIB table is consulted, using the destination IP address as an index. The longest match in the table is found (both address and mask), and the resulting next-hop Layer 3 address is obtained. The FIB also contains each next-hop entry's Layer 2 MAC address and the egress switch port (and VLAN ID) so that further table lookups are not necessary.

- **Security ACLs**—Inbound and outbound access lists are compiled into TCAM entries so that decisions of whether to forward a packet can be determined as a single table lookup.

- **QoS ACLs**—Packet classification, policing, and marking all can be performed as single table lookups in the QoS TCAM.

As with Layer 2 switching, the packet finally must be placed in the appropriate egress queue on the appropriate egress switch port.

However, recall that during the multilayer switching process, the next-hop destination was obtained from the FIB table, just as a router would do. The Layer 3 address identified the next hop and found its Layer 2 address. Only the Layer 2 address would be used, so the Layer 2 frames could be sent on.

The next-hop Layer 2 address must be put into the frame in place of the original destina-
tion address (the multilayer switch). The frame's Layer 2 source address also must become that of the multilayer switch before it is sent on to the next hop. As any good router must do, the Time-To-Live (TTL) value in the Layer 3 packet must be decremented by one.

Because the contents of the Layer 3 packet (the TTL value) have changed, the Layer 3 header checksum must be recalculated. And because both Layers 2 and 3 contents have changed, the Layer 2 checksum must be recalculated. In other words, the entire Ethernet frame must be rewritten before it goes into the egress queue. This also is accomplished efficiently in hardware.

Multilayer Switching Exceptions

To forward packets using the simultaneous decision processes described in the preceding section, the packet must be "MLS-ready" and must require no additional decisions. For example, CEF can directly forward most IP packets between hosts. This occurs when the source and destination addresses (both MAC and IP) are known already and no other IP parameters must be manipulated.

Other packets cannot be directly forwarded by CEF and must be handled in more detail. This is done by a quick inspection during the forwarding decisions. If a packet meets criteria such as the following, it is flagged for further processing and sent or "punted" to the switch CPU for *process switching*:

- ARP requests and replies

- IP packets requiring a response from a router (TTL has expired, MTU is exceeded, fragmentation is needed, and so on)

- IP broadcasts that will be relayed as unicast (DHCP requests, IP helper-address functions)

- Routing protocol updates

- Cisco Discovery Protocol packets

- IPX routing protocol and service advertisements

- Packets needing encryption

- Packets triggering Network Address Translation (NAT)

- Other non-IP and non-IPX protocol packets (AppleTalk, DECnet, and so on)

Tables Used in Switching

Catalyst switches maintain several types of tables to be used in the switching process. The tables are tailored for Layer 2 switching or MLS and are kept in very fast memory so that many fields within a frame or packet can be compared in parallel.

Content-Addressable Memory

All Catalyst switch models use a CAM table for Layer 2 switching. As frames arrive on switch ports, the source MAC addresses are learned and recorded in the CAM table. The port of arrival and the VLAN both are recorded in the table, along with a time stamp. If a MAC address learned on one switch port has moved to a different port, the MAC address and time stamp are recorded for the most recent arrival port. Then, the previous entry is deleted. If a MAC address is found already present in the table for the correct arrival port, only its time stamp is updated.

Key Topic

Switches generally have large CAM tables so that many addresses can be looked up for frame forwarding. However, there is not enough table space to hold every possible address on large networks. To manage the CAM table space, *stale entries* (addresses that have not been heard from for a period of time) are aged out. By default, idle CAM table entries are kept for 300 seconds before they are deleted. You can change the default setting using the following configuration command:

```
Switch(config)# mac address-table aging-time seconds
```

By default, MAC addresses are learned dynamically from incoming frames. You also can configure static CAM table entries that contain MAC addresses that might not be learned otherwise. To do this, use the following configuration command:

```
Switch(config)# mac address-table static mac-address vlan vlan-id interface type
   mod/num
```

Here, the MAC address (in dotted triplet hex format) is identified with the VLAN and the switch interface where it appears.

Note: You should be aware that there is a slight discrepancy in the CAM table command syntax. Until Catalyst IOS version 12.1(11)EA1, the syntax for CAM table commands used the keywords **mac-address-table**. In more recent Cisco IOS versions, the syntax has changed to use the keywords **mac address-table** (first hyphen omitted). The Catalyst 4500 and 6500 IOS Software are exceptions, however, and continue to use the **mac-address-table** keyword form. Many switch platforms support either syntax to ease the transition.

Exactly what happens when a host's MAC address is learned on one switch port, and then the host moves so that it appears on a different switch port? Ordinarily, the host's original CAM table entry would have to age out after 300 seconds, while its address was learned on the new port. To avoid having duplicate CAM table entries, a switch purges any existing entries for a MAC address that has just been learned on a different switch port. This is a safe assumption because MAC addresses are unique, and a single host should never be seen on more than one switch port unless problems exist in the network. If a switch notices that a MAC address is being learned on alternating switch ports, it generates an error message that flags the MAC address as "flapping" between interfaces.

Ternary Content-Addressable Memory

In traditional routing, ACLs can match, filter, or control specific traffic. Access lists are made up of one or more access control entities (ACE) or matching statements that are evaluated in sequential order. Evaluating an access list can take up additional time, adding to the latency of forwarding packets.

In multilayer switches, however, all the matching process that ACLs provide is implemented in hardware. TCAM allows a packet to be evaluated against an entire access list in a single table lookup. Most switches have multiple TCAMs so that both inbound and outbound security and QoS ACLs can be evaluated simultaneously, or entirely in parallel with a Layer 2 or Layer 3 forwarding decision.

The Catalyst IOS Software has two components that are part of the TCAM operation:

- **Feature Manager (FM)**—After an access list has been created or configured, the Feature Manager software compiles, or merges, the ACEs into entries in the TCAM table. The TCAM then can be consulted at full frame-forwarding speed.

- **Switching Database Manager (SDM)**—You can partition the TCAM on some Catalyst switches into areas for different functions. The SDM software configures or tunes the TCAM partitions, if needed. (The TCAM is fixed on Catalyst 4500 and 6500 platforms and cannot be repartitioned.)

TCAM Structure

The TCAM is an extension of the CAM table concept. Recall that a CAM table takes in an index or key value (usually a MAC address) and looks up the resulting value (usually a switch port or VLAN ID). Table lookup is fast and always based on an exact key match consisting of two input values: 0 and 1 bits.

TCAM also uses a table-lookup operation but is greatly enhanced to allow a more abstract operation. For example, binary values (0s and 1s) make up a key into the table, but a mask value also is used to decide which bits of the key are actually relevant. This effectively makes a key consisting of three input values: 0, 1, and X (don't care) bit values—a three-fold or *ternary* combination.

TCAM entries are composed of Value, Mask, and Result (VMR) combinations. Fields from frame or packet headers are fed into the TCAM, where they are matched against the value and mask pairs to yield a result. As a quick reference, these can be described as follows:

■ **Values** are always 134-bit quantities, consisting of source and destination addresses and other relevant protocol information—all patterns to be matched. The information concatenated to form the value depends on the type of access list, as shown in Table 2-2. Values in the TCAM come directly from any address, port, or other protocol information given in an ACE.

Table 2-2   *TCAM Value Pattern Components*

Access List Type	Value and Mask Components, 134 Bits Wide (Number of Bits)
Ethernet	Source MAC (48), destination MAC (48), Ethertype (16)
ICMP	Source IP (32), destination IP (32), protocol (16), ICMP code (8), ICMP type (4), IP type of service (ToS) (8)
Extended IP using TCP/UDP	Source IP (32), destination IP (32), protocol (16), IP ToS (8), source port (16), source operator (4), destination port (16), destination operator (4)
Other IP	Source IP (32), destination IP (32), protocol (16), IP ToS (8)
IGMP	Source IP (32), destination IP (32), protocol (16), IP ToS (8), IGMP message type (8)
IPX	Source IPX network (32), destination IPX network (32), destination node (48), IPX packet type (16)

■ **Masks** are also 134-bit quantities, in exactly the same format, or bit order, as the values. Masks select only the value bits of interest; a mask bit is set to exactly match a value bit or is not set for value bits that do not matter. The masks used in the TCAM stem from address or bit masks in ACEs.

■ **Results** are numeric values that represent what action to take after the TCAM lookup occurs. Whereas traditional access lists offer only a *permit* or *deny* result, TCAM lookups offer a number of possible results or actions. For example, the result can be a permit or deny decision, an index value to a QoS policer, a pointer to a next-hop routing table, and so on.

The TCAM always is organized by masks, where each unique mask has eight value patterns associated with it. For example, the Catalyst 6500 TCAM (one for security ACLs

Key Topic

and one for QoS ACLs) holds up to 4096 masks and 32,768 value patterns. The trick is that each of the mask-value pairs is evaluated *simultaneously*, or in parallel, revealing the best or longest match in a single table lookup.

TCAM Example

Figure 2-5 shows how the TCAM is built and used. This is a simple example and might or might not be identical to the results that the Feature Manager produces because the ACEs might need to be optimized or rewritten to achieve certain TCAM algorithm requirements.

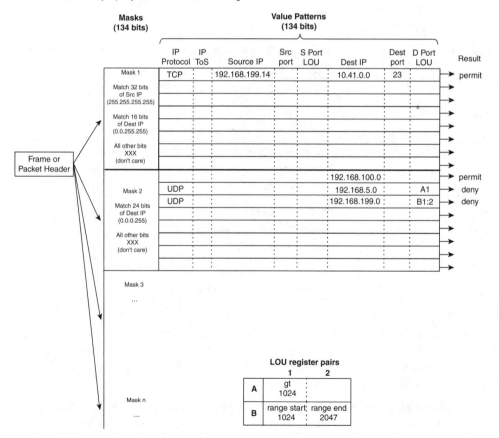

```
access-list 100 permit tcp host 192.168.199.14 10.41.0.0 0.0.255.255 eq telnet
access-list 100 permit ip any 192.168.100.0 0.0.0.255
access-list 100 deny udp any 192.168.5.0 0.0.0.255 gt 1024
access-list 100 deny udp any 192.168.199.0 0.0.0.255 range 1024 2047
```

Figure 2-5   *How an Access List Is Merged into TCAM*

The sample access list 100 (extended IP) is configured and merged into TCAM entries. First, the mask values must be identified in the access list. When an address value and a corresponding address mask are specified in an ACE, those mask bits must be set for matching. All other mask bits can remain in the "don't care" state. The access list contains only three unique masks: one that matches all 32 bits of the source IP address (found with an address mask of 0.0.0.0 or the keyword **host**), one that matches 16 bits of the destination address (found with an address mask of 0.0.255.255), and one that matches only 24 bits of the destination address (found with an address mask of 0.0.0.255). The keyword **any** in the ACEs means "match anything" or "don't care."

The unique masks are placed into the TCAM. Then, for each mask, all possible value patterns are identified. For example, a 32-bit source IP mask (Mask 1) can be found only in ACEs with a source IP address of 192.168.199.14 and a destination of 10.41.0.0. (The rest of Mask 1 is the destination address mask 0.0.255.255.) Those address values are placed into the first value pattern slot associated with Mask 1. Mask 2 has three value patterns: destination addresses 192.168.100.0, 192.168.5.0, and 192.168.199.0. Each of these is placed in the three pattern positions of Mask 2. This process continues until all ACEs have been merged.

When a mask's eighth pattern position has been filled, the next pattern with the same mask must be placed under a new mask. A bit of a balancing act occurs to try to fit all ACEs into the available mask and pattern entries without an overflow.

Port Operations in TCAM

You might have noticed that matching strictly based on values and masks covers only ACE statements that involve exact matches (either the **eq** port operation keyword or no Layer 4 port operations). For example, ACEs such as the following involve specific address values, address masks, and port numbers:

```
access-list test permit ip 192.168.254.0 0.0.0.255 any
access-list test permit tcp any host 192.168.199.10 eq www
```

What about ACEs that use port operators, where a comparison must be made? Consider the following:

```
access-list test permit udp any host 192.168.199.50 gt 1024
access-list test permit tcp any any range 2000 2002
```

A simple logical operation between a mask and a pattern cannot generate the desired result. The TCAM also provides a mechanism for performing a Layer 4 operation or comparison, also done during the single table lookup. If an ACE has a port operator, such as **gt**, **lt**, **neq**, or **range**, the Feature Manager software compiles the TCAM entry to include the use of the operator and the operand in a logical operation unit (LOU) register. Only a limited number of LOUs are available in the TCAM. If there are more ACEs with comparison operators than there are LOUs, the Feature Manager must break up the ACEs into multiple ACEs with only regular matching (using the **eq** operator).

In Figure 2-5, two ACEs require a Layer 4 operation:

■ One that checks for UDP destination ports greater than 1024

■ One that looks for the UDP destination port range 1024 to 2047

The Feature Manager checks all ACEs for Layer 4 operation and places these into LOU register pairs. These can be loaded with operations, independent of any other ACE parameters. The LOU contents can be reused if other ACEs need the same comparisons and values. After the LOUs are loaded, they are referenced in the TCAM entries that need them. This is shown by LOUs A1 and the B1:2 pair. A finite number (actually, a rather small number) of LOUs are available in the TCAM, so the Feature Manager software must use them carefully.

Monitoring Switching Tables

You can display or query the switching tables to verify the information that the switch has learned. As well, you might want to check the tables to find out on which switch port a specific MAC address has been learned.

CAM Table Operation

To view the contents of the CAM table, you can use the following form of the **show mac address-table** EXEC command:

```
Switch# show mac address-table dynamic [address mac-address | interface type
  mod/num | vlan vlan-id]
```

The entries that have been learned dynamically will be shown. You can add the **address** keyword to specify a single MAC address, or the **interface** or **vlan** keyword to see addresses that have been learned on a specific interface or VLAN.

For example, assume that you need to find the learned location of the host with MAC address 0050.8b11.54da. The **show mac address-table dynamic address 0050.8b11.54da** command might produce the output in Example 2-1.

Example 2-1 *Determining Host Location by MAC Address*

```
Switch# show mac address-table dynamic address 0050.8b11.54da
          Mac Address Table
-------------------------------------------------

Vlan     Mac Address       Type        Ports
----     -----------       ----        -----
  54     0050.8b11.54da    DYNAMIC     Fa1/0/1
Total Mac Addresses for this criterion: 1
Switch#
```

From this, you can see that the host somehow is connected to interface Fast Ethernet 1/0/1, on VLAN 54.

Tip: If your Catalyst IOS switch is not accepting commands of the form **mac address-table**, try adding a hyphen between the keywords. For example, the Catalyst 4500 and 6500 most likely will accept **show mac-address-table** instead.

Suppose that this same command produced no output, showing nothing about the interface and VLAN where the MAC address is found. What might that mean? Either the host has not sent a frame that the switch can use for learning its location, or something odd is going on. Perhaps the host is using two network interface cards (NIC) to load balance traffic; one NIC is only receiving traffic, whereas the other is only sending. Therefore, the switch never hears and learns the receiving-only NIC address.

To see all the MAC addresses that are currently found on interface GigabitEthernet1/0/29, you could use the **show mac address-table dynamic interface gig1/0/29** command. The output shown in Example 2-2 indicates that only one host has been learned on the interface. Perhaps only a single PC connects to that interface.

Example 2-2 *Determining Hosts Active on an Interface*

```
Switch# show mac address-table dynamic interface gigabitethernet1/0/29
          Mac Address Table
-------------------------------------------------

Vlan    Mac Address       Type        Ports
----    -----------       ----        -----
 537    0013.7297.3d4b    DYNAMIC     Gi1/0/29
Total Mac Addresses for this criterion: 1
Switch#
```

However, suppose the same command is used to check interface GigabitEthernet1/0/49. The output shown in Example 2-3 lists many MAC addresses—all found on a single interface. How can so many addresses be learned on one switch interface? This interface must lead to another switch or another part of the network where other devices are located.

Example 2-3 *Finding Many Hosts on an Interface*

```
Switch# show mac address-table dynamic interface gig1/0/49
          Mac Address Table
-------------------------------------------------

Vlan    Mac Address       Type        Ports
----    -----------       ----        -----
 580    0000.0c07.ac01    DYNAMIC     Gi1/0/49
 580    0007.0e0b.f918    DYNAMIC     Gi1/0/49
 580    000f.1f78.1094    DYNAMIC     Gi1/0/49
 580    0011.43ac.b083    DYNAMIC     Gi1/0/49
 580    0011.bb2d.3f6e    DYNAMIC     Gi1/0/49
 580    0014.6a86.1f1e    DYNAMIC     Gi1/0/49
 580    0014.6a86.1f3d    DYNAMIC     Gi1/0/49
 580    0014.6a86.1f3f    DYNAMIC     Gi1/0/49
 580    0014.6a86.1f47    DYNAMIC     Gi1/0/49
—More—
```

To see the CAM table's size, use the **show mac address-table count** command, as shown in Example 2-4. MAC address totals are shown for each active VLAN on the switch. This can give you a good idea of the size of the CAM table and how many hosts are using the network.

Example 2-4   *Checking the Size of the CAM Table*

```
Switch# show mac address-table count
Mac Entries for Vlan 1:
--------------------------
Dynamic Address Count  : 0
Static  Address Count  : 0
Total Mac Addresses    : 0

Mac Entries for Vlan 2:
--------------------------
Dynamic Address Count  : 89
Static  Address Count  : 0
Total Mac Addresses    : 89

Mac Entries for Vlan 580:
--------------------------
Dynamic Address Count  : 600
Static  Address Count  : 0
Total Mac Addresses    : 600

Total Mac Address Space Available: 4810
Switch#
```

CAM table entries can be cleared manually, if needed, by using the following EXEC command:

```
Switch# clear mac address-table dynamic [address mac-address | interface type
  mod/num | vlan vlan-id]
```

Tip: Frequently, you need to know where a user with a certain MAC address is connected. In a large network, discerning at which switch and switch port a MAC address can be found might be difficult. Start at the network's center, or core, and display the CAM table entry for the MAC address. Look at the switch port shown in the entry and find the neighboring switch connected to that port using CDP neighbor information. Then move to that switch and repeat the CAM table process. Keep moving from switch to switch until you reach the edge of the network where the MAC address connects.

TCAM Operation

The TCAM in a switch is more or less self-sufficient. Access lists are compiled or merged automatically into the TCAM, so there is nothing to configure. The only concept you need to be aware of is how the TCAM resources are being used.

TCAMs have a limited number of usable mask, value pattern, and LOU entries. If access lists grow to be large or many Layer 4 operations are needed, the TCAM tables and registers can overflow. If that happens while you are configuring an ACL, the switch will generate syslog messages that flag the TCAM overflow situation as it tries to compile the ACL into TCAM entries.

Exam Preparation Tasks

Review All Key Topics

Review the most important topics in the chapter, noted with the Key Topic icon in the outer margin of the page. Table 2-3 lists a reference of these key topics and the page numbers on which each is found.

Key Topic

Table 2-3   *Key Topics for Chapter 2*

Key Topic Element	Description	Page Number
Paragraph	Discusses collision domain	22
Paragraph	Discusses flooding and unknown unicast flooding	24
List	Describes topology-based switching	26
Paragraph	Discusses the CAM table	29
Paragraph	Explains TCAM operation	31

Define Key Terms

Define the following key terms from this chapter, and check your answers in the glossary:

collision domain, flooding, unknown unicast flooding, CEF, FIB, CAM, TCAM

Use Command Reference to Check Your Memory

This section includes the most important configuration and EXEC commands covered in this chapter. It might not be necessary to memorize the complete syntax of every command, but you should remember the basic keywords that are needed.

To test your memory of the CAM-related commands, cover the right side of Table 2-4 with a piece of paper, read the description on the left side, and then see how much of the command you can remember.

Remember that the CCNP exam focuses on practical or hands-on skills that are used by a networking professional. For the skills covered in this chapter, remember that the commands always involve the keywords **mac address-table**.

Table 2-4   *Commands Used to Monitor and Manipulate the CAM Table*

Function	Command
Find the location of a specific MAC address.	**show mac address-table dynamic address** *mac-address*
Display all MAC addresses learned on a specific interface.	**show mac address-table dynamic interface** *type number*
Display the current CAM table size.	**show mac address-table count**
Enter a static CAM table entry.	**mac address-table static** *mac-address* **vlan** *vlan-id* **interface** *type number*
Clear a CAM entry.	**clear mac address-table dynamic [address** *mac-address* | **interface** *type number* | **vlan** *vlan-id*]

This chapter covers the following topics that you need to master for the CCNP SWITCH exam:

Ethernet Concepts—This section discusses the concepts and technology behind various forms of Ethernet media.

Connecting Switches and Devices—This section discusses the physical cabling and connectivity used with Catalyst switches.

Switch Port Configuration—This section covers the configuration steps and commands needed to use Catalyst Ethernet, Fast Ethernet, and Gigabit and 10-Gigabit Ethernet switch ports in a network.

CHAPTER 3

Switch Port Configuration

This chapter presents the various Ethernet network technologies used to establish switched connections within the campus network. You can connect a switch to an end device such as a PC or to another switch. The chapter also details the switch commands required for configuring and troubleshooting Ethernet LAN ports.

"Do I Know This Already?" Quiz

The "Do I Know This Already?" quiz allows you to assess whether you should read this entire chapter thoroughly or jump to the "Exam Preparation Tasks" section. If you are in doubt based on your answers to these questions or your own assessment of your knowledge of the topics, read the entire chapter. Table 3-1 outlines the major headings in this chapter and the "Do I Know This Already?" quiz questions that go with them. You can find the answers in Appendix A, "Answers to the 'Do I Know This Already?' Quizzes."

Table 3-1 *"Do I Know This Already?" Foundation Topics Section-to-Question Mapping*

Foundation Topics Section	Questions Covered in This Section
Ethernet Concepts	1–6
Connecting Switches and Devices	7–8
Switch Port Configuration	9–11

1. What does the IEEE 802.3 standard define?

   a. Spanning Tree Protocol

   b. Token Ring

   c. Ethernet

   d. Switched Ethernet

2. At what layer are traditional 10-Mbps Ethernet, Fast Ethernet, and Gigabit Ethernet the same?

   a. Layer 1

   b. Layer 2

   c. Layer 3

   d. Layer 4

3. At what layer are traditional 10-Mbps Ethernet, Fast Ethernet, and Gigabit Ethernet different?

    a. Layer 1

    b. Layer 2

    c. Layer 3

    d. Layer 4

4. What is the maximum cable distance for a Category 5 100BASE-TX connection?

    a. 100 feet

    b. 100 m

    c. 328 m

    d. 500 m

5. Ethernet autonegotiation determines which of the following?

    a. Spanning-tree mode

    b. Duplex mode

    c. Quality of service mode

    d. Error threshold

6. Which of the following cannot be automatically determined and set if the far end of a connection doesn't support autonegotiation?

    a. Link speed

    b. Link duplex mode

    c. Link media type

    d. MAC address

7. Which of these is not a standard type of gigabit interface converter (GBIC) or small form factor pluggable (SFP) module?

    a. 1000BASE-LX/LH

    b. 1000BASE-T

    c. 1000BASE-FX

    d. 1000BASE-ZX

8. What type of cable should you use to connect two switches back to back using their Fast Ethernet 10/100 ports?

    a. Rollover cable

    b. Transfer cable

    c. Crossover cable

    d. Straight-through cable

9. Assume that you have just entered the **configure terminal** command. To configure the speed of the first Fast Ethernet interface on Cisco Catalyst switch module number one to 100 Mbps, which one of these commands should you enter first?

   a. speed 100 mbps

   b. speed 100

   c. interface fastethernet 1/0/1

   d. interface fast ethernet 1/0/1

10. If a switch port is in the errdisable state, what is the first thing you should do?

    a. Reload the switch.

    b. Use the **clear errdisable port** command.

    c. Use the **shut** and **no shut** interface-configuration commands.

    d. Determine the cause of the problem.

11. Which of the following **show interface** output information can you use to diagnose a switch port problem?

    a. Port state.

    b. Port speed.

    c. Input errors.

    d. Collisions.

    e. All these answers are correct.

Foundation Topics

Ethernet Concepts

This section reviews the varieties of Ethernet and their application in a campus network. The bandwidth requirements for a network segment are determined by the types of applications in use, the traffic flows within the network, and the size of the user community served. Ethernet scales to support increasing bandwidths; the Ethernet medium should be chosen to match the need at each point in the campus network. As network bandwidth requirements grow, you can scale the links between access, distribution, and core layers to match the load.

Other network media technologies available include Fiber Distribution Data Interface (FDDI), Copper Distribution Data Interface (CDDI), Token Ring, and Asynchronous Transfer Mode (ATM). Although some networks still use these media, Ethernet has emerged as the most popular choice in installed networks. Ethernet is chosen because of its low cost, market availability, and scalability to higher bandwidths.

Ethernet (10 Mbps)

Ethernet is a LAN technology based on the Institute of Electrical and Electronics Engineers (IEEE) 802.3 standard. Ethernet (in contrast to Fast Ethernet and later versions) offers a bandwidth of 10 Mbps between end users. In its most basic form, Ethernet is a shared medium that becomes both a collision and a broadcast domain. As the number of users on the shared media increases, so does the probability that a user is trying to transmit data at any given time. When one user transmits at about the same time as another, a *collision* occurs. In other words, both users can't transmit data at the same time if they both are sharing the same network media.

Ethernet is based on the *carrier sense multiple access collision detect (CSMA/CD)* technology, which requires that transmitting stations back off for a random period of time when a collision occurs. If a station must wait its turn to transmit, it cannot transmit and receive at the same time. This is called *half-duplex* operation.

The more crowded an Ethernet segment becomes, the number of stations likely to be transmitting at a given time increases. Imagine standing in a crowded room trying to tell a story. Instead of attempting to talk over the crowd, you stop and politely wait while other people talk. The more people there are in the room, the more difficult talking becomes. Likewise, as an Ethernet segment becomes more crowded, it becomes more inefficient.

Key Topic

Ethernet switching addresses this problem by dynamically allocating a dedicated 10-Mbps bandwidth to each of its ports. The resulting increased network performance occurs by reducing the number of users connected to an Ethernet segment. In effect, collisions are less probable and the collision domain is reduced in size.

Although switched Ethernet's job is to offer fully dedicated bandwidth to each connected device, assuming that network performance will improve across the board when switching is introduced is a common mistake. For example, consider a workgroup of users connected by a shared-media Ethernet hub. These users regularly access an enterprise server located elsewhere in the campus network. To improve performance, the decision is made to replace the hub with an Ethernet switch so that all users get dedicated 10-Mbps connections. Because the switch offers dedicated bandwidth for connections between the end-user devices connected to its ports, any user-to-user traffic probably would see improved performance. However, the enterprise server still is located elsewhere in the network, and all the switched users still must share available bandwidth across the campus to reach it. As discussed earlier in the book, instead of throwing raw bandwidth at a problem, a design based on careful observation of traffic patterns and flows offers a better solution.

Because switched Ethernet can remove the possibility of collisions, stations do not have to listen to each other to take a turn transmitting on the wire. Instead, stations can operate in *full-duplex* mode—transmitting and receiving simultaneously. Full-duplex mode further increases network performance, with a net throughput of 10 Mbps in each direction, or 20 Mbps total throughput on each port.

Another consideration when dealing with 10-Mbps Ethernet is the physical cabling. Ethernet cabling involves the use of unshielded twisted-pair (UTP) wiring (10BASE-T Ethernet), usually restricted to an end-to-end distance of 100 meters (328 feet) between active devices. Keeping cable lengths as short as possible in the wiring closet also reduces noise and crosstalk when many cables are bundled together.

In a campus network environment, Ethernet can be found in the access layer, between end user devices and the access-layer switch. However, in modern networks, faster generations of Ethernet are usually used in the access layer. Ethernet typically is not used at either the distribution or the core layer due to its relatively low bandwidth capacity.

Note: Ethernet applications (10BASE2, 10BASE5, 10BASE-F, and so on) use other cabling technologies, although they are not discussed here. For the most part, 10BASE-T with UTP wiring is the most commonly used. A useful website for further reading about Ethernet technology is Charles Spurgeon's Ethernet Web Site, at www.ethermanage.com/ethernet/.

Fast Ethernet

Instead of requiring campuses to invest in a completely new technology to gain increased bandwidth, the networking industry developed a higher-speed Ethernet based on existing Ethernet standards. Fast Ethernet operates at 100 Mbps and is defined in the IEEE 802.3u standard. The Ethernet cabling schemes, CSMA/CD operation, and all upper-layer protocol operations are maintained with Fast Ethernet. The net result is the same data link Media Access Control (MAC) layer (OSI Layer 2) merged with a new physical layer (OSI Layer 1).

The campus network can use Fast Ethernet to link access- and distribution-layer switches, if no higher-speed links are available. These links can support the aggregate traffic from multiple Ethernet segments in the access layer. Fast Ethernet generally is used to connect end user workstations to the access-layer switch and to provide improved connectivity to enterprise servers.

Cabling for Fast Ethernet can involve either UTP or fiber. Table 3-2 lists the specifications for Fast Ethernet that define the media types and distances.

Table 3-2   *Cabling Specifications for Fast Ethernet*

Technology	Wiring Type	Pairs	Cable Length
100BASE-TX	EIA/TIA Category 5 UTP	2	100 m
100BASE-T2	EIA/TIA Category 3, 4, 5 UTP	2	100 m
100BASE-T4	EIA/TIA Category 3, 4, 5 UTP	4	100 m
100BASE-FX	Multimode fiber (MMF); 62.5-micron core, 125-micron outer cladding (62.5/125)	1	400 m half duplex or 2000 m full duplex
	Single-mode fiber (SMF)	1	10 km

Full-Duplex Fast Ethernet

As with traditional Ethernet, the natural progression to improve performance is to use full-duplex operation. Fast Ethernet can provide up to 100 Mbps in each direction on a switched connection, for 200 Mbps total throughput.

This maximum throughput is possible only when one device (a workstation, server, router, or another switch) is connected directly to a switch port. In addition, the devices at each end of the link must both support full-duplex operation, allowing each to transmit at will without having to detect and recover from collisions.

The Fast Ethernet specification also offers backward compatibility to support traditional 10-Mbps Ethernet. In the case of 100BASE-TX, switch ports often are called "10/100" ports, to denote the dual speed. To provide this support, the two devices at each end of a network connection automatically can negotiate link capabilities so that they both can operate at a maximum common level. This negotiation involves detecting and selecting the highest physical layer technology (available bandwidth) and half-duplex or full-duplex operation. To properly negotiate a connection, *both* ends should be configured for autonegotiation.

Key Topic

The link speed is determined by electrical signaling so that either end of a link can determine what speed the other end is trying to use. If both ends of the link are configured to autonegotiate, they will use the highest speed that is common to them.

A link's duplex mode, however, is negotiated through an exchange of information. This means that for one end to successfully autonegotiate the duplex mode, the other end also must be set to autonegotiate. Otherwise, one end never will see duplex information from the other end and won't be capable of determining the correct mode to use. If duplex autonegotiation fails, a switch port always falls back to its default setting: half-duplex.

Caution: Beware of a duplex mismatch when both ends of a link are not set for autonegotiation. During a mismatch, one end uses full duplex while the other end uses half duplex. The result is that the half-duplex station will detect a collision when both ends transmit; it will back off appropriately. The full-duplex station, however, will assume that it has the right to transmit at any time. It will not stop and wait for any reason. This can cause errors on the link and poor response times between the stations.

Autonegotiation uses the priorities shown in Table 3-3 for each mode of Ethernet to determine which technology to agree on. If both devices can support more than one technology, the technology with the highest priority is used. For example, if two devices can support both 10BASE-T and 100BASE-TX, both devices will use the higher-priority 100BASE-TX mode.

Table 3-3 *Autonegotiation Selection Priorities*

Priority	Ethernet Mode
7	100BASE-T2 (full duplex)
6	100BASE-TX (full duplex)
5	100BASE-T2 (half duplex)
4	100BASE-T4
3	100BASE-TX
2	10BASE-T (full duplex)
1	10BASE-T

To ensure proper configuration at both ends of a link, Cisco recommends that the appropriate values for transmission speed and duplex mode be configured manually on switch ports. This precludes any possibility that one end of the link will change its settings, resulting in an unusable connection. If you manually set the switch port, don't forget to manually set the device on the other end of the link accordingly. Otherwise, a speed or duplex mismatch between the two devices might occur.

Cisco provides one additional capability to Fast Ethernet, which allows several Fast Ethernet links to be bundled together for increased throughput. *Fast EtherChannel (FEC)* allows two to eight full-duplex Fast Ethernet links to act as a single physical link, for 400- to 1600-Mbps duplex bandwidth. This technology is described in greater detail in Chapter 6, "Aggregating Switch Links."

Gigabit Ethernet

You can scale Fast Ethernet by an additional order of magnitude with Gigabit Ethernet (which supports 1000 Mbps or 1 Gbps) using the same IEEE 802.3 Ethernet frame format as before. This scalability allows network designers and managers to leverage existing

Key
Topic

knowledge and technologies to install, migrate, manage, and maintain Gigabit Ethernet networks.

However, the physical layer has been modified to increase data-transmission speeds. Two technologies were merged to gain the benefits of each: the IEEE 802.3 Ethernet standard and the American National Standards Institute (ANSI) X3T11 FibreChannel. IEEE 802.3 provided the foundation of frame format, CSMA/CD, full duplex, and other Ethernet characteristics. FibreChannel provided a base of high-speed ASICs, optical components, and encoding/decoding and serialization mechanisms. The resulting protocol is termed IEEE 802.3z Gigabit Ethernet.

Gigabit Ethernet supports several cabling types, referred to as *1000BASE-X*. Table 3-4 lists the cabling specifications for each type.

Table 3-4   *Gigabit Ethernet Cabling and Distance Limitations*

GE Type	Wiring Type	Pairs	Cable Length
1000BASE-CX	Shielded twisted pair (STP)	1	25 m
1000BASE-T	EIA/TIA Category 5 UTP	4	100 m
1000BASE-SX	Multimode fiber (MMF) with 62.5-micron core; 850-nm laser	1	275 m
	MMF with 50-micron core; 850-nm laser	1	550 m
1000BASE-LX/LH	MMF with 62.5-micron core; 1300-nm laser	1	550 m
	MMF with 50-micron core; 1300-nm laser	1	550 m
	SMF with 9-micron core; 1300-nm laser	1	10 km
1000BASE-ZX	SMF with 9-micron core; 1550-nm laser	1	70 km
	SMF with 8-micron core; 1550-nm laser	1	100 km

In a campus network, you can use Gigabit Ethernet to connect individual devices to a switch or to connect two switches together.

The "Gigabit over copper" solution that the 1000BASE-T media provides is based on the IEEE 802.3ab standard. Most Gigabit Ethernet switch ports used between switches are fixed at 1000 Mbps. However, other switch ports can support a fallback to Fast or Legacy Ethernet speeds. Here, speed can be autonegotiated between end nodes to the highest common speed—10 Mbps, 100 Mbps, or 1000 Mbps. These ports are often called 10/100/1000 ports to denote the triple speed. Here, the autonegotiation supports the same priority scheme as Fast Ethernet, although 1000BASE-T full duplex becomes the highest priority, followed by 1000BASE-T half duplex. Gigabit Ethernet's port duplex mode always is set to full duplex on Cisco switches, so duplex autonegotiation is not possible.

Finally, Cisco has extended the concept of Fast EtherChannel to bundle several Gigabit Ethernet links to act as a single physical connection. With *Gigabit EtherChannel (GEC)*, two to eight full-duplex Gigabit Ethernet connections can be aggregated, for a single logical link of up to 16-Gbps throughput. Port aggregation and the EtherChannel technology are described further in Chapter 6.

> **Note:** The 10-Gigabit Ethernet Alliance offers further reading about Gigabit Ethernet and its operation, migration, and standards. Refer to the "Archive White Papers" section on its website at http://www.10gea.org.

10-Gigabit Ethernet

Key
Topic

Ethernet scales by orders of magnitude, beginning with 10 Mbps, progressing to 100 Mbps, and then to 1000 Mbps. To meet the demand for aggregating many Gigabit Ethernet links over a single connection, 10-Gigabit Ethernet was developed. Again, the Layer 2 characteristics of Ethernet have been preserved; the familiar 802.3 frame format and size, along with the MAC protocol, remain unchanged.

The 10-Gigabit Ethernet, also known as *10GbE*, and the IEEE 802.3ae standard differ from their predecessors only at the physical layer (PHY); 10GbE operates only at full duplex. The standard defines several different transceivers that can be used as Physical Media Dependent (PMD) interfaces. These are classified into the following:

- **LAN PHY**—Interconnects switches in a campus network, predominantly in the core layer

- **WAN PHY**—Interfaces with existing synchronous optical network (SONET) or synchronous digital hierarchy (SDH) networks typically found in metropolitan-area networks (MAN)

The PMD interfaces also have a common labeling scheme, much as Gigabit Ethernet does. Whereas Gigabit Ethernet uses 1000BASE-X to indicate the media type, 10-Gigabit Ethernet uses 10GBASE-X. Table 3-5 lists the different PMDs defined in the standard, along with the type of fiber and distance limitations. All the fiber-optic PMDs can be used as either a LAN or a WAN PHY, except for the 10GBASE-LX4, which is only a LAN PHY. Be aware that the long-wavelength PMDs carry a significantly greater expense than the others.

Table 3-5   *10-Gigabit Ethernet PMD Types and Characteristics*

PMD Type	Fiber Medium	Maximum Distance
10GBASE-SR/SW (850 nm serial)	MMF: 50 micron	66 m
	MMF: 50 micron (2GHz km modal bandwidth)	300 m
	MMF: 62.5 micron	33 m
10GBASE-LR/LW (1310 nm serial)	SMF: 9 micron	10 km
10GBASE-ER/EW (1550 nm serial)	SMF: 9 micron	40 km

continues

Table 3-5 *10-Gigabit Ethernet PMD Types and Characteristics (Continued)*

PMD Type·	Fiber Medium	Maximum Distance
10GBASE-LX4/LW4 (1310 nm WWDM)	MMF: 50 micron	300 m
	MMF: 62.5 micron	300 m
	SMF: 9 micron	10 km
10GBASE-CX4	Copper: CX4 with Infiniband connectors	15 m

Transceiver types are denoted by a two-letter suffix. The first letter specifies the wavelength used: S = short, L = long, E = extra-long wavelength. The second letter specifies the PHY type: R = LAN PHY, W = WAN PHY. For LX4 and LW4, L refers to a long wavelength, X and W refer to the coding used, and 4 refers to the number of wavelengths transmitted. WWDM is wide-wavelength division multiplexing.

Cisco Catalyst switches supported 10-Gigabit Ethernet PMDs in the form of XENPAK, X2, and SFP+ transceivers. Generally, the X2 form factor is smaller than the XENPAK, and the SFP+ is smaller still, allowing more port density on a switch module.

For the most current switch compatibility listing, refer to the "Cisco 10-Gigabit Ethernet Transceiver Modules Compatibility Matrix" document at http://www.cisco.com/en/US/docs/interfaces_modules/transceiver_modules/compatibility/matrix/OL_6974.html.

Connecting Switches and Devices

Switch deployment in a network involves two steps: physical connectivity and switch configuration. This section describes the connections and cabling requirements for devices in a switched network.

Ethernet Port Cables and Connectors

Catalyst switches support a variety of network connections, including all forms of Ethernet. In addition, Catalyst switches support several types of cabling, including UTP and optical fiber.

Fast Ethernet (100BASE-FX) ports use two-strand multimode fiber (MMF) with MT-RJ or SC connectors to provide connectivity. The MT-RJ connectors are small and modular, each containing a pair of fiber-optic strands. The connector snaps into position, but you must press a tab to remove it. The SC connectors on the fiber cables are square in shape. These connectors snap in and out of the switch port connector as the connector is pushed in or pulled out. One fiber strand is used as a transmit path and the other as a receive path. The transmit fiber on one switch device should connect to the receive fiber on the other end.

All Catalyst switch families support 10/100 autosensing (using Fast Ethernet autonegotiation) and 10/100/1000 autosensing for Gigabit Ethernet. These ports use RJ-45 connectors on Category 5 UTP cabling to complete the connections. These ports can connect to other UTP-based Ethernet autosensing devices. UTP cabling is arranged so that RJ-45 pins 1,2 and 3,6 form two twisted pairs. These pairs connect straight through to the far end.

To connect two 10/100 switch ports back to back, as in an access-layer to distribution-layer link, you must use a Category 5 UTP crossover cable. In this case, RJ-45 pins 1,2 and 3,6 are still twisted pairs, but 1,2 on one end connects to 3,6 on the other end, and 3,6 on one end connects to 1,2 on the other end.

Note: Because UTP Ethernet connections use only pairs 1,2 and 3,6, some cable plant installers connect only these pairs and leave the remaining two pair positions empty. Although this move provides Ethernet connectivity, it is not good practice for future needs. Instead, all four RJ-45 connector pairs should be connected end to end. For example, a full four-pair UTP cable plant can be used for either Ethernet or Token Ring connectivity, without rewiring. (Token Ring UTP connections use pairs 3,6 and 4,5.)
Also, to be compatible with the new IEEE 802.3ab standard for Gigabit Ethernet over copper (1000BASE-T), you must use all four pairs end to end.

Gigabit Ethernet Port Cables and Connectors

Gigabit Ethernet connections take a different approach by providing modular connectivity options. Catalyst switches with Gigabit Ethernet ports have standardized rectangular openings that can accept gigabit interface converter (GBIC) or small form factor pluggable (SFP) modules. The GBIC and SFP modules provide the media personality for the port so that various cable media can connect. In this way, the switch chassis is completely modular and requires no major change to accept a new media type. Instead, the appropriate module is hot-swappable and is plugged into the switch to support the new media. GBIC modules can use SC fiber-optic and RJ-45 UTP connectors. SFP modules can use LC and MT-RJ fiber-optic and RJ-45 UTP connectors. GBIC and SFP modules are available for the following Gigabit Ethernet media:

- **1000BASE-SX**—Short-wavelength connectivity using SC fiber connectors and MMF for distances up to 550 m (1804 feet).

- **1000BASE-LX/LH**—Long-wavelength/long-haul connectivity using SC fiber connectors and either MMF or single-mode fiber (SMF); MMF can be used for distances up to 550 m (1804 feet), and SMF can be used for distances up to 10 km (32,810 feet). MMF requires a special mode-conditioning cable for fiber distances less than 100 m (328 feet) or greater than 300 m (984 feet). This keeps the GBIC from overdriving the far-end receiver on a short cable and lessens the effect of differential mode delay on a long cable.

- **1000BASE-ZX**—Extended-distance connectivity using SC fiber connectors and SMF; works for distances up to 70 km, and even to 100 km when used with premium-grade SMF.

- **GigaStack**—Uses a proprietary connector with a high-data-rate copper cable with enhanced signal integrity and electromagnetic interference (EMI) performance; provides a GBIC-to-GBIC connection between stacking Catalyst switches or between any two Gigabit switch ports over a short distance. The connection is full duplex if only one of the two stacking connectors is used; if both connectors are used, they each become half duplex over a shared bus.

■ **1000BASE-T**—Sports an RJ-45 connector for four-pair UTP cabling; works for distances up to 100 m (328 feet).

Note: You must use a four-pair Category 5 (or greater) UTP crossover cable to connect two 1000BASE-T switch ports back to back. In this case, RJ-45 pins 1,2, 3,6, 4,5, and 7,8 are still twisted pairs on one end, connecting to pins 3,6, 1,2, 7,8, and 4,5 respectively on the other end.

Caution: The fiber-based modules always have the receive fiber on the left connector and the transmit fiber on the right connector, as you face the connectors. These modules could produce invisible laser radiation from the transmit connector. Therefore, always keep unused connectors covered with the rubber plugs, and don't ever look directly into the connectors.

Switch Port Configuration

You can configure the individual ports on a switch with various information and settings, as detailed in the following sections.

Selecting Ports to Configure

Before you can modify port settings, you must select one or more switch ports. Even though they have traditionally been called *ports*, Catalyst switches running the Cisco IOS Software refer to them as *interfaces*.

Key Topic

To select a single switch port, enter the following command in global configuration mode:

```
Switch(config)# interface type module/number
```

The port is identified by its Ethernet type (**fastethernet**, **gigabitethernet**, **tengigabitethernet**, or **vlan**), the physical module or "blade" where it is located, and the port number within the module. Some switches, such as the Catalyst 2950 and 3560, do not have multiple modules. For those models, ports have a module number of 0 (zero). As an example, the Fast Ethernet 0/14 interface is selected for configuration using the following command:

```
Switch(config)# interface fastethernet 0/14
```

The Catalyst 3750 is also a fixed-configuration switch, but it can be stacked with other switches in the 3750 family. Interfaces are referenced by module and port number, where the module number represents the switch position in the stack. For example, port 24 on the switch at position 2 in the stack would be referenced as Fast Ethernet 2/0/24.

Naturally, you can select and configure multiple interfaces in this fashion, one at a time. If you need to make many configuration changes for each interface in a 48-port switch or module, however, this can get very tedious. The Catalyst IOS Software also allows multiple interfaces to be selected in a single pass through the **interface range** configuration command. After you select the range, any interface configuration commands entered are applied to each of the interfaces in the range.

To select several arbitrary ports for a common configuration setting, you can identify them as a "range" entered as a list. All port numbers and the commas that separate them must be separated with spaces. Use the following command in global configuration mode:

```
Switch(config)# interface range type module/number [, type module/number ...]
```

For example, to select interfaces Fast Ethernet 1/0/3, 1/0/7, 1/0/9, and 1/0/48 for configuration, you could use this command:

```
Switch(config)# interface range fastethernet 1/0/3 , fastethernet 1/0/7 ,
  fastethernet 1/0/9 , fastethernet 1/0/48
```

You also can select a continuous range of ports, from a beginning interface to an ending interface. Enter the interface type and module, followed by the beginning and ending port number separated by a dash with spaces. Use this command in global configuration mode:

```
Switch(config)# interface range type module/first-number - last-number
```

For example, you could select all 48 Fast Ethernet interfaces on module 1 with the following command:

```
Switch(config)# interface range fastethernet 1/0/1 - 48
```

Finally, you sometimes need to make configuration changes to several groups or ranges of ports at the same time. You can define a macro that contains a list of interfaces or ranges of interfaces or both. Then, you can invoke the interface-range macro just before configuring the port settings. This applies the port settings to each interface that is identified by the macro. The steps for defining and applying this macro are as follows:

Step 1. Define the macro name and specify as many lists and ranges of interfaces as needed. The command syntax is open ended but follows the list and range syntax of the **interface range** commands defined previously:

```
Switch(config)# define interface-range macro-name type module/number
[, type module/ number ...] [type module/first-number - last-number]
[...]
```

Step 2. Invoke the macro called *macro-name* just as you would with a regular interface, just before entering any interface-configuration commands:

```
Switch(config)# interface range macro macro-name
```

As an example, suppose that you need to configure Gigabit Ethernet 2/0/1, 2/0/3 through 2/0/5, 3/0/1, 3/0/10, and 3/0/32 through 3/0/48 with a set of identical interface configurations. You could use the following commands to define and apply a macro, respectively:

```
Switch(config)# define interface-range MyGroup gig 2/0/1 , gig 2/0/3 - 2/0/5 ,
  gig 3/0/1 , gig 3/0/10, gig 3/0/32 - 3/0/48
Switch(config)# interface range macro MyGroup
```

Remember to surround any commas and hyphens with spaces when you enter **interface range** commands.

Identifying Ports

You can add a text description to a switch port's configuration to help identify it. This description is meant as a comment field only, as a record of port use or other unique information. The port description is included when displaying the switch configuration and interface information.

To assign a comment or description to a port, enter the following command in interface configuration mode:

```
Switch(config-if)# description description-string
```

The description string can have embedded spaces between words, if needed. To remove a description, use the **no description** interface-configuration command.

As an example, interface Fast Ethernet 1/0/11 is labeled with "Printer in Bldg A, room 213":

```
Switch(config)# interface fast 1/0/11
Switch(config-if)# description Printer in Bldg A, room 213
```

Port Speed

Key Topic

You can assign a specific speed to switch ports through switch-configuration commands. Fast Ethernet 10/100 ports can be set to speeds of 10, 100, and Auto (the default) for autonegotiate mode. Gigabit Ethernet GBIC ports always are set to a speed of 1000, whereas 1000BASE-T ports can be set to speeds of 10, 100, 1000, and Auto (the default).

Note: If a 10/100 or a 10/100/1000 port is assigned a speed of Auto, both its speed and duplex mode will be negotiated.

To specify the port speed on a particular Ethernet port, use the following interface-configuration command:

```
Switch(config-if)# speed {10 | 100 | 1000 | auto}
```

Port Duplex Mode

Key Topic

You also can assign a specific link mode to Ethernet-based switch ports. Therefore, the port operates in half-duplex, full-duplex, or autonegotiated mode. Autonegotiation is allowed only on UTP Fast Ethernet and Gigabit Ethernet ports. In this mode, the port *participates* in a negotiation by attempting full-duplex operation first and then half-duplex operation if full duplex is not successful. The autonegotiation process repeats whenever the link status changes. Be sure to set both ends of a link to the same speed and duplex settings to eliminate any chance that the two ends will be mismatched.

Note: A 10-Mbps Ethernet link (fixed speed) defaults to half duplex, whereas a 100-Mbps Fast Ethernet (dual speed 10/100) link defaults to full duplex. Multispeed links default to autonegotiate the duplex mode.

To set the link mode on a switch port, enter the following command in interface configuration mode:

```
Switch(config-if)# duplex {auto | full | half}
```

For instance, you could use the commands in Example 3-1 to configure 10/100/1000 interfaces Gigabit Ethernet 3/1 for autonegotiation and 3/2 for 100-Mbps full duplex (no autonegotiation).

Example 3-1 *Configuring the Link Mode on a Switch Port*

```
Switch(config)# interface gig 3/1
Switch(config-if)# speed auto
Switch(config-if)# duplex auto
Switch(config-if)# interface gig 3/2
Switch(config-if)# speed 100
Switch(config-if)# duplex full
```

Managing Error Conditions on a Switch Port

A network-management application can be used to detect a serious error condition on a switch port. A switch can be polled periodically so that its port error counters can be examined to see whether an error condition has occurred. If so, an alert can be issued so that someone can take action to correct the problem.

Catalyst switches can detect error conditions automatically, without any further help. If a serious error occurs on a switch port, that port can be shut down automatically until someone manually enables the port again, or until a predetermined time has elapsed.

Detecting Error Conditions

By default, a Catalyst switch detects an error condition on every switch port for every possible cause. If an error condition is detected, the switch port is put into the errdisable state and is disabled. You can tune this behavior on a global basis so that only certain causes trigger any port being disabled. Use the following command in global configuration mode, where the **no** keyword is added to disable the specified cause:

```
Switch(config)# [no] errdisable detect cause [all | cause-name]
```

You can repeat this command to enable or disable more than one cause. One of the following triggers the errdisable state:

- **all**—Detects every possible cause

- **arp-inspection**—Detects errors with dynamic ARP inspection

- **bpduguard**—Detects when a spanning-tree bridge protocol data unit (BPDU) is received on a port configured for STP PortFast

- **channel-misconfig**—Detects an error with an EtherChannel bundle

- **dhcp-rate-limit**—Detects an error with DHCP snooping

- **dtp-flap**—Detects when trunking encapsulation is changing from one type to another

- **gbic-invalid**—Detects the presence of an invalid GBIC or SFP module

- **ilpower**—Detects an error with offering inline power

- **l2ptguard**—Detects an error with Layer 2 Protocol Tunneling

- **link-flap**—Detects when the port link state is "flapping" between the up and down states

- **loopback**—Detects when an interface has been looped back

- **pagp-flap**—Detects when an EtherChannel bundle's ports no longer have consistent configurations

- **psecure-violation**—Detects conditions that trigger port security configured on a port

- **rootguard**—Detects when an STP BPDU is received from the root bridge on an unexpected port

- **security-violation**—Detects errors related to port security

- **storm-control**—Detects when a storm control threshold has been exceeded on a port

- **udld**—Detects when a link is seen to be *unidirectional* (data passing in only one direction)

- **unicast-flood**—Detects conditions that trigger unicast flood blocking on a port

- **vmps**—Detects errors when assigning a port to a dynamic VLAN through VLAN membership policy server (VMPS)

Automatically Recover from Error Conditions

By default, ports put into the errdisable state must be re-enabled manually. This is done by issuing the **shutdown** command in interface configuration mode, followed by the **no shutdown** command. Before you re-enable a port from the errdisable condition, you always should determine the cause of the problem so that the errdisable condition doesn't occur again.

You can decide to have a switch automatically reenable an errdisabled port if it is more important to keep the link up until the problem can be resolved. To automatically reenable an errdisabled port, you first must specify the errdisable causes that can be reenabled. Use this command in global configuration mode, with a *cause-name* from the preceding list:

```
Switch(config)# errdisable recovery cause [all | cause-name]
```

If any errdisable causes are configured for automatic recovery, the errdisabled port stays down for 300 seconds, by default. To change the recovery timer, use the following command in global configuration mode:

```
Switch(config)# errdisable recovery interval seconds
```

You can set the interval from 30 to 86,400 seconds (24 hours).

As an example, you could use the following commands to configure all switch ports to be reenabled automatically in 1 hour after a port security violation has been detected:

```
Switch(config)# errdisable recovery cause psecurity-violation
Switch(config)# errdisable recovery interval 3600
```

Remember that the errdisable causes and automatic recovery are configured globally—the settings apply to all switch ports.

Enable and Use the Switch Port

If the port is not enabled or activated automatically, use the **no shutdown** interface-configuration command. To view a port's current speed and duplex state, use the **show interface** command. You can see a brief summary of all interface states with the **show interfaces status** command.

Troubleshooting Port Connectivity

Suppose that you are experiencing problems with a switch port. How would you troubleshoot it? The following sections cover a few common troubleshooting techniques.

Looking for the Port State

Use the **show interfaces** EXEC command to see complete information about the switch port. The port's current state is given in the first line of output, as in Example 3-2.

Key Topic

Example 3-2   *Determining Port State Information*

```
Switch# show interfaces fastethernet 1/0/1
FastEthernet1/0/1 is up, line protocol is up
  Hardware is Fast Ethernet, address is 0009.b7ee.9801 (bia 0009.b7ee.9801)
  MTU 1500 bytes, BW 100000 Kbit, DLY 100 usec,
     reliability 255/255, txload 1/255, rxload 1/255
```

The first **up** tells the state of the port's physical or data link layer. If this is shown as **down**, the link is physically disconnected or a link cannot be detected. The second state, given as **line protocol is up**, shows the Layer 2 status. If the state is given as **errdisable**, the switch has detected a serious error condition on this port and has automatically disabled it.

To quickly see a list of states for all switch ports, use the **show interface status** EXEC command. Likewise, you can see a list of all ports in the errdisable state (and the cause) by using the **show interface status err-disabled** EXEC command.

Looking for Speed and Duplex Mismatches

If a user notices slow response time or low throughput on a 10/100 or 10/100/1000 switch port, the problem could be a mismatch of the port speed or duplex mode between the switch and the host. This is particularly common when one end of the link is set to autonegotiate the link settings and the other end is not.

Key Topic

Use the **show interface** command for a specific interface and look for any error counts that are greater than 0. For example, in the following output in Example 3-3, the switch port is set to autonegotiate the speed and duplex mode. It has decided on 100 Mbps at half duplex. Notice that there are many *runts* (packets that were truncated before they were fully received) and input errors. These are symptoms that a setting mismatch exists between the two ends of the link.

Example 3-3   *Determining Link Speed and Duplex Mode*

```
Switch# show interfaces fastethernet 1/0/13
FastEthernet1/0/13 is up, line protocol is up
  Hardware is Fast Ethernet, address is 00d0.589c.3e8d (bia 00d0.589c.3e8d)
  MTU 1500 bytes, BW 10000 Kbit, DLY 1000 usec,
      reliability 255/255, txload 2/255, rxload 1/255
  Encapsulation ARPA, loopback not set
  Keepalive not set
  Auto-duplex (Half), Auto Speed (100), 100BASETX/FX  ARP type: ARPA, ARP
      Timeout 04:00:00
Last input never, output 00:00:01, output hang never
Last clearing of "show interface" counters never
Queueing strategy: fifo
Output queue 0/40, 0 drops; input queue 0/75, 0 drops
5 minute input rate 0 bits/sec, 0 packets/sec
5 minute output rate 81000 bits/sec, 49 packets/sec
    500867 packets input, 89215950 bytes
    Received 12912 broadcasts, 374879 runts, 0 giants, 0 throttles
    374879 input errors, 0 CRC, 0 frame, 0 overrun, 0 ignored
    0 watchdog, 0 multicast
    0 input packets with dribble condition detected
    89672388 packets output, 2205443729 bytes, 0 underruns
    0 output errors, 0 collisions, 3 interface resets
    0 babbles, 0 late collision, 0 deferred
    0 lost carrier, 0 no carrier
    0 output buffer failures, 0 output buffers swapped out
```

Because this port is autonegotiating the link speed, it must have detected an electrical signal that indicated 100 Mbps in common with the host. However, the host most likely was configured for 100 Mbps at full duplex (not autonegotiating). The switch was incapable of exchanging duplex information, so it fell back to its default of half duplex. Again, always make sure both ends of a connection are set to the same speed and duplex.

Exam Preparation Tasks

Review All Key Topics

Review the most important topics in the chapter, noted with the Key Topic icon in the outer margin of the page. Table 3-6 lists a reference of these key topics and the page numbers on which each is found.

Key
Topic

Table 3-6   *Key Topics for Chapter 3*

Key Topic Element	Description	Page Number
Paragraph	Describes the characteristics of Ethernet switching	44
Paragraph	Explains Ethernet autonegotiation	46
Paragraph	Discusses similarities and differences of Ethernet types	47
Paragraph	Describes 10-Gigabit Ethernet	49
Paragraph	Covers interface selection for configuration	52
Paragraph	Explains how to configure the port speed	54
Paragraph	Explains how to configure the port duplex mode	54
Paragraph	Explains how to configure port error detection	55
Paragraph	Explains how to verify the port state	57
Paragraph	Explains how to verify port speed and duplex mode	57

Define Key Terms

Define the following key terms from this chapter, and check your answers in the glossary:

CSMA/CD, duplex mode, autonegotiation, duplex mismatch, IEEE 802.3

Use Command Reference to Check Your Memory

This section includes the most important configuration and EXEC commands covered in this chapter. It might not be necessary to memorize the complete syntax of every command, but you should remember the basic keywords that are needed.

To test your memory of the port configuration commands, cover the right side of Table 3-7 with a piece of paper, read the description on the left side, and then see how much of the command you can remember.

Remember that the CCNP exam focuses on practical or hands-on skills that are used by a networking professional. Therefore, you should remember the commands needed to configure and test a switch interface.

Table 3-7 *Switch Port Configuration Commands*

Task	Command Syntax
Select a port.	interface *type module/number*
Select multiple ports.	interface range *type module/number* [, *type module/number ...*]
	or
	interface range *type module/first-number – last-number*
Define an interface macro.	define interface-range *macro-name type module/number* [, *type module/number ...*] [*type module/first-number – last-number*] [...]
	interface range macro *macro-name*
Identify port.	description *description-string*
Set port speed.	speed {10 | 100 | 1000 | auto}
Set port mode.	duplex {auto | full | half}
Detect port error conditions.	errdisable detect cause [all | *cause-name*]
Automatically recover from errdisable.	errdisable recovery cause [all | *cause-name*]
	errdisable recovery interval *seconds*
Manually recover from errdisable.	shutdown
	no shutdown

This chapter covers the following topics that you need to master for the CCNP SWITCH exam:

Virtual LANs—This section reviews VLANs, VLAN membership, and VLAN configuration on a Catalyst switch.

VLAN Trunks—This section covers transporting multiple VLANs over single links and VLAN trunking with Ethernet.

VLAN Trunk Configuration—This section outlines the Catalyst switch commands that configure VLAN trunks.

Troubleshooting VLANs and Trunks—This section provides commands to use when a VLAN or trunk is not operating properly.

CHAPTER 4

VLANs and Trunks

Switched campus networks can be broken up into distinct broadcast domains or virtual LANs (VLAN). A flat network topology, or a network with a single broadcast domain, can be simple to implement and manage. However, flat network topology is not scalable. Instead, the campus can be divided into segments using VLANs, while Layer 3 routing protocols manage interVLAN communication.

This chapter details the process of defining common workgroups within a group of switches. It covers switch configuration for VLANs, along with the method of identifying and transporting VLANs on various types of links.

"Do I Know This Already?" Quiz

The "Do I Know This Already?" quiz allows you to assess whether you should read this entire chapter thoroughly or jump to the "Exam Preparation Tasks" section. If you are in doubt based on your answers to these questions or your own assessment of your knowledge of the topics, read the entire chapter. Table 4-1 outlines the major headings in this chapter and the "Do I Know This Already?" quiz questions that go with them. You can find the answers in Appendix A, "Answers to the 'Do I Know This Already?' Quizzes."

Table 4-1 *"Do I Know This Already?" Foundation Topics Section-to-Question Mapping*

Foundation Topics Section	Questions Covered in This Section
Virtual LANs	1–4
VLAN Trunks	5–12
VLAN Trunk Configuration	
Troubleshooting VLANs and Trunks	13–14

1. A VLAN is which of the following?

   a. Collision domain

   b. Spanning-tree domain

   c. Broadcast domain

   d. VTP domain

2. Switches provide VLAN connectivity at which layer of the OSI model?

    a. Layer 1

    b. Layer 2

    c. Layer 3

    d. Layer 4

3. Which one of the following is needed to pass data between two PCs, each connected to a different VLAN?

    a. Layer 2 switch

    b. Layer 3 switch

    c. Trunk

    d. Tunnel

4. Which Catalyst IOS switch command is used to assign a port to a VLAN?

    a. access vlan *vlan-id*

    b. switchport access vlan *vlan-id*

    c. vlan *vlan-id*

    d. set port vlan *vlan-id*

5. Which of the following is a standardized method of trunk encapsulation?

    a. 802.1d

    b. 802.1Q

    c. 802.3z

    d. 802.1a

6. What is the Cisco proprietary method for trunk encapsulation?

    a. CDP

    b. EIGRP

    c. ISL

    d. DSL

7. Which of these protocols dynamically negotiates trunking parameters?

    a. PAgP

    b. STP

    c. CDP

    d. DTP

8. How many different VLANs can an 802.1Q trunk support?

    a. 256

    b. 1024

    c. 4096

    d. 32,768

    e. 65,536

9. Which of the following incorrectly describes a native VLAN?

    a. Frames are untagged on an 802.1Q trunk.

    b. Frames are untagged on an ISL trunk.

    c. Frames can be interpreted by a nontrunking host.

    d. The native VLAN can be configured for each trunking port.

10. If two switches each support all types of trunk encapsulation on a link between them, which one will be negotiated?

    a. ISL

    b. 802.1Q

    c. DTP

    d. VTP

11. Which VLANs are allowed on a trunk link by default?

    a. None

    b. Only the native VLAN

    c. All active VLANs

    d. Only negotiated VLANs

12. Which command configures a switch port to form a trunk without using negotiation?

    a. **switchport mode trunk**

    b. **switchport mode trunk nonegotiate**

    c. **switchport mode dynamic auto**

    d. **switchport mode dynamic desirable**

13. Two hosts are connected to switch interfaces Fast Ethernet 0/1 and 0/33, but they cannot communicate with each other. Their IP addresses are in the 192.168.10.0/24 subnet, which is carried over VLAN 10. The **show vlan id 10** command generates the following output:

```
Switch# show vlan id 10
VLAN Name                              Status    Ports
---- -------------------------------   -----. ----------------
-
Users                            active    Fa0/1, Fa0/2, Fa0/3, Fa0/4,
                                           Fa0/5, Fa0/6, Fa0/7, Fa0/8,
                                           Fa0/9, Fa0/10, Fa0/11, Fa0/12,
```

```
Fa0/13, Fa0/14, Fa0/15, Fa0/16,
Fa0/17, Fa0/18, Fa0/19, Fa0/20,
Fa0/21, Fa0/22, Fa0/23, Fa0/25,
Fa0/26, Fa0/27, Fa0/28, Fa0/31,
Fa0/32, Fa0/34, Fa0/35, Fa0/36,
Fa0/37, Fa0/39, Fa0/40, Fa0/41,
Fa0/42, Fa0/43, Fa0/46
```

The hosts are known to be up and connected. Which of the following reasons might be causing the problem?

- **a.** The two hosts are assigned to VLAN 1.
- **b.** The two hosts are assigned to different VLANs.
- **c.** Interface FastEthernet0/33 is a VLAN trunk.
- **d.** The two hosts are using unregistered MAC addresses.

14. A trunk link between two switches did not come up as expected. The configuration on Switch A is as follows:

```
Switch A# show running-config interface gigabitethernet0/1
interface GigabitEthernet0/1
  switchport trunk encapsulation dot1q
  switchport trunk allowed vlan 1-10
  switchport mode dynamic auto
  no shutdown
```

The interface configuration on Switch B is as follows:

```
Switch B# show running-config interface gigabitethernet0/1
interface GigabitEthernet0/1
  switchport trunk encapsulation dot1q
  switchport mode dynamic auto
  switchport access vlan 5
  no shutdown
```

Which one of the following reasons is probably causing the problem?

- **a.** The two switches don't have matching **switchport trunk allowed vlan** commands.
- **b.** Neither switch has a native VLAN configured.
- **c.** Both switches are configured in the dynamic auto mode.
- **d.** Switch B is configured to use access VLAN 5.

Foundation Topics

Virtual LANs

Consider a network design that consists of Layer 2 devices only. For example, this design could be a single Ethernet segment, an Ethernet switch with many ports, or a network with several interconnected Ethernet switches. A full Layer 2–only switched network is referred to as a *flat network topology*. A flat network is a single broadcast domain, such that every connected device sees every broadcast packet that is transmitted. As the number of stations on the network increases, so does the number of broadcasts.

Because of the Layer 2 foundation, flat networks cannot contain redundant paths for load balancing or fault tolerance. The reason for this is explained in Chapters 7, "Traditional Spanning Tree Protocol," through 10, "Advanced Spanning Tree Protocol." To gain any advantage from additional paths to a destination, Layer 3 routing functions must be introduced.

A switched environment offers the technology to overcome flat network limitations. Switched networks can be subdivided into VLANs. By definition, a VLAN is a single broadcast domain. All devices connected to the VLAN receive broadcasts sent by any other VLAN members. However, devices connected to a different VLAN will not receive those same broadcasts. (Naturally, VLAN members also receive unicast packets directed toward them from other VLAN members.)

Key Topic

A VLAN consists of hosts defined as members, communicating as a *logical* network segment. In contrast, a physical segment consists of devices that must be connected to a physical cable segment. A VLAN can have connected members located anywhere in the campus network, as long as VLAN connectivity is provided among all members. Layer 2 switches are configured with a VLAN mapping and provide the logical connectivity among the VLAN members.

Figure 4-1 shows how a VLAN can provide logical connectivity between switch ports. Two workstations on the left Catalyst switch are assigned to VLAN 1, whereas a third workstation is assigned to VLAN 100. In this example, no communication can occur between VLAN 1 and VLAN 100. Both ends of the link between the Catalysts are assigned to VLAN 1. One workstation on the right Catalyst also is assigned to VLAN 1. Because there is end-to-end connectivity of VLAN 1, any of the workstations on VLAN 1 can communicate as if they were connected to a physical network segment.

VLAN Membership

When a VLAN is provided at an access-layer switch, an end user must have some means of gaining membership to it. Two membership methods exist on Cisco Catalyst switches:

- Static VLAN configuration

- Dynamic VLAN assignment

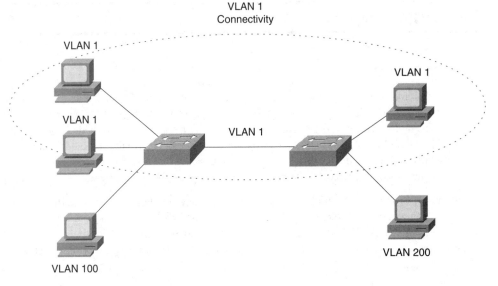

Figure 4-1 *VLAN Functionality*

Static VLANs

Static VLANs offer *port-based* membership, in which switch ports are assigned to specific VLANs. End-user devices become members in a VLAN based on the physical switch port to which they are connected. No handshaking or unique VLAN membership protocol is needed for the end devices; they automatically assume VLAN connectivity when they connect to a port. Normally, the end device is not even aware that the VLAN exists. The switch port and its VLAN simply are viewed and used as any other network segment, with other "locally attached" members on the wire.

Switch ports are assigned to VLANs by the manual intervention of the network administrator, hence the static nature. Each port receives a Port VLAN ID (PVID) that associates it with a VLAN number. The ports on a single switch can be assigned and grouped into many VLANs. Even though two devices are connected to the same switch, traffic will not pass between them if they are connected to ports on different VLANs. To perform this function, you could use either a Layer 3 device to route packets or an external Layer 2 device to bridge packets between the two VLANs.

The static port-to-VLAN membership normally is handled in hardware with application-specific integrated circuits (ASIC) in the switch. This membership provides good performance because all port mappings are done at the hardware level, with no complex table lookups needed.

Configuring Static VLANs

This section describes the switch commands needed to configure static VLANs. By default, all switch ports are assigned to VLAN 1, are set to be a VLAN type of Ethernet, and have a maximum transmission unit (MTU) size of 1500 bytes.

First, the VLAN must be created on the switch, if it does not already exist. Then, the VLAN must be assigned to specific switch ports. VLANs always are referenced by a VLAN number, which can range from 1 to 1005. VLANs 1 and 1002 through 1005 automatically are created and are set aside for special uses. For example, VLAN 1 is the default VLAN for every switch port. VLANs 1002 to 1005 are reserved for legacy functions related to Token Ring and FDDI switching.

Catalyst IOS switches also can support extended-range VLANs, in which the VLAN number can be 1 to 4094, for compatibility with the IEEE 802.1Q standard. The extended range is enabled only when the switch is configured for VTP transparent mode with the **vtp mode transparent** global configuration command. This is because of limitations with VTP Versions 1 and 2. VTP Version 3 does allow extended range VLANs to be used and advertised, but this version is not available in any IOS-based Catalyst switches at press time. (VTP is covered in Chapter 5, "VLAN Trunking Protocol.")

Tip: Although the extended range of VLAN numbers enables you to support more VLANs in your network, some limitations exist. For example, a switch normally maintains VLAN definitions in a special database file, separate from the switch configuration. The VLAN Trunking Protocol (VTP) uses the VLAN database so that VLAN definitions can be advertised and shared between switches over trunk links. When extended-range VLANs are created, they are not stored in the VLAN database file.

Why does this matter? As long as the switch remains in VTP transparent mode, the extended VLANs can be used. However, if the switch is later configured to participate in VTP as either a server or a client, you must manually delete the extended VLANs. For any switch ports that were assigned to the extended VLANs, you also must reconfigure them for VLAN membership within the normal VLAN range.

To configure static VLANs, begin by defining the VLAN with the following command in global configuration mode:

```
Switch(config)# vlan vlan-num
Switch(config-vlan)# name vlan-name
```

The VLAN numbered *vlan-num* is immediately created and stored in the database, along with a descriptive text string defined by *vlan-name* (up to 32 characters with no embedded spaces). The **name** command is optional; if it is not used, the default VLAN name is of the form **VLAN** *XXX*, where *XXX* represents the VLAN number. If you need to include spaces to separate words in the VLAN name, use underscore characters instead.

As an example, you can use the following commands to create VLANs 2 and 101:

```
Switch(config)# vlan 2
Switch(config-vlan)# name Engineering
Switch(config-vlan)# vlan 101
Switch(config-vlan)# name Marketing
```

To delete a VLAN from the switch configuration, you can use the **no vlan** *vlan-num* command.

Next, you should assign one or more switch ports to the VLAN. Use the following configuration commands:

```
Switch(config)# interface type module/number
Switch(config-if)# switchport
Switch(config-if)# switchport mode access
Switch(config-if)# switchport access vlan vlan-num
```

The initial **switchport** command configures the port for Layer 2 operation. Switch ports on most Catalyst switch platforms default to Layer 2 operation. In that case, the **switchport** command will already be present in the configuration and you won't have to enter it explicitly. Otherwise, the switch will reject any Layer 2 configuration command if the port is not already configured for Layer 2 operation.

The **switchport mode access** command forces the port to be assigned to only a single VLAN, providing VLAN connectivity to the access layer or end user. The port is given a static VLAN membership by the **switchport access vlan** command. Here, the logical VLAN is referenced by the *vlan-num* setting (1 to 1005 or 1 to 4094).

To verify VLAN configuration, use the **show vlan** command to output a list of all VLANs defined in the switch, along with the ports that are assigned to each VLAN. Example 4-1 shows some sample output from the **show vlan** command.

Example 4-1   *Verifying VLAN Configuration with the show vlan Command*

```
Switch#
show vlan
VLAN Name                             Status    Ports
---- -------------------------------- -------   -------------------------------
1    default                          active    Gi1/1, Gi1/2, Gi3/20, Gi4/20
2    Engineering                      active    Gi4/2, Gi4/3, Gi4/4, Gi4/5
                                                Gi4/6, Gi4/7, Gi4/8, Gi4/9
                                                Gi4/10, Gi4/11, Gi4/12
101  Marketing                        active    Gi2/5, Gi2/6, Gi2/7, Gi2/8
                                                Gi2/9, Gi2/10, Gi2/11, Gi2/12
                                                Gi2/13, Gi2/14, Gi2/15, Gi2/16
                                                Gi2/17, Gi2/18
```

Dynamic VLANs

Dynamic VLANs provide membership based on the MAC address of an end-user device. When a device is connected to a switch port, the switch must, in effect, query a database to establish VLAN membership. A network administrator also must assign the user's MAC address to a VLAN in the database of a VLAN Membership Policy Server (VMPS).

With Cisco switches, dynamic VLANs are created and managed using network-management tools such as CiscoWorks. Dynamic VLANs allow a great deal of flexibility and mobility for end users but require more administrative overhead.

Note: Dynamic VLANs are not covered in this text or in the SWITCH course or exam (at press time). For more information, refer to the "Configuring VMPS" section in a Catalyst

configuration guide such as http://www.cisco.com/en/US/docs/switches/lan/catalyst3560/
software/release/12.2_25_see/configuration/guide/swvlan.html#wp1212223.

Deploying VLANs

To implement VLANs, you must consider the number of VLANs you need and how best
to place them. As usual, the number of VLANs depends on traffic patterns, application
types, segmentation of common workgroups, and network-management requirements.

**Key
Topic**

An important factor to consider is the relationship between VLANs and the IP addressing
schemes used. Cisco recommends a one-to-one correspondence between VLANs and IP
subnets. This recommendation means that if a subnet with a 24-bit mask (255.255.255.0) is
used for a VLAN, no more than 254 devices should be in the VLAN. In addition, you
should not allow VLANs to extend beyond the Layer 2 domain of the distribution switch.
In other words, the VLAN should not reach across a network's core and into another
switch block. The idea again is to keep broadcasts and unnecessary traffic movement out
of the core block.

VLANs can be scaled in the switch block by using two basic methods:

- End-to-end VLANs

- Local VLANs

End-to-End VLANs

End-to-end VLANs, also called *campuswide VLANs*, span the entire switch fabric of a
network. They are positioned to support maximum flexibility and mobility of end devices. Users can be assigned to VLANs regardless of their physical location. As a user
moves around the campus, that user's VLAN membership stays the same. This means that
each VLAN must be made available at the access layer in every switch block.

End-to-end VLANs should group users according to common requirements. All users in a
VLAN should have roughly the same traffic flow patterns, following the 80/20 rule. Recall
that this rule estimates that 80 percent of user traffic stays within the local workgroup,
whereas 20 percent is destined for a remote resource in the campus network. Although
only 20 percent of the traffic in a VLAN is expected to cross the network core, end-to-
end VLANs make it possible for 100 percent of the traffic within a single VLAN to cross
the core.

Because all VLANs must be available at each access-layer switch, VLAN trunking must be
used to carry all VLANs between the access- and distribution-layer switches.

Tip: End-to-end VLANs are not recommended in an enterprise network, unless there is a
good reason. In an end-to-end VLAN, broadcast traffic is carried over from one end of the
network to the other, creating the possibility for a broadcast storm or Layer 2 bridging
loop to spread across the whole extent of a VLAN. This can exhaust the bandwidth of dis-
tribution- and core-layer links, as well as switch CPU resources. Now the storm or loop has

disrupted users on the end-to-end VLAN, in addition to users on other VLANs that might be crossing the core.

When such a problem occurs, troubleshooting becomes more difficult. In other words, the risks of end-to-end VLANs outweigh the convenience and benefits.

Local VLANs

Because most enterprise networks have moved toward the 20/80 rule (where server and intranet/Internet resources are centralized), end-to-end VLANs have become cumbersome and difficult to maintain. The 20/80 rule reverses the traffic pattern of the end-to-end VLAN: Only 20 percent of traffic is local, whereas 80 percent is destined to a remote resource across the core layer. End users usually require access to central resources outside their VLAN. Users must cross into the network core more frequently. In this type of network, VLANs should be designed to contain user communities based on geographic boundaries, with little regard to the amount of traffic leaving the VLAN.

Local or geographic VLANs range in size from a single switch in a wiring closet to an entire building. Arranging VLANs in this fashion enables the Layer 3 function in the campus network to intelligently handle the interVLAN traffic loads, where traffic passes into the core. This scenario provides maximum availability by using multiple paths to destinations, maximum scalability by keeping the VLAN within a switch block, and maximum manageability.

VLAN Trunks

At the access layer, end-user devices connect to switch ports that provide simple connectivity to a single VLAN each. The attached devices are unaware of any VLAN structure and simply attach to what appears to be a normal physical network segment. Remember, sending information from an access link on one VLAN to another VLAN is not possible without the intervention of an additional device—either a Layer 3 router or an external Layer 2 bridge.

Note that a single switch port can support more than one IP subnet for the devices attached to it. For example, consider a shared Ethernet hub that is connected to a single Ethernet switch port. One user device on the hub might be configured for 192.168.1.1 255.255.255.0, whereas another is assigned 192.168.17.1 255.255.255.0. Although these subnets are discontiguous and unique, and both are communicating on one switch port, they cannot be considered separate VLANs. The switch port supports one VLAN, but multiple subnets can exist on that single VLAN.

A *trunk link*, however, can transport more than one VLAN through a single switch port. Trunk links are most beneficial when switches are connected to other switches or switches are connected to routers. A trunk link is not assigned to a specific VLAN. Instead, one, many, or all active VLANs can be transported between switches using a single physical trunk link.

Connecting two switches with separate physical links for each VLAN is possible. The top half of Figure 4-2 shows how two switches might be connected in this fashion.

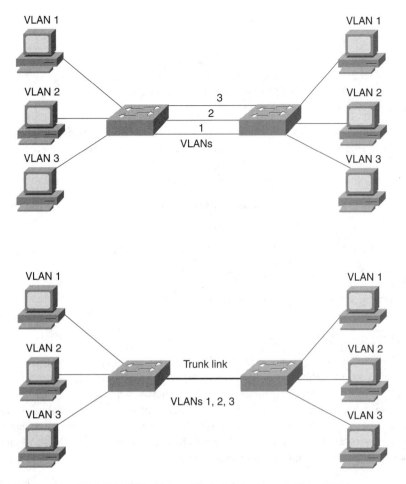

Figure 4-2 *Passing VLAN Traffic Using Single Links Versus Trunk Links*

As VLANs are added to a network, the number of links can grow quickly. A more efficient use of physical interfaces and cabling involves the use of trunking. The bottom half of the figure shows how one trunk link can replace many individual VLAN links.

Cisco supports trunking on both Fast Ethernet and Gigabit Ethernet switch links, and aggregated Fast and Gigabit EtherChannel links. To distinguish between traffic belonging to different VLANs on a trunk link, the switch must have a method of identifying each frame with the appropriate VLAN. The switches on *each end* of a trunk link both must have the same method for correlating frames with VLAN numbers. The next section covers several available identification methods.

VLAN Frame Identification

Because a trunk link can transport many VLANs, a switch must identify frames with their respective VLANs as they are sent and received over a trunk link. Frame identification, or *tagging*, assigns a unique user-defined ID to each frame transported on a trunk link.

Think of this ID as the VLAN number or VLAN "color," as if each VLAN were drawn on a network diagram in a unique color.

VLAN frame identification was developed for switched networks. As each frame is transmitted over a trunk link, a unique identifier is placed in the frame header. As each switch along the way receives these frames, the identifier is examined to determine to which VLAN the frames belong and then is removed.

If frames must be transported out another trunk link, the VLAN identifier is added back into the frame header. Otherwise, if frames are destined out an access (nontrunk) link, the switch removes the VLAN identifier before transmitting the frames to the end station. Therefore, all traces of VLAN association are hidden from the end station.

VLAN identification can be performed using two methods, each using a different frame identifier mechanism:

- Inter-Switch Link (ISL) protocol
- IEEE 802.1Q protocol

These methods are described in the sections that follow.

Inter-Switch Link Protocol

The Inter-Switch Link (ISL) protocol is a Cisco-proprietary method for preserving the source VLAN identification of frames passing over a trunk link. ISL performs frame identification in Layer 2 by encapsulating each frame between a header and a trailer. Any Cisco switch or router device configured for ISL can process and understand the ISL VLAN information. ISL primarily is used for Ethernet media, although Cisco has included provisions to carry Token Ring, FDDI, and ATM frames over Ethernet ISL. (A Frame-Type field in the ISL header indicates the source frame type.)

When a frame is destined out a trunk link to another switch or router, ISL adds a 26-byte header and a 4-byte trailer to the frame. The source VLAN is identified with a 15-bit VLAN ID field in the header. The trailer contains a cyclic redundancy check (CRC) value to ensure the data integrity of the new encapsulated frame. Figure 4-3 shows how Ethernet frames are encapsulated and forwarded out a trunk link. Because tagging information is added at the beginning and end of each frame, ISL sometimes is referred to as *double tagging*.

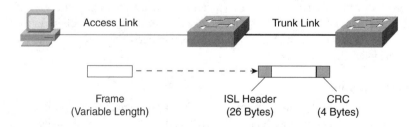

Access Link   Trunk Link

Frame   ISL Header   CRC
(Variable Length)   (26 Bytes)   (4 Bytes)

Figure 4-3   *ISL Frame Identification*

If a frame is destined for an access link, the ISL encapsulation (both header and trailer) is not rewritten into the frame before transmission. This removal preserves ISL information only for trunk links and devices that can understand the protocol.

Tip: The ISL method of VLAN identification or trunking encapsulation no longer is supported across all Cisco Catalyst switch platforms. Even so, you should still be familiar with it and know how it compares to the standards-based IEEE 802.1Q method.

IEEE 802.1Q Protocol

The IEEE 802.1Q protocol also can carry VLAN associations over trunk links. However, this frame-identification method is standardized, allowing VLAN trunks to exist and operate between equipment from multiple vendors.

Key Topic

In particular, the IEEE 802.1Q standard defines an architecture for VLAN use, services provided with VLANs, and protocols and algorithms used to provide VLAN services. You can find further information about the 802.1Q standard at http://grouper.ieee.org/groups/802/1/pages/802.1Q.html.

As with Cisco ISL, IEEE 802.1Q can be used for VLAN identification with Ethernet trunks. However, instead of encapsulating each frame with a VLAN ID header and trailer, 802.1Q embeds its tagging information within the Layer 2 frame. This method is referred to as *single tagging* or *internal tagging*.

802.1Q also introduces the concept of a *native VLAN* on a trunk. Frames belonging to this VLAN are *not* encapsulated with any tagging information. If an end station is connected to an 802.1Q trunk link, the end station can receive and understand only the native VLAN frames. This provides a simple way to offer full trunk encapsulation to the devices that can understand it, while giving normal-access stations some inherent connectivity over the trunk.

In an Ethernet frame, 802.1Q adds a 4-byte tag just after the source Address field, as shown in Figure 4-4.

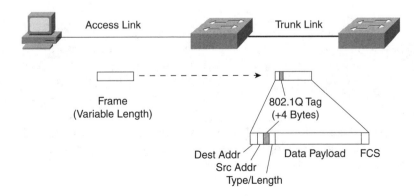

Figure 4-4 *IEEE 802.1Q Frame-Tagging Standard*

The first two bytes are used as a Tag Protocol Identifier (TPID) and always have a value of 0x8100 to signify an 802.1Q tag. The remaining two bytes are used as a Tag Control Information (TCI) field. The TCI information contains a three-bit Priority field, which is used to implement class-of-service (CoS) functions in the accompanying 802.1Q/802.1p prioritization standard. One bit of the TCI is a Canonical Format Indicator (CFI), flagging whether the MAC addresses are in Ethernet or Token Ring format. (This also is known as *canonical format*, or *little-endian* or *big-endian format*.)

The last 12 bits are used as a VLAN identifier (VID) to indicate the source VLAN for the frame. The VID can have values from 0 to 4095, but VLANs 0, 1, and 4095 are reserved.

Note that both ISL and 802.1Q tagging methods have one implication—they add to the length of an existing Ethernet frame. ISL adds a total of 30 bytes to each frame, whereas 802.1Q adds 4 bytes. Because Ethernet frames cannot exceed 1518 bytes, the additional VLAN tagging information can cause the frame to become too large. Frames that barely exceed the MTU size are called *baby giant frames*. Switches usually report these frames as Ethernet errors or oversize frames.

Note: Baby giant, or oversize, frames can exceed the frame size set in various standards. To properly handle and forward them anyway, Catalyst switches use proprietary hardware with the ISL encapsulation method. In the case of 802.1Q encapsulation, switches can comply with the IEEE 802.3ac standard, which extends the maximum frame length to 1522 bytes.

Dynamic Trunking Protocol

You can manually configure trunk links on Catalyst switches for either ISL or 802.1Q mode. In addition, Cisco has implemented a proprietary, point-to-point protocol called *Dynamic Trunking Protocol (DTP)* that negotiates a common trunking mode between two switches. The negotiation covers the encapsulation (ISL or 802.1Q) and whether the link becomes a trunk at all. This allows trunk links to be used without a great deal of manual configuration or administration. The use of DTP is explained in the next section.

Tip: You should disable DTP negotiation if a switch has a trunk link connected to a non-trunking router or firewall interface because those devices cannot participate in DTP negotiation. A trunk link can be negotiated between two switches only if both switches belong to the same VLAN Trunking Protocol (VTP) management domain or if one or both switches have not defined their VTP domain (that is, the NULL domain). VTP is discussed in Chapter 5.

If the two switches are in different VTP domains and trunking is desired between them, you must set the trunk links to on mode or nonegotiate mode. This setting forces the trunk to be established. These options are explained in the next section.

VLAN Trunk Configuration

By default, all switch ports in Layer 2 mode are nontrunking and operate as access links until some intervention changes the mode. Specifically, ports actively try to become trunks as long as the far end agrees. In that case, a common encapsulation is chosen, favoring ISL if both support it. The sections that follow demonstrate the commands necessary to configure VLAN trunks.

VLAN Trunk Configuration

Use the following commands to create a VLAN trunk link:

```
Switch(config)# interface type mod/port
Switch(config-if)# switchport
Switch(config-if)# switchport trunk encapsulation {isl | dot1q | negotiate}
Switch(config-if)# switchport trunk native vlan vlan-id
Switch(config-if)# switchport trunk allowed vlan {vlan-list | all |
   {add | except | remove} vlan-list}
Switch(config-if)# switchport mode {trunk | dynamic {desirable | auto}}
```

A switch port must be in Layer 2 mode before it can support a trunk. To accomplish this, you use the **switchport** command with no other keywords. You then can configure the trunk encapsulation with the **switchport trunk encapsulation** command, as one of the following:

- **Isl**—VLANs are tagged by encapsulating each frame using the Cisco ISL protocol.

- **dot1q**—VLANs are tagged in each frame using the IEEE 802.1Q standard protocol. The only exception is the native VLAN, which is sent normally and is not tagged.

- **negotiate (the default)**—The encapsulation is negotiated to select either ISL or IEEE 802.1Q, whichever both ends of the trunk support. If both ends support both types, ISL is favored.

In the case of an IEEE 802.1Q trunk, you should configure the native VLAN with the **switchport trunk native vlan** command, identifying the untagged or native VLAN number as *vlan-id* (1 to 4094). By default, an 802.1Q trunk uses VLAN 1 as the native VLAN. In the case of an ISL trunk, using this command has no effect because ISL doesn't support an untagged VLAN.

The last command, **switchport trunk allowed vlan**, defines which VLANs can be trunked over the link. By default, a switch transports all active VLANs (1 to 4094) over a trunk link. An active VLAN is one that has been defined on the switch and has ports assigned to carry it.

There might be times when the trunk link should not carry all VLANs. For example, broadcasts are forwarded to every switch port on a VLAN—including the trunk link because it, too, is a member of the VLAN. If the VLAN does not extend past the far end of the trunk link, propagating broadcasts across the trunk makes no sense.

Key Topic

You can tailor the list of allowed VLANs on the trunk by using the **switchport trunk allowed vlan** command with one of the following:

- **vlan-list**—An explicit list of VLAN numbers, separated by commas or dashes.

- **all**—All active VLANs (1 to 4094) will be allowed.

- **add *vlan-list***—A list of VLAN numbers will be added to the already configured list; this is a shortcut to keep from typing a long list of numbers.

- **except *vlan-list***—All VLANs (1 to 4094) will be allowed, except for the VLAN numbers listed; this is a shortcut to keep from typing a long list of numbers.

- **remove *vlan-list***—A list of VLAN numbers will be removed from the already configured list; this is a shortcut to keep from typing a long list of numbers.

In the **switchport mode** command, you can set the trunking mode to any of the following:

- **trunk**—This setting places the port in permanent trunking mode. DTP is still operational, so if the far-end switch port is configured to trunk, dynamic desirable, or dynamic auto mode, trunking will be negotiated successfully.

  The trunk mode is usually used to establish an unconditional trunk. Therefore, the corresponding switch port at the other end of the trunk should be configured similarly. In this way, both switches always expect the trunk link to be operational without any negotiation. You also should manually configure the encapsulation mode to eliminate its negotiation.

- **dynamic desirable (the default)**—The port actively attempts to convert the link into trunking mode. In other words, it "asks" the far-end switch to bring up a trunk. If the far-end switch port is configured to trunk, dynamic desirable, or dynamic auto mode, trunking is negotiated successfully.

- **dynamic auto**—The port can be converted into a trunk link, but only if the far-end switch actively requests it. Therefore, if the far-end switch port is configured to trunk or dynamic desirable mode, trunking is negotiated. Because of the passive negotiation behavior, the link never becomes a trunk if both ends of the link are left to the dynamic auto default.

Tip: In all these modes, DTP frames are sent out every 30 seconds to keep neighboring switch ports informed of the link's mode. On critical trunk links in a network, manually configuring the trunking mode on both ends is best so that the link never can be negotiated to any other state.

If you decide to configure *both ends* of a trunk link as a fixed trunk (**switchport mode trunk**), you can disable DTP completely so that these frames are not exchanged. To do this, add the **switchport nonegotiate** command to the interface configuration. Be aware that after DTP frames are disabled, no future negotiation is possible until this configuration is reversed.

To view the trunking status on a switch port, use the **show interface** *type mod/port* **trunk** command, as demonstrated in Example 4-2.

Example 4-2   *Determining Switch Port Trunking Status*

```
Switch# show interface gigabitethernet 2/1 trunk
Port        Mode        Encapsulation  Status        Native vlan
Gi2/1       on          802.1q         trunking      1


Port        Vlans allowed on trunk
Gi2/1       1-4094


Port        Vlans allowed and active in management domain
Gi2/1       1-2,526,539,998,1002-1005


Port        Vlans in spanning tree forwarding state and not pruned
Gi2/1       1-2,526,539,998,1002-1005
```

Trunk Configuration Example

As an example of trunk configuration, consider two switches, Switch D and Switch A, which are distribution-layer and access-layer switches, respectively. The two switches are connected by a link between their Gigabit Ethernet 2/1 interfaces. This link should be configured to be a trunk carrying only VLAN numbers 100 through 105, although more VLANs exist and are used.

The trunk link should use 802.1Q encapsulation, with VLAN 100 as the native VLAN. First, configure Switch-D to actively negotiate a trunk with the far-end switch. You could use the following configuration commands on Switch-D:

```
Switch-D(config)# interface gigabitethernet 2/1
Switch-D(config-if)# switchport trunk encapsulation dot1q
Switch-D(config-if)# switchport trunk native vlan 100
Switch-D(config-if)# switchport trunk allowed vlan 100-105
Switch-D(config-if)# switchport mode dynamic desirable
```

At this point, you assume that Switch A is configured correctly, too. Now, you should try to verify that the trunk is working as expected. On Switch D, you can view the trunk status with the following command:

```
Switch-D# show interface gigabitethernet 2/1 trunk
Port        Mode        Encapsulation  Status        Native vlan

Gi1/1       desirable   802.1q         not-trunking  100
Port        Vlans allowed on trunk
Gi1/1       100
Port        Vlans allowed and active in management domain
Gi1/1       100
Port        Vlans in spanning tree forwarding state and not pruned
Gi1/1       none
```

To your surprise, the trunk's status is not-trunking. Next, you should verify that the physical link is up:

```
Switch-D# show interface status
Port        Name            Status       Vlan       Duplex  Speed Type
Gi1/1                       notconnect   1          auto    1000  1000BaseSX
Gi1/2                       notconnect   1          auto    1000  1000BaseSX
Gi2/1                       connected    100        full    1000  1000BaseSX
```

What could be preventing the trunk from being established? If Switch D is in dynamic desirable negotiation mode, it is actively asking Switch A to bring up a trunk. Obviously, Switch A must not be in agreement. The desirable mode can negotiate a trunk with all other trunking modes, so Switch A's interface must not be configured for trunking. Instead, it is most likely configured as an access port (**switchport mode access**).

Switch A can be corrected by configuring its Gigabit Ethernet 2/1 interface to negotiate a trunk. Switch D is in dynamic desirable mode, so Switch A could use either trunk, dynamic desirable, or dynamic auto mode.

Now, suppose that you realize VLAN 103 should not be passed between these switches. You can use either of the following command sequences to manually prune VLAN 103 from the trunk:

```
Switch-D(config)# interface gigabitethernet 2/1
Switch-D(config-if)# switchport trunk allowed vlan 100-102,104-105
```

or

```
Switch-D(config-if)# switchport trunk allowed vlan remove 103
```

In the latter case, the previous range of 100 to 105 is kept in the configuration, and only 103 is automatically removed from the list.

When you manually prune VLANs from being allowed on a trunk, the same operation should be performed at both ends of the trunk link. Otherwise, one of the two switches still could flood broadcasts from that VLAN onto the trunk, using unnecessary bandwidth in only one direction.

For completeness, the configuration of Switch A at this point would look like the following:

```
Switch-A(config)# interface gigabitethernet 2/1
Switch-A(config-if)# switchport trunk encapsulation dot1q
Switch-A(config-if)# switchport trunk native vlan 100
Switch-A(config-if)# switchport trunk allowed vlan 100-105
Switch-A(config-if)# switchport trunk allowed vlan remove 103
Switch-A(config-if)# switchport mode dynamic desirable
```

Troubleshooting VLANs and Trunks

Remember that a VLAN is nothing more than a logical network segment that can be spread across many switches. If a PC in one location cannot communicate with a PC in another location, where both are assigned to the same IP subnet, make sure that both of their switch ports are configured for the same VLAN. If they are, examine the path between the two. Is the VLAN carried continuously along the path? If there are trunks along the way, is the VLAN being carried across the trunks?

To verify a VLAN's configuration on a switch, use the **show vlan id** *vlan-id* EXEC command, as demonstrated in Example 4-3. Make sure that the VLAN is shown to have an active status and that it has been assigned to the correct switch ports.

Key Topic

Example 4-3   *Verifying Switch VLAN Configuration*

```
Switch# show vlan id 2
VLAN Name                             Status    Ports
---- -------------------------------- --------- -------
2    Engineering                      active    Gi2/1, Gi2/2, Gi2/3, Gi2/4
                                                Gi4/2, Gi4/3, Gi4/4, Gi4/5
                                                Gi4/6, Gi4/7, Gi4/8, Gi4/9
                                                Gi4/10, Gi4/11, Gi4/12


VLAN Type  SAID       MTU   Parent RingNo BridgeNo Stp  BrdgMode Trans1 Trans2
---- ----- ---------- ----- ------- ------ -------- ---- -------- ------ -------
2    enet  100002     1500  -       -      -        -    -        0      0

Primary Secondary Type               Ports
------- --------- ------------------ -------------------------------------------


Switch#
```

For a trunk, these parameters must be agreeable on both ends before the trunk can operate correctly:

■ Trunking mode (unconditional trunking, negotiated, or non-negotiated).

■ Trunk encapsulation (ISL, IEEE 802.1Q, or negotiated through DTP).

■ Native VLAN. You can bring up a trunk with different native VLANs on each end; however, both switches will log error messages about the mismatch, and the potential exists that traffic will not pass correctly between the two native VLANs.

■ The native VLAN mismatch is discovered through the exchange of CDP messages, not through examination of the trunk itself. Also, the native VLAN is configured independently of the trunk encapsulation, so it is possible to have a native VLAN mismatch even if the ports use ISL encapsulation. In this case, the mismatch is only cosmetic and won't cause a trunking problem.

■   Allowed VLANs. By default, a trunk allows all VLANs to be transported across it. If one end of the trunk is configured to disallow a VLAN, that VLAN will not be contiguous across the trunk.

Key Topic

To see a comparison of how a switch port is configured for trunking versus its active state, use the **show interface** *type mod/num* **switchport** command, as demonstrated in Example 4-4. Look for the administrative versus operational values, respectively, to see whether the trunk is working the way you configured it.

Notice that the port has been configured to negotiate a trunk through DTP (dynamic auto), but the port is operating in the static access (nontrunking) mode. This should tell you that both ends of the link probably are configured for the auto mode so that neither actively will request a trunk.

Example 4-4   *Comparing Switch Port Trunking Configuration and Active State*

```
Switch# show interface fastethernet 0/2 switchport
Name: Fa0/2
Switchport: Enabled
Administrative Mode: dynamic auto

Operational Mode: static access
Administrative Trunking Encapsulation: dot1q
Operational Trunking Encapsulation: native
Negotiation of Trunking: On
Access Mode VLAN: 1 (default)
Trunking Native Mode VLAN: 1 (default)
Administrative private-vlan host-association: none
Administrative private-vlan mapping: none
Operational private-vlan: none
Trunking VLANs Enabled: ALL
Pruning VLANs Enabled: 2-1001

Protected: false
Unknown unicast blocked: disabled
Unknown multicast blocked: disabled

Voice VLAN: none (Inactive)
Appliance trust: none
Switch#
```

For more concise information about a trunking port, you can use the **show interface** [*type mod/num*] **trunk** command, as demonstrated in Example 4-5.

Example 4-5   *Viewing Concise Information About a Trunking Port*

```
Switch# show interface fastethernet 0/2 trunk
Port       Mode          Encapsulation  Status        Native vlan
Fa0/2      auto          802.1q         not-trunking  1


Port       Vlans allowed on trunk
Fa0/2      1


Port       Vlans allowed and active in management domain
Fa0/2      1


Port       Vlans in spanning tree forwarding state and not pruned
Fa0/2      1
Switch#
```

Again, notice that the port is in the autonegotiation mode, but it is currently not-trunking. Because the port is not trunking, only the access VLAN (VLAN 1 in this example) is listed as allowed and active on the trunk.

To see whether and how DTP is being used on a switch, use the **show dtp** [**interface** *type mod/num*] command. Specifying an interface shows the DTP activity in greater detail.

Exam Preparation Tasks

Review All Key Topics

Review the most important topics in the chapter, noted with the Key Topic icon in the outer margin of the page. Table 4-2 lists a reference of these key topics and the page numbers on which each is found.

Table 4-2   *Key Topics for Chapter 4*

Key Topic Element	Description	Page Number
Paragraph	Explains VLAN characteristics	67
Paragraph	Discusses how to configure a VLAN	68
Paragraph	Discusses planning strategies for VLAN implementation	71
Paragraph	Explains the 802.1Q trunking protocol	75
Paragraph	Describes VLAN trunk link configuration	77
Paragraph	Discusses how to verify VLAN configuration	81
Paragraph	Explains how to verify that a trunk link is working properly	82

Define Key Terms

Define the following key terms from this chapter, and check your answers in the glossary:

VLAN, broadcast domain, VLAN number, end-to-end VLAN, local VLAN, 20/80 rule, VLAN trunk, ISL, 802.1Q, DTP, native VLAN

Use Command Reference to Check Your Memory

This section includes the most important configuration and EXEC commands covered in this chapter. It might not be necessary to memorize the complete syntax of every command, but you should remember the basic keywords that are needed .

To test your memory of the VLAN and trunk-related commands, cover the right side of Tables 4-3 and 4-4 with a piece of paper, read the description on the left side, and then see how much of the command you can remember.

Remember that the CCNP exam focuses on practical or hands-on skills that are used by a networking professional. For the skills covered in this chapter, notice that most of the commands involve the keyword **switchport**.

Table 4-3   *VLAN and Trunking Configuration Commands*

Task	Command Syntax
Create VLAN.	**vlan** *vlan-num* **name** *vlan-name*
Assign port to VLAN.	**interface** *type module/number* **switchport mode access** **switchport access vlan** *vlan-num*
Configure trunk.	**interface** *type mod/port* **switchport trunk encapsulation** {isl | dot1q | negotiate} **switchport trunk native vlan** *vlan-id* **switchport trunk allowed vlan** {*vlan-list* | **all** | {**add** | **except** | **remove**} *vlan-list*} **switchport mode** {**trunk** | **dynamic** {**desirable** | **auto**}}

Table 4-4   *VLAN and Trunking Troubleshooting Commands*

Task	Command Syntax
Verify VLAN configuration.	**show vlan id** *vlan-id*
Verify active trunk parameters.	**show interface** *type mod/num* **trunk**
Compare trunk configuration and active parameters.	**show interface** *type mod/num* **switchport**
Verify DTP operation.	**show dtp** [**interface** *type mod/num*]

This chapter covers the following topics that you need to master for the CCNP SWITCH exam:

VLAN Trunking Protocol—This section presents Cisco VLAN Trunking Protocol (VTP) for VLAN management in a campus network.

VTP Configuration—This section covers the Catalyst switch commands used to configure VTP.

VTP Pruning—This section details traffic management by pruning within VTP domains, along with the commands needed for configuration.

Troubleshooting VTP—This section gives a brief summary of things to consider and commands to use when VTP is not operating properly.

CHAPTER 5

VLAN Trunking Protocol

When VLANs are defined and used on switches throughout an enterprise or campus network, the administrative overhead can easily increase. Using the VLAN Trunking Protocol (VTP) makes VLAN administration more organized and manageable. This chapter covers VTP and its configuration.

A similar standards-based VLAN-management protocol for IEEE 802.1Q trunks is called *GARP VLAN Registration Protocol (GVRP)*. The GARP and GVRP protocols are defined in the IEEE 802.1D and 802.1Q (clause 11) standards, respectively. At press time, GVRP was not supported in any of the Cisco IOS Software–based Catalyst switches. Therefore, it is not covered in this text or in the SWITCH course.

"Do I Know This Already?" Quiz

The "Do I Know This Already?" quiz allows you to assess whether you should read this entire chapter thoroughly or jump to the "Exam Preparation Tasks" section. If you are in doubt based on your answers to these questions or your own assessment of your knowledge of the topics, read the entire chapter. Table 5-1 outlines the major headings in this chapter and the "Do I Know This Already?" quiz questions that go with them. You can find the answers in Appendix A, "Answers to the 'Do I Know This Already?' Quizzes."

Table 5-1 *"Do I Know This Already?" Foundation Topics Section-to-Question Mapping*

Foundation Topics Section	Questions Covered in This Section
VLAN Trunking Protocol	1–8
VTP Configuration	
VTP Pruning	9–10
Troubleshooting VTP	11–12

 1. Which of the following is not a Catalyst switch VTP mode?

   a. Server

   b. Client

   c. Designated

   d. Transparent

2. A switch in VTP transparent mode can do which one of the following?

   a. Create a new VLAN

   b. Only listen to VTP advertisements

   c. Send its own VTP advertisements

   d. Cannot make VLAN configuration changes

3. Which one of the following is a valid VTP advertisement?

   a. Triggered update

   b. VLAN database

   c. Subset

   d. Domain

4. Which one of the following is needed for VTP communication?

   a. A Management VLAN

   b. A Trunk link

   c. An Access VLAN

   d. An IP address

5. Which one of the following VTP modes does not allow any manual VLAN configuration changes?

   a. Server

   b. Client

   c. Designated

   d. Transparent

6. Select all the parameters that decide whether to accept new VTP information:

   a. VTP priority

   b. VTP domain name

   c. Configuration revision number

   d. VTP server name

7. How many VTP management domains can a Catalyst switch participate in?

   a. 1

   b. 2

   c. Unlimited

   d. 4096

8. Which IOS command configures a Catalyst switch for VTP client mode?

   a. set vtp mode client

   b. vtp client

   c. vtp mode client

   d. vtp client mode

9. What is the purpose of VTP pruning?

   a. Limit the number of VLANs in a domain

   b. Stop unnecessary VTP advertisements

   c. Limit the extent of broadcast traffic

   d. Limit the size of the virtual tree

10. Which VLAN number is never eligible for VTP pruning?

   a. 0

   b. 1

   c. 1000

   d. 1001

11. Which of the following might present a VTP problem?

   a. Two or more VTP servers in a domain

   b. Two servers with the same configuration revision number

   c. A server in two domains

   d. A new server with a higher configuration revision number

12. If a VTP server is configured for VTP version 2, what else must happen for successful VTP communication in a domain?

   a. A VTP version 2 password must be set.

   b. All other switches in the domain must be version 2 capable.

   c. All other switches must be configured for VTP version 2.

   d. The VTP configuration revision number must be reset.

Foundation Topics

VLAN Trunking Protocol

As the previous chapter demonstrated, VLAN configuration and trunking on a switch or a small group of switches is fairly intuitive. Campus network environments, however, usually consist of many interconnected switches. Configuring and managing a large number of switches, VLANs, and VLAN trunks quickly can get out of control.

Cisco has developed a method to manage VLANs across the campus network. The VLAN Trunking Protocol (VTP) uses Layer 2 trunk frames to communicate VLAN information among a group of switches. VTP manages the addition, deletion, and renaming of VLANs across the network from a central point of control. Any switch participating in a VTP exchange is aware of and can use any VLAN that VTP manages.

VTP Domains

VTP is organized into *management domains*, or areas with common VLAN requirements. A switch can belong to only one VTP domain, in addition to sharing VLAN information with other switches in the domain. Switches in different VTP domains, however, do not share VTP information.

Switches in a VTP domain advertise several attributes to their domain neighbors. Each advertisement contains information about the VTP management domain, VTP revision number, known VLANs, and specific VLAN parameters. When a VLAN is added to a switch in a management domain, other switches are notified of the new VLAN through *VTP advertisements*. In this way, all switches in a domain can prepare to receive traffic on their trunk ports using the new VLAN.

VTP Modes

Key Topic

To participate in a VTP management domain, each switch must be configured to operate in one of several modes. The VTP mode determines how the switch processes and advertises VTP information. You can use the following modes:

- **Server mode**—VTP servers have full control over VLAN creation and modification for their domains. All VTP information is advertised to other switches in the domain, while all received VTP information is synchronized with the other switches. By default, a switch is in VTP server mode. Note that each VTP domain must have at least one server so that VLANs can be created, modified, or deleted, and VLAN information can be propagated.

- **Client mode**—VTP clients do not allow the administrator to create, change, or delete any VLANs. Instead, they listen to VTP advertisements from other switches and modify their VLAN configurations accordingly. In effect, this is a passive listening mode. Received VTP information is forwarded out trunk links to neighboring switches in the domain, so the switch also acts as a VTP relay.

- **Transparent mode**—VTP transparent switches do not participate in VTP. While in transparent mode, a switch does not advertise its own VLAN configuration, and a switch does not synchronize its VLAN database with received advertisements. In VTP version 1, a transparent mode switch does not even relay VTP information it receives to other switches unless its VTP domain names and VTP version numbers match those of the other switches. In VTP version 2, transparent switches do forward received VTP advertisements out of their trunk ports, acting as VTP relays. This occurs regardless of the VTP domain name setting.

Tip: While a switch is in VTP transparent mode, it can create and delete VLANs that are local only to itself. These VLAN changes, however, are not propagated to any other switch.

VTP Advertisements

Each Cisco switch participating in VTP advertises VLANs (only VLANs 1 to 1005), revision numbers, and VLAN parameters on its trunk ports to notify other switches in the management domain. VTP advertisements are sent as multicast frames. The switch intercepts frames sent to the VTP multicast address and processes them with its supervisory processor. VTP frames are forwarded out trunk links as a special case.

Because all switches in a management domain learn of new VLAN configuration changes, a VLAN must be created and configured on only one VTP server switch in the domain.

By default, management domains are set to use nonsecure advertisements without a password. You can add a password to set the domain to secure mode. The same password must be configured on every switch in the domain so that all switches exchanging VTP information use identical encryption methods.

VTP switches use an index called the *VTP configuration revision number* to keep track of the most recent information. Every switch in a VTP domain stores the configuration revision number that it last heard from a VTP advertisement. The VTP advertisement process always starts with configuration revision number 0 (zero).

When subsequent changes are made on a VTP server, the revision number is incremented before the advertisements are sent. When listening switches (configured as members of the same VTP domain as the advertising switch) receive an advertisement with a greater revision number than is stored locally, the advertisement overwrites any stored VLAN information.

Because of this, it is very important to always force any newly added network switches to have revision number 0 before being attached to the network. Otherwise, a switch might have stored a revision number that is greater than the value currently in use in the domain.

The VTP revision number is stored in NVRAM and is not altered by a power cycle of the switch. Therefore, the revision number can be initialized to 0 only by using one of the following methods:

- Change the switch's VTP mode to transparent and then change the mode back to server.

- Change the switch's VTP domain to a bogus name (a nonexistent VTP domain), and then change the VTP domain back to the original name.

If the VTP revision number is not reset to 0, the switch might enter the network as a VTP server and have a pre-existing revision number (from a previous life) that is higher than in previous legitimate advertisements. The new switch's VTP information would be seen as more recent, so all other switches in the VTP domain would gladly accept its database of VLANs and overwrite their good VLAN database entries with null or deleted VLAN status information.

Key Topic

In other words, a new server switch might inadvertently cause every other working switch to flush all records of every VLAN in production. The VLANs would be deleted from the VTP database and from the switches, causing any switch port assigned to them to become inactive. This is referred to as a *VTP synchronization problem.* For critical portions of your network, you should consider using transparent VTP mode to prevent the synchronization problem from ever becoming an issue.

> **Tip:** It might seem intuitive that a switch acting as a VTP server could come online with a higher configuration revision number and wreak havoc on the whole domain. You should also be aware that this same thing can happen if a VTP client comes online with a higher revision, too!
>
> Even though it seems as if a client should strictly listen to advertisements from servers, a client can and does send out its own advertisements. When it first powers up, a client sends a summary advertisement from its own stored database. It realizes that it has a greater revision number if it receives an inferior advertisement from a server. Therefore, it sends out a subset advertisement with the greater revision number, which VTP servers will accept as more up-to-date information.

VTP advertisements can originate as requests from client mode switches that want to learn about the VTP database at boot. Advertisements also can originate from server mode switches as VLAN configuration changes occur.

VTP advertisements can occur in three forms:

- **Summary advertisements**—VTP domain servers send summary advertisements every 300 seconds and every time a VLAN database change occurs. The summary advertisement lists information about the management domain, including VTP version, domain name, configuration revision number, time stamp, MD5 encryption hash code, and the number of subset advertisements to follow. For VLAN configuration changes, summary advertisements are followed by one or more subset advertisements with more specific VLAN configuration data. Figure 5-1 shows the summary advertisement format.

- **Subset advertisements**—VTP domain servers send subset advertisements after a VLAN configuration change occurs. These advertisements list the specific changes that have been performed, such as creating or deleting a VLAN, suspending or activating a VLAN, changing the name of a VLAN, and changing a VLAN's maximum transmission unit (MTU). Subset advertisements can list the following VLAN parameters: status of the VLAN, VLAN type (such as Ethernet or Token Ring), MTU, length of the VLAN name, VLAN number, security association identifier (SAID) value, and

VLAN name. VLANs are listed individually in sequential subset advertisements. Figure 5-2 shows the VTP subset advertisement format.

Version (1 byte)	Type (Summary Adv) (1 byte)	Number of subset advertisements to follow (1 byte)	Domain name length (1 byte)
Management Domain Name (zero-padded to 32 bytes)			
Configuration Revision Number (4 bytes)			
Updater Identity (orginating IP address: 4 bytes)			
Update Time Stamp (12 bytes)			
MD5 Digest hash code (16 bytes)			

Figure 5-1   *VTP Summary Advertisement Format*

VTP Subset Advertisement

0	1	2	3
Version (1 byte)	Type (Subset Adv) (1 byte)	Subset sequence number (1 byte)	Domain name length (1 byte)
Management Domain Name (zero-padded to 32 bytes)			
Configuration Revision Number (4 bytes)			
VLAN Info Field 1 (see below)			
VLAN Info Field ...			
VLAN Info Field N			

VTP VLAN Info Field

0	1	2	3
Info Length	VLAN Status	VLAN Type	VLAN Name Length
VLAN ID		MTU Size	
802.10 SAID			
VLAN Name (padded with zeros to multiple of 4 bytes)			

Figure 5-2   *VTP Subset Advertisement and VLAN Info Field Formats*

■ **Advertisement requests from clients**—A VTP client can request any VLAN information it lacks. For example, a client switch might be reset and have its VLAN database cleared, and its VTP domain membership might be changed, or it might hear a VTP summary advertisement with a higher revision number than it currently has. After a client advertisement request, the VTP domain servers respond with summary and subset advertisements to bring it up to date. Figure 5-3 shows the advertisement request format.

0	1	2	3
Version (1 byte)	Type (Adv request) (1 byte)	Reserved (1 byte)	Domain name length (1 byte)
Management Domain Name (zero-padded to 32 bytes)			
Starting advertisement to request			

Figure 5-3 *VTP Advertisement Request Format*

Catalyst switches in server mode store VTP information separately from the switch configuration in NVRAM. VLAN and VTP data are saved in the vlan.dat file on the switch's flash memory file system. All VTP information, including the VTP configuration revision number, is retained even when the switch power is off. In this manner, a switch can recover the last known VLAN configuration from its VTP database after it reboots.

Tip: Remember that even in VTP client mode, a switch will store the last known VTP information—including the configuration revision number. Don't assume that a VTP client will start with a clean slate when it powers up.

VTP Configuration

By default, every switch operates in VTP server mode for the management domain NULL (a blank string), with no password or secure mode. If the switch hears a VTP summary advertisement on a trunk port from any other switch, it automatically learns the VTP domain name, VLANs, and the configuration revision number it hears. This makes it easy to bring up a new switch in an existing VTP domain. However, be aware that the new switch stays in VTP server mode, something that might not be desirable.

Tip: You should get into the habit of double-checking the VTP configuration of any switch before you add it into your network. Make sure that the VTP configuration revision number is set to 0. You can do this by isolating the switch from the network, powering it up, and using the **show vtp status** command, as demonstrated in the following output:

```
Switch# show vtp status
VTP Version                      : 2
Configuration Revision           : 0
Maximum VLANs supported locally : 1005
Number of existing VLANs        : 5
```

```
VTP Operating Mode             : Server
VTP Domain Name                :
VTP Pruning Mode               : Disabled
VTP V2 Mode                    : Disabled
VTP Traps Generation           : Disabled
MD5 digest                     : 0x57 0xCD 0x40 0x65 0x63 0x59 0x47 0xBD
Configuration last modified by 0.0.0.0 at 0-0-00 00:00:00
Switch#
```

Here, the switch has a configuration revision number of 0, and is in the default state of VTP server mode with an undefined VTP domain name. This switch would be safe to add to a network.

The following sections discuss the commands and considerations that you should use to configure a switch for VTP operation.

You should be aware that there are two supported ways to configure VLAN and VTP information in Catalyst IOS switches:

- Global configuration mode commands (for example, **vlan**, **vtp mode**, and **vtp domain**)

- VLAN database mode commands

The **vlan database** EXEC command still is supported in Catalyst IOS Software only for backward compatibility, but this is not covered in the SWITCH course or the exam.

Configuring a VTP Management Domain

Before a switch is added into a network, the VTP management domain should be identified. If this switch is the first one on the network, the management domain must be created. Otherwise, the switch might have to join an existing management domain with other existing switches.

You can use the following global configuration command to assign a switch to a management domain, where the *domain-name* is a text string up to 32 characters long:

```
Switch(config)# vtp domain domain-name
```

Configuring the VTP Mode

Next, you need to choose the VTP mode for the new switch. The three VTP modes of operation and their guidelines for use are as follows:

- **Server mode**—Server mode can be used on any switch in a management domain, even if other server and client switches are in use. This mode provides some redundancy in case of a server failure in the domain. Each VTP management domain should have at least one server. The first server defined in a network also defines the management domain that will be used by future VTP servers and clients. Server mode is the default VTP mode and allows VLANs to be created and deleted.

Note: Multiple VTP servers can coexist in a domain. This usually is recommended for redundancy. The servers do not elect a primary or secondary server; they all simply function as servers. If one server is configured with a new VLAN or VTP parameter, it advertises the changes to the rest of the domain. All other servers synchronize their VTP databases to this advertisement, just as any VTP client would.

- **Client mode**—If other switches are in the management domain, you should configure a new switch for client mode operation. In this way, the switch is forced to learn any existing VTP information from a reliable existing server. After the switch has learned the current VTP information, you can reconfigure it for server mode if it will be used as a redundant server.

- **Transparent mode**—This mode is used if a switch will not share VLAN information with any other switch in the network. VLANs still can be created, deleted, and modified on the transparent switch. However, they are not advertised to other neighboring switches. VTP advertisements received by a transparent switch, however, are forwarded to other switches on trunk links.

  Keeping switches in transparent mode can eliminate the chance for duplicate, overlapping VLANs in a large network with many network administrators. For example, two administrators might configure VLANs on switches in their respective areas but use the same VLAN identification or VLAN number. Even though the two VLANs have different meanings and purposes, they could overlap if both administrators advertised them using VTP servers.

Key Topic

You can configure the VTP mode with the following sequence of global configuration commands:

```
Switch(config)# vtp mode {server | client | transparent}
Switch(config)# vtp password password
```

If the domain is operating in secure mode, a password also can be defined. The password can be configured only on VTP servers and clients. The password itself is not sent; instead, an MD5 digest or hash code is computed and sent in VTP advertisements (servers) and is used to validate received advertisements (clients). The password is a string of 1 to 32 characters (case sensitive).

If secure VTP is implemented using passwords, begin by configuring a password on the VTP servers. The client switches retain the last-known VTP information but cannot process received advertisements until the same password is configured on them, too.

Table 5-2 shows a summary of the VTP modes. You can use this table for quick review as you study VTP operation.

Table 5-2 *Catalyst VTP Modes*

VTP Mode	Characteristics
Server	All VLAN and VTP configuration changes occur here. The server advertises settings and changes to all other servers and clients in a VTP domain. (This is the default mode for Catalyst switches.)
Client	Listens to all VTP advertisements from servers in a VTP domain. Advertisements are relayed out other trunk links. No VLAN or VTP configuration changes can be made on a client.
Transparent	VLAN configuration changes are made locally, independent of any VTP domain. VTP advertisements are not received but merely are relayed out other trunk links, if possible.

Configuring the VTP Version

Two versions of VTP are available for use in a management domain. Catalyst switches are capable of running either VTP version 1 or VTP version 2. Within a management domain, the two versions are not interoperable. Therefore, the same VTP version must be configured on every switch in a domain. VTP version 1 is the default protocol on a switch.

If a switch is capable of running VTP version 2, however, a switch can coexist with other version 1 switches, as long as its VTP version 2 is not enabled. This situation becomes important if you want to use version 2 in a domain. Then only one server mode switch needs to have VTP version 2 enabled. The new version number is propagated to all other version 2–capable switches in the domain, causing them all to automatically enable version 2 for use.

> **Tip:** A third version of VTP addresses some of the traditional shortcomings. For example, VTP version 3 supports extended VLAN numbers (1 to 4095) that are compatible with the IEEE 802.1Q trunking standard. At the time of this writing, VTPv3 is available only on Cisco Catalyst platforms running the CatOS (non-IOS) operating system. Therefore, only VTP versions 1 and 2 are covered on the SWITCH exam and in this text.

The two versions of VTP differ in the features they support. VTP version 2 offers the following additional features over Version 1:

- **Version-dependent transparent mode**—In transparent mode, VTP version 1 matches the VTP version and domain name before forwarding the information to other switches using VTP. VTP version 2 in transparent mode forwards the VTP messages without checking the version number. Because only one domain is supported in a switch, the domain name doesn't have to be checked.

- **Consistency checks**—VTP version 2 performs consistency checks on the VTP and VLAN parameters entered from the command-line interface (CLI) or by the Simple Network Management Protocol (SNMP). This checking helps prevent errors in such things as VLAN names and numbers from being propagated to other switches in the domain. However, no consistency checks are performed on VTP messages that are received on trunk links or on configuration and database data that is read from NVRAM.

- **Token Ring support**—VTP version 2 supports the use of Token Ring switching and Token Ring VLANs. (If Token Ring switching is being used, VTP version 2 must be enabled.)

- **Unrecognized Type-Length-Value (TLV) support**—VTP version 2 switches propagate received configuration change messages out other trunk links, even if the switch supervisor cannot parse or understand the message. For example, a VTP advertisement contains a Type field to denote what type of VTP message is being sent. VTP message type 1 is a summary advertisement, and message type 2 is a subset advertisement. An extension to VTP that utilizes other message types and other message length values could be in use. Instead of dropping the unrecognized VTP message, version 2 still propagates the information and keeps a copy in NVRAM.

The VTP version number is configured using the following global configuration command:

```
Switch(config)# vtp version {1 | 2}
```

By default, a switch uses VTP Version 1.

VTP Configuration Example

As an example, a switch is configured as the VTP server in a domain named MyCompany. The domain uses secure VTP with the password **bigsecret**. You can use the following configuration commands to accomplish this:

```
Switch(config)# vtp domain MyCompany
Switch(config)# vtp mode server
Switch(config)# vtp password bigsecret
```

VTP Status

Key Topic

The current VTP parameters for a management domain can be displayed using the **show vtp status** command. Example 5-1 demonstrates some sample output of this command from a switch acting as a VTP client in the VTP domain called CampusDomain.

Example 5-1 show vtp status *Reveals VTP Parameters for a Management Domain*

```
Switch# show vtp status
VTP Version                    : 2
Configuration Revision         : 89
Maximum VLANs supported locally : 1005
Number of existing VLANs       : 74
VTP Operating Mode             : Client
VTP Domain Name                : CampusDomain
VTP Pruning Mode               : Enabled VTP V2 Mode : Disabled VTP
  Traps Generation             : Disabled
```

```
MD5 digest                        : 0x4B 0x07 0x75 0xEC 0xB1 0x3D 0x6F 0x1F
                                    Configuration
  last modified by 192.168.199.1 at 11-19-02 09:29:56
Switch#
```

VTP message and error counters also can be displayed with the **show vtp counters** command. You can use this command for basic VTP troubleshooting to see whether the switch is interacting with other VTP nodes in the domain. Example 5-2 demonstrates some sample output from the **show vtp counters** command.

Example 5-2   show vtp counters *Reveals VTP Message and Error Counters*

```
Switch# show vtp counters
VTP statistics:
Summary advertisements received    : 1
Subset advertisements received     : 2
Request advertisements received    : 1
Summary advertisements transmitted : 1630
Subset advertisements transmitted  : 0
Request advertisements transmitted : 4
Number of config revision errors   : 0
Number of config digest errors     : 0
Number of V1 summary errors        : 0


VTP pruning statistics:

Trunk            Join Transmitted Join Received    Summary advts received from
                                                   non-pruning-capable device
---------------- ---------------- ---------------- -------------------------------
Gi0/1            82352            82931            0
Switch#
```

VTP Pruning

Recall that, by definition, a switch must forward broadcast frames out all available ports in the broadcast domain because broadcasts are destined everywhere there is a listener. Unless forwarded by more intelligent means, multicast frames follow the same pattern.

In addition, frames destined for an address that the switch has not yet learned or has *forgotten* (the MAC address has aged out of the address table) must be forwarded out all ports in an attempt to find the destination. These frames are referred to as *unknown unicast*.

When forwarding frames out all ports in a broadcast domain or VLAN, trunk ports are included if they transport that VLAN. By default, a trunk link transports traffic from all VLANs, unless specific VLANs are removed from the trunk. Generally, in a network with several switches, trunk links are enabled between switches, and VTP is used to manage the propagation of VLAN information. This scenario causes the trunk links between switches to carry traffic from *all* VLANs, not just from the specific VLANs created.

Consider the network shown in Figure 5-4. When end user Host PC in VLAN 3 sends a broadcast, Catalyst switch C forwards the frame out all VLAN 3 ports, including the trunk link to Catalyst A. Catalyst A, in turn, forwards the broadcast on to Catalysts B and D over those trunk links. Catalysts B and D forward the broadcast out only their access links that have been configured for VLAN 3. If Catalysts B and D do not have any active users in VLAN 3, forwarding that broadcast frame to them would consume bandwidth on the trunk links and processor resources in both switches, only to have switches B and D discard the frames.

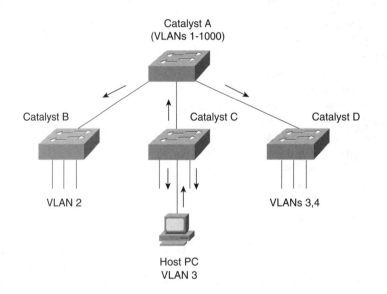

Figure 5-4 *Flooding in a Catalyst Switch Network*

Key Topic

VTP pruning makes more efficient use of trunk bandwidth by reducing unnecessary flooded traffic. Broadcast and unknown unicast frames on a VLAN are forwarded over a trunk link only if the switch on the receiving end of the trunk has ports in that VLAN.

VTP pruning occurs as an extension to VTP version 1, using an additional VTP message type. When a Catalyst switch has a port associated with a VLAN, the switch sends an advertisement to its neighbor switches that it has active ports on that VLAN. The neighbors keep this information, enabling them to decide whether flooded traffic from a VLAN should use a trunk port.

Figure 5-5 shows the network from Figure 5-4 with VTP pruning enabled. Because Catalyst B has not advertised its use of VLAN 3, Catalyst A will prune VLAN 3 from the trunk to B and will choose not to flood VLAN 3 traffic to Catalyst B over the trunk link. Catalyst D has advertised the need for VLAN 3, so traffic will be flooded to it.

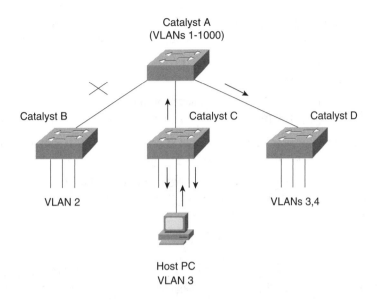

Figure 5-5 *Flooding in a Catalyst Switch Network Using VTP Pruning*

> **Tip:** Even when VTP pruning has determined that a VLAN is not needed on a trunk, an
> instance of the Spanning Tree Protocol (STP) will run for every VLAN that is allowed on
> the trunk link. To reduce the number of STP instances, you manually should "prune"
> unneeded VLANs from the trunk and allow only the needed ones. Use the **switchport
> trunk allowed vlan** command to identify the VLANs that should be added or removed
> from a trunk.

Enabling VTP Pruning

By default, VTP pruning is disabled on IOS-based switches. To enable pruning, use the following global configuration command:

```
Switch(config)# vtp pruning
```

If you use this command on a VTP server, it also advertises that pruning needs to be enabled for the entire management domain. All other switches listening to that advertisement
also will enable pruning.

When pruning is enabled, all general-purpose VLANs become eligible for pruning on all
trunk links, if needed. However, you can modify the default list of pruning eligibility with
the following interface-configuration command:

```
Switch(config)# interface type mod/num
Switch(config-if)# switchport trunk pruning vlan {{{add | except |  remove}
  vlan-list} | none}
```

By default, VLANs 2 through 1001 are eligible, or "enabled," for potential pruning on every trunk. Use one of the following keywords with the command to tailor the list:

- *vlan-list*—An explicit list of eligible VLAN numbers (anything from 2 to 1001), separated by commas or by dashes.

- **add** *vlan-list*—A list of VLAN numbers (anything from 2 to 1001) is added to the already configured list; this is a shortcut to keep from typing a long list of numbers.

- **except** *vlan-list*—All VLANs are eligible except for the VLAN numbers listed (anything from 2 to 1001); this is a shortcut to keep from typing a long list of numbers.

- **remove** *vlan-list*—A list of VLAN numbers (anything from 2 to 1001) is removed from the already configured list; this is a shortcut to keep from typing a long list of numbers.

- **none**—No VLAN will be eligible for pruning.

Tip: Be aware that VTP pruning has no effect on switches in the VTP transparent mode. Instead, those switches must be configured manually to "prune" VLANs from trunk links. In this case, pruning is always configured on the upstream side of a trunk. (The downstream side switch doesn't have any ports that belong to the pruned VLAN, so there is no need to prune from that end.)

By default, VLANs 2 to 1001 are eligible for pruning. VLAN 1 has a special meaning because it sometimes is used for control traffic and is the default access VLAN on switch ports. Because of these historical reasons, VLAN 1 is never eligible for pruning. In addition, VLANs 1002 through 1005 are reserved for Token Ring and FDDI VLANs and are never eligible for pruning.

Troubleshooting VTP

If a switch does not seem to be receiving updated information from a VTP server, consider these possible causes:

- The switch is configured for VTP transparent mode. In this mode, incoming VTP advertisements are not processed; they are relayed only to other switches in the domain.

- If the switch is configured as a VTP client, there might not be another switch functioning as a VTP server. In this case, configure the local switch to become a VTP server itself.

- The link toward the VTP server is not in trunking mode. VTP advertisements are sent only over trunks. Use the **show interface** *type mod/num* **switchport** to verify the operational mode as a trunk.

- Make sure the VTP domain name is configured correctly to match that of the VTP server.

- Make sure the VTP version is compatible with other switches in the VTP domain.

- Make sure the VTP password matches others in the VTP domain. If the server doesn't use a password, make sure the password is disabled or cleared on the local switch.

Tip: Above all else, verify a switch's VTP configuration before connecting it to a production network. If the switch has been configured previously or used elsewhere, it might already be in VTP server mode and have a VTP configuration revision number that is higher than that of other switches in the production VTP domain. In that case, other switches will listen and learn from the new switch because it has a higher revision number and must know more recent information. This could cause the new switch to introduce bogus VLANs into the domain or, worse yet, to cause all other switches in the domain to delete all their active VLANs.

To prevent this from happening, reset the configuration revision number of every new switch before it is added to a production network.

Table 5-3 lists and describes the commands that are useful for verifying or troubleshooting VTP configuration.

Table 5-3 *VTP Configuration Troubleshooting Commands*

Function	Command Syntax
Displays current VTP parameters, including the last advertising server	**show vtp status**
Displays VTP advertisement and pruning statistics	**show vtp counters**
Displays defined VLANs	**show vlan brief**
Displays trunk status, including pruning eligibility	**show interface** *type mod/num* **switchport**
Displays VTP pruning state	**show interface** *type mod/num* **pruning**

Exam Preparation Tasks

Review All Key Topics

Review the most important topics in the chapter, noted with the Key Topic icon in the outer margin of the page. Table 5-4 lists a reference of these key topics and the page numbers on which each is found.

Table 5-4 *Key Topics for Chapter 5*

Key Topic Element	Description	Page Number
Paragraph	Describes VTP modes	90
Paragraph	Explains the VPN configuration revision number	91
Paragraph	Discusses the VTP synchronization problem and how to prevent it from occurring	92
Paragraph	Explains how to configure the VTP domain	95
Paragraph	Explains how to configure the VTP mode	96
Paragraph	Describes VTP version operation	97
Paragraph	Discusses how to verify VTP operation	98
Paragraph	Explains VTP pruning	100

Complete Tables and Lists from Memory

Print a copy of Appendix C, "Memory Tables," (found on the CD), or at least the section for this chapter, and complete the tables and lists from memory. Appendix D, "Memory Tables Answer Key," also on the CD, includes completed tables and lists to check your work.

Define Key Terms

Define the following key terms from this chapter, and check your answers in the glossary:

VTP, VTP domain, VTP configuration revision number, VTP synchronization problem, VTP pruning

Use Command Reference to Check Your Memory

This section includes the most important configuration and EXEC commands covered in this chapter. It might not be necessary to memorize the complete syntax of every command, but you should remember the basic keywords that are needed.

To test your memory of the VTP-related commands, cover the right side of Table 5-5 with a piece of paper, read the description on the left side, and then see how much of the command you can remember.

Remember that the CCNP exam focuses on practical or hands-on skills that are used by a networking professional. For the skills covered in this chapter, remember that the commands always involve the **vtp** keyword.

Table 5-5 *VTP Configuration Commands*

Task	Command Syntax
Define the VTP domain.	**vtp domain** *domain-name*
Set the VTP mode.	**vtp mode** {**server**	**client**	**transparent**}
Define an optional VTP password.	**vtp password** *password*
Configure VTP version.	**vtp version** {**1**	**2**}
Enable VTP pruning.	**vtp pruning**
Select VLANs eligible for pruning on a trunk interface.	**interface** *type mod/num* **switchport trunk pruning vlan** {**add**	**except**	**none**	**remove**} *vlan-list*

This chapter covers the following topics that you need to master for the CCNP SWITCH exam:

Switch Port Aggregation with EtherChannel—This section discusses the concept of aggregating, or "bundling," physical ports into a single logical link. Methods for load balancing traffic across the physical links also are covered.

EtherChannel Negotiation Protocols—This section discusses two protocols that dynamically negotiate and control EtherChannels: Port Aggregation Protocol (PAgP), a Cisco proprietary protocol, and Link Aggregation Control Protocol (LACP), a standards-based protocol.

EtherChannel Configuration—This section discusses the Catalyst switch commands needed to configure EtherChannel.

Troubleshooting an EtherChannel—This section gives a brief summary of things to consider and commands to use when an aggregated link is not operating properly.

CHAPTER 6

Aggregating Switch Links

In previous chapters, you learned about connecting switches and organizing users and devices into common workgroups. Using these principles, end users can be given effective access to resources both on and off the campus network. However, today's mission-critical applications and services demand networks that provide high availability and reliability.

This chapter presents technologies that you can use in a campus network to provide higher bandwidth and reliability between switches.

"Do I Know This Already?" Quiz

The "Do I Know This Already?" quiz allows you to assess whether you should read this entire chapter thoroughly or jump to the "Exam Preparation Tasks" section. If you are in doubt based on your answers to these questions or your own assessment of your knowledge of the topics, read the entire chapter. Table 6-1 outlines the major headings in this chapter and the "Do I Know This Already?" quiz questions that go with them. You can find the answers in Appendix A, "Answers to the 'Do I Know This Already?' Quizzes."

Table 6-1 *"Do I Know This Already?" Foundation Topics Section-to-Question Mapping*

Foundation Topics Section	Questions Covered in This Section
Switch Port Aggregation with EtherChannel	1–7
EtherChannel Negotiation Protocols	8–11
EtherChannel Configuration	11–12
Troubleshooting an EtherChannel	13

1. If Fast Ethernet ports are bundled into an EtherChannel, what is the maximum throughput supported on a Catalyst switch?

    a. 100 Mbps

    b. 200 Mbps

    c. 400 Mbps

    d. 800 Mbps

    e. 1600 Mbps

2. Which of these methods distributes traffic over an EtherChannel?

    a. Round robin

    b. Least-used link

    c. A function of address

    d. A function of packet size

3. What type of interface represents an EtherChannel as a whole?

    a. Channel

    b. Port

    c. Port channel

    d. Channel port

4. Which of the following is not a valid method for EtherChannel load balancing?

    a. Source MAC address

    b. Source and destination MAC addresses

    c. Source IP address

    d. IP precedence

    e. UDP/TCP port

5. How can the EtherChannel load-balancing method be set?

    a. Per switch port

    b. Per EtherChannel

    c. Globally per switch

    d. Can't be configured

6. What logical operation is performed to calculate EtherChannel load balancing as a function of two addresses?

    a. OR

    b. AND

    c. XOR

    d. NOR

7. Which one of the following is a valid combination of ports for an EtherChannel?

    a. Two access links (one VLAN 5, one VLAN 5)

    b. Two access links (one VLAN 1, one VLAN 10)

    c. Two trunk links (one VLANs 1 to 10, one VLANs 1, 11 to 20)

    d. Two Fast Ethernet links (both full duplex, one 10 Mbps)

8. Which of these is a method for negotiating an EtherChannel?

    a. PAP

    b. CHAP

    c. LAPD

    d. LACP

9. Which of the following is a valid EtherChannel negotiation mode combination between two switches?

    a. PAgP auto, PAgP auto

    b. PAgP auto, PAgP desirable

    c. on, PAgP auto

    d. LACP passive, LACP passive

10. When is PAgP's "desirable silent" mode useful?

    a. When the switch should not send PAgP frames

    b. When the switch should not form an EtherChannel

    c. When the switch should not expect to receive PAgP frames

    d. When the switch is using LACP mode

11. Which of the following EtherChannel modes does not send or receive any negotiation frames?

    a. channel-group 1 mode passive

    b. channel-group 1 mode active

    c. channel-group 1 mode on

    d. channel-group 1 mode desirable

    e. channel-group 1 mode auto

12. Two computers are the only hosts sending IP data across an EtherChannel between two switches. Several different applications are being used between them. Which of these load-balancing methods would be more likely to use the most links in the EtherChannel?

    a. Source and destination MAC addresses.

    b. Source and destination IP addresses.

    c. Source and destination TCP/UDP ports.

    d. None of the other answers is correct.

13. Which command can be used to see the status of an EtherChannel's links?

    a. show channel link

    b. show etherchannel status

    c. show etherchannel summary

    d. show ether channel status

Foundation Topics

Switch Port Aggregation with EtherChannel

Key Topic

As discussed in Chapter 3, "Switch Port Configuration," switches can use Ethernet, Fast Ethernet, Gigabit, or 10-Gigabit Ethernet ports to scale link speeds by a factor of ten. Cisco offers another method of scaling link bandwidth by aggregating, or *bundling*, parallel links, termed the *EtherChannel* technology. Two to eight links of either Fast Ethernet (FE), Gigabit Ethernet (GE), or 10-Gigabit Ethernet (10GE) are bundled as one logical link of *Fast EtherChannel (FEC)*, *Gigabit EtherChannel (GEC)*, or *10-Gigabit Etherchannel (10GEC)*, respectively. This bundle provides a full-duplex bandwidth of up to 1600 Mbps (eight links of Fast Ethernet), 16 Gbps (eight links of Gigabit Ethernet), or 160 Gbps (eight links of 10-Gigabit Ethernet).

This also provides an easy means to "grow," or expand, a link's capacity between two switches, without having to continually purchase hardware for the next magnitude of throughput. For example, a single Fast Ethernet link (200 Mbps throughput) can be incrementally expanded up to eight Fast Ethernet links (1600 Mbps) as a single Fast EtherChannel. If the traffic load grows beyond that, the growth process can begin again with a single Gigabit Ethernet link (2 Gbps throughput), which can be expanded up to eight Gigabit Ethernet links as a Gigabit EtherChannel (16 Gbps). The process repeats again by moving to a single 10-Gigabit Ethernet link, and so on.

Ordinarily, having multiple or parallel links between switches creates the possibility of bridging loops, an undesirable condition. EtherChannel avoids this situation by bundling parallel links into a single, logical link, which can act as either an access or a trunk link. Switches or devices on each end of the EtherChannel link must understand and use the EtherChannel technology for proper operation.

Although an EtherChannel link is seen as a single logical link, the link doesn't necessarily have an inherent total bandwidth equal to the sum of its component physical links. For example, suppose that an FEC link is made up of four full-duplex, 100-Mbps Fast Ethernet links. Although it is possible for the FEC link to carry a total throughput of 800 Mbps (if each link becomes fully loaded), the single resulting FEC bundle does not operate at this speed.

Instead, traffic is distributed across the individual links within the EtherChannel. Each of these links operates at its inherent speed (200 Mbps full duplex for FE) but carries only the frames placed on it by the EtherChannel hardware. If one link within the bundle is favored by the load-distribution algorithm, that link will carry a disproportionate amount of traffic. In other words, the load isn't always distributed equally among the individual links. The load-balancing process is explained further in the next section.

EtherChannel also provides redundancy with several bundled physical links. If one of the links within the bundle fails, traffic sent through that link automatically is moved to an adjacent link. Failover occurs in less than a few milliseconds and is transparent to the end user. As more links fail, more traffic is moved to further adjacent links. Likewise, as links are restored, the load automatically is redistributed among the active links.

Bundling Ports with EtherChannel

EtherChannel bundles can consist of up to eight physical ports of the same Ethernet media type and speed. Some configuration restrictions exist to ensure that only similarly configured links are bundled.

Generally, all bundled ports first must belong to the same VLAN. If used as a trunk, bundled ports must be in trunking mode, have the same native VLAN, and pass the same set of VLANs. Each of the ports should have the same speed and duplex settings before being bundled. Bundled ports also must be configured with identical spanning-tree settings.

Distributing Traffic in EtherChannel

Traffic in an EtherChannel is distributed across the individual bundled links in a deterministic fashion; however, the load is not necessarily balanced equally across all the links. Instead, frames are forwarded on a specific link as a result of a hashing algorithm. The algorithm can use source IP address, destination IP address, or a combination of source and destination IP addresses, source and destination MAC addresses, or TCP/UDP port numbers. The hash algorithm computes a binary pattern that selects a link number in the bundle to carry each frame.

Key Topic

If only one address or port number is hashed, a switch forwards each frame by using one or more low-order bits of the hash value as an index into the bundled links. If two addresses or port numbers are hashed, a switch performs an exclusive-OR (XOR) operation on one or more low-order bits of the addresses or TCP/UDP port numbers as an index into the bundled links.

For example, an EtherChannel consisting of two links bundled together requires a 1-bit index. If the index is 0, link 0 is selected; if the index is 1, link 1 is used. Either the lowest-order address bit or the XOR of the last bit of the addresses in the frame is used as the index. A four-link bundle uses a hash of the last 2 bits. Likewise, an eight-link bundle uses a hash of the last 3 bits. The hashing operation's outcome selects the EtherChannel's outbound link. Table 6-2 shows the results of an XOR on a two-link bundle, using the source and destination addresses.

Table 6-2 *Frame Distribution on a Two-Link EtherChannel*

Binary Address	Two-Link EtherChannel XOR and Link Number
Addr1: ... xxxxxxx0 Addr2: ... xxxxxxx0	... xxxxxxx0: Use link 0
Addr1: ... xxxxxxx0 Addr2: ... xxxxxxx1	... xxxxxxx1: Use link 1
Addr1: ... xxxxxxx1 Addr2: ... xxxxxxx0	... xxxxxxx1: Use link 1

continues

Table 6-2 *Frame Distribution on a Two-Link EtherChannel* *(Continued)*

Binary Address	Two-Link EtherChannel XOR and Link Number
Addr1: ... xxxxxxx1 Addr2: ... xxxxxxx1	... xxxxxxx0: Use link 0

The XOR operation is performed independently on each bit position in the address value. If the two address values have the same bit value, the XOR result is always 0. If the two address bits differ, the XOR result is always 1. In this way, frames can be distributed statistically among the links with the assumption that MAC or IP addresses themselves are distributed statistically throughout the network. In a four-link EtherChannel, the XOR is performed on the lower 2 bits of the address values, resulting in a 2-bit XOR value (each bit is computed separately) or a link number from 0 to 3.

As an example, consider a packet being sent from IP address 192.168.1.1 to 172.31.67.46. Because EtherChannels can be built from two to eight individual links, only the rightmost (least-significant) 3 bits are needed as a link index. From the source and destination addresses, these bits are 001 (1) and 110 (6), respectively. For a two-link EtherChannel, a 1-bit XOR is performed on the rightmost address bit: 1 XOR 0 = 1, causing Link 1 in the bundle to be used. A four-link EtherChannel produces a 2-bit XOR: 01 XOR 10 = 11, causing Link 3 in the bundle to be used. Finally, an eight-link EtherChannel requires a 3-bit XOR: 001 XOR 110 = 111, where Link 7 in the bundle is selected.

A conversation between two devices always is sent through the same EtherChannel link because the two endpoint addresses stay the same. However, when a device talks to several other devices, chances are that the destination addresses are distributed equally with 0s and 1s in the last bit (even and odd address values). This causes the frames to be distributed across the EtherChannel links.

Note that the load distribution is still proportional to the volume of traffic passing between pairs of hosts or link indexes. For example, suppose that there are two pairs of hosts talking across a two-link channel, and each pair of addresses results in a unique link index. Frames from one pair of hosts always travel over one link in the channel, whereas frames from the other pair travel over the other link. The links are both being used as a result of the hash algorithm, so the load is being distributed across every link in the channel.

However, if one pair of hosts has a much greater volume of traffic than the other pair, one link in the channel will be used much more than the other. This still can create a load imbalance. To remedy this condition, you should consider other methods of hashing algorithms for the channel. For example, a method that combines the source and destination addresses along with UDP or TCP port numbers in a single XOR operation can distribute traffic much differently. Then, packets are placed on links within the bundle based on the applications (port numbers) used within conversations between two hosts. The possible hashing methods are discussed in the following section.

Configuring EtherChannel Load Balancing

The hashing operation can be performed on either MAC or IP addresses and can be based solely on source or destination addresses, or both. Use the following command to configure frame distribution for all EtherChannel switch links:

```
Switch(config)# port-channel load-balance method
```

Notice that the load-balancing method is set with a global configuration command. You must set the method globally for the switch, not on a per-port basis. Table 6-3 lists the possible values for the *method* variable, along with the hashing operation and some sample supporting switch models.

Table 6-3 *Types of EtherChannel Load-Balancing Methods*

method Value	Hash Input	Hash Operation	Switch Model
src-ip	Source IP address	bits	All models
dst-ip	Destination IP address	bits	All models
src-dst-ip	Source and destination IP address	XOR	All models
src-mac	Source MAC address	bits	All models
dst-mac	Destination MAC address	bits	All models
src-dst-mac	Source and destination MAC	XOR	All models
src-port	Source port number	bits	6500, 4500
dst-port	Destination port number	bits	6500, 4500
src-dst-port	Source and destination port	XOR	6500, 4500

The default configuration is to use source XOR destination IP addresses, or the **src-dst-ip** method. The default for the Catalyst 2970 and 3560 is **src-mac** for Layer 2 switching. If Layer 3 switching is used on the EtherChannel, the **src-dst-ip** method will always be used, even though it is not configurable.

Normally, the default action should result in a statistical distribution of frames; however, you should determine whether the EtherChannel is imbalanced according to the traffic patterns present. For example, if a single server is receiving most of the traffic on an EtherChannel, the server's address (the destination IP address) always will remain constant in the many conversations. This can cause one link to be overused if the destination IP address is used as a component of a load-balancing method. In the case of a four-link EtherChannel, perhaps two of the four links are overused. Configuring the use of MAC addresses, or only the source IP addresses, might cause the distribution to be more balanced across all the bundled links.

Tip: To verify how effectively a configured load-balancing method is performing, you can use the **show etherchannel port-channel** command. Each link in the channel is displayed, along with a hex "Load" value. Although this information is not intuitive, you can use the hex values to get an idea of each link's traffic loads relative to the others.

In some applications, EtherChannel traffic might consist of protocols other than IP. For example, IPX or SNA frames might be switched along with IP. Non-IP protocols need to be distributed according to MAC addresses because IP addresses are not applicable. Here, the switch should be configured to use MAC addresses instead of the IP default.

Tip: A special case results when a router is connected to an EtherChannel. Recall that a router always uses its burned-in MAC address in Ethernet frames, even though it is forwarding packets to and from many different IP addresses. In other words, many end stations send frames to their local router address with the router's MAC address as the destination. This means that the destination MAC address is the same for all frames destined through the router.

Usually, this will not present a problem because the source MAC addresses are all different. When two routers are forwarding frames to each other, however, both source and destination MAC addresses remains constant, and only one link of the EtherChannel is used. If the MAC addresses remain constant, choose IP addresses instead. Beyond that, if most of the traffic is between the same two IP addresses, as in the case of two servers talking, choose IP port numbers to disperse the frames across different links.

You should choose the load-balancing method that provides the greatest distribution or variety when the channel links are indexed. Also consider the type of addressing that is being used on the network. If most of the traffic is IP, it might make sense to load balance according to IP addresses or TCP/UDP port numbers.

But if IP load balancing is being used, what happens to non-IP frames? If a frame can't meet the load-balancing criteria, the switch automatically falls back to the "next lowest" method. With Ethernet, MAC addresses must always be present, so the switch distributes those frames according to their MAC addresses.

A switch also provides some inherent protection against bridging loops with EtherChannels. When ports are bundled into an EtherChannel, no inbound (received) broadcasts and multicasts are sent back out over any of the remaining ports in the channel. Outbound broadcast and multicast frames are load-balanced like any other: The broadcast or multicast address becomes part of the hashing calculation to choose an outbound channel link.

EtherChannel Negotiation Protocols

EtherChannels can be negotiated between two switches to provide some dynamic link configuration. Two protocols are available to negotiate bundled links in Catalyst switches. The Port Aggregation Protocol (PAgP) is a Cisco-proprietary solution, and the Link

Aggregation Control Protocol (LACP) is standards based. Table 6-4 summarizes the negotiation protocols and their operation.

Table 6-4   *EtherChannel Negotiation Protocols*

Negotiation Mode		Negotiation Packets Sent?	Characteristics
PAgP	**LACP**		
On	On	No	All ports channeling
Auto	Passive	Yes	Waits to channel until asked
Desirable	Active	Yes	Actively asks to form a channel

Port Aggregation Protocol

To provide automatic EtherChannel configuration and negotiation between switches, Cisco developed the *Port Aggregation Protocol*. PAgP packets are exchanged between switches over EtherChannel-capable ports. Neighbors are identified and port group capabilities are learned and compared with local switch capabilities. Ports that have the same neighbor device ID and port group capability are bundled together as a bidirectional, point-to-point EtherChannel link.

Key Topic

PAgP forms an EtherChannel only on ports that are configured for either identical static VLANs or trunking. PAgP also dynamically modifies parameters of the EtherChannel if one of the bundled ports is modified. For example, if the configured VLAN, speed, or duplex mode of a port in an established bundle is changed, PAgP reconfigures that parameter for all ports in the bundle.

PAgP can be configured in active mode (desirable), in which a switch actively asks a far-end switch to negotiate an EtherChannel, or in passive mode (auto, the default), in which a switch negotiates an EtherChannel only if the far end initiates it.

Link Aggregation Control Protocol

LACP is a standards-based alternative to PAgP, defined in IEEE 802.3ad (also known as IEEE 802.3 Clause 43, "Link Aggregation"). LACP packets are exchanged between switches over EtherChannel-capable ports. As with PAgP, neighbors are identified and port group capabilities are learned and compared with local switch capabilities. However, LACP also assigns roles to the EtherChannel's endpoints.

Key Topic

The switch with the lowest *system priority* (a 2-byte priority value followed by a 6-byte switch MAC address) is allowed to make decisions about what ports actively are participating in the EtherChannel at a given time.

Ports are selected and become active according to their *port priority* value (a 2-byte priority followed by a 2-byte port number), where a low value indicates a higher priority. A set of up to 16 potential links can be defined for each EtherChannel. Through LACP, a switch selects up to eight of these having the lowest port priorities as active EtherChannel links at any given time. The other links are placed in a standby state and will be enabled in the EtherChannel if one of the active links goes down.

Like PAgP, LACP can be configured in active mode (active), in which a switch actively asks a far-end switch to negotiate an EtherChannel, or in passive mode (passive), in which a switch negotiates an EtherChannel only if the far end initiates it.

EtherChannel Configuration

For each EtherChannel on a switch, you must choose the EtherChannel negotiation protocol and assign individual switch ports to the EtherChannel. Both PAgP- and LACP-negotiated EtherChannels are described in the following sections. You also can configure an EtherChannel to use the on mode, which unconditionally bundles the links. In this case, neither PAgP nor LACP packets are sent or received.

As ports are configured to be members of an EtherChannel, the switch automatically creates a logical port-channel interface. This interface represents the channel as a whole.

Configuring a PAgP EtherChannel

Key Topic

To configure switch ports for PAgP negotiation (the default), use the following commands:

```
Switch(config)# interface type mod/num
Switch(config-if)# channel-protocol pagp
Switch(config-if)# channel-group number mode {on | {{auto | desirable}
  [non-silent]}}
```

On all Cisco IOS–based Catalyst models, you can select between PAgP and LACP as a channel-negotiation protocol. Some older models, however, offer only PAgP, so the **channel-protocol** command is not available. Each interface that will be included in a single EtherChannel bundle must be configured and assigned to the same unique channel group *number* (1 to 64). Channel negotiation must be set to on (unconditionally channel, no PAgP negotiation), auto (passively listen and wait to be asked), or desirable (actively ask).

Note: IOS-based Catalyst switches do not assign interfaces to predetermined channel groups by default. In fact, the interfaces are not assigned to channel groups until you configure them manually.

This is different from Catalyst OS (CatOS) switches, such as the Catalyst 4000 (Supervisors I and II), 5000, and 6500 (hybrid mode). On those platforms, Ethernet line cards are broken up into default channel groups.

By default, PAgP operates in silent submode with the desirable and auto modes, and allows ports to be added to an EtherChannel even if the other end of the link is silent and never transmits PAgP packets. This might seem to go against the idea of PAgP, in which two endpoints are supposed to negotiate a channel. After all, how can two switches negotiate anything if no PAgP packets are received?

The key is in the phrase "*if* the other end is silent." The silent submode listens for any PAgP packets from the far end, looking to negotiate a channel. If none is received, silent submode assumes that a channel should be built anyway, so no more PAgP packets are expected from the far end.

This allows a switch to form an EtherChannel with a device such as a file server or a network analyzer that doesn't participate in PAgP. In the case of a network analyzer connected to the far end, you also might want to see the PAgP packets generated by the switch, as if you were using a normal PAgP EtherChannel.

If you expect a PAgP-capable switch to be on the far end, you should add the **non-silent** keyword to the desirable or auto mode. This requires each port to receive PAgP packets before adding them to a channel. If PAgP isn't heard on an active port, the port remains in the up state, but PAgP reports to the Spanning Tree Protocol (STP) that the port is down.

Tip: In practice, you might notice a delay from the time the links in a channel group are connected until the time the channel is formed and data can pass over it. You will encounter this if both switches are using the default PAgP auto mode and silent submode. Each interface waits to be asked to form a channel, and each interface waits and listens before accepting silent channel partners. The silent submode amounts to approximately a 15-second delay.

Even if the two interfaces are using PAgP auto mode, the link will still eventually come up, although not as a channel. You might notice that the total delay before data can pass over the link is actually approximately 45 or 50 seconds. The first 15 seconds are the result of PAgP silent mode waiting to hear inbound PAgP messages, and the final 30 seconds are the result of the STP moving through the listening and learning stages.

As an example of PAgP configuration, suppose that you want a switch to use an Ether-Channel load-balancing hash of both source and destination port numbers. A Gigabit EtherChannel will be built from interfaces Gigabit Ethernet 3/1 through 3/4, with the switch actively negotiating a channel. The switch should not wait to listen for silent partners. You can use the following configuration commands to accomplish this:

```
Switch(config)# port-channel load-balance src-dst-port
Switch(config)# interface range gig 3/1 - 4
Switch(config-if)# channel-protocol pagp
Switch(config-if)# channel-group 1 mode desirable non-silent
```

Configuring a LACP EtherChannel

To configure switch ports for LACP negotiation, use the following commands:

Key
Topic

```
Switch(config)# lacp system-priority priority
Switch(config)# interface type mod/num
Switch(config-if)# channel-protocol lacp
Switch(config-if)# channel-group number mode {on | passive | active}
Switch(config-if)# lacp port-priority priority
```

First, the switch should have its LACP system priority defined (1 to 65,535; default 32,768). If desired, one switch should be assigned a lower system priority than the other so that it can make decisions about the EtherChannel's makeup. Otherwise, both switches will have the same system priority (32,768), and the one with the lower MAC address will become the decision maker.

Each interface included in a single EtherChannel bundle must be assigned to the same unique channel group *number* (1 to 64). Channel negotiation must be set to on (unconditionally channel, no LACP negotiation), passive (passively listen and wait to be asked), or active (actively ask).

You can configure more interfaces in the channel group *number* than are allowed to be active in the channel. This prepares extra standby interfaces to replace failed active ones. Use the **lacp port-priority** command to configure a lower port priority (1 to 65,535; default 32,768) for any interfaces that must be active, and a higher priority for interfaces that might be held in the standby state. Otherwise, just use the default scenario, in which all ports default to 32,768 and the lower port numbers (in interface number order) are used to select the active ports.

As an example of LACP configuration, suppose that you want to configure a switch to negotiate a Gigabit EtherChannel using interfaces Gigabit Ethernet 2/1 through 2/4 and 3/1 through 3/4. Interfaces Gigabit Ethernet 2/5 through 2/8 and 3/5 through 3/8 are also available, so these can be used as standby links to replace failed links in the channel. This switch actively should negotiate the channel and should be the decision maker about the channel operation.

You can use the following configuration commands to accomplish this:

```
Switch(config)# lacp system-priority 100
Switch(config)# interface range gig 2/1 - 4 , gig 3/1 - 4
Switch(config-if)# channel-protocol lacp
Switch(config-if)# channel-group 1 mode active
Switch(config-if)# lacp port-priority 100
Switch(config-if)# exit
Switch(config)# interface range gig 2/5 - 8 , gig 3/5 - 8
Switch(config-if)# channel-protocol lacp
Switch(config-if)# channel-group 1 mode active
```

Notice that interfaces Gigabit Ethernet 2/5-8 and 3/5-8 have been left to their default port priorities of 32,768. This is higher than the others, which were configured for 100, so they will be held as standby interfaces.

Troubleshooting an EtherChannel

Key Topic

If you find that an EtherChannel is having problems, remember that the whole concept is based on consistent configurations on *both* ends of the channel. Here are some reminders about EtherChannel operation and interaction:

- EtherChannel on mode does not send or receive PAgP or LACP packets. Therefore, both ends should be set to on mode before the channel can form.

- EtherChannel desirable (PAgP) or active (LACP) mode attempts to ask the far end to bring up a channel. Therefore, the other end must be set to either desirable or auto mode.

- EtherChannel auto (PAgP) or passive (LACP) mode participates in the channel protocol, but only if the far end asks for participation. Therefore, two switches in the auto or passive mode will not form an EtherChannel.

- PAgP desirable and auto modes default to the silent submode, in which no PAgP packets are expected from the far end. If ports are set to nonsilent submode, PAgP packets must be received before a channel will form.

First, verify the EtherChannel state with the **show etherchannel summary** command. Each port in the channel is shown, along with flags indicating the port's state, as shown in Example 6-1.

Example 6-1   show etherchannel summary *Command Output*

```
Switch# show etherchannel summary
Flags:  D - down        P - in port-channel
        I - stand-alone s - suspended
        H - Hot-standby (LACP only)
        R - Layer3       S - Layer2
        u - unsuitable for bundling
        U - in use       f - failed to allocate aggregator
        d - default port
Number of channel-groups in use: 1
Number of aggregators:           1


Group  Port-channel  Protocol    Ports
------+-------------+-----------+------------------------------------------------


1      Po1(SU)        PAgP         Fa0/41(P)  Fa0/42(P)  Fa0/43  Fa0/44(P)
                                  Fa0/45(P)  Fa0/46(P)  Fa0/47(P)  Fa0/48(P)
```

The status of the port channel shows the EtherChannel logical interface as a whole. This should show SU (Layer 2 channel, in use) if the channel is operational. You also can examine the status of each port within the channel. Notice that most of the channel ports have flags (P), indicating that they are active in the port-channel. One port shows because it is physically not connected or down. If a port is connected but not bundled in the channel, it will have an independent, or (I), flag.

You can verify the channel negotiation mode with the **show etherchannel port** command, as shown in Example 6-2. The local switch is shown using desirable mode with PAgP (Desirable-Sl is desirable silent mode). Notice that you also can see the far end's negotiation mode under the Partner Flags heading, as A, or auto mode.

Example 6-2   show etherchannel port *Command Output*

```
Switch# show etherchannel port
                 Channel-group listing:
                 ---------------------
```

```
Group: 1
-----------
                    Ports in the group:
                    --------------------
Port: Fa0/41
------------

Port state     = Up Mstr In-Bndl
Channel group = 1           Mode = Desirable-Sl     Gcchange = 0
Port-channel  = Po1         GC   = 0x00010001              Pseudo port-channel = Po1
Port index    = 0           Load = 0x00           Protocol =   PAgP

Flags:  S - Device is sending Slow hello.  C - Device is in Consistent state.
        A - Device is in Auto mode.        P - Device learns on physical port.
        d - PAgP is down.
Timers: H - Hello timer is running.        Q - Quit timer is running.
        S - Switching timer is running.    I - Interface timer is running.

Local information:
                                    Hello    Partner  PAgP       Learning  Group
Port          Flags State  Timers   Interval Count    Priority   Method    Ifindex
Fa0/41        SC    U6/S7  H        30s      1        128        Any       55

Partner's information:

              Partner             Partner          Partner             Partner Group
Port          Name                Device ID        Port      Age Flags  Cap.

Fa0/41        FarEnd              00d0.5849.4100   3/1       19s SAC     11

Age of the port in the current state: 00d:08h:05m:28s
```

Within a switch, an EtherChannel cannot form unless each of the component or member ports is configured consistently. Each must have the same switch mode (access or trunk), native VLAN, trunked VLANs, port speed, port duplex mode, and so on.

You can display a port's configuration by looking at the **show running-config interface** *type mod/ num* output. Also, the **show interface** *type mod/num* **etherchannel** shows all active EtherChannel parameters for a single port. If you configure a port inconsistently with others for an EtherChannel, you see error messages from the switch.

Some messages from the switch might look like errors but are part of the normal Ether-Channel process. For example, as a new port is configured as a member of an existing EtherChannel, you might see this message:

```
4d00h: %EC-5-L3DONTBNDL2: FastEthernet0/2 suspended: incompatible partner port
  with FastEthernet0/1
```

When the port first is added to the EtherChannel, it is incompatible because the STP runs on the channel and the new port. After STP takes the new port through its progression of states, the port is automatically added into the EtherChannel.

Other messages do indicate a port-compatibility error. In these cases, the cause of the error is shown. For example, the following message tells that Fast Ethernet0/3 has a different duplex mode than the other ports in the EtherChannel:

```
4d00h: %EC-5-CANNOT_BUNDLE2: FastEthernet0/3 is not compatible with
   FastEthernet0/1 and will be suspended (duplex of Fa0/3 is full, Fa0/1 is half)
```

Finally, you can verify the EtherChannel load-balancing or hashing algorithm with the **show etherchannel load-balance** command. Remember that the switches on either end of an EtherChannel can have different load-balancing methods. The only drawback to this is that the load balancing will be asymmetric in the two directions across the channel.

Table 6-5 lists the commands useful for verifying or troubleshooting EtherChannel operation.

Table 6-5   *EtherChannel Troubleshooting Commands*

Display Function	Command Syntax
Current EtherChannel status of each member port	show etherchannel summary show etherchannel port
Time stamps of EtherChannel changes	show etherchannel port-channel
Detailed status about each EtherChannel component	show etherchannel detail
Load-balancing hashing algorithm	show etherchannel load-balance
Load-balancing port index used by hashing algorithm	show etherchannel port-channel
EtherChannel neighbors on each port	show {pagp	lacp} neighbor
LACP system ID	show lacp sys-id

Exam Preparation Tasks

Review All Key Topics

Review the most important topics in the chapter, noted with the key topics icon in the outer margin of the page. Table 6-6 lists a reference of these key topics and the page numbers on which each is found.

Table 6-6   *Key Topics for Chapter 6*

Key Topic Element	Description	Page Number
Paragraph	Discusses aggregating links into EtherChannels	110
Paragraph	Explains how traffic is distributed in an EtherChannel	111
Table 6-3	Lists EtherChannel load-balancing methods	113
Paragraph	Describes the PAgP negotiation protocol	115
Paragraph	Describes the LACP negotiation protocol	115
Paragraph	Explains PAgP configuration	116
Paragraph	Explains LACP configuration	117
Paragraph	Discusses rules of thumb for proper EtherChannel operation	118

Complete Tables and Lists from Memory

Print a copy of Appendix C, "Memory Tables," (found on the CD), or at least the section for this chapter, and complete the tables and lists from memory. Appendix D, "Memory Tables Answer Key," also on the CD, includes completed tables and lists to check your work.

Define Key Terms

Define the following key terms from this chapter, and check your answers in the glossary:

EtherChannel, PAgP, LACP

Command Reference to Check Your Memory

This section includes the most important configuration and EXEC commands covered in this chapter. It might not be necessary to memorize the complete syntax of every command, but you should be able to remember the basic keywords that are needed.

To test your memory of the commands related to EtherChannels, cover the right side of Table 6-7 with a piece of paper, read the description on the left side, and then see how much of the command you can remember.

Remember that the CCNP exam focuses on practical or hands-on skills that are used by a networking professional. For the skills covered in this chapter, remember that an Ether-Channel is called a port-channel interface when you are configuring it. When you are displaying information about an EtherChannel, begin the commands with the **show etherchannel** keywords.

Table 6-7 *EtherChannel Configuration Commands*

Task	Command Syntax
Select a load-balancing method for the switch.	**port-channel load-balance** *method*
Use a PAgP mode on an interface.	**channel-protocol pagp**
	channel-group *number* **mode {on** | **{{auto** | **desirable} [non-silent]}}**
Assign the LACP system priority.	**lacp system-priority** *priority*
Use an LACP mode on an interface.	**channel-protocol lacp**
	channel-group *number* **mode {on** | **passive** | **active}**
	lacp port-priority *priority*

This chapter covers the following topics that you need to master for the CCNP SWITCH exam:

IEEE 802.1D Overview—This section discusses the original, or more traditional, Spanning Tree Protocol (STP). This protocol is the foundation for the default Catalyst STP and for all the enhancements that are described in Chapters 8, "Spanning-Tree Configuration," through 10, "Advanced Spanning Tree Protocol."

Types of STP—This section discusses other types of STP that might be running on a Catalyst switch—specifically, the Common Spanning Tree, Per-VLAN Spanning Tree (PVST), and PVST+.

CHAPTER 7

Traditional Spanning Tree Protocol

Previous chapters covered ways to connect two switches together with a VLAN trunk link. What if something happens to the trunk link? The two switches would be isolated from each other. A more robust network design would add redundant links between switches. Although this increases the network availability, it also opens up the possibility for conditions that would impair the network. In a Layer 2 switched network, preventing bridging loops from forming over redundant paths is important. Spanning Tree Protocol (STP) was designed to monitor and control the Layer 2 network so that a loop-free topology is maintained.

This chapter discusses the theory and operation of the STP. More specifically, the original, or traditional, STP is covered, as defined in IEEE 802.1D. Several chapters explain STP topics in this book. Here is a brief roadmap so that you can chart a course:

- **Chapter 7, "Traditional Spanning Tree Protocol"**—Covers the theory of IEEE 802.1D

- **Chapter 8, "Spanning-Tree Configuration"**—Covers the configuration commands needed for IEEE 802.1D

- **Chapter 9, "Protecting the Spanning Tree Protocol Topology"**—Covers the features and commands to filter and protect a converged STP topology from conditions that could destabilize it

- **Chapter 10, "Advanced Spanning Tree Protocol"**—Covers the newer 802.1w and 802.1s enhancements to STP, allowing more scalability and faster convergence

"Do I Know This Already?" Quiz

The "Do I Know This Already?" quiz allows you to assess whether you should read this entire chapter thoroughly or jump to the "Exam Preparation Tasks" section. If you are in doubt based on your answers to these questions or your own assessment of your knowledge of the topics, read the entire chapter. Table 7-1 outlines the major headings in this chapter and the "Do I Know This Already?" quiz questions that go with them. You can find the answers in Appendix A, "Answers to the 'Do I Know This Already?' Quizzes."

Table 7-1 *"Do I Know This Already?" Foundation Topics Section-to-Question Mapping*

Foundation Topics Section	Questions Covered in This Section
IEEE 802.1D Overview	1–10
Types of STP	11–12

1. How is a bridging loop best described?

    a. A loop formed between switches for redundancy

    b. A loop formed by the Spanning Tree Protocol

    c. A loop formed between switches where frames circulate endlessly

    d. The round-trip path a frame takes from source to destination

2. Which of these is one of the parameters used to elect a root bridge?

    a. Root path cost

    b. Path cost

    c. Bridge priority

    d. BPDU revision number

3. If all switches in a network are left at their default STP values, which one of the following is not true?

    a. The root bridge will be the switch with the lowest MAC address.

    b. The root bridge will be the switch with the highest MAC address.

    c. One or more switches will have a bridge priority of 32,768.

    d. A secondary root bridge will be present on the network.

4. Configuration BPDUs are originated by which of the following?

    a. All switches in the STP domain

    b. Only the root bridge switch

    c. Only the switch that detects a topology change

    d. Only the secondary root bridge when it takes over

5. Which of these is the single most important design decision to be made in a network running STP?

    a. Removing any redundant links

    b. Making sure all switches run the same version of IEEE 802.1D

    c. Root bridge placement

    d. Making sure all switches have redundant links

6. What happens to a port that is neither a root port nor a designated port?

    a. It is available for normal use.

    b. It can be used for load balancing.

    c. It is put into the Blocking state.

    d. It is disabled.

7. What is the maximum number of root ports that a Catalyst switch can have?

    a. 1

    b. 2

    c. Unlimited

    d. None

8. What mechanism is used to set STP timer values for all switches in a network?

    a. Configuring the timers on every switch in the network.

    b. Configuring the timers on the root bridge switch.

    c. Configuring the timers on both primary and secondary root bridge switches.

    d. The timers can't be adjusted.

9. MAC addresses can be placed into the CAM table, but no data can be sent or received if a switch port is in which of the following STP states?

    a. Blocking

    b. Forwarding

    c. Listening

    d. Learning

10. What is the default "hello" time for IEEE 802.1D?

    a. 1 second

    b. 2 seconds

    c. 30 seconds

    d. 60 seconds

11. Which of the following is the Spanning Tree Protocol defined in the IEEE 802.1Q standard?

    a. PVST

    b. CST

    c. EST

    d. MST

12. If a switch has 10 VLANs defined and active, how many instances of STP will run using PVST+ versus CST?

    a. 1 for PVST+, 1 for CST

    b. 1 for PVST+, 10 for CST

    c. 10 for PVST+, 1 for CST

    d. 10 for PVST+, 10 for CST

Foundation Topics

IEEE 802.1D Overview

A robust network design not only includes efficient transfer of packets or frames, but also considers how to recover quickly from faults in the network. In a Layer 3 environment, the routing protocols in use keep track of redundant paths to a destination network so that a secondary path can be used quickly if the primary path fails. Layer 3 routing allows many paths to a destination to remain up and active, and allows load sharing across multiple paths.

In a Layer 2 environment (switching or bridging), however, no routing protocols are used, and active redundant paths are neither allowed nor desirable. Instead, some form of bridging provides data transport between networks or switch ports. The Spanning Tree Protocol (STP) provides network link redundancy so that a Layer 2 switched network can recover from failures without intervention in a timely manner. The STP is defined in the IEEE 802.1D standard.

STP is discussed in relation to the problems it solves in the sections that follow.

Bridging Loops

Recall that a Layer 2 switch mimics the function of a transparent bridge. A transparent bridge must offer segmentation between two networks while remaining transparent to all the end devices connected to it. For the purpose of this discussion, consider a two-port Ethernet switch and its similarities to a two-port transparent bridge.

A transparent bridge (and the Ethernet switch) must operate as follows:

Key Topic

- The bridge has no initial knowledge of any end device's location; therefore, the bridge must "listen" to frames coming into each of its ports to figure out on which network each device resides. The bridge assumes that a device using the source MAC address is located behind the port that the frame arrives on. As the listening process continues, the bridge builds a table that correlates source MAC addresses with the bridge port numbers where they were detected.

- The bridge can constantly update its bridging table on detecting the presence of a new MAC address or on detecting a MAC address that has changed location from one Bridge Port to another. The bridge then can forward frames by looking at the destination MAC address, looking up that address in the bridge table, and sending the frame out the port where the destination device is known to be located.

- If a frame arrives with the broadcast address as the destination address, the bridge must forward, or flood, the frame out all available ports. However, the frame is not forwarded out the port that initially received the frame. In this way, broadcasts can reach all available Layer 2 networks. A bridge segments only collision domains—it does not segment broadcast domains.

- If a frame arrives with a destination address that is not found in the bridge table, the bridge cannot determine which port to forward the frame to for transmission. This type of frame is known as an *unknown unicast*. In this case, the bridge treats the frame as if it were a broadcast and floods it out all remaining ports. When a reply to that frame is overheard, the bridge can learn the location of the unknown station and can add it to the bridge table for future use.

■ Frames forwarded across the bridge cannot be modified by the bridge itself. Therefore, the bridging process is effectively *transparent*.

Bridging or switching in this fashion works well. Any frame forwarded, whether to a known or unknown destination, is forwarded out the appropriate port or ports so that it is likely to be received successfully at the end device. Figure 7-1 shows a simple two-port switch functioning as a bridge, forwarding frames between two end devices. However, this network design offers no additional links or paths for redundancy if the switch or one of its links fails. In that case, the networks on either side of the bridge would become isolated from each other.

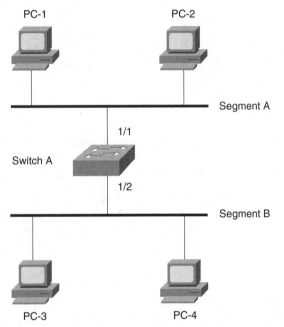

Figure 7-1 *Transparent Bridging with a Switch*

To add some redundancy, you can add a second switch between the two original network segments, as shown in Figure 7-2. Now, two switches offer the transparent bridging function in parallel. In theory, a single switch or a single link can fail without causing end-to-end connectivity to fail.

Consider what happens when PC-1 sends a frame to PC-4. For now, assume that both PC-1 and PC-4 are known to the switches and are in their address tables. PC-1 sends the frame onto network Segment A. Switch A and switch B both receive the frame on their 1/1 ports. Because PC-4 already is known to the switches, the frame is forwarded out ports 2/1 on each switch onto Segment B. The end result is that PC-4 receives two copies of the frame from PC-1. This is not ideal, but it is not disastrous, either.

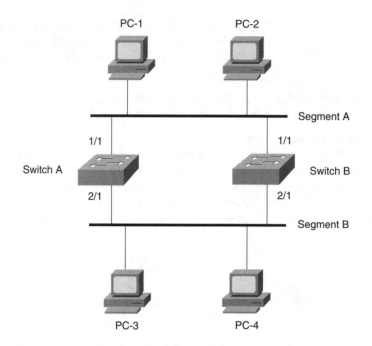

Figure 7-2   *Redundant Bridging with Two Switches*

Now, consider the same process of sending a frame from PC-1 to PC-4. This time, however, neither switch knows anything about the location of PC-1 or PC-4. PC-1 sends the frame to PC-4 by placing it on Segment A. The sequence of events is as follows:

Step 1.   Both switch A and switch B receive the frame on their 1/1 ports. Because the MAC address of PC-1 has not yet been seen or recorded, each switch records PC-1's MAC address in its address table along with the receiving port number, 1/1. From this information, both switches infer that PC-1 must reside on Segment A.

Step 2.   Because the location of PC-4 is unknown, both switches correctly decide that they must flood the frame out all available ports. This is an unknown unicast condition and is their best effort to make sure that the frame eventually reaches its destination.

Step 3.   Each switch floods or copies the frame to its 2/1 port on Segment B. PC-4, located on Segment B, receives the two frames destined for it. However, on Segment B, switch A now hears the new frame forwarded by switch B, and switch B hears the new frame forwarded by switch A.

Step 4.   Switch A sees that the "new" frame is from PC-1 to PC-4. From the address table, the switch previously learned that PC-1 was on port 1/1, or Segment A. However, the source address of PC-1 has just been heard on port 2/1, or Segment B. By definition, the switch must relearn the location of PC-1 with the most recent information, which it now incorrectly assumes to be Segment B. (Switch B follows the same procedure, based on the "new" frame from switch A.)

Step 5.   At this point, neither switch A nor switch B has learned the location of PC-4 because no frames have been received with PC-4 as the source address. Therefore, the new frame must be flooded out all available ports in an attempt to find PC-4. This frame then is sent out switch A's 1/1 port and onto Segment A, as well as switch B's 1/1 port and onto Segment A.

Step 6.   Now both switches relearn the location of PC-1 as Segment A and forward the "new" frames back onto Segment B; then the entire process repeats.

This process of forwarding a single frame around and around between two switches is known as a *bridging loop*. Neither switch is aware of the other, so each happily forwards the same frame back and forth between its segments. Also note that because two switches are involved in the loop, the original frame has been duplicated and now is sent around in two counter-rotating loops. What stops the frame from being forwarded in this fashion forever? Nothing! PC-4 begins receiving frames addressed to it as fast as the switches can forward them.

Notice how the learned location of PC-1 keeps changing as frames get looped. Even a simple unicast frame has caused a bridging loop to form, and each switch's bridge table is repeatedly corrupted with incorrect data.

What would happen if PC-1 sent a broadcast frame instead? The bridging loops (remember that two of them are produced by the two parallel switches) form exactly as before. The broadcast frames continue to circulate forever. Now, however, every end-user device located on both Segments A and B receives and processes every broadcast frame. This type of broadcast storm can easily saturate the network segments and bring every host on the segments to a halt.

The only way to end the bridging loop condition is to physically break the loop by disconnecting switch ports or shutting down a switch. Obviously, it would be better to *prevent* bridging loops than to be faced with finding and breaking them after they form.

Preventing Loops with Spanning Tree Protocol

Bridging loops form because parallel switches (or bridges) are unaware of each other. STP was developed to overcome the possibility of bridging loops so that redundant switches and switch paths could be used for their benefits. Basically, the protocol enables switches to become aware of each other so they can negotiate a loop-free path through the network.

Note: Because STP is involved in loop detection, many people refer to the catastrophic loops as "spanning-tree loops." This is technically incorrect because the Spanning Tree Protocol's entire function is to prevent bridging loops. The correct terminology for this condition is a *bridging loop*.

Loops are discovered before they are made available for use, and redundant links are effectively shut down to prevent the loops from forming. In the case of redundant links, switches can be made aware that a link shut down for loop prevention should be brought up quickly in case of a link failure. The section "Redundant Link Convergence" in Chapter 8 provides more information.

STP is communicated among all connected switches on a network. Each switch executes the spanning-tree algorithm based on information received from other neighboring switches. The algorithm chooses a reference point in the network and calculates all the redundant paths to that reference point. When redundant paths are found, the spanning-tree algorithm picks one path by which to forward frames and disables, or blocks, forwarding on the other redundant paths.

As its name implies, STP computes a tree structure that spans all switches in a subnet or network. Redundant paths are placed in a Blocking or Standby state to prevent frame forwarding. The switched network is then in a loop-free condition. However, if a forwarding port fails or becomes disconnected, the spanning-tree algorithm recomputes the spanning-tree topology so that the appropriate blocked links can be reactivated.

Spanning-Tree Communication: Bridge Protocol Data Units

Key Topic

STP operates as switches communicate with one another. Data messages are exchanged in the form of *bridge protocol data units* (BPDU). A switch sends a BPDU frame out a port, using the unique MAC address of the port itself as a source address. The switch is unaware of the other switches around it, so BPDU frames are sent with a destination address of the well-known STP multicast address 01-80-c2-00-00-00.

Two types of BPDU exist:

■   **Configuration BPDU**, used for spanning-tree computation

■   **Topology Change Notification (TCN) BPDU**, used to announce changes in the network topology

The Configuration BPDU message contains the fields shown in Table 7-2. The TCN BPDU is discussed in the "Topology Changes" section later in this chapter.

Table 7-2 *Configuration BPDU Message Content*

Field Description	Number of Bytes
Protocol ID (always 0)	2
Version (always 0)	1
Message Type (Configuration or TCN BPDU)	1
Flags	1
Root Bridge ID	8
Root Path Cost	4
Sender Bridge ID	8

Table 7-2 *Configuration BPDU Message Content (Continued)*

Field Description	Number of Bytes
Port ID	2
Message Age (in 256ths of a second)	2
Maximum Age (in 256ths of a second)	2
Hello Time (in 256ths of a second)	2
Forward Delay (in 256ths of a second)	2

The exchange of BPDU messages works toward the goal of electing reference points as a foundation for a stable spanning-tree topology. Loops also can be identified and removed by placing specific redundant ports in a Blocking or Standby state. Notice that several key fields in the BPDU are related to bridge (or switch) identification, path costs, and timer values. These all work together so that the network of switches can converge on a common spanning-tree topology and select the same reference points within the network. These reference points are defined in the sections that follow.

By default, BPDUs are sent out all switch ports every 2 seconds so that current topology information is exchanged and loops are identified quickly.

Electing a Root Bridge

For all switches in a network to agree on a loop-free topology, a common frame of reference must exist to use as a guide. This reference point is called the *root bridge*. (The term *bridge* continues to be used even in a switched environment because STP was developed for use in bridges. Therefore, when you see *bridge*, think *switch*.)

Key Topic

An election process among all connected switches chooses the root bridge. Each switch has a unique *bridge ID* that identifies it to other switches. The bridge ID is an 8-byte value consisting of the following fields:

- **Bridge Priority (2 bytes)**—The priority or weight of a switch in relation to all other switches. The Priority field can have a value of 0 to 65,535 and defaults to 32,768 (or 0x8000) on every Catalyst switch.

- **MAC Address (6 bytes)**—The MAC address used by a switch can come from the Supervisor module, the backplane, or a pool of 1,024 addresses that are assigned to every supervisor or backplane, depending on the switch model. In any event, this address is hard-coded and unique, and the user cannot change it.

When a switch first powers up, it has a narrow view of its surroundings and assumes that it is the root bridge itself. (This notion probably will change as other switches check in and enter the election process.) The election process then proceeds as follows: Every switch begins by sending out BPDUs with a root bridge ID equal to its own bridge ID and a sender bridge ID that is its own bridge ID. The sender bridge ID simply tells other switches who is the actual sender of the BPDU message. (After a root bridge is decided on, configuration BPDUs are sent only by the root bridge. All other bridges must forward or relay the BPDUs, adding their own sender bridge IDs to the message.)

Received BPDU messages are analyzed to see if a "better" root bridge is being announced. A root bridge is considered better if the root bridge ID value is *lower* than another. Again, think of the root bridge ID as being broken into Bridge Priority and MAC Address fields. If two bridge priority values are equal, the lower MAC address makes the bridge ID better. When a switch hears of a better root bridge, it replaces its own root bridge ID with the root bridge ID announced in the BPDU. The switch then is required to recommend or advertise the new root bridge ID in its own BPDU messages, although it still identifies itself as the sender bridge ID.

Sooner or later, the election converges and all switches agree on the notion that one of them is the root bridge. As might be expected, if a new switch with a lower bridge priority powers up, it begins advertising itself as the root bridge. Because the new switch does indeed have a lower bridge ID, all the switches soon reconsider and record it as the new root bridge. This also can happen if the new switch has a bridge priority equal to that of the existing root bridge but has a lower MAC address. root bridge election is an ongoing process, triggered by root bridge ID changes in the BPDUs every 2 seconds.

As an example, consider the small network shown in Figure 7-3. For simplicity, assume that each Catalyst switch has a MAC address of all 0s, with the last hex digit equal to the switch label.

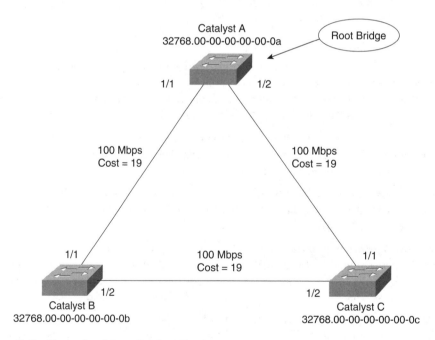

Figure 7-3 *Example of Root Bridge Election*

In this network, each switch has the default bridge priority of 32,768. The switches are interconnected with Fast Ethernet links. All three switches try to elect themselves as the root, but all of them have equal Bridge Priority values. The election outcome produces the root bridge, determined by the lowest MAC address—that of Catalyst A.

Electing Root Ports

Now that a reference point has been nominated and elected for the entire switched
work, each nonroot switch must figure out where it is in relation to the root bridge
action can be performed by selecting only one *root port* on each nonroot switch. The
root port always points toward the current root bridge.

STP uses the concept of cost to determine many things. Selecting a root port involves
evaluating the *root path cost*. This value is the cumulative cost of all the links leading to
the root bridge. A particular switch link also has a cost associated with it, called the *path
cost*. To understand the difference between these values, remember that only the root path
cost is carried inside the BPDU. (Refer to Table 7-2.) As the root path cost travels along,
other switches can modify its value to make it cumulative. The path cost, however, is not
contained in the BPDU. It is known only to the local switch where the port (or "path" to a
neighboring switch) resides.

Path costs are defined as a 1-byte value, with the default values shown in Table 7-3. Generally, the higher the bandwidth of a link, the lower the cost of transporting data across it.
The original IEEE 802.1D standard defined path cost as 1000 Mbps divided by the link
bandwidth in megabits per second. These values are shown in the center column of the
table. Modern networks commonly use Gigabit Ethernet and OC-48 ATM, which are both
either too close to or greater than the maximum scale of 1000 Mbps. The IEEE now uses
a nonlinear scale for path cost, as shown in the right column of the table.

Tip: Be aware that there are two STP path cost scales, one that is little used with a linear
scale and one commonly used that is nonlinear. If you decide to memorize some common
path cost values, learn only the ones in the New STP Cost column of the table.

Table 7-3 *STP Path Cost*

Link Bandwidth	Old STP Cost	New STP Cost
4 Mbps	250	250
10 Mbps	100	100
16 Mbps	63	62
45 Mbps	22	39
100 Mbps	10	19
155 Mbps	6	14
622 Mbps	2	6
1 Gbps	1	4
10 Gbps	0	2

The root path cost value is determined in the following manner:

1. The root bridge sends out a BPDU with a root path cost value of 0 because its ports sit directly on the root bridge.

2. When the next-closest neighbor receives the BPDU, it adds the path cost of its own port where the BPDU arrived. (This is done as the BPDU is *received*.)

3. The neighbor sends out BPDUs with this new cumulative value as the root path cost.

4. The root path cost is incremented by the ingress port path cost as the BPDU is received at each switch down the line.

5. Notice the emphasis on incrementing the root path cost as BPDUs are *received*. When computing the spanning-tree algorithm manually, remember to compute a new root path cost as BPDUs *come in* to a switch port, not as they go out.

After incrementing the root path cost, a switch also records the value in its memory. When a BPDU is received on another port and the new root path cost is lower than the previously recorded value, this lower value becomes the new root path cost. In addition, the lower cost tells the switch that the path to the root bridge must be better using this port than it was on other ports. The switch has now determined which of its ports has the best path to the root: the root port.

Figure 7-4 shows the same network from Figure 7-3 in the process of root port selection.

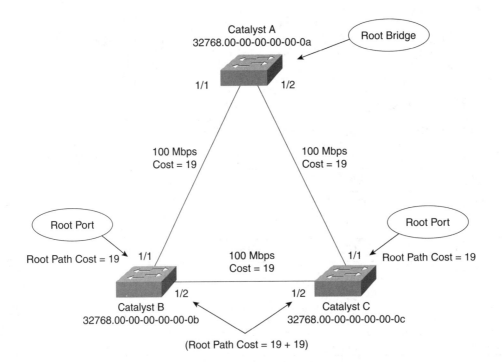

Figure 7-4 *Example of Root Port Selection*

The root bridge, Catalyst A, already has been elected. Therefore, every other switch in the network must choose one port that has the best path to the root bridge. Catalyst B selects its port 1/1, with a root path cost of 0 plus 19. Port 1/2 is not chosen because its root path cost is 0 (BPDU from Catalyst A) plus 19 (path cost of A–C link), plus 19 (path cost of C–B link), or a total of 38. Catalyst C makes an identical choice of port 1/1.

Electing Designated Ports

By now, you should begin to see the process unfolding: A starting or reference point has been identified, and each switch "connects" itself toward the reference point with the single link that has the best path. A tree structure is beginning to emerge, but links have only been identified at this point. All links still are connected and could be active, leaving bridging loops.

To remove the possibility of bridging loops, STP makes a final computation to identify one *designated port* on each network segment. Suppose that two or more switches have ports connected to a single common network segment. If a frame appears on that segment, all the bridges attempt to forward it to its destination. Recall that this behavior was the basis of a bridging loop and should be avoided.

Instead, only one of the links on a segment should forward traffic to and from that segment—the one that is selected as the designated port. Switches choose a designated port based on the lowest cumulative root path cost to the root bridge. For example, a switch always has an idea of its own root path cost, which it announces in its own BPDUs. If a neighboring switch on a shared LAN segment sends a BPDU announcing a lower root path cost, the neighbor must have the designated port. If a switch learns only of higher root path costs from other BPDUs received on a port, however, it then correctly assumes that its own receiving port is the designated port for the segment.

Notice that the entire STP determination process has served only to identify bridges and ports. All ports are still active, and bridging loops still might lurk in the network. STP has a set of progressive states that each port must go through, regardless of the type or identification. These states actively prevent loops from forming and are described in the next section.

In each determination process discussed so far, two or more links might have identical root path costs. This results in a tie condition, unless other factors are considered. All tie-breaking STP decisions are based on the following sequence of four conditions:

1. Lowest root bridge ID

2. Lowest root path cost to root bridge

3. Lowest sender bridge ID

4. Lowest sender port ID

Figure 7-5 demonstrates an example of designated port selection. This figure is identical to Figure 7-3 and Figure 7-4, with further spanning-tree development shown. The only changes are the choices of designated ports, although seeing all STP decisions shown on one network diagram is handy.

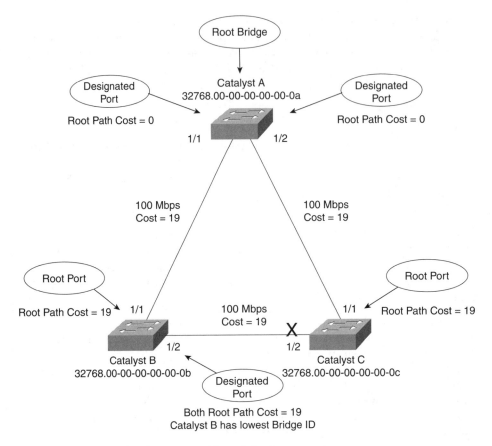

Figure 7-5 *Example of Designated Port Selection*

The three switches have chosen their designated ports (DP) for the following reasons:

- **Catalyst A**—Because this switch is the root bridge, all its active ports are designated ports, by definition. At the root bridge, the root path cost of each port is 0.

- **Catalyst B**—Catalyst A port 1/1 is the DP for the Segment A–B because it has the lowest root path cost (0). Catalyst B port 1/2 is the DP for segment B–C. The root path cost for each end of this segment is 19, determined from the incoming BPDU on port 1/1. Because the root path cost is equal on both ports of the segment, the DP must be chosen by the next criteria—the lowest sender bridge ID. When Catalyst B sends a BPDU to Catalyst C, it has the lowest MAC address in the bridge ID. Catalyst C also sends a BPDU to Catalyst B, but its sender bridge ID is higher. Therefore, Catalyst B port 1/2 is selected as the segment's DP.

- **Catalyst C**—Catalyst A port 1/2 is the DP for Segment A–C because it has the lowest root path cost (0). Catalyst B port 1/2 is the DP for Segment B–C. Therefore, Catalyst C port 1/2 will be neither a root port nor a designated port. As discussed in the next section, any port that is not elected to either position enters the Blocking state. Where blocking occurs, bridging loops are broken.

STP States

To participate in STP, each port of a switch must progress through several states. A port begins its life in a Disabled state, moving through several passive states and, finally, into an active state if allowed to forward traffic. The STP port states are as follows:

Key Topic

- **Disabled**—Ports that are administratively shut down by the network administrator, or by the system because of a fault condition, are in the Disabled state. This state is special and is not part of the normal STP progression for a port.

- **Blocking**—After a port initializes, it begins in the Blocking state so that no bridging loops can form. In the Blocking state, a port cannot receive or transmit data and cannot add MAC addresses to its address table. Instead, a port is allowed to receive only BPDUs so that the switch can hear from other neighboring switches. In addition, ports that are put into standby mode to remove a bridging loop enter the Blocking state.

- **Listening**—A port is moved from Blocking to Listening if the switch thinks that the port can be selected as a root port or designated port. In other words, the port is on its way to begin forwarding traffic.

  In the Listening state, the port still cannot send or receive data frames. However, the port is allowed to receive and send BPDUs so that it can actively participate in the Spanning Tree topology process. Here, the port finally is allowed to become a root port or designated port because the switch can advertise the port by sending BPDUs to other switches. If the port loses its root port or designated port status, it returns to the Blocking state.

- **Learning**—After a period of time called the *Forward Delay* in the Listening state, the port is allowed to move into the Learning state. The port still sends and receives BPDUs as before. In addition, the switch now can learn new MAC addresses to add to its address table. This gives the port an extra period of silent participation and allows the switch to assemble at least some address information. The port cannot yet send any data frames, however.

- **Forwarding**—After another Forward Delay period of time in the Learning state, the port is allowed to move into the Forwarding state. The port now can send and receive data frames, collect MAC addresses in its address table, and send and receive BPDUs. The port is now a fully functioning switch port within the spanning-tree topology.

Remember that a switch port is allowed into the Forwarding state only if no redundant links (or loops) are detected and if the port has the best path to the root bridge as the root port or designated port.

Table 7-4 summarizes the STP port states and what can and cannot be done in those states.

Table 7-4   *STP States and Port Activity*

STP State	The Port Can...	The Port Cannot...	Duration
Disabled	N/A	Send or receive data	N/A
Blocking	Receive BPDUs	Send or receive data or learn MAC addresses	Indefinite if loop has been detected
Listening	Send and receive BPDUs	Send or receive data or learn MAC addresses	Forward Delay timer (15 seconds)
Learning	Send and receive BPDUs and learn MAC addresses	Send or receive data	Forward Delay timer (15 seconds)
Forwarding	Send and receive BPDUs, learn MAC addresses, and send and receive data		Indefinite as long as port is up and loop is not detected

Example 7-1 shows the output from a switch as one of its ports progresses through the STP port states.

Example 7-1   *Port Progressing Through the STP Port States*

```
*Mar 16 14:31:00 UTC: STP SW: Fa0/1 new disabled req for 1 vlans
Switch(config)# interface fastethernet 0/1
Switch(config-if)#no shutdown
Switch(config-if)#^-Z
*Mar 16 14:31:00 UTC: STP SW: Fa0/1 new blocking req for 1 vlans

Switch# show spanning interface fastethernet 0/1

Vlan            Port ID                   Designated              Port ID
Name            Prio.Nbr    Cost Sts      Cost Bridge ID          Prio.Nbr
---------------- ------------- --------------- ---------------------------- --------
VLAN0001        128.1          19 LIS       0 32769 000a.f40a.2980 128.1

*Mar 16 14:31:15 UTC: STP SW: Fa0/1 new learning req for 1 vlans

Switch# show spanning interface fastethernet 0/1
Vlan            Port ID                   Designated              Port ID
Name            Prio.Nbr    Cost Sts      Cost Bridge ID          Prio.Nbr
---------------- ------------- --------------- ---------------------------- --------
VLAN0001        128.1          19 LRN       0 32768 00d0.5849.4100   32.129

*Mar 16 14:31:30 UTC: STP SW: Fa0/1 new forwarding req for 1 vlans
```

```
Switch# show spanning interface fastethernet 0/1

Vlan                Port ID                     Designated              Port ID
Name                Prio.Nbr    Cost Sts        Cost Bridge ID          Prio.Nbr
----------------    ------------ --------------  ------------------------- --------

VLAN0001            128.1        19 FWD          0 32768 00d0.5849.4100   32.129
```

The example begins as the port is administratively disabled from the command line. When the port is enabled, successive **show spanning-tree interface** *type mod/port* commands display the port state as Listening, Learning, and then Forwarding. These are shown in the shaded text of the example. Notice also the time stamps and port states provided by the **debug spanning-tree switch state** command, which give a sense of the timing between port states. Because this port was eligible as a root port, the **show** command never could execute fast enough to show the port in the Blocking state.

You can manually work out a spanning-tree topology using a network diagram. Follow the basic steps listed in Table 7-5 to add information to the network diagram. By the time you reach step 5, your STP will have converged, just like the switches in a live network would do.

Table 7-5 *Manual STP Computation*

Task	Description
1. Identify path costs on links.	For each link between switches, write the path cost that each switch uses for the link.
2. Identify the root bridge.	Find the switch with the lowest bridge ID; mark it on the drawing.
3. Select root ports (1 per switch).	For each switch, find the one port that has the best path to the root bridge. This is the one with the lowest root path cost. Mark the port with an RP label.
4. Select designated ports (1 per segment).	For each link between switches, identify which end of the link will be the designated port. This is the one with the lowest root path cost; if equal on both ends, use STP tie-breakers. Mark the port with a DP label.
5. Identify the blocking ports.	Every switch port that is neither a root nor a designated port will be put into the Blocking state. Mark these with an X.

STP Timers

STP operates as switches send BPDUs to each other in an effort to form a loop-free topology. The BPDUs take a finite amount of time to travel from switch to switch. In addition, news of a topology change (such as a link or root bridge failure) can suffer from propagation delays as the announcement travels from one side of a network to the other. Because of the possibility of these delays, keeping the spanning-tree topology from settling out or converging until all switches have had time to receive accurate information is important.

Key Topic

STP uses three timers to make sure that a network converges properly before a bridging loop can form. The timers and their default values are as follows:

- **Hello Time**—The time interval between Configuration BPDUs sent by the root bridge. The Hello Time value configured in the root bridge switch determines the Hello Time for all nonroot switches because they just relay the Configuration BPDUs as they are received from the root. However, all switches have a locally configured Hello Time that is used to time TCN BPDUs when they are retransmitted. The IEEE 802.1D standard specifies a default Hello Time value of 2 seconds.

- **Forward Delay**—The time interval that a switch port spends in both the Listening and Learning states. The default value is 15 seconds.

- **Max (maximum) Age**—The time interval that a switch stores a BPDU before discarding it. While executing the STP, each switch port keeps a copy of the "best" BPDU that it has heard. If the switch port loses contact with the BPDU's source (no more BPDUs are received from it), the switch assumes that a topology change must have occurred after the Max Age time elapsed and so the BPDU is aged out. The default Max Age value is 20 seconds.

The STP timers can be configured or adjusted from the switch command line. However, the timer values never should be changed from the defaults without careful consideration. Then the values should be changed only on the root bridge switch. Recall that the timer values are advertised in fields within the BPDU. The root bridge ensures that the timer values propagate to all other switches.

Tip: The default STP timer values are based on some assumptions about the size of the network and the length of the Hello Time. A reference model of a network having a diameter of seven switches derives these values. The diameter is measured from the root bridge switch outward, including the root bridge.

In other words, if you draw the STP topology, the diameter is the number of switches connected in series from the root bridge out to the end of any branch in the tree. The Hello Time is based on the time it takes for a BPDU to travel from the root bridge to a point seven switches away. This computation uses a Hello Time of 2 seconds.

The network diameter can be configured on the root bridge switch to more accurately reflect the true size of the physical network. Making that value more accurate reduces the total STP convergence time during a topology change. Cisco also recommends that if changes need to be made, only the network diameter value should be modified on the root bridge switch. When the diameter is changed, the switch calculates new values for all three timers automatically.

Table 7-6 summarizes the STP timers, their functions, and their default values.

Table 7-6   *STP Timers*

Timer	Function	Default Value
Hello	Interval between configuration BPDUs.	2 seconds
Forward Delay	Time spent in Listening and Learning states before transitioning toward Forwarding state.	15 seconds
Max Age	Maximum length of time a BPDU can be stored without receiving an update. Timer expiration signals an indirect failure with designated or root bridge.	20 seconds

Topology Changes

To announce a change in the active network topology, switches send a TCN BPDU. Table 7-7 shows the format of these messages.

Table 7-7   *Topology Change Notification BPDU Message Content*

Field Description	# of Bytes
Protocol ID (always 0)	2
Version (always 0)	1
Message Type (Configuration or TCN BPDU)	1

A topology change occurs when a switch either moves a port into the Forwarding state or moves a port from the Forwarding or Learning states into the Blocking state. In other words, a port on an active switch comes up or goes down. The switch sends a TCN BPDU out its root port so that, ultimately, the root bridge receives news of the topology change. Notice that the TCN BPDU carries no data about the change but informs recipients only that a change has occurred. Also notice that the switch will not send TCN BPDUs if the port has been configured with PortFast enabled.

Key Topic

The switch continues sending TCN BPDUs every Hello Time interval until it gets an acknowledgment from its upstream neighbor. As the upstream neighbors receive the TCN BPDU, they propagate it on toward the root bridge and send their own acknowledgments. When the root bridge receives the TCN BPDU, it also sends out an acknowledgment. However, the root bridge sets the Topology Change flag in its Configuration BPDU, which is relayed to every other bridge in the network. This is done to signal the topology change and cause all other bridges to shorten their bridge table aging times from the default (300 seconds) to the Forward Delay value (default 15 seconds).

This condition causes the learned locations of MAC addresses to be flushed out much sooner than they normally would, easing the bridge table corruption that might occur because of the change in topology. However, any stations that are actively communicating during this time are kept in the bridge table. This condition lasts for the sum of the Forward Delay and the Max Age (default 15 + 20 seconds).

The theory behind topology changes is fairly straightforward, but it's often difficult to grasp how a working network behaves during a change. For example, suppose that you have a Layer 2 network (think of a single VLAN or a single instance of STP) that is stable and loop free. If a switch uplink suddenly failed or a new uplink was added, how would the various switches in the network react? Would users all over the network lose connectivity while the STP "recomputes" or reconverges?

Examples of different types of topology changes are presented in the following sections, along with the sequence of STP events. Each type has a different cause and a different effect. To provide continuity as the STP concepts are presented, the same network previously shown in Figures 7-3 through 7-5 is used in each of these examples.

Direct Topology Changes

A direct topology change is one that can be detected on a switch interface. For example, if a trunk link suddenly goes down, the switch on each end of the link can immediately detect a link failure. The absence of that link changes the bridging topology, so other switches should be notified.

Figure 7-6 shows a network that has converged into a stable STP topology. The VLAN is forwarding on all trunk links except port 1/2 on Catalyst C, where it is in the Blocking state.

This network has just suffered a link failure between Catalyst A and Catalyst C. The sequence of events unfolds as follows:

1. Catalyst C detects a link down on its port 1/1; Catalyst A detects a link down on its port 1/2.

2. Catalyst C removes the previous "best" BPDU it had received from the root over port 1/1. Port 1/1 is now down so that BPDU is no longer valid.

   Normally, Catalyst C would try to send a TCN message out its root port, to reach the root bridge. Here, the root port is broken, so that isn't possible. Without an advanced feature such as STP UplinkFast, Catalyst C isn't yet aware that another path exists to the root.

   Also, Catalyst A is aware of the link down condition on its own port 1/2. It normally would try to send a TCN message out its root port to reach the root bridge. Here, Catalyst A *is* the root, so that isn't really necessary.

3. The root bridge, Catalyst A, sends a Configuration BPDU with the TCN bit set out its port 1/1. This is received and relayed by each switch along the way, informing each one of the topology change.

4. Catalysts B and C receive the TCN message. The only reaction these switches take is to shorten their bridging table aging times to the Forward Delay time. At this point, they don't know how the topology has changed; they only know to force fairly recent bridging table entries to age out.

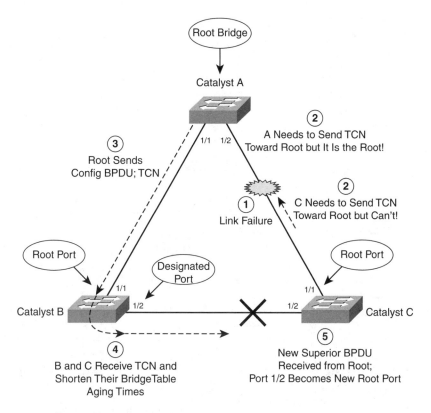

Figure 7-6 *Effects of a Direct Topology Change*

5. Catalyst C basically just sits and waits to hear from the root bridge again. The Config
    BPDU TCN message is received on port 1/2, which was previously in the Blocking
    state. This BPDU becomes the "best" one received from the root, so port 1/2
    becomes the new root port.

    Catalyst C now can progress port 1/2 from Blocking through the Listening, Learning,
    and Forwarding states.

As a result of a direct link failure, the topology has changed and STP has converged
again. Notice that only Catalyst C has undergone any real effects from the failure.
Switches A and B heard the news of the topology change but did not have to move any
links through the STP states. In other words, the whole network did not go through a
massive STP reconvergence.

The total time that users on Catalyst C lost connectivity was roughly the time that port
1/2 spent in the Listening and Learning states. With the default STP timers, this amounts
to about two times the Forward Delay period (15 seconds), or 30 seconds total.

Indirect Topology Changes

Figure 7-7 shows the same network as Figure 7-6, but this time the link failure indirectly
involves Catalysts A and C. The link status at each switch stays up, but something between

them has failed or is filtering traffic. This could be another device, such as a service provider's switch, a firewall, and so on. As a result, no data (including BPDUs) can pass between those switches.

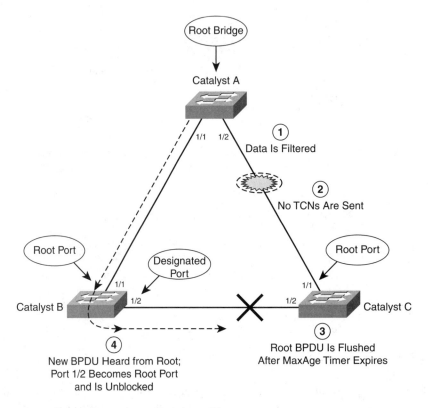

Figure 7-7   *Effects of an Indirect Topology Change*

STP can detect and recover from indirect failures, thanks to timer mechanisms. The sequence of events unfolds as follows:

1. Catalysts A and C both show a link up condition; data begins to be filtered elsewhere on the link.

2. No link failure is detected, so no TCN messages are sent.

3. Catalyst C already has stored the "best" BPDU it had received from the root over port 1/1. No further BPDUs are received from the root over that port. After the Max Age timer expires, no other BPDU is available to refresh the "best" entry, so it is flushed. Catalyst C now must wait to hear from the Root again on any of its ports.

4. The next Configuration BPDU from the root is heard on Catalyst C port 1/2. This BPDU becomes the new "best" entry, and port 1/2 becomes the root port. Now the port is progressed from Blocking through the Listening, Learning, and finally Forwarding states.

As a result of the indirect link failure, the topology doesn't change immediately. The absence of BPDUs from the root causes Catalyst C to take some action. Because this type of failure relies on STP timer activity, it generally takes longer to detect and mitigate.

In this example, the total time that users on Catalyst C lost connectivity was roughly the time until the Max Age timer expired (20 seconds), plus the time until the next Configuration BPDU was received (2 seconds) on port 1/2, plus the time that port 1/2 spent in the Listening (15 seconds) and Learning (15 seconds) states. In other words, 52 seconds elapse if the default timer values are used.

Insignificant Topology Changes

Figure 7-8 shows the same network topology as Figure 7-6 and Figure 7-7, with the addition of a user PC on access-layer switch Catalyst C. The user's switch port, 2/12, is just another link as far as the switch is concerned. If the link status goes up or down, the switch must view that as a topology change and inform the root bridge.

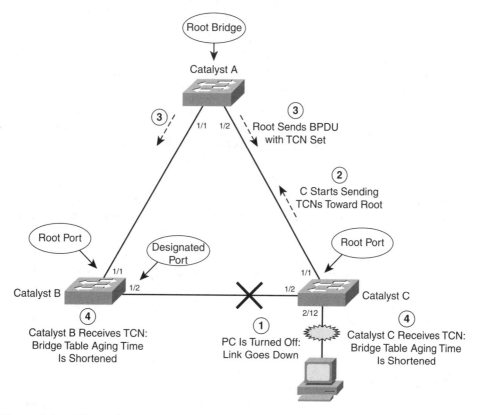

Figure 7-8 *Effects of an Insignificant Topology Change*

Obviously, user ports are expected to go up and down as the users reboot their machines, turn them on and off as they go to and from work, and so on. Regardless, TCN messages are sent by the switch, just as if a trunk link between switches had changed state.

To see what effect this has on the STP topology and the network, consider the following sequence of events:

1. The PC on Catalyst port 2/12 is turned off. The switch detects the link status going down.

2. Catalyst C begins sending TCN BPDUs toward the root, over its root port (1/1).

3. The root sends a TCN acknowledgment back to Catalyst C and then sends a Configuration BPDU with the TCN bit set to all downstream switches. This is done to inform every switch of a topology change somewhere in the network.

4. The TCN flag is received from the root, and both Catalysts B and C shorten their bridge table aging times. This causes recently idle entries to be flushed, leaving only the actively transmitting stations in the table. The aging time stays short for the duration of the Forward Delay and Max Age timers.

Notice that this type of topology change is mostly cosmetic. No actual topology change occurred because none of the switches had to change port states to reach the root bridge. Instead, powering off the PC caused all the switches to age out entries from their bridge or CAM tables much sooner than normal.

At first, this doesn't seem like a major problem because the PC link state affects only the "newness" of the CAM table contents. If CAM table entries are flushed as a result, they probably will be learned again. This becomes a problem when every user PC is considered. Now every time *any* PC in the network powers up or down, *every* switch in the network must age out CAM table entries.

Given enough PCs, the switches could be in a constant state of flushing bridge tables. Also remember that when a switch doesn't have a CAM entry for a destination, the packet must be flooded out all its ports. Flushed tables mean more unknown unicasts, which mean more broadcasts or flooded packets throughout the network.

Fortunately, Catalyst switches have a feature that can designate a port as a special case. You can enable the STP PortFast feature on a port with a single attached PC. As a result, TCNs aren't sent when the port changes state, and the port is brought right into the Forwarding state when the link comes up. The section "Redundant Link Convergence," in Chapter 8, covers PortFast in more detail.

Types of STP

So far, this chapter has discussed STP in terms of its operation to prevent loops and to recover from topology changes in a timely manner. STP was originally developed to operate in a bridged environment, basically supporting a single LAN (or one VLAN). Implementing STP into a switched environment has required additional consideration and modification to support multiple VLANs. Because of this, the IEEE and Cisco have approached

STP differently. This section reviews the three traditional types of STP that are encountered in switched networks and how they relate to one another. No specific configuration commands are associated with the various types of STP here. Instead, you need a basic understanding of how they interoperate in a network.

Note: The IEEE has produced additional standards for spanning-tree enhancements that greatly improve on its scalability and convergence aspects. These are covered in Chapter 10. When you have a firm understanding of the more traditional forms of STP presented in this chapter, you can grasp the enhanced versions much easier.

Common Spanning Tree

The IEEE 802.1Q standard specifies how VLANs are to be trunked between switches. It also specifies only a single instance of STP that encompasses all VLANs. This instance is referred to as the *Common Spanning Tree* (CST). All CST BPDUs are transmitted over trunk links using the native VLAN with untagged frames.

Having a single STP for many VLANs simplifies switch configuration and reduces switch CPU load during STP calculations. However, having only one STP instance can cause limitations, too. Redundant links between switches will be blocked with no capability for load balancing. Conditions also can occur that would cause CST to mistakenly enable forwarding on a link that does not carry a specific VLAN, whereas other links would be blocked.

Per-VLAN Spanning Tree

Cisco has a proprietary version of STP that offers more flexibility than the CST version. *Per-VLAN Spanning Tree* (PVST) operates a separate instance of STP for each individual VLAN. This allows the STP on each VLAN to be configured independently, offering better performance and tuning for specific conditions. Multiple spanning trees also make load balancing possible over redundant links when the links are assigned to different VLANs. One link might forward one set of VLANs, while another redundant link might forward a different set.

Because of its proprietary nature, PVST requires the use of Cisco Inter-Switch Link (ISL) trunking encapsulation between switches. In networks where PVST and CST coexist, interoperability problems occur. Each requires a different trunking method, so BPDUs are never exchanged between STP types.

Per-VLAN Spanning Tree Plus

Cisco has a second proprietary version of STP that allows devices to interoperate with both PVST and CST. *Per-VLAN Spanning Tree Plus* (PVST+) effectively supports three groups of STP operating in the same campus network:

- Catalyst switches running PVST

- Catalyst switches running PVST+

- Switches running CST over 802.1Q

Table 7-8 summarizes the three STP types and their basic functions.

Table 7-8 *Types of STP*

Type of STP	Function
CST	1 instance of STP, over the native VLAN; 802.1Q-based
PVST	1 instance of STP per VLAN; Cisco ISL-based
PVST+	Provides interoperability between CST and PVST; operates over both 802.1Q and ISL

To do this, PVST+ acts as a translator between groups of CST switches and groups of PVST switches. PVST+ can communicate directly with PVST by using ISL trunks. To communicate with CST, however, PVST+ exchanges BPDUs with CST as untagged frames over the native VLAN. BPDUs from other instances of STP (other VLANs) are propagated across the CST portions of the network by tunneling. PVST+ sends these BPDUs by using a unique multicast address so that the CST switches forward them on to downstream neighbors without interpreting them first. Eventually, the tunneled BPDUs reach other PVST+ switches where they are understood.

Exam Preparation Tasks

Review All Key Topics

Review the most important topics in the chapter, noted with the Key Topic icon in the outer margin of the page. Table 7-9 lists a reference of these key topics and the page numbers on which each is found.

Key Topic

Table 7-9 *Key Topics for Chapter 7*

Key Topic Element	Description	Page Number
List	Describes transparent bridge operation	128
List	Explains a bridging loop	130
Paragraph	Discusses BPDUs	132
Paragraph	Discusses root bridge election	133
Paragraph	Explains root port selection and root path cost	135
Paragraph	Discusses designated port selection	137
List	Explains tie-breaking decision process	137
List	Discusses the sequence of STP port states	139
List	Explains the three STP timers and their uses	142
Paragraph	Explains STP topology changes	143
Paragraph	Describes the Common Spanning Tree	149
Paragraph	Describes Per-VLAN Spanning Tree	149

Complete Tables and Lists from Memory

Print a copy of Appendix C, "Memory Tables," (found on the CD), or at least the section for this chapter, and complete the tables and lists from memory. Appendix D, "Memory Tables Answer Key," also on the CD, includes completed tables and lists to check your work.

Define Key Terms

Define the following key terms from this chapter, and check your answers in the glossary:

transparent bridge, bridging loop, Spanning Tree Protocol (STP), BPDU, root bridge, root port, root path cost, designated port, Hello Time, Forward Delay, Max Age time, TCN, Common Spanning Tree (CST), PVST, PVST+

This chapter covers the following topics that you need to master for the CCNP SWITCH exam:

STP Root Bridge—This section discusses the importance of identifying a root bridge and suggestions for its placement in the network. This section also presents the root bridge configuration commands.

Spanning-Tree Customization—This section covers the configuration commands that enable you to alter the spanning-tree topology.

Tuning Spanning-Tree Convergence—This section discusses how to alter, or tune, the STP timers to achieve optimum convergence times in a network.

Redundant Link Convergence—This section describes the methods that cause a network to converge more quickly after a topology change.

Monitoring STP—This section offers a brief summary of the commands you can use to verify that an STP instance is working properly.

CHAPTER 8

Spanning-Tree Configuration

This chapter presents the design and configuration considerations necessary to implement the IEEE 802.1D Spanning Tree Protocol (STP) in a campus network. This chapter also discusses the commands needed to configure the STP features, previously described in Chapter 7, "Traditional Spanning Tree Protocol."

You can also tune STP or make it converge more efficiently in a given network. This chapter presents the theory and commands needed to accomplish this.

"Do I Know This Already?" Quiz

The "Do I Know This Already?" quiz allows you to assess whether you should read this entire chapter thoroughly or jump to the "Exam Preparation Tasks" section. If you are in doubt based on your answers to these questions or your own assessment of your knowledge of the topics, read the entire chapter. Table 8-1 outlines the major headings in this chapter and the "Do I Know This Already?" quiz questions that go with them. You can find the answers in Appendix A, "Answers to the 'Do I Know This Already?' Quizzes."

Table 8-1 *"Do I Know This Already?" Foundation Topics Section-to-Question Mapping*

Foundation Topics Section	Questions Covered in This Section
STP Root Bridge	1–5
Spanning-Tree Customization	6–7
Tuning Spanning-Tree Convergence	8–9
Redundant Link Convergence	10–12
Monitoring STP	13

1. Where should the root bridge be placed on a network?

    a. On the fastest switch

    b. Closest to the most users

    c. Closest to the center of the network

    d. On the least-used switch

2. Which of the following is a result of a poorly placed root bridge in a network?

   a.   Bridging loops form.

   b.   STP topology can't be resolved.

   c.   STP topology can take unexpected paths.

   d.   Root bridge election flapping occurs.

3. Which of these parameters should you change to make a switch become a root bridge?

   a.   Switch MAC address

   b.   Path cost

   c.   Port priority

   d.   Bridge priority

4. What is the default 802.1D STP bridge priority on a Catalyst switch?

   a.   0

   b.   1

   c.   32,768

   d.   65,535

5. Which of the following commands is most likely to make a switch become the root bridge for VLAN 5, assuming that all switches have the default STP parameters?

   a.   spanning-tree root

   b.   spanning-tree root vlan 5

   c.   spanning-tree vlan 5 priority 100

   d.   spanning-tree vlan 5 root

6. What is the default path cost of a Gigabit Ethernet switch port?

   a.   1

   b.   2

   c.   4

   d.   19

   e.   1000

7. What command can change the path cost of interface Gigabit Ethernet 3/1 to a value of 8?

   a.   spanning-tree path-cost 8

   b.   spanning-tree cost 8

   c.   spanning-tree port-cost 8

   d.   spanning-tree gig 3/1 cost 8

8. What happens if the root bridge switch and another switch are configured with different STP Hello timer values?

    a. Nothing—each sends hellos at different times.

    b. A bridging loop could form because the two switches are out of sync.

    c. The switch with the lower Hello timer becomes the root bridge.

    d. The other switch changes its Hello timer to match the root bridge

9. What network diameter value is the basis for the default STP timer calculations?

    a. 1

    b. 3

    c. 7

    d. 9

    e. 15

10. Where should the STP PortFast feature be used?

    a. An access-layer switch port connected to a PC

    b. An access-layer switch port connected to a hub

    c. A distribution-layer switch port connected to an access layer switch

    d. A core-layer switch port

11. Where should the STP UplinkFast feature be enabled?

    a. An access-layer switch.

    b. A distribution-layer switch.

    c. A core-layer switch.

    d. All these answers are correct.

12. If used, the STP BackboneFast feature should be enabled on which of these?

    a. All backbone- or core-layer switches

    b. All backbone- and distribution-layer switches

    c. All access-layer switches

    d. All switches in the network

13. Which one of the following commands can be used to verify the current root bridge in VLAN 10?

    a. show root vlan 10

    b. show root-bridge vlan 10

    c. show spanning-tree vlan 10 root

    d. show running-config

Foundation Topics

STP Root Bridge

Spanning Tree Protocol (STP) and its computations are predictable; however, other factors might subtly influence STP decisions, making the resulting tree structure neither expected nor ideal.

As the network administrator, you can make adjustments to the spanning-tree operation to control its behavior. The location of the root bridge should be determined as part of the design process. You can use redundant links for load balancing in parallel, if configured correctly. You can also configure STP to converge quickly and predictably if a major topology change occurs.

Tip: By default, STP is enabled for all active VLANs and on all ports of a switch. STP should remain enabled in a network to prevent bridging loops from forming. However, you might find that STP has been disabled in some way.

If an entire instance of STP has been disabled, you can reenable it with the following global configuration command:

```
Switch(config)# spanning-tree vlan vlan-id
```

If STP has been disabled for a specific VLAN on a specific port, you can reenable it with the following interface configuration command:

```
Switch (config-if)# spanning-tree vlan vlan-id
```

Root Bridge Placement

Although STP is wonderfully automatic with its default values and election processes, the resulting tree structure might perform quite differently than expected. The root bridge election is based on the idea that one switch is chosen as a common reference point, and all other switches choose ports that have the best-cost path to the root. The root bridge election is also based on the idea that the root bridge can become a central hub that interconnects other legs of the network. Therefore, the root bridge can be faced with heavy switching loads in its central location.

Key Topic

If the root bridge election is left to its default state, several things can occur to result in a poor choice. For example, the *slowest* switch (or bridge) could be elected as the root bridge. If heavy traffic loads are expected to pass through the root bridge, the slowest switch is not the ideal candidate. Recall that the only criteria for root bridge election is that the switch must have the lowest bridge ID (bridge priority and MAC address), which is not necessarily the best choice to ensure optimal performance. If the slowest switch has the same bridge priority as the others and has the lowest MAC address, the slowest switch will be chosen as the root.

A second factor to consider relates to redundancy. If all switches are left at their default states, only one root bridge is elected, with no clear choice for a backup. What happens if that switch fails? Another root bridge election occurs, but again, the choice might not be the ideal switch or the ideal location.

The final consideration is the location of the root bridge switch. As before, an election with default switch values could place the root bridge in an unexpected location in the network. More important, an inefficient spanning-tree structure could result, causing traffic from a large portion of the network to take a long and winding path just to pass through the root bridge.

Figure 8-1 shows a portion of a real-world hierarchical campus network.

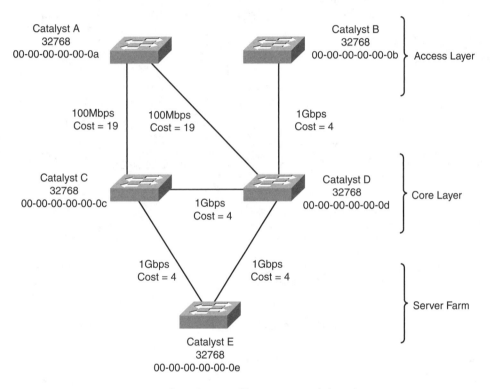

Figure 8-1 *Campus Network with an Inefficient Root Bridge Election*

Catalyst switches A and B are two access-layer devices; Catalysts C and D form the core layer, and Catalyst E connects a server farm into the network core. Notice that most of the switches use redundant links to other layers of the hierarchy. At the time of this example, however, many switches, such as Catalyst B, still have only a single connection into the core. These switches are slated for an "upgrade," in which a redundant link will be added to the other half of the core.

As you will see, Catalyst A will become the root bridge because of its low MAC address. All switches have been left to their default STP states—the bridge priority of each is 32,768 (or 32,768 plus the VLAN ID, if the extended system ID is enabled). Figure 8-2 shows the converged state of STP. For the purposes of this discussion, the root ports and designated ports are simply shown on the network diagram. As an exercise, you should work through the spanning-tree process yourself, based on the information shown in the figure. The more examples you can work out by hand, the better you will understand the entire spanning-tree process.

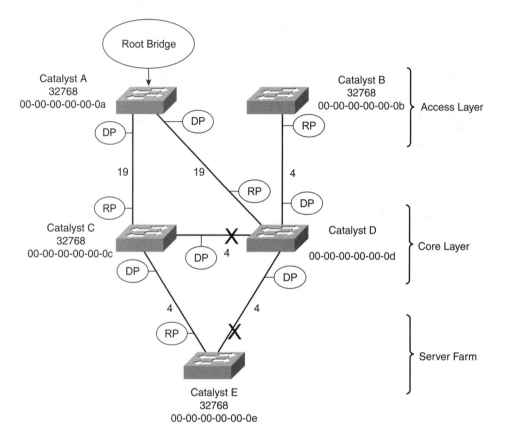

Figure 8-2   *Campus Network with STP Converged*

Notice that Catalyst A, one of the access-layer switches, has been elected the root bridge. Unfortunately, Catalyst A cannot take advantage of the 1-Gbps links, unlike the other switches. Also note the location of the *X* symbols over the ports that are neither root ports nor designated ports. These ports will enter the Blocking state, and no data packets will pass through them.

Finally, Figure 8-3 shows the same network with the blocking links removed. Now you can see the true structure of the final spanning tree.

Catalyst A, an access-layer switch, is the root bridge. Workstations on Catalyst A can reach servers on Catalyst E by crossing through the core layer (Catalyst C), as expected. However, notice what has happened to the other access-layer switch, Catalyst B. Workstations on this switch must cross into the core layer (Catalyst D), back into the access layer (Catalyst A), back through the core (Catalyst C), and finally to the server farm (Catalyst E).

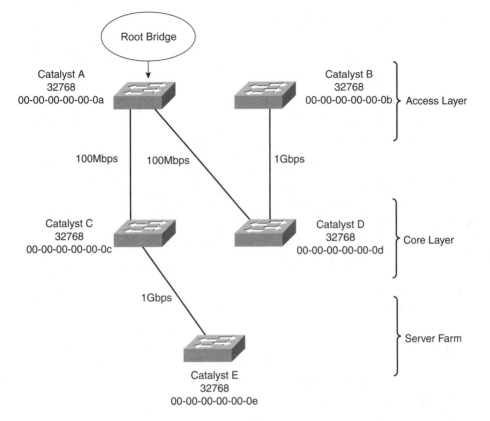

Figure 8-3   *Final Spanning-Tree Structure for the Campus Network*

This action is obviously inefficient. For one thing, Catalyst A is probably not a high-end switch because it is used in the access layer. However, the biggest issue is that other access-layer areas are forced to thread through the relatively slow uplinks on Catalyst A. This winding path will become a major bottleneck to the users.

Root Bridge Configuration

To prevent the surprises outlined in the previous section, you should *always* do two things:

■   Configure one switch as a root bridge in a determined fashion.

■   Configure another switch as a secondary root bridge, in case of a primary root bridge failure.

As the common reference point, the root bridge (and the secondary) should be placed near the center of the Layer 2 network. For example, a switch in the distribution layer would make a better root bridge choice than one in the access layer because more traffic is expected to pass through the distribution-layer devices. In a flat switched network (no Layer 3 devices), a switch near a server farm would be a more efficient root bridge than switches elsewhere. Most traffic will be destined to and from the server farm and will benefit from a predetermined, direct path.

Tip: A Catalyst switch can be configured to use one of the following formats for its STP bridge ID:

■ Traditional 802.1D bridge priority value (16 bits), followed by the unique switch MAC address for the VLAN

■ The 802.1t extended system ID (4-bit priority multiplier, plus a 12-bit VLAN ID), followed by a nonunique switch MAC address for the VLAN

If the switch can't support 1024 unique MAC addresses for its own use, the extended system ID is always enabled by default. Otherwise, the traditional method is enabled by default.

To begin using the extended system ID method, you can use the following global configuration command:

```
Switch(config)# spanning-tree extend system-id
```

Otherwise, you can use the traditional method by beginning the command with the **no** keyword.

You can configure a Catalyst switch to become the root bridge using one of two methods, which are configured as follows:

■ Manually setting the bridge priority value so that a switch is given a lower-than-default bridge ID value to win a root bridge election. You must know the bridge priorities of every other switch in a VLAN so that you can choose a value that is less than all the others. The command to accomplish this is as follows:

```
Switch(config)# spanning-tree vlan vlan-list priority bridge-priority
```

The *bridge-priority* value defaults to 32,768, but you can also assign a value of 0 to 65,535. If STP extended system ID is enabled, the default *bridge-priority* is 32,768 plus the VLAN number. In that case, the value can range from 0 to 61,440, but only as multiples of 4096. A lower bridge priority is preferable.

Remember that Catalyst switches run one instance of STP for each VLAN (PVST+), so the VLAN ID must always be given. You should designate an appropriate root bridge for each VLAN. For example, you could use the following command to set the bridge priority for VLAN 5 and VLANs 100 through 200 to 4096:

```
Switch(config)# spanning-tree vlan 5,100-200 priority 4096
```

■ Causing the would-be root bridge switch to choose its own priority, based on some assumptions about other switches in the network. You can accomplish this with the following command:

```
Switch(config)# spanning-tree vlan vlan-id root {primary | secondary}
  [diameter diameter]
```

This command is actually a macro on the Catalyst that executes several other commands. The result is a more direct and automatic way to force one switch to become the root bridge. Notice that the actual bridge priorities are not given in the command. Instead, the switch modifies its STP values according to the current values in use within the active network. *These values are modified only once, when the macro command is issued.* Use

the **primary** keyword to make the switch attempt to become the primary roo'
This command modifies the switch's bridge priority value to become less th'
priority of the current root bridge. If the current root priority is more thar
cal switch sets its priority to 24,576. If the current root priority is less than tı.
switch sets its priority to 4096 less than the current root.

For the **secondary** root bridge, the root priority is set to an artificially low value of
28,672. There is no way to query or listen to the network to find another potential secondary root simply because there are no advertisements or elections of secondary root
bridges. Instead, the fixed secondary priority is used under the assumption that it will be
less than the default priorities (32,768) that might be used on switches elsewhere. You can
also modify the network diameter by adding the **diameter** keyword to this command. This
modification is discussed further in the "Tuning Spanning-Tree Convergence" section,
later in the chapter.

As a final example, consider a switch that is currently using its default bridge priority for
VLAN 100. In the extended system-id mode, the default priority is 32,768 plus 100 (the
VLAN number). The output in Example 8-1 demonstrates this under the bridge ID information. The default priority is greater than the current root bridge priority of 4200, so the
local switch cannot become the root.

Example 8-1 *Displaying the STP Bridge Priority Values*

```
Switch# show spanning-tree vlan 100
VLAN0100
  Spanning tree enabled protocol ieee
  Root  ID  Priority  4200

            Address     000b.5f65.1f80
            Cost        4
            Port        1 (GigabitEthernet0/1)
            Hello Time   2 sec  Max Age 20 sec  Forward Delay 15 sec


  Bridge  ID  Priority  32868  (priority  32768  sys-id-ext  100)

            Address     000c.8554.9a80
            Hello Time   2 sec  Max Age 20 sec  Forward Delay 15 sec
            Aging Time 300
[output omitted]
```

Now, the automatic method is used to attempt to make the switch become root for VLAN
100, using the command demonstrated in Example 8-2.

Example 8-2 *Using a Macro Command to Configure a Root Bridge*

```
Switch(config)# spanning-tree vlan 100 root primary
% Failed to make the bridge root for vlan 100
% It may be possible to make the bridge root by setting the priority
% for some (or all) of these instances to zero.
Switch(config)#
```

Why did this method fail? The current root bridge has a bridge priority of 4200. Because that priority is less than 24,576, the local switch will try to set its priority to 4096 less than the current root. Although the resulting priority would be 104, the local switch is using an extended system ID, which requires bridge priority values that are multiples of 4096. The only value that would work is 0, but the automatic method will not use it. Instead, the only other option is to manually configure the bridge priority to 0 with the following command:

```
Switch(config)# spanning-tree vlan 100 priority 0
```

Remember that on switches that use an extended system ID, the bridge priority is the configured priority (multiple of 4096) plus the VLAN number. Even though the priority was set to 0 with the previous command, the switch is actually using a value of 100—priority 0 plus VLAN number 100, as the output in Example 8-3 reveals.

Example 8-3 *Displaying Bridge Priorities with Extended System IDs*

```
Switch# show spanning-tree vlan 100
VLAN0100
  Spanning tree enabled protocol ieee
  Root  ID  Priority  100

            Address      000c.8554.9a80
            This bridge is the root

            Hello Time    2 sec  Max Age 20 sec  Forward Delay 15 sec


  Bridge  ID  Priority  100  (priority  0  sys-id-ext  100)

            Address      000c.8554.9a80
            Hello Time    2 sec  Max Age 20 sec  Forward Delay 15 sec
            Aging Time 300
[output omitted]
```

Note: The **spanning-tree vlan** *vlan-id* **root** command will not be shown in a Catalyst switch configuration because the command is actually a macro executing other switch commands. The actual commands and values produced by the macro will be shown, however. For example, the macro can potentially adjust the four STP values as follows:

```
Switch(config)# spanning-tree vlan 1 root primary
vlan 1 bridge priority set to 24576
vlan 1 bridge max aging time unchanged at 20
vlan 1 bridge hello time unchanged at 2
vlan 1 bridge forward delay unchanged at 15
```

Be aware that this macro doesn't guarantee that the switch will become the root and maintain that status. After the macro is used, it is entirely possible for another switch in the network to have its bridge priority configured to a lower value. The other switch would become the new root, displacing the switch that ran the macro.

On the root, it is usually good practice to directly modify the bridge priority to an artificially low value (even priority 1 or 0) with the **spanning-tree vlan** *vlan-id* **priority** *bridge-priority* command. This makes it more difficult for another switch in the network to win the root bridge election, unless it is manually configured with a priority that is even lower.

Spanning-Tree Customization

The most important decision you can make when designing your spanning-tree topology is the placement of the root bridge. Other decisions, such as the exact loop-free path structure, will occur automatically as a result of the spanning-tree algorithm (STA). Occasionally, the path might need additional tuning, but only under special circumstances and after careful consideration.

Recall the sequence of four criteria that STP uses to choose a path:

1. Lowest bridge ID

2. Lowest root path cost

3. Lowest sender bridge ID

4. Lowest sender port ID

The previous section discussed how to tune a switch's bridge ID to force it to become the root bridge in a network. You can also change the bridge priority on a switch to influence the value it uses in the sender bridge ID that it announced as it relays BPDUs to other neighboring switches.

Only the automatic STP computation has been discussed, using the default switch port costs to make specific path decisions. The following sections discuss ways you can influence the exact topology that results.

Tuning the Root Path Cost

The root path cost for each active port of a switch is determined by the cumulative cost as a BPDU travels along. As a switch *receives* a BPDU, the port cost of the receiving port is added to the root path cost in the BPDU. The port or port path cost is inversely proportional to the port's bandwidth. If desired, a port's cost can be modified from the default value.

Note: Before modifying a switch port's path cost, you should always calculate the root path costs of other alternative paths through the network. Changing one port's cost might influence STP to choose that port as a root port, but other paths still could be preferred. You also should calculate a port's existing path cost to determine what the new cost value should be. Careful calculation will ensure that the desired path indeed will be chosen.

Key Topic

Use the following interface configuration command to set a switch port's path cost:

```
Switch (config-if)# spanning-tree [vlan vlan-id] cost cost
```

If the **vlan** parameter is given, the port cost is modified only for the specified VLAN. Otherwise, the cost is modified for the port as a whole (all active VLANs). The *cost* value can range from 1 to 65,535. There are standard or default values that correspond to port bandwidth, as shown in Table 8-2.

Table 8-2   *STP Port Cost*

Link Bandwidth	STP Cost
4 Mbps	250
10 Mbps	100
16 Mbps	62
45 Mbps	39
100 Mbps	19
155 Mbps	14
622 Mbps	6
1 Gbps	4
10 Gbps	2

For example, a Gigabit Ethernet interface has a default port cost of 4. You can use the following command to change the cost to 2, but only for VLAN 10:

```
Switch(config-if)# spanning-tree vlan 10 cost 2
```

You can see the port cost of an interface by using the following command:

```
Switch# show spanning-tree interface type mod/num [cost]
```

As an example, Gigabit Ethernet 0/1 is configured as a trunk port, carrying VLANs 1, 10, and 20. Example 8-4 shows the port cost for each of the VLANs.

Example 8-4   *Displaying STP Port Cost Values on an Interface*

```
Switch# show spanning-tree interface gigabitEthernet 0/1
Vlan            Role Sts Cost       Prio.Nbr Type
--------------- ---- --- ---------- -------- --------------------------------
VLAN0001        Root FWD 4          128.1    P2p
VLAN0010        Desg FWD 2          128.1    P2p
VLAN0020        Root FWD 4          128.1    P2p
```

Tuning the Port ID

The fourth criteria of an STP decision is the port ID. The port ID value that a switch uses is actually a 16-bit quantity: 8 bits for the port priority and 8 bits for the port number. The port priority is a value from 0 to 255 and defaults to 128 for all ports. The port number can range from 0 to 255 and represents the port's actual physical mapping. Port numbers begin with 1 at port 0/1 and increment across each module. (The numbers might not be consecutive because each module is assigned a particular range of numbers.)

Tip: Port numbers are usually intuitive on a fixed configuration switch, such as a 48-port Catalyst 3560. The STP port number is simply the interface number, from 1 to 48.

However, it is not easy to find the STP port number in a switch with many modules and many ports. Notice how Gigabit Ethernet 3/16 is also known as port number 144 in the following example:

```
Switch# show spanning-tree interface gigabitEthernet 3/16
Vlan              Role Sts Cost       Prio.Nbr Type
----------------  ---- --- ---------  -------- ------------------------------
VLAN0010          Desg FWD 4          128.144  Edge P2p
VLAN0100          Desg FWD 4          128.144  Edge P2p
VLAN0200          Desg FWD 4          128.144  Edge P2p
Switch#
```

The entire port ID consists of the port priority followed by the port number. In the preceding example output, the port ID is 128.144. As a 16-bit quantity in hex, it is 8090. In addition, ports that are bundled into an EtherChannel or Port-channel interface always have a higher port ID than they would if they were not bundled.

Obviously, a switch port's port number is fixed because it is based only on its hardware location or index. The port ID, however, can be modified to influence an STP decision by using the port priority. You can configure the port priority with this interface-configuration command:

```
Switch(config-if)# spanning-tree [vlan vlan-list] port-priority port-priority
```

You can modify the port priority for one or more VLANs by using the **vlan** parameter. The VLAN numbers are given as *vlan-list*, a list of single values or ranges of values separated by commas. Otherwise, the port priority is set for the port as a whole (all active VLANs). The value of *port-priority* can range from 0 to 255 and defaults to 128. A lower port priority value indicates a more preferred path toward the root bridge.

As an example, you can use the following command sequence to change the port priority of Gigabit Ethernet 3/16 from 128 (the default) to 64 for VLANs 10 and 100:

```
Switch(config)# interface gigabitethernet 3/16
Switch(config-if)# spanning-tree vlan 10,100 port-priority 64
```

You can confirm the changes with the **show spanning-tree interface** command, as demonstrated in Example 8-5.

Example 8-5 *Confirming STP Port Priority Values After Configuration*

```
Switch# show spanning-tree interface gigabitEthernet 3/16
Vlan            Role Sts Cost      Prio.Nbr Type
---------------- ---- --- --------- -------- --------------------------
VLAN0010         Desg FWD 4         64.144   Edge P2p
VLAN0100         Desg FWD 4         64.144   Edge P2p
VLAN0200         Desg FWD 4         128.144  Edge P2p
Switch#
```

Tuning Spanning-Tree Convergence

STP uses several timers, a sequence of states that ports must move through, and specific topology change conditions to prevent bridging loops from forming in a complex network. Each of these parameters or requirements is based on certain default values for a typical network size and function. For the majority of cases, the default STP operation is sufficient to keep the network loop free and enable users to communicate.

However, in certain situations, the default STP can cause network access to be delayed while timers expire and while preventing loops on links where loops are not possible. For example, when a single PC is connected to a switch port, a bridging loop is simply not possible. Another situation relates to the size of a Layer 2 switched network: The default STP timers are based on a benchmark network size.

In a network that is smaller, waiting until the default timer values expire might not make sense when they could be safely set to shorter values. In situations like this, you can safely make adjustments to the STP convergence process for more efficiency.

Modifying STP Timers

Key Topic

Recall that STP uses three timers to keep track of various port operation states and communication between bridges. The three STP timers can be adjusted by using the commands documented in the sections that follow. Remember that the timers need to be modified only on the root bridge because the root bridge propagates all three timer values throughout the network as fields in the configuration BPDU.

Manually Configuring STP Timers

Use one or more of the following global configuration commands to modify STP timers:

```
Switch(config)# spanning-tree [vlan vlan-id] hello-time seconds
Switch(config)# spanning-tree [vlan vlan-id] forward-time seconds
Switch(config)# spanning-tree [vlan vlan-id] max-age seconds
```

Notice that the timers can be changed for a single instance (VLAN) of STP on the switch by using the **vlan** *vlan-id* parameters. If you omit the **vlan** keyword, the timer values are configured for *all* instances (all VLANs) of STP on the switch.

The *Hello timer* triggers periodic "hello" (actually, the configuration BPDU) messages that are sent from the root to other bridges in the network. This timer also sets the interval in which a bridge expects to hear a hello relayed from its neighboring bridges. Configuration

BPDUs are sent every 2 seconds, by default. You can modify the Hello timer with the **hello-time** keyword, along with a value of 1 to 10 seconds, as in the following command:

```
Switch(config)# spanning-tree hello-time 1
```

The *Forward Delay timer* determines the amount of time a port stays in the Listening state before moving into the Learning state, and how long it stays in the Learning state before moving to the Forwarding state. You can modify the Forward Delay timer with the **forward-time** keyword. The default value is 15 seconds, but this can be set to a value of 4 to 30 seconds. This timer should be modified only under careful consideration because the value depends on the diameter of the network and the propagation of BPDUs across all switches. A value that is too low allows loops to form, possibly crippling a network.

The Max Age timer specifies a stored BPDU's lifetime that has been received from a neighboring switch with a designated port. Suppose that BPDUs are being received on a nondesignated switch port every 2 seconds, as expected. Then an indirect failure, or one that doesn't involve a physical link going down, occurs that prevents BPDUs from being sent. The receiving switch waits until the Max Age timer expires to listen for further BPDUs. If none is received, the nondesignated port moves into the Listening state, and the receiving switch generates configuration BPDUs. This port then becomes the designated port to restore connectivity on the segment.

To modify the Max Age timer, use the **max-age** keyword. The timer value defaults to 20 seconds but can be set from 6 to 40 seconds.

Automatically Configuring STP Timers

Modifying STP timers can be tricky, given the conservative nature of the default values and the calculations needed to derive proper STP operation. Timer values are basically dependent on the Hello Time and the switched network's diameter, in terms of switch hops. Catalyst switches offer a single command that can change the timer values in a more controlled fashion. As described earlier, the **spanning-tree vlan** *vlan-list* **root** macro command is a better tool to use than setting the timers with the individual commands. This global configuration command has the following syntax:

```
Switch(config)# spanning-tree vlan vlan-list root {primary | secondary} [diameter
   diameter [hello-time hello-time]]
```

Here, STP timers will be adjusted according to the formulas specified in the 802.1D standard by giving only the network's diameter (the maximum number of switches that traffic will traverse across a Layer 2 network) and an optional *hello-time*. If you do not specify a Hello Time, the default value of 2 seconds is assumed.

This command can be used only on a per-VLAN basis to modify the timers for a particular VLAN's spanning tree instance. The network diameter can be a value from one to seven switch hops. Because this command makes a switch become the root bridge, all the modified timer values resulting from this command will be propagated to other switches through the configuration BPDU.

As an example, suppose that a small network consists of three switches connected in a triangle fashion. The command output in Example 8-6 shows the current (default) STP timer values that are in use for VLAN 100.

Example 8-6 *Displaying the STP Timer Values in Use*

```
Switch# show spanning-tree vlan 100
VLAN0100
  Spanning tree enabled protocol ieee
  Root ID    Priority    100
             Address     000c.8554.9a80
             This bridge is the root
             Hello Time  2  sec  Max Age  20  sec  Forward  Delay 15  sec


  Bridge ID  Priority    100    (priority 0 sys-id-ext 100)
             Address     000c.8554.9a80
             Hello Time   2 sec  Max Age 20 sec  Forward Delay 15 sec
             Aging Time 300
[output omitted]
```

The longest path that a packet can take through the sample network is three switches. This is considerably less than the reference diameter of seven that is used to calculate the default timer values. Therefore, you can safely assume that this network diameter is three, provided that no additional switches will be added to lengthen the longest path. Suppose that a Hello Time of 1 second is also desired, to shorten the time needed to detect a dead neighbor. The following command attempts to make the local switch become the root bridge and automatically adjusts the STP timers:

```
Switch(config)# spanning-tree vlan 100 root primary diameter 3 hello-time 1
```

You can confirm the new timer values with the **show spanning-tree vlan** *vlan-id* command, as demonstrated in Example 8-7.

Example 8-7 *Confirming STP Timer Configuration Changes*

```
Switch# show spanning-tree vlan 100
VLAN0100
  Spanning tree enabled protocol ieee
  Root ID    Priority    100
             Address     000c.8554.9a80
             This bridge is the root
             Hello Time  1  sec  Max Age  7  sec  Forward  Delay  5  sec

  Bridge ID  Priority    100    (priority 0 sys-id-ext 100)
             Address     000c.8554.9a80
             Hello Time   1 sec  Max Age  7 sec  Forward Delay  5 sec
             Aging Time 300
```

Redundant Link Convergence

Some additional methods allow faster STP convergence if a link failure occurs:

- **PortFast**—Enables fast connectivity to be established on access-layer switch ports to workstations that are booting

- **UplinkFast**—Enables fast-uplink failover on an access-layer switch when dual up-links are connected into the distribution layer

- **BackboneFast**—Enables fast convergence in the network backbone or core layer switches after a spanning-tree topology change occurs

Instead of modifying timer values, these methods work by controlling convergence on specifically located ports within the network hierarchy.

> **Tip:** The STP has been enhanced to allow almost instantaneous topology changes instead of having to rely on these Cisco-proprietary extensions. This enhancement is known as the Rapid Spanning Tree Protocol, or IEEE 802.1w, and is covered in Chapter 10, "Advanced Spanning Tree Protocol." You should become familiar with the topics in this chapter first because they provide the basis for the concepts in Chapter 10.

PortFast: Access-Layer Nodes

An end-user workstation is usually connected to a switch port in the access layer. If the workstation is powered off and then turned on, the switch will sense that the port link status has gone down and back up. The port will not be in a usable state until STP cycles from the Blocking state to the Forwarding state. With the default STP timers, this transition takes at least 30 seconds (15 seconds for Listening to Learning, and 15 seconds for Learning to Forwarding). Therefore, the workstation cannot transmit or receive any useful data until the Forwarding state finally is reached on the port.

> **Tip:** Port initialization delays of up to 50 seconds can be observed. As discussed, 30 of these seconds are due to the STP state transitions. If a switch port is running Port Aggregation Protocol (PAgP) to negotiate EtherChannel configuration, an additional 20-second delay can occur.

On switch ports that connect only to single workstations or specific devices, bridging loops never should be possible. The potential for a loop exists only if the workstation had additional connections back into the network and if it were bridging traffic itself. For ex-ample, this can happen on PCs that are running Windows XP when network bridging has been enabled. In most situations, this is not very likely to happen.

Catalyst switches offer the PortFast feature, which shortens the Listening and Learning states to a negligible amount of time. When a workstation link comes up, the switch im-mediately moves the PortFast port into the Forwarding state. Spanning-tree loop detection is still in operation, however, and the port moves into the Blocking state if a loop is ever detected on the port.

By default, PortFast is disabled on all switch ports. You can configure PortFast as a global default, affecting all switch ports with a single command. All ports that are configured for access mode (nontrunking) will have PortFast automatically enabled. You can use the following global configuration command to enable PortFast as the default:

```
Switch(config)# spanning-tree portfast default
```

You can also enable or disable the PortFast feature on specific switch ports by using the following interface configuration command:

```
Switch(config-if)# [no] spanning-tree portfast
```

Obviously, you should not enable PortFast on a switch port that is connected to a hub or another switch because bridging loops could form. One other benefit of PortFast is that Topology Change Notification (TCN) BPDUs are not sent when a switch port in PortFast mode goes up or down. This simplifies the TCN transmission on a large network when end-user workstations are coming up or shutting down.

Tip: You can also use a macro configuration command to force a switch port to support a single host. The following command enables STP PortFast, sets the port to access (nontrunking) mode, and disables PAgP to prevent the port from participating in an EtherChannel:

```
Switch(config)# interface type mod/num
Switch(config-if)# switchport host
switchport mode will be set to access
spanning-tree portfast will be enabled
channel group will be disabled
```

You can display the current PortFast status with the following command:

```
Switch# show spanning-tree interface type mod/num portfast
```

For example, the following output shows that port Fast Ethernet 0/1 supports only access VLAN 10 and has PortFast enabled:

```
Switch# show spanning-tree interface fastethernet 0/1 portfast
VLAN0010          enabled
Switch#
```

UplinkFast: Access-Layer Uplinks

Consider an access-layer switch that has redundant uplink connections to two distribution-layer switches. Normally, one uplink would be in the Forwarding state and the other would be in the Blocking state. If the primary uplink went down, up to 50 seconds could elapse before the redundant uplink could be used.

The UplinkFast feature on Catalyst switches enables leaf-node switches or switches at the ends of the spanning-tree branches to have a functioning root port while keeping *one or more* redundant or potential root ports in Blocking mode. When the primary root port uplink fails, another blocked uplink immediately can be brought up for use.

Tip: Many Catalyst switches have two built-in, high-speed uplink ports (Gigabit Ethernet, for example). You might get the idea that UplinkFast can only toggle between two leaf-node uplink ports. This is entirely untrue. UplinkFast keeps a record of *all* parallel paths to the root bridge. All uplink ports but one are kept in the Blocking state. If the root port fails, the uplink with the next-lowest root path cost is unblocked and used without delay.

To enable the UplinkFast feature, use the following global configuration command:

```
Switch(config)# spanning-tree uplinkfast [max-update-rate pkts-per-second]
```

When UplinkFast is enabled, it is enabled for the entire switch and all VLANs. UplinkFast works by keeping track of possible paths to the root bridge. Therefore, the command *is not allowed on the root bridge switch*. UplinkFast also makes some modifications to the local switch to ensure that it does not become the root bridge and that the switch is not used as a transit switch to get to the root bridge. In other words, the goal is to keep Up-linkFast limited to leaf-node switches that are farthest from the root.

First, the switch's bridge priority is raised to 49,152, making it unlikely that the switch will be elected to root bridge status. The port cost of all local switch ports is incremented by 3000, making the ports undesirable as paths to the root for any downstream switches.

The command also includes a **max-update-rate** parameter. When an uplink on a switch goes down, UplinkFast makes it easy for the local switch to update its bridging table of MAC addresses to point to the new uplink. However, UplinkFast also provides a mechanism for the local switch to notify other upstream switches that stations downstream (or within the access layer) can be reached over the newly activated uplink.

The switch accomplishes this by sending dummy multicast frames to destination 0100.0ccd.cdcd on behalf of the stations contained in its Content-Addressable Memory (CAM) table. The MAC addresses are used as the source addresses in the dummy frames, as if the stations actually had sent them. The idea is to quickly send the multicast frames over the new uplink, giving upstream hosts a chance to receive the frames and learn of the new path to those source addresses.

These multicast frames are sent out at a rate specified by the **max-update-rate** parameter in packets per second. This limits the amount of bandwidth used for the dummy multi-casts if the CAM table is quite large. The default is 150 packets per second (pps), but the rate can range from 0 to 65,535 pps. If the value is 0, no dummy multicasts are sent.

Tip: You can use the following command to display the current status of STP UplinkFast:

```
Switch# show spanning-tree uplinkfast
UplinkFast is enabled
Station update rate set to 150 packets/sec.
UplinkFast statistics
Number of transitions via uplinkFast (all VLANs)           : 2
Number of proxy multicast addresses transmitted (all VLANs)  : 52
```

```
Name                      Interface List
--------------------      ------------------------------
VLAN0001                  Gi0/1(fwd)
VLAN0010                  Gi0/1(fwd)
VLAN0100                  Gi0/1(fwd)
Switch#
```

BackboneFast: Redundant Backbone Paths

In the network backbone, or core layer, a different method is used to shorten STP convergence. BackboneFast works by having a switch actively determine whether alternative paths exist to the root bridge, in case the switch detects an *indirect link failure*. Indirect link failures occur when a link that is not directly connected to a switch fails.

A switch detects an indirect link failure when it receives inferior BPDUs from its designated bridge on either its root port or a blocked port. (Inferior BPDUs are sent from a designated bridge that has lost its connection to the root bridge, making it announce itself as the new root.)

Normally, a switch must wait for the Max Age timer to expire before responding to the inferior BPDUs. However, BackboneFast begins to determine whether other alternative paths to the root bridge exist according to the following port types that received the inferior BPDU:

- If the inferior BPDU arrives on a port in the Blocking state, the switch considers the root port and all other blocked ports to be alternative paths to the root bridge.

- If the inferior BPDU arrives on the root port itself, the switch considers all blocked ports to be alternative paths to the root bridge.

- If the inferior BPDU arrives on the root port and no ports are blocked, however, the switch assumes that it has lost connectivity with the root bridge. In this case, the switch assumes that it has become the root bridge, and BackboneFast allows it to do so before the Max Age timer expires.

Detecting alternative paths to the root bridge also involves an interactive process with other bridges. If the local switch has blocked ports, BackboneFast begins to use the *Root Link Query (RLQ)* protocol to see whether upstream switches have stable connections to the root bridge.

First, RLQ Requests are sent out. If a switch receives an RLQ Request and either is the root bridge or has lost connection to the root, it sends an RLQ Reply. Otherwise, the RLQ Request is propagated on to other switches until an RLQ Reply can be generated. On the local switch, if an RLQ Reply is received on its current root port, the path to the root bridge is intact and stable. If it is received on a nonroot port, an alternative root path must be chosen. The Max Age timer immediately is expired so that a new root port can be found.

Key Topic

BackboneFast is simple to configure and operates by short-circuiting the Max Age timer when needed. Although this function shortens the time a switch waits to detect a root path failure, ports still must go through full-length Forward Delay timer intervals during the Listening and Learning states. Where PortFast and UplinkFast enable immediate transitions, BackboneFast can reduce the maximum convergence delay only from 50 to 30 seconds.

To configure BackboneFast, use the following global configuration command:

```
Switch(config)# spanning-tree backbonefast
```

When used, BackboneFast should be enabled on *all* switches in the network because BackboneFast requires the use of the RLQ Request and Reply mechanism to inform switches of Root Path stability. The RLQ protocol is active only when BackboneFast is enabled on a switch. By default, BackboneFast is disabled.

Tip: You can verify the current BackboneFast state with the following command:

```
Switch# show spanning-tree backbonefast
BackboneFast is enabled
Switch#
```

Monitoring STP

Because the STP running in a network uses several timers, costs, and dynamic calculations, predicting the current state is difficult. You can use a network diagram and work out the STP topology by hand, but any change on the network could produce an entirely different outcome. Then, figure in something like PVST+, in which you have one instance of STP running for each VLAN present. Obviously, simply viewing the STP status on the active network devices would be better.

You can display information about many aspects of the STP from a Catalyst switch command-line interface (CLI). Specifically, you need to find out the current root bridge and its location in the network. You also might want to see the bridge ID of the switch where you are connected, to see how it participates in STP. Use the information in Table 8-3 to determine what command is useful for what situation.

Table 8-3 *Commands for Displaying Spanning-Tree Information*

Task	Command Syntax
View all possible STP parameters for all VLANs. Port information is summarized.	Switch# **show spanning-tree**
View all possible STP information for all VLANs. Port information is very detailed.	Switch# **show spanning-tree detail**
View the total number of switch ports currently in each of the STP states.	Switch# **show spanning-tree [vlan** *vlan-id]* **summary**
Find the root bridge ID, the root port, and the root path cost.	Switch# **show spanning-tree [vlan** *vlan-id]* **root**
Show the bridge ID and STP timers for the local switch.	Switch# **show spanning-tree [vlan** *vlan-id]* **bridge**

continues

Table 8-3 *Commands for Displaying Spanning-Tree Information* *(Continued)*

Task	Command Syntax
Show the STP activity on a specific interface.	Switch# **show spanning-tree interface** *type port*
Show the STP UplinkFast status.	Switch# **show spanning-tree uplinkfast**
Show the STP BackboneFast status.	Switch# **show spanning-tree backbonefast**

Exam Preparation Tasks

Review All Key Topics

Review the most important topics in the chapter, noted with the Key Topic icon in the outer margin of the page. Table 8-4 lists a reference of these key topics and the page numbers on which each is found.

Key
Topic

Table 8-4   *Key Topics for Chapter 8*

Key Topic Element	Description	Page Number
Paragraph	Explains the pitfalls of a default root bridge election	156
Paragraph	Covers best practice for root bridge placement	159
Bullet	Discusses manual root bridge configuration	160
Bullet	Discusses automatic root bridge configuration	160
Paragraph	Explains how to configure the root path cost on an interface	164
Paragraph	Explains how STP timers can be adjusted on the root bridge	166
Paragraph	Explains the PortFast feature	169
Paragraph	Explains the UplinkFast feature	170
Paragraph	Explains the BackboneFast feature	172

Complete Tables and Lists from Memory

Print a copy of Appendix C, "Memory Tables," (found on the CD), or at least the section for this chapter, and complete the tables and lists from memory. Appendix D, "Memory Tables Answer Key," also on the CD, includes completed tables and lists to check your work.

Define Key Terms

Define the following key terms from this chapter, and check your answers in the glossary:

PortFast, UplinkFast, BackboneFast

Use Command Reference to Check Your Memory

This section includes the most important configuration and EXEC commands covered in this chapter. It might not be necessary to memorize the complete syntax of every command, but you should remember the basic keywords that are needed.

To test your memory of the STP configuration commands, cover the right side of Table 8-5 with a piece of paper, read the description on the left side, and then see how much of the command you can remember.

Remember that the CCNP exam focuses on practical or hands-on skills that are used by a networking professional. For the skills covered in this chapter, notice that the commands always begin with the keyword **spanning-tree**.

Table 8-5   *STP Configuration Commands*

Task	Command Syntax
Enable STP.	Switch(config)# **spanning-tree** *vlan-id*
Set bridge priority.	Switch(config)# **spanning-tree vlan** *vlan-id* **priority** *bridge-priority*
Set root bridge (macro).	Switch(config)# **spanning-tree vlan** *vlan-id* **root** {**primary** | **secondary**} [**diameter** *diameter*]
Set port cost.	Switch(config-if)# **spanning-tree** [**vlan** *vlan-id*] **cost** *cost*
Set port priority.	Switch(config-if)# **spanning-tree** [**vlan** *vlan-id*] **port-priority** *port-priority*
Set STP timers.	Switch(config)# **spanning-tree** [**vlan** *vlan-id*] **hello-time** *seconds*
	Switch(config)# **spanning-tree** [**vlan** *vlan-id*] **forward-time** *seconds*
	Switch(config)# **spanning-tree** [**vlan** *vlan-id*] **max-age** *seconds*
Set PortFast on an interface.	Switch(config-if)# **spanning-tree portfast**
Set UplinkFast on a switch.	Switch(config)# **spanning-tree uplinkfast** [**max-update-rate** *pkts-per-second*]
Set BackboneFast on a switch.	Switch(config)# **spanning-tree backbonefast**

This chapter covers the following topics that you need to master for the CCNP SWITCH exam:

Protecting Against Unexpected BPDUs—This section covers the Root Guard and BPDU Guard features, which protect against unexpected root candidates and unexpected BPDUs, respectively.

Protecting Against Sudden Loss of BPDUs—This section discusses the Loop Guard and UDLD features, which detect and protect against the loss of root bridge BPDUs and conditions causing unidirectional links, respectively.

Using BPDU Filtering to Disable STP on a Port—This section explains how to filter BPDUs on a switch port to prevent the port from participating in STP altogether. Bridging loops are neither detected nor prevented.

Troubleshooting STP Protection—This section summarizes the commands that diagnose or verify actions to protect the topology.

CHAPTER 9

Protecting the Spanning Tree Protocol Topology

Achieving and maintaining a loop-free Spanning Tree Protocol (STP) topology revolves around the simple process of sending and receiving bridge protocol data units (BPDU). Under normal conditions, with all switches playing fairly and according to the rules, a loop-free topology is determined dynamically.

This chapter discusses two basic conditions that can occur to disrupt the loop-free topology (even while STP is running):

On a port that has not been receiving BPDUs, BPDUs are not expected. When BPDUs suddenly appear for some reason, the STP topology can reconverge to give unexpected results.

On a port that normally receives BPDUs, BPDUs always are expected. When BPDUs suddenly disappear for some reason, a switch can make incorrect assumptions about the topology and unintentionally create loops.

"Do I Know This Already?" Quiz

The "Do I Know This Already?" quiz allows you to assess whether you should read this entire chapter thoroughly or jump to the "Exam Preparation Tasks" section. If you are in doubt based on your answers to these questions or your own assessment of your knowledge of the topics, read the entire chapter. Table 9-1 outlines the major headings in this chapter and the "Do I Know This Already?" quiz questions that go with them. You can find the answers in Appendix A, "Answers to the 'Do I Know This Already?' Quizzes."

Table 9-1 *"Do I Know This Already?" Foundation Topics Section-to-Question Mapping*

Foundation Topics Section	Questions Covered in This Section
Protecting Against Unexpected BPDUs	1–5
Protecting Against Sudden Loss of BPDUs	6–11
Using BPDU Filtering to Disable STP on a Port	12
Troubleshooting STP Protection	13

1. Why is it important to protect the placement of the root bridge?

    a. To keep two root bridges from becoming active

    b. To keep the STP topology stable

    c.   So all hosts have the correct gateway

    d.   So the root bridge can have complete knowledge of the STP topology

2. Which of the following features protects a switch port from accepting superior BPDUs?

    a.   STP Loop Guard

    b.   STP BPDU Guard

    c.   STP Root Guard

    d.   UDLD

3. Which of the following commands can you use to enable STP Root Guard on a switch port?

    a.   **spanning-tree root guard**

    b.   **spanning-tree root-guard**

    c.   **spanning-tree guard root**

    d.   **spanning-tree rootguard enable**

4. Where should the STP Root Guard feature be enabled on a switch?

    a.   All ports

    b.   Only ports where the root bridge should never appear

    c.   Only ports where the root bridge should be located

    d.   Only ports with PortFast enabled

5. Which of the following features protects a switch port from accepting BPDUs when PortFast is enabled?

    a.   STP Loop Guard

    b.   STP BPDU Guard

    c.   STP Root Guard

    d.   UDLD

6. To maintain a loop-free STP topology, which one of the following should a switch uplink be protected against?

    a.   A sudden loss of BPDUs

    b.   Too many BPDUs

    c.   The wrong version of BPDUs

    d.   BPDUs relayed from the root bridge

7. Which of the following commands can enable STP Loop Guard on a switch port?

    a.   **spanning-tree loop guard**

    b.   **spanning-tree guard loop**

    c.   **spanning-tree loop-guard**

    d.   **spanning-tree loopguard enable**

8. STP Loop Guard detects which of the following conditions?

    a. The sudden appearance of superior BPDUs

    b. The sudden lack of BPDUs

    c. The appearance of duplicate BPDUs

    d. The appearance of two root bridges

9. Which of the following features can actively test for the loss of the receive side of a link between switches?

    a. POST

    b. BPDU

    c. UDLD

    d. STP

10. UDLD must detect a unidirectional link before which of the following?

    a. The Max Age timer expires.

    b. STP moves the link to the Blocking state.

    c. STP moves the link to the Forwarding state.

    d. STP moves the link to the Listening state.

11. What must a switch do when it receives a UDLD message on a link?

    a. Relay the message on to other switches

    b. Send a UDLD acknowledgment

    c. Echo the message back across the link

    d. Drop the message

12. Which of the following features effectively disables spanning-tree operation on a switch port?

    a. STP PortFast

    b. STP BPDU filtering

    c. STP BPDU Guard

    d. STP Root Guard

13. To reset switch ports that have been put into the errdisable mode by UDLD, which one of the following commands should be used?

    a. clear errdisable udld

    b. udld reset

    c. no udld

    d. show udld errdisable

Foundation Topics

Protecting Against Unexpected BPDUs

A network running STP uses BPDUs to communicate between switches (bridges). Switches become aware of each other and of the topology that interconnects them. After a root bridge is elected, BPDUs are generated by the root and are relayed down through the spanning-tree topology. Eventually, all switches in the STP domain receive the root's BPDUs so that the network converges and a stable loop-free topology forms.

To maintain an efficient topology, the placement of the root bridge must be predictable. Hopefully, you configured one switch to become the root bridge and a second one to be the secondary root. What happens when a "foreign" or rogue switch is connected to the network, and that switch suddenly is capable of becoming the root bridge? Cisco added two STP features that help prevent the unexpected: Root Guard and BPDU Guard.

Root Guard

After an STP topology has converged and becomes loop free, switch ports are assigned the following roles:

- **Root port**—The one port on a switch that is closest (with the lowest root path cost) to the root bridge.

- **Designated port**—The port on a LAN segment that is closest to the root. This port relays, or transmits, BPDUs down the tree.

- **Blocking port**—Ports that are neither root nor designated ports.

- **Alternate port**—Ports that are candidate root ports (they are also close to the root bridge) but are in the Blocking state. These ports are identified for quick use by the STP UplinkFast feature.

- **Forwarding port**—Ports where no other STP activity is detected or expected. These are ports with normal end-user connections.

The root bridge always is expected to be seen on the root port and the alternative ports because these are "closest" (have the best-cost path) to it.

Suppose that another switch is introduced into the network with a bridge priority that is more desirable (lower) than that of the current root bridge. The new switch then would become the root bridge, and the STP topology might reconverge to a new shape. This is entirely permissible by the STP because the switch with the lowest bridge ID always wins the root election.

However, this is not always desirable for you, the network administrator, because the new STP topology might be something totally unacceptable. In addition, while the topology is reconverging, your production network might become unavailable.

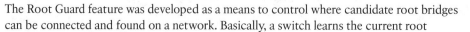

The Root Guard feature was developed as a means to control where candidate root bridges can be connected and found on a network. Basically, a switch learns the current root

bridge's bridge ID. If another switch advertises a *superior BPDU*, or on
bridge ID, on a port where Root Guard is enabled, the local switch will
switch to become the root. As long as the superior BPDUs are being re
the port will be kept in the *root-inconsistent* STP state. No data can '
that state, but the switch can listen to BPDUs received on the port to
vertising itself.

In essence, Root Guard designates that a port can only forward or relay BPDUs; ᴛ…
can't be used to receive BPDUs. Root Guard prevents the port from ever becoming a root
port where BPDUs normally would be received from the root bridge.

You can enable Root Guard only on a per-port basis. By default, it is disabled on all switch
ports. To enable it, use the following interface configuration command:

```
Switch(config-if)# spanning-tree guard root
```

When the superior BPDUs no longer are received, the port is cycled through the normal
STP states to return to normal use.

Use Root Guard on switch ports where you never expect to find the root bridge for a
VLAN. In fact, Root Guard affects the entire port so that a root bridge never can be allowed on *any* VLAN on the port. When a superior BPDU is heard on the port, the entire
port, in effect, becomes blocked.

Tip: You can display switch ports that Root Guard has put into the root-inconsistent state
with the following command:

```
Switch# show spanning-tree inconsistentports
```

BPDU Guard

Recall that the traditional STP offers the PortFast feature, in which switch ports are allowed to immediately enter the Forwarding state as soon as the link comes up. Normally,
PortFast provides quick network access to end-user devices, where bridging loops never
are expected to form. Even while PortFast is enabled on a port, STP still is running and can
detect a bridging loop. However, a loop can be detected only in a finite amount of time—
the length of time required to move the port through the normal STP states.

Note: Remember that enabling PortFast on a port is not the same as disabling the STP
on it.

By definition, if you enable PortFast, you do not expect to find anything that can cause a
bridging loop—especially another switch or device that produces BPDUs. Suppose that a
switch is connected by mistake to a port where PortFast is enabled. Now there is a potential for a bridging loop to form. An even greater consequence is that the potential now exists for the newly connected device to advertise itself and become the new root bridge.

The BPDU Guard feature was developed to further protect the integrity of switch ports
that have PortFast enabled. If any BPDU (whether superior to the current root or not) is

**Key
Topic**

received on a port where BPDU Guard is enabled, that port immediately is put into the errdisable state. The port is shut down in an error condition and must be either manually re-enabled or automatically recovered through the errdisable timeout function.

By default, BPDU Guard is disabled on all switch ports. You can configure BPDU Guard as a global default, affecting all switch ports with a single command. All ports that have Port-Fast enabled also have BPDU Guard automatically enabled. You can use the following global configuration command to enable BPDU Guard as the default:

```
Switch(config)# spanning-tree portfast bpduguard default
```

You also can enable or disable BPDU Guard on a per-port basis, using the following interface configuration command:

```
Switch(config-if)# [no] spanning-tree bpduguard enable
```

When the BPDUs no longer are received, the port still remains in the errdisable state. See Chapter 3, "Switch Port Configuration," for more information about recovering from the errdisable state.

You should use BPDU Guard on all switch ports where STP PortFast is enabled. This prevents any possibility that a switch will be added to the port, either intentionally or by mistake. An obvious application for BPDU Guard is on access-layer switch ports where users and end devices connect. BPDUs normally would not be expected there and would be detected if a switch or hub inadvertently were connected.

Naturally, BPDU Guard does not prevent a bridging loop from forming if an Ethernet hub is connected to the PortFast port. This is because a hub doesn't transmit BPDUs itself; it merely repeats Ethernet frames from its other ports. A loop could form if the hub became connected to two locations in the network, providing a path for frames to be looped without any STP activity.

You never should enable BPDU Guard on any switch uplink where the root bridge is located. If a switch has multiple uplinks, any of those ports could receive legitimate BPDUs from the root—even if they are in the Blocking state as a result of the UplinkFast feature. If BPDU Guard is enabled on an uplink port, BPDUs will be detected and the uplink will be put into the Errdisable state. This will preclude that uplink port from being used as an uplink into the network.

Protecting Against Sudden Loss of BPDUs

STP BPDUs are used as probes to learn about a network topology. When the switches participating in STP converge on a common and consistent loop-free topology, BPDUs still must be sent by the root bridge and must be relayed by every other switch in the STP domain. The STP topology's integrity then depends on a continuous and regular flow of BPDUs from the root.

What happens if a switch doesn't receive BPDUs in a timely manner or when it doesn't receive any? The switch can view that condition as acceptable—perhaps an upstream switch or an upstream link is dead. In that case, the topology must have changed, so blocked ports eventually can be unblocked again.

However, if the absence of BPDUs is actually a mistake and BPDUs are not being received even though there is no topology change, bridging loops easily can form.

Cisco has added two STP features that help detect or prevent the unexpected loss of BPDUs:

■   Loop Guard

■   Unidirectional Link Detection (UDLD)

Loop Guard

Suppose that a switch port is receiving BPDUs and the switch port is in the Blocking state. The port makes up a redundant path; it is blocking because it is neither a root port nor a designated port. It will remain in the Blocking state as long as a steady flow of BPDUs is received.

If BPDUs are being sent over a link but the flow of BPDUs stops for some reason, the last-known BPDU is kept until the Max Age timer expires. Then that BPDU is flushed, and the switch thinks there is no longer a need to block the port. After all, if no BPDUs are received, there must not be another STP device connected there.

The switch then moves the port through the STP states until it begins to forward traffic— and forms a bridging loop. In its final state, the port becomes a designated port where it begins to relay or send BPDUs downstream, when it actually should be receiving BPDUs from upstream.

To prevent this situation, you can use the Loop Guard STP feature. When enabled, Loop Guard keeps track of the BPDU activity on nondesignated ports. While BPDUs are received, the port is allowed to behave normally. When BPDUs go missing, Loop Guard moves the port into the loop-inconsistent state. The port is effectively blocking at this point to prevent a loop from forming and to keep it in the nondesignated role.

Key Topic

When BPDUs are received on the port again, Loop Guard allows the port to move through the normal STP states and become active. In this fashion, Loop Guard automatically governs ports without the need for manual intervention.

By default, Loop Guard is disabled on all switch ports. You can enable Loop Guard as a global default, affecting all switch ports, with the following global configuration command:

```
Switch(config)# spanning-tree loopguard default
```

You also can enable or disable Loop Guard on a specific switch port by using the following interface-configuration command:

```
Switch(config-if)# [no] spanning-tree guard loop
```

Although Loop Guard is configured on a switch port, its corrective blocking action is taken on a per-VLAN basis. In other words, Loop Guard doesn't block the entire port; only the offending VLANs are blocked.

You can enable Loop Guard on all switch ports, regardless of their functions. The switch figures out which ports are nondesignated and monitors the BPDU activity to keep them nondesignated. Nondesignated ports are generally the alternative root ports and ports that normally are blocking.

UDLD

In a campus network, switches are connected by bidirectional links, where traffic can flow in two directions. Clearly, if a link has a physical layer problem, the two switches it connects detect a problem, and the link is shown as not connected.

What would happen if just one side of the link (receive or transmit) had an odd failure, such as malfunctioning transmit circuitry in a gigabit interface converter (GBIC) or small form factor pluggable (SFP) modules? In some cases, the two switches still might see a functional bidirectional link, although traffic actually would be delivered in only one direction. This is known as a *unidirectional link*.

A unidirectional link poses a potential danger to STP topologies because BPDUs will not be received on one end of the link. If that end of the link normally would be in the Blocking state, it will not be that way for long. A switch interprets the absence of BPDUs to mean that the port can be moved safely through the STP states so that traffic can be forwarded. However, if that is done on a unidirectional link, a bridging loop forms and the switch never realizes the mistake.

Key Topic

To prevent this situation, you can use the Cisco-proprietary Unidirectional Link Detection (UDLD) STP feature. When enabled, UDLD interactively monitors a port to see whether the link is truly bidirectional. A switch sends special Layer 2 UDLD frames identifying its switch port at regular intervals. UDLD expects the far-end switch to echo those frames back across the same link, with the far-end switch port's identification added.

If a UDLD frame is received in return and both neighboring ports are identified in the frame, the link must be bidirectional. However, if the echoed frames are not seen, the link must be unidirectional for some reason.

Naturally, an echo process such as this requires *both ends* of the link to be configured for UDLD. Otherwise, one end of the link will not echo the frames back to the originator. In addition, each switch at the end of a link sends its own UDLD messages independently, expecting echoes from the far end. This means that two echo processes are occurring on any given link.

UDLD messages are sent at regular intervals, as long as the link is active. You can configure the message interval UDLD uses. (The default is 15 seconds.) The objective behind UDLD is to detect a unidirectional link condition before STP has time to move a blocked port into the Forwarding state. To do this, the target time must be less than the Max Age timer plus two intervals of the Forward Delay timer, or 50 seconds. UDLD can detect a unidirectional link after about three times the UDLD message interval (45 seconds total, using the default).

UDLD has two modes of operation:

- **Normal mode**—When a unidirectional link condition is detected, the port is allowed to continue its operation. UDLD merely marks the port as having an undetermined state and generates a syslog message.

- **Aggressive mode**—When a unidirectional link condition is detected, the switch takes action to reestablish the link. UDLD messages are sent out once a second for 8 seconds. If none of those messages is echoed back, the port is placed in the Errdisable state so that it cannot be used.

You configure UDLD on a per-port basis, although you can enable it globally for all fiber-optic switch ports (either native fiber or fiber-based GBIC or SFP modules). By default, UDLD is disabled on all switch ports. To enable it globally, use the following global configuration command:

```
Switch(config)# udld {enable | aggressive | message time seconds}
```

For normal mode, use the **enable** keyword; for aggressive mode, use the **aggressive** keyword. You can use the **message time** keywords to set the message interval to *seconds*, ranging from 7 to 90 seconds. (The default interval varies according to switch platform. For example, the Catalyst 3550 default is 7 seconds; the Catalyst 4500 and 6500 default is 15 seconds.)

You also can enable or disable UDLD on individual switch ports, if needed, using the following interface configuration command:

```
Switch(config-if)# udld {enable | aggressive | disable}
```

Here, you can use the **disable** keyword to completely disable UDLD on a fiber-optic interface.

Note: The default UDLD message interval times differ among Catalyst switch platforms. Although two neighbors might have mismatched message time values, UDLD still works correctly. This is because each of the two neighbors simply echoes UDLD messages back as they are received, without knowledge of their neighbor's own time interval. The time interval is used only to decide when to send UDLD messages and as a basis for detecting a unidirectional link from the absence of echoed messages.

If you decide to change the default message time, make sure that UDLD still can detect a fault *before* STP decides to move a link to the Forwarding state.

You safely can enable UDLD on all switch ports. The switch globally enables UDLD only on ports that use fiber-optic media. Twisted-pair or copper media does not suffer from the physical layer conditions that allow a unidirectional link to form. However, you can enable UDLD on nonfiber links individually, if you want.

At this point, you might be wondering how UDLD can be enabled gracefully on the two end switches. Recall that in aggressive mode, UDLD disables the link if the neighbor does not reflect the messages back within a certain time period. If you are enabling UDLD on a production network, is there a chance that UDLD will disable working links before you can get the far end configured?

The answer is no. UDLD makes some intelligent assumptions when it is enabled on a link for the first time. First, UDLD has no record of any neighbor on the link. It starts sending out messages, hoping that a neighboring switch will hear them and echo them back. Obviously, the device at the far end also must support UDLD so that the messages will be echoed back.

If the neighboring switch does not yet have UDLD enabled, no messages will be echoed. UDLD will keep trying (indefinitely) to detect a neighbor and will not disable the link. After the neighbor has UDLD configured also, both switches become aware of each other and the bidirectional state of the link through their UDLD message exchanges. From then on, if messages are not echoed, the link can accurately be labeled as unidirectional.

Finally, be aware that if UDLD detects a unidirectional condition on a link, it takes action on only that link. This becomes important in an EtherChannel: If one link within the channel becomes unidirectional, UDLD flags or disables only the offending link in the bundle, not the entire EtherChannel. UDLD sends and echoes its messages on each link within an EtherChannel channel independently.

Using BPDU Filtering to Disable STP on a Port

Ordinarily, STP operates on all switch ports in an effort to eliminate bridging loops before they can form. BPDUs are sent on all switch ports—even ports where PortFast has been enabled. BPDUs also can be received and processed if any are sent by neighboring switches.

You always should allow STP to run on a switch to prevent loops. However, in special cases when you need to prevent BPDUs from being sent or processed on one or more switch ports, you can use BPDU filtering to effectively disable STP on those ports.

By default, BPDU filtering is disabled on all switch ports. You can configure BPDU filtering as a global default, affecting all switch ports with the following global configuration command:

```
Switch(config)# spanning-tree portfast bpdufilter default
```

The **default** keyword indicates that BPDU filtering will be enabled automatically on all ports that have PortFast enabled. If PortFast is disabled on a port, then BPDU filtering will not be enabled there.

You also can enable or disable BPDU filtering on specific switch ports by using the following interface configuration command:

```
Switch(config-if)# spanning-tree bpdufilter {enable | disable}
```

Be very careful to enable BPDU filtering only under controlled circumstances in which you are absolutely sure that a switch port will have a single host connected and that a loop will be impossible. Enable BPDU filtering only if the connected device cannot allow BPDUs to be accepted or sent. Otherwise, you should permit STP to operate on the switch ports as a precaution.

Troubleshooting STP Protection

With several different types of STP protection features available, you might need to know which (if any) has been configured on a switch port. Table 9-2 lists and describes the EXEC commands useful for verifying the features presented in this chapter.

Table 9-2 *Commands for Verifying and Troubleshooting STP Protection Features*

Display Function	Command Syntax
List the ports that have been labeled in an inconsistent state.	Switch# **show spanning-tree inconsistentports**
Look for detailed reasons for inconsistencies.	Switch# **show spanning-tree interface** *type mod/num* [**detail**]
Display the global BPDU Guard, BPDU filter, and Loop Guard states.	Switch# **show spanning-tree summary**
Display the UDLD status on one or all ports.	Switch# **show udld** [*type mod/num*]
Reenable ports that UDLD aggressive mode has errdisabled.	Switch# **udld reset**

Exam Preparation Tasks

Review All Key Topics

Review the most important topics in the chapter, noted with the Key Topic icon in the outer margin of the page. Table 9-3 lists a reference of these key topics and the page numbers on which each is found.

Table 9-3 *Key Topics for Chapter 9*

Key Topic Element	Description	Page Number
Paragraph	Discusses the Root Guard feature	182
Paragraph	Discusses the BPDU Guard feature	183
Paragraph	Discusses the Loop Guard feature	185
Paragraph	Discusses the UDLD feature	186
Paragraph	Explains BPDU filtering	188

Complete Tables and Lists from Memory

Print a copy of Appendix C, "Memory Tables," (found on the CD), or at least the section for this chapter, and complete the tables and lists from memory. Appendix D, "Memory Tables Answer Key," also on the CD, includes completed tables and lists to check your work.

Define Key Terms

Define the following key terms from this chapter, and check your answers in the glossary:

Root Guard, superior BPDU, BPDU Guard, Loop Guard, UDLD, BPDU filtering

Use Command Reference to Check Your Memory

This section includes the most important configuration and EXEC commands covered in this chapter. It might not be necessary to memorize the complete syntax of every command, but you should remember the basic keywords that are needed.

With so many similar and mutually exclusive STP protection features available, you might have a hard time remembering which ones to use where. Use Figure 9-1 as a quick reference.

Figure 9-1 shows two backbone switches (Catalyst A and B), along with an access-layer switch (Catalyst C), with redundant uplinks. Users are connected to the access switch, where PortFast is in use. An additional access switch (Catalyst D) has an uplink to access-layer switch C. All switch-to-switch links are fiber-based Gigabit Ethernet. Obviously, a root bridge never should appear out of Catalyst D.

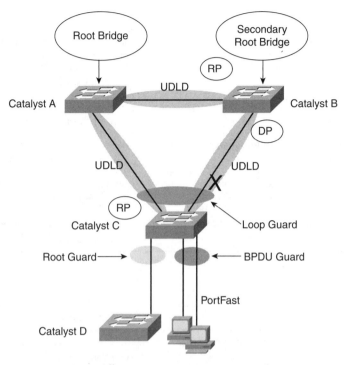

Root guard: Apply to ports where root is never expected.

BPDU guard: Apply to all user ports where PortFast is enabled.

Loop guard: Apply to nondesignated ports but okay to apply to all ports.

UDLD: Apply to all fiber-optic links between switches (must be enabled on both ends).

Permissible combinations on a switch port:
Loop guard and UDLD
Root guard and UDLD

Not permissible on a switch port:

Root guard and Loop guard
Root guard and BPDU guard

Figure 9-1   *Guidelines for Applying STP Protection Features in a Network*

To test your memory of the STP protection feature commands, cover the rightmost columns of Tables 9-4 and 9-5 with a piece of paper, read the description on the left side, then see how much of the command you can remember.

Remember that the CCNP exam focuses on practical or hands-on skills that are used by a networking professional.

Table 9-4 *STP Protection Configuration Commands*

Task	Global Command Syntax	Interface Command Syntax
Enable Root Guard	—	Switch(config-if)# **spanning-tree guard root**
Enable BPDU Guard	Switch(config)# **spanning-tree portfast bpduguard default**	Switch(config-if)# **spanning-tree bpduguard enable**
Enable Loop Guard	Switch(config)# **spanning-tree loopguard default**	Switch(config-if)# **spanning-tree guard loop**
Enable UDLD	Switch(config)# **udld {enable	aggressive	message time seconds}**	Switch(config-if)# **udld {enable	aggressive	disable}**
Enable BPDU filtering	Switch(config)# **spanning-tree bpdufilter default**	Switch(config-if)# **spanning-tree bpdufilter enable**

Table 9-5 *STP Protection Activity Commands*

Task	Command Syntax
Look for ports that have been put in an inconsistent state	Switch# **show spanning-tree inconsistentports**
Display the global BPDU Guard, BPDU filter, and Loop Guard states	Switch# **show spanning-tree summary**
Show UDLD status	Switch# **show udld** [*type mod/num*]
Reenable all ports that UDLD has errdisabled	Switch# **udld reset**

This chapter covers the following topics that you need to master for the CCNP SWITCH exam:

Rapid Spanning Tree Protocol—This section discusses the enhancements that allow switches to run STP efficiently, offering fast convergence.

Multiple Spanning Tree Protocol—This section discusses the latest IEEE standard that supports a reduced number of STP instances for a campus network while using RSTP for efficient operation.

CHAPTER 10

Advanced Spanning Tree Protocol

Familiarity with the IEEE 802.1D STP standard is essential because that protocol is used universally to maintain loop-free bridged and switched networks. However, it now is considered a legacy protocol, offering topology change and convergence times that are not as acceptable as they once were.

This chapter discusses the many STP enhancements that are available in new standards. Rapid STP (RSTP) is presented first because it provides the foundation for efficient STP activity. RSTP can be coupled with either per-VLAN STP (PVST+) or Multiple STP modes. This allows a Layer 2 campus network to undergo change quickly and efficiently, with little downtime for today's applications.

This chapter also covers Multiple STP (MST or MSTP). MST allows VLANs to be individually mapped into arbitrary STP instances while RSTP operates in the background. You can use MST to greatly simplify the Layer 2 topologies and STP operations when many VLANs (and many instances of STP) are present in a network.

"Do I Know This Already?" Quiz

The "Do I Know This Already?" quiz allows you to assess whether you should read this entire chapter thoroughly or jump to the "Exam Preparation Tasks" section. If you are in doubt based on your answers to these questions or your own assessment of your knowledge of the topics, read the entire chapter. Table 10-1 outlines the major headings in this chapter and the "Do I Know This Already?" quiz questions that go with them. You can find the answers in Appendix A, "Answers to the 'Do I Know This Already?' Quizzes."

Table 10-1 *"Do I Know This Already?" Foundation Topics Section-to-Question Mapping*

Foundation Topics Section	Questions Covered in This Section
Rapid Spanning Tree Protocol	1–8
Multiple Spanning Tree Protocol	9–12

1. Which one of the following commands enables the use of RSTP?

    a. spanning-tree mode rapid-pvst

    b. no spanning-tree mode pvst

    c. spanning-tree rstp

    d. spanning-tree mode rstp

    e. None. RSTP is enabled by default.

2. On which standard is RSTP based?

    a. 802.1Q

    b. 802.1D

    c. 802.1w

    d. 802.1s

3. Which of the following is not a port state in RSTP?

    a. Listening

    b. Learning

    c. Discarding

    d. Forwarding

4. When a switch running RSTP receives an 802.1D BPDU, what happens?

    a. The BPDU is discarded or dropped.

    b. An ICMP message is returned.

    c. The switch begins to use 802.1D rules on that port.

    d. The switch disables RSTP.

5. When does an RSTP switch consider a neighbor to be down?

    a. After three BPDUs are missed

    b. After six BPDUs are missed

    c. After the Max Age timer expires

    d. After the Forward timer expires

6. Which process is used during RSTP convergence?

    a. BPDU propagation

    b. Synchronization

    c. Forward timer expiration

    d. BPDU

7. What causes RSTP to view a port as a point-to-point port?

    a. Port speed

    b. Port media

    c. Port duplex

    d. Port priority

8. Which of the following events triggers a topology change with RSTP on a nonedge port?

    a. A port comes up or goes down.

    b. A port comes up.

    c. A port goes down.

    d. A port moves to the Forwarding state.

9. Which of the following is *not* a characteristic of MST?

    a. A reduced number of STP instances

    b. Fast STP convergence

    c. Eliminated need for CST

    d. Interoperability with PVST+

10. Which of the following standards defines the MST protocol?

    a. 802.1Q

    b. 802.1D

    c. 802.1w

    d. 802.1s

11. How many instances of STP are supported in the Cisco implementation of MST?

    a. 1

    b. 16

    c. 256

    d. 4096

12. What switch command can be used to change from PVST+ to MST?

    a. spanning-tree mst enable

    b. no spanning-tree pvst+

    c. spanning-tree mode mst

    d. spanning-tree mst

Foundation Topics

Rapid Spanning Tree Protocol

The IEEE 802.1D Spanning Tree Protocol was designed to keep a switched or bridged network loop free, with adjustments made to the network topology dynamically. A topology change typically takes 30 seconds, with a port moving from the Blocking state to the Forwarding state after two intervals of the Forward Delay timer. As technology has improved, 30 seconds has become an unbearable length of time to wait for a production network to fail over or "heal" itself during a problem.

The IEEE 802.1w standard was developed to use 802.1D's principal concepts and make the resulting convergence much faster. This is also known as the Rapid Spanning Tree Protocol (RSTP), which defines how switches must interact with each other to keep the network topology loop free in a very efficient manner.

As with 802.1D, RSTP's basic functionality can be applied as a single instance or multiple instances. This can be done by using RSTP as the underlying mechanism for the Cisco-proprietary Per-VLAN Spanning Tree Protocol (PVST+). The resulting combination is called *Rapid PVST+* (RPVST+). RSTP also is used as part of the IEEE 802.1s Multiple Spanning Tree (MST) operation. RSTP operates consistently in each, but replicating RSTP as multiple instances requires different approaches.

RSTP Port Behavior

In 802.1D, each switch port is assigned a role and a state at any given time. Depending on the port's proximity to the Root Bridge, it takes on one of the following roles:

- Root port
- Designated port
- Blocking port (neither root nor designated)

The Cisco-proprietary UplinkFast feature also reserved a hidden alternate port role for ports that offered parallel paths to the root but were in the Blocking state.

Recall that each switch port also is assigned one of five possible states:

- Disabled
- Blocking
- Listening
- Learning
- Forwarding

Only the Forwarding state allows data to be sent and received. A port's state is somewhat tied to its role. For example, a blocking port cannot be a root port or a designated port.

RSTP achieves its rapid nature by letting each switch interact with its neighbors through each port. This interaction is performed based on a port's role, not strictly on the BPDUs that are relayed from the root bridge. After the role is determined, each port can be given a state that determines what it does with incoming data.

The root bridge in a network using RSTP is elected just as with 802.1D—by the lowest Bridge ID. After all switches agree on the identity of the root, the following port roles are determined:

- **Root port**—The one switch port on each switch that has the best root path cost to the root. This is identical to 802.1D. (By definition, the root bridge has no root ports.)

- **Designated port**—The switch port on a network segment that has the best root path cost to the root.

- **Alternate port**—A port that has an alternative path to the root, different from the path the root port takes. This path is less desirable than that of the root port. (An example of this is an access-layer switch with two uplink ports; one becomes the root port, and the other is an alternate port.)

- **Backup port**—A port that provides a redundant (but less desirable) connection to a segment where another switch port already connects. If that common segment is lost, the switch might or might not have a path back to the root.

RSTP defines port states only according to what the port does with incoming frames. (Naturally, if incoming frames are ignored or dropped, so are outgoing frames.) Any port role can have any of these port states:

- **Discarding**—Incoming frames simply are dropped; no MAC addresses are learned. (This state combines the 802.1D Disabled, Blocking, and Listening states because all three did not effectively forward anything. The Listening state is not needed because RSTP quickly can negotiate a state change without listening for BPDUs first.)

- **Learning**—Incoming frames are dropped, but MAC addresses are learned.

- **Forwarding**—Incoming frames are forwarded according to MAC addresses that have been (and are being) learned.

BPDUs in RSTP

In 802.1D, BPDUs basically originate from the root bridge and are relayed by all switches down through the tree. Because of this propagation of BPDUs, 802.1D convergence must wait for steady-state conditions before proceeding.

RSTP uses the 802.1D BPDU format for backward compatibility. However, some previously unused bits in the Message Type field are used. The sending switch port identifies itself by its RSTP role and state. The BPDU version also is set to 2 to distinguish RSTP BPDUs from 802.1D BPDUs. In addition, RSTP uses an interactive process so that two neighboring switches can negotiate state changes. Some BPDU bits are used to flag messages during this negotiation.

BPDUs are sent out every switch port at Hello Time intervals, regardless of whether BPDUs are received from the root. In this way, any switch anywhere in the network can play an active role in maintaining the topology. Switches also can expect to receive regular BP-DUs from their neighbors. When three BPDUs are missed in a row, that neighbor is presumed to be down, and all information related to the port leading to the neighbor immediately is aged out. This means that a switch can detect a neighbor failure in three Hello intervals (default 6 seconds), versus the Max Age timer interval (default 20 seconds) for 802.1D.

Key Topic

Because RSTP distinguishes its BPDUs from 802.1D BPDUs, it can coexist with switches still using 802.1D. Each port attempts to operate according to the STP BPDU that is received. For example, when an 802.1D BPDU (version 0) is received on a port, that port begins to operate according to the 802.1D rules.

However, each port has a measure that locks the protocol in use, in case BPDUs from both 802.1D and RSTP are received within a short time frame. This can occur if the switches in a network are being migrated from one STP type to another. Instead of flapping or toggling the STP type during a migration, the switch holds the protocol type for the duration of a migration delay timer. After this timer expires, the port is free to change protocols if needed.

RSTP Convergence

The convergence of STP in a network is the process that takes all switches from a state of independence (each thinks it must be the STP root) to one of uniformity, in which each switch has a place in a loop-free tree topology. You can think of convergence as a two-stage process:

1. One common root bridge must be "elected," and all switches must know about it.

2. The state of every switch port in the STP domain must be brought from a Blocking state to the appropriate state to prevent loops.

Convergence generally takes time because messages are propagated from switch to switch. The traditional 802.1D STP also requires the expiration of several timers before switch ports can safely be allowed to forward data.

RSTP takes a different approach when a switch needs to decide how to participate in the tree topology. When a switch first joins the topology (perhaps it was just powered up) or has detected a failure in the existing topology, RSTP requires it to base its forwarding decisions on the type of port.

Port Types

Key Topic

Every switch port can be considered one of the following types:

■ **Edge port**—A port at the "edge" of the network, where only a single host connects. Traditionally, this has been identified by enabling the STP PortFast feature. RSTP keeps the PortFast concept for familiarity. By definition, the port cannot form a loop as it connects to one host, so it can be placed immediately in the Forwarding state. However, if a BPDU ever is received on an edge port, the port immediately loses its edge port status.

- **Root port**—The port that has the best cost to the root of the STP instance. Only one root port can be selected and active at any time, although alternative paths to the root can exist through other ports. If alternative paths are detected, those ports are identified as alternative root ports and immediately can be placed in the Forwarding state when the existing root port fails.

- **Point-to-point port**—Any port that connects to another switch and becomes a designated port. A quick handshake with the neighboring switch, rather than a timer expiration, decides the port state. BPDUs are exchanged back and forth in the form of a proposal and an agreement. One switch proposes that its port becomes a designated port; if the other switch agrees, it replies with an agreement message.

Point-to-point ports automatically are determined by the duplex mode in use. Full-duplex ports are considered point to point because only two switches can be present on the link. STP convergence can occur quickly over a point-to-point link through RSTP handshake messages.

Half-duplex ports, on the other hand, are considered to be on a shared medium with possibly more than two switches present. They are not point-to-point ports. STP convergence on a half-duplex port must occur between several directly connected switches. Therefore, the traditional 802.1D style convergence must be used. This results in a slower response because the shared-medium ports must go through the fixed Listening and Learning state time periods.

It's easy to see how two switches quickly can converge to a common idea of which one is the root and which one will have the designated port after just a single exchange of BPDUs. What about a larger network, where 802.1D BPDUs normally would have to be relayed from switch to switch?

RSTP handles the complete STP convergence of the network as a propagation of handshakes over point-to-point links. When a switch needs to make an STP decision, a handshake is made with the nearest neighbor. When that is successful, the handshake sequence is moved to the next switch and the next, as an ever-expanding wave moving toward the network's edges.

During each handshake sequence, a switch must take measures to completely ensure that it will not introduce a bridging loop before moving the handshake outward. This is done through a synchronization process.

Synchronization

To participate in RSTP convergence, a switch must decide the state of each of its ports. Nonedge ports begin in the Discarding state. After BPDUs are exchanged between the switch and its neighbor, the Root Bridge can be identified. If a port receives a superior BPDU from a neighbor, that port becomes the root port.

For each nonedge port, the switch exchanges a proposal-agreement handshake to decide the state of each end of the link. Each switch assumes that its port should become the designated port for the segment, and a proposal message (a configuration BPDU) is sent to the neighbor suggesting this.

When a switch receives a proposal message on a port, the following sequence of events occurs. Figure 10-1 shows the sequence, based on the center Catalyst switch:

1. If the proposal's sender has a superior BPDU, the local switch realizes that the sender should be the designated switch (having the designated port) and that its own port must become the new root port.

2. Before the switch agrees to anything, it must synchronize itself with the topology.

3. All nonedge ports immediately are moved into the Discarding (blocking) state so that no bridging loops can form.

4. An agreement message (a configuration BPDU) is sent back to the sender, indicating that the switch is in agreement with the new designated port choice. This also tells the sender that the switch is in the process of synchronizing itself.

5. The root port immediately is moved to the Forwarding state. The sender's port also immediately can begin forwarding.

6. For each nonedge port that is currently in the Discarding state, a proposal message is sent to the respective neighbor.

7. An agreement message is expected and received from a neighbor on a nonedge port.

8. The nonedge port immediately is moved to the Forwarding state.

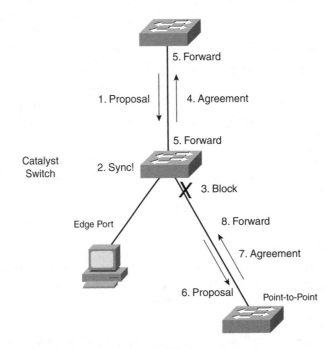

Figure 10-1 *Sequence of Events During RSTP Convergence*

Notice that the RSTP convergence begins with a switch sending a proposal message. The recipient of the proposal must synchronize itself by effectively isolating itself from the rest of the topology. All nonedge ports are blocked until a proposal message can be sent, causing the nearest neighbors to synchronize themselves. This creates a moving "wave" of synchronizing switches, which quickly can decide to start forwarding on their links only if their neighbors agree. Figure 10-2 shows how the synchronization wave travels through a network at three successive time intervals. Isolating the switches along the traveling wave inherently prevents bridging loops.

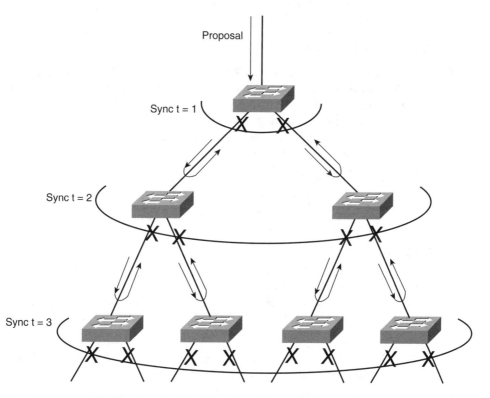

Figure 10-2   *RSTP Synchronization Traveling Through a Network*

The entire convergence process happens quickly, at the speed of BPDU transmission, without the use of any timers. However, a designated port that sends a proposal message might not receive an agreement message reply. Suppose that the neighboring switch does not understand RSTP or has a problem replying. The sending switch then must become overly cautious and must begin playing by the 802.1D rules—the port must be moved through the legacy Listening and Learning states (using the Forward Delay timer) before moving to the Forwarding state.

Topology Changes and RSTP

Recall that when an 802.1D switch detects a port state change (either up or down), it signals the root bridge by sending Topology Change Notification (TCN) BPDUs. The root bridge, in turn, must signal the topology change by sending out a TCN message that is relayed to all switches in the STP domain.

RSTP detects a topology change only when a nonedge port transitions to the Forwarding state. This might seem odd because a link failure is not used as a trigger. RSTP uses all its rapid convergence mechanisms to prevent bridging loops from forming. Therefore, topology changes are detected only so that bridging tables can be updated and corrected as hosts appear first on a failed port and then on a different functioning port.

When a topology change is detected, a switch must propagate news of the change to other switches in the network so that they can correct their bridging tables, too. This process is similar to the convergence and synchronization mechanism; topology change (TC) messages propagate through the network in an ever-expanding wave.

BPDUs, with their TC bit set, are sent out all the nonedge designated ports. This is done until the TC timer expires, after two intervals of the Hello time. This notifies neighboring switches of the new link and the topology change. In addition, all MAC addresses associated with the nonedge designated ports are flushed from the content-addressable memory (CAM) table. This forces the addresses to be relearned after the change, in case hosts now appear on a different link.

All neighboring switches that receive the TC messages also must flush the MAC addresses learned on all ports except the one that received the TC message. Those switches then must send TC messages out their nonedge designated ports, and so on.

RSTP Configuration

By default, a switch operates in Per-VLAN Spanning Tree Plus (PVST+) mode using traditional 802.1D STP. Therefore, RSTP cannot be used until a different spanning-tree mode (MST or RPVST+) is enabled. Remember that RSTP is just the underlying mechanism that a spanning-tree mode can use to detect topology changes and converge a network into a loop-free topology.

The only configuration changes related to RSTP affect the port or link type. The link type is used to determine how a switch negotiates topology information with its neighbors.

To configure a port as an RSTP edge port, use the following interface configuration command:

```
Switch(config-if)# spanning-tree portfast
```

You already should be familiar with this command from the 802.1D STP configuration. After PortFast is enabled, the port is considered to have only one host and is positioned at the edge of the network.

By default, RSTP automatically decides that a port is a point-to-point link if it is operating in full-duplex mode. Ports connecting to other switches are usually full duplex because there are only two switches on the link. However, you can override the automatic determination, if needed. For example, a port connecting to one other switch might be operating at half duplex, for some reason. To force the port to act as a point-to-point link, use the following interface configuration command:

```
Switch(config-if)# spanning-tree link-type point-to-point
```

Rapid Per-VLAN Spanning Tree Protocol

Chapter 7, "Traditional Spanning Tree Protocol," describes PVST+ as the default STP mode on Catalyst switches. In PVST+, one spanning tree instance is created and used for each active VLAN that is defined on the switch. Each STP instance behaves according to the traditional 802.1D STP rules.

You can improve the efficiency of each STP instance by configuring a switch to begin using RSTP instead. This means that each VLAN will have its own independent instance of RSTP running on the switch. This mode is known as *Rapid PVST+* (RPVST+).

You need only one configuration step to change the STP mode and begin using RPVST+. You can use the following global configuration command to accomplish this:

```
Switch(config)# spanning-tree mode rapid-pvst
```

Be careful when you use this command on a production network because any STP process that is currently running must be restarted. This can cause functioning links to move through the traditional STP states, preventing data from flowing for a short time.

Tip: To revert back to the default PVST+ mode, using traditional 802.1D STP, you can use the following command:
```
Switch(config)# spanning-tree mode pvst
```

After you enable the RPVST+ mode, the switch must begin supporting both RSTP and 802.1D STP neighbors. The switch can detect the neighbor's STP type by the BPDU version that is received. You can see the neighbor type in the output of the **show spanning-tree vlan** *vlan-id* command, as demonstrated in Example 10-1.

Example 10-1   *Detecting a Neighboring Switch's STP Type*

```
Switch# show spanning-tree vlan 171
VLAN0171
  Spanning tree enabled protocol rstp

  Root ID    Priority    4267
             Address     00d0.0457.38aa
             Cost        3

             Port        833 (Port-channel1)
             Hello Time   2 sec  Max Age 20 sec  Forward Delay 15 sec

  Bridge ID  Priority    32939   (priority 32768 sys-id-ext 171)
             Address     0007.0d55.a800
```

```
                    Hello Time    2 sec   Max Age 20 sec   Forward Delay 15 sec
                    Aging Time 300


   Interface           Role Sts Cost         Prio.Nbr Type
   ---------------     ---- ---- ----------   -------- -------------------------------
   Gi7/8               Desg FWD 4              128.392  P2p
   Gi9/6               Altn BLK 4              128.518  P2p Peer(STP)
   Po1                 Root FWD 3              128.833  P2p
   Po2                 Desg FWD 3              128.834  P2p
   Po3                 Desg FWD 3              128.835  P2p
   Switch#
```

The output in Example 10-1 shows information about the RSTP instance for VLAN 171. The first shaded line confirms that the local switch indeed is running RSTP. (The only other way to confirm the STP mode is to locate the **spanning-tree mode** command in the running configuration.)

In addition, this output displays all the active ports participating in the VLAN 171 instance of RSTP, along with their port types. The string **P2p** denotes a point-to-point RSTP port type in which a full-duplex link connects two neighboring switches that both are running RSTP. If you see **P2p Peer(STP)**, the port is a point-to-point type but the neighboring device is running traditional 802.1D STP.

Multiple Spanning Tree Protocol

Chapter 7 covered two "flavors" of spanning-tree implementations—IEEE 802.1Q and PVST+—both based on the 802.1D STP. These also represent the two extremes of STP operation in a network:

- **802.1Q**—Only a single instance of STP is used for all VLANs. If there are 500 VLANs, only 1 instance of STP will be running. This is called the Common Spanning Tree (CST) and operates over the trunk's native VLAN.

- **PVST+**—One instance of STP is used for each active VLAN in the network. If there are 500 VLANs, 500 independent instances of STP will be running.

In most networks, each switch has a redundant path to another switch. For example, an access-layer switch usually has two uplinks, each connecting to a different distribution- or core-layer switch. If 802.1Q's CST is used, only one STP instance will run. This means that there is only one loop-free topology at any given time and that only one of the two uplinks in the access-layer switch will be forwarding. The other uplink always will be blocking.

Obviously, arranging the network so that both uplinks can be used simultaneously would be best. One uplink should carry one set of VLANs, whereas the other should carry a different set as a type of load balancing.

PVST+ seems more attractive to meet that goal because it allows different VLANs to have different topologies so that each uplink can be forwarding. But think of the consequences: As the number of VLANs increases, so does the number of independent STP instances.

Each instance uses some amount of the switch CPU and memory resources. The more instances that are in use, the fewer CPU resources will be available for switching.

Beyond that, what is the real benefit of having 500 STP topologies for 500 VLANs, when only a small number of possible topologies exist for a switch with two uplinks? Figure 10-3 shows a typical network with an access-layer switch connecting to a pair of core switches. Two VLANs are in use, with the root bridges configured to support load balancing across the two uplinks. The right portion of the figure shows every possible topology for VLANs A and B. Notice that because the access-layer switch has only two uplinks, only two topologies actually matter—one in which the left uplink forwards, and one in which the right uplink forwards.

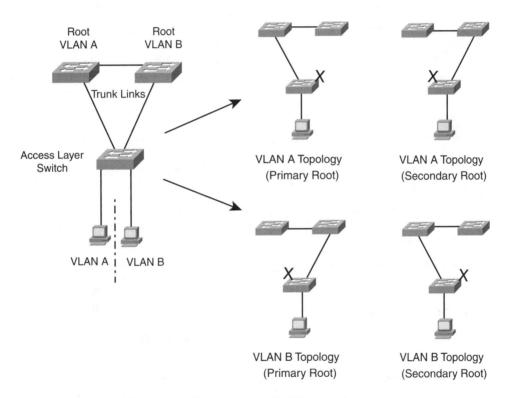

Figure 10-3 *Possible STP Topologies for Two VLANs*

Notice also that the number of useful topologies is independent of the number of VLANs. If 10 or 100 VLANs were used in the figure, there would still be only two possible outcomes at the access-layer switch. Therefore, running 10 or 100 instances of STP when only a couple would suffice is rather wasteful.

The Multiple Spanning Tree Protocol was developed to address the lack of and surplus of STP instances. As a result, the network administrator can configure exactly the number of

STP instances that makes sense for the enterprise network, no matter how many VLANs are in use. MST is defined in the IEEE 802.1s standard.

MST Overview

MST is built on the concept of mapping one or more VLANs to a single STP instance. Multiple instances of STP can be used (hence the name MST), with each instance supporting a different group of VLANs.

For the network shown in Figure 10-3, only two MST instances would be needed. Each could be tuned to result in a different topology so that Instance 1 would forward on the left uplink, whereas Instance 2 would forward on the right uplink. Therefore, VLAN A would be mapped to Instance 1, and VLAN B would be mapped to Instance 2.

To implement MST in a network, you need to determine the following:

■ The number of STP instances needed to support the desired topologies

■ Whether to map a set of VLANs to each instance

MST Regions

Key Topic

MST is different from 802.1Q and PVST+, although it can interoperate with them. If a switch is configured to use MST, it somehow must figure out which of its neighbors are using which type of STP. This is done by configuring switches into common MST regions, where every switch in a region runs MST with compatible parameters.

In most networks, a single MST region is sufficient, although you can configure more than one region. Within the region, all switches must run the instance of MST that is defined by the following attributes:

■ MST configuration name (32 characters)

■ MST configuration revision number (0 to 65535)

■ MST instance-to-VLAN mapping table (4096 entries)

If two switches have the same set of attributes, they belong to the same MST region. If not, they belong to two independent regions.

MST BPDUs contain configuration attributes so that switches receiving BPDUs can compare them against their local MST configurations. If the attributes match, the STP instances within MST can be shared as part of the same region. If not, a switch is seen to be at the MST region boundary, where one region meets another or one region meets traditional 802.1D STP.

Note: The entire MST instance-to-VLAN mapping table is not sent in the BPDUs because the instance mappings must be configured on each switch. Instead, a digest, or a hash code computed from the table contents, is sent. As the contents of the table change, the digest value will be different. Therefore, a switch quickly can compare a received digest to its own to see if the advertised table is the same.

Spanning-Tree Instances Within MST

MST was designed to interoperate with all other forms of STP. Therefore, it also must support STP instances from each. This is where MST can get confusing. Think of the entire enterprise network as having a single CST topology so that one instance of STP represents any and all VLANs and MST regions present. The CST maintains a common loop-free topology while integrating all forms of STP that might be in use.

To do this, CST must regard each MST region as a single "black box" bridge because it has no idea what is inside the region, nor does it care. CST maintains a loop-free topology only with the links that connect the regions to each other and to standalone switches running 802.1Q CST.

IST Instances

Something other than CST must work out a loop-free topology inside each MST region. Within a single MST region, an Internal Spanning Tree (IST) instance runs to work out a loop-free topology between the links where CST meets the region boundary and all switches inside the region. Think of the IST instance as a locally significant CST, bounded by the edges of the region.

The IST presents the entire region as a single virtual bridge to the CST outside. BPDUs are exchanged at the region boundary only over the native VLAN of trunks, as if a single CST were in operation. And, indeed, it is.

Figure 10-4 shows the basic concept behind the IST instance. The network at the left has an MST region, where several switches are running compatible MST configurations. Another switch is outside the region because it is running only the CST from 802.1Q.

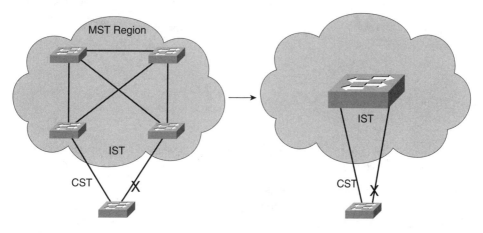

Figure 10-4   *Concepts Behind the IST Instance*

The same network is shown at the right, where the IST has produced a loop-free topology for the network inside the region. The IST makes the internal network look like a single bridge (the "big switch" in the cloud) that can interface with the CST running outside the region.

MST Instances

Recall that the whole idea behind MST is the capability to map multiple VLANs to a smaller number of STP instances. Inside a region, the actual MST instances (MSTI) exist alongside the IST. Cisco supports a maximum of 16 MSTIs in each region. The IST always exists as MSTI number 0, leaving MSTIs 1 through 15 available for use.

Figure 10-5 shows how different MSTIs can exist within a single MST region. The left portion of the figure is identical to that of Figure 10-4. In this network, two MST instances, MSTI 1 and MSTI 2, are configured with different VLANs mapped to each. Their topologies follow the same structure as the network on the left side of the figure, but each has converged differently.

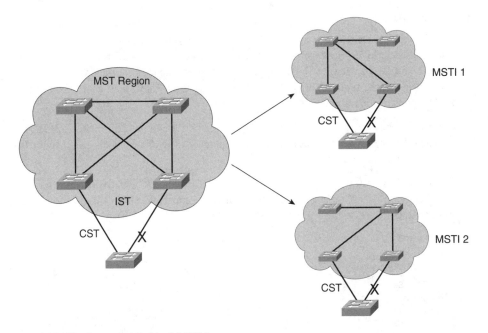

Figure 10-5   *Concepts Behind MST Instances*

Notice that within the MST cloud, there are now three independent STP instances coexisting: MSTI1, MSTI 2, and the IST.

Only the IST (MSTI 0) is allowed to send and receive MST BPDUs. Information about each of the other MSTIs is appended to the MST BPDU as an M-record. Therefore, even if a region has all 16 instances active, only 1 BPDU is needed to convey STP information about them all.

Each of the MSTIs is significant only within a region, even if an adjacent region has the same MSTIs in use. In other words, the MSTIs combine with the IST only at the region boundary to form a subtree of the CST. That means only IST BPDUs are sent into and out of a region.

What if an MST region connects with a switch running traditional PVST+? MST can detect this situation by listening to the received BPDUs. If BPDUs are heard from more than one VLAN (the CST), PVST+ must be in use. When the MST region sends a BPDU toward the PVST+ switch, the IST BPDUs are replicated into all the VLANs on the PVST+ switch trunk.

Tip: Keep in mind that the IST instance is active on *every* port on a switch. Even if a port does not carry VLANs that have been mapped to the IST, IST must be running on the port. Also, by default, all VLANs are mapped to the IST instance. You must explicitly map them to other instances, if needed.

MST Configuration

You must manually configure the MST configuration attributes on each switch in a region. There is currently no method to propagate this information from one switch to another, as is done with a protocol such as VLAN Trunking Protocol (VTP). To define the MST region, use the following configuration commands in the order shown:

Key
Topic

Step 1. Enable MST on the switch:

```
Switch(config)# spanning-tree mode mst
```

Step 2. Enter the MST configuration mode:

```
Switch(config)# spanning-tree mst configuration
```

Step 3. Assign a region configuration name (up to 32 characters):

```
Switch(config-mst)# name name
```

Step 4. Assign a region configuration revision number (0 to 65,535):

```
Switch(config-mst)# revision version
```

The configuration revision number gives you a means of tracking changes to the MST region configuration. Each time you make changes to the configuration, you should increase the number by one. Remember that the region configuration (including the revision number) must match on all switches in the region. Therefore, you also need to update the revision numbers on the other switches to match.

Step 5. Map VLANs to an MST instance:

```
Switch(config-mst)# instance instance-id vlan vlan-list
```

The *instance-id* (0 to 15) carries topology information for the VLANs listed in *vlan-list*. The list can contain one or more VLANs separated by commas. You also can add a range of VLANs to the list by separating numbers with a hyphen. VLAN numbers can range from 1 to 4,094. (Remember that, by default, all VLANs are mapped to instance 0, the IST.)

Step 6. Show the pending changes you have made:

```
Switch(config-mst)# show pending
```

Step 7.   Exit the MST configuration mode; commit the changes to the active MST region configuration:

```
Switch(config-mst)# exit
```

After MST is enabled and configured, PVST+ operation stops and the switch changes to RSTP operation. A switch cannot run both MST and PVST+ at the same time.

You also can tune the parameters that MST uses when it interacts with CST or traditional 802.1D. The parameters and timers are identical to those discussed in Chapter 8, "Spanning-Tree Configuration." In fact, the commands are very similar except for the addition of the **mst** keyword and the *instance-id*. Instead of tuning STP for a VLAN instance, you use an MST instance.

Table 10-2 summarizes the commands as a quick reference. Notice that the timer configurations are applied to MST as a whole, not to a specific MST instance. This is because all instance timers are defined through the IST instance and BPDUs.

Table 10-2   *MST Configuration Commands*

Task	Command Syntax
Set root bridge (macro).	Switch(config)# **spanning-tree mst** *instance-id* **root** {**primary** | **secondary**} [**diameter** *diameter*]
Set bridge priority.	Switch(config)# **spanning-tree mst** *instance-id* **priority** *bridge-priority*
Set port cost.	Switch(config)# **spanning-tree mst** *instance-id* **cost** *cost*
Set port priority.	Switch(config)# **spanning-tree mst** *instance-id* **port-priority** *port-priority*
Set STP timers.	Switch(config)# **spanning-tree mst hello-time** *seconds*
	Switch(config)# **spanning-tree mst forward-time** *seconds*
	Switch(config)# **spanning-tree mst max-age** *seconds*

Exam Preparation Tasks

Review All Key Topics

Review the most important topics in the chapter, noted with the Key Topic icon in the outer margin of the page. Table 10-3 lists a reference of these key topics and the page numbers on which each is found.

Key Topic

Table 10-3   *Key Topics for Chapter 10*

Key Topic Element	Description	Page Number
Paragraph	Describes RSTP root bridge election and port states	199
Paragraph	Describes RSTP port states	199
Paragraph	Discusses RSTP compatibility with 802.1D STP	200
Paragraph	Describes RSTP port types	200
Paragraph	Explains the RSTP synchronization process	201
Paragraph	Discusses how RSTP detects topology changes	204
Paragraph	Explains how to configure an RSTP edge port	204
Paragraph	Explains how to enable the RPVST+ mode, using RSTP	205
Paragraph	Discusses how MST is organized into regions	208
Paragraph	Describes the IST instance	209
Paragraph	Describes MST instances	210
List	Explains how to configure MST	211

Complete Tables and Lists from Memory

Print a copy of Appendix C, "Memory Tables," (found on the CD), or at least the section for this chapter, and complete the tables and lists from memory. Appendix D, "Memory Tables Answer Key," also on the CD, includes completed tables and lists to check your work.

Define Key Terms

Define the following key terms from this chapter, and check your answers in the glossary:

RSTP, RPVST+, alternate port, backup port, discarding state, edge port, point-to-point port, synchronization, MST, MST region, IST instance, MST instance (MSTI)

Use Command Reference to Check Your Memory

This section includes the most important configuration and EXEC commands covered in this chapter. It might not be necessary to memorize the complete syntax of every command, but you should remember the basic keywords that are needed.

To test your memory of the Rapid STP and MST commands, cover the right side of Tables 10-4 and 10-5 with a piece of paper, read the description on the left side, and then see how much of the command you can remember.

Table 10-4   *RSTP Configuration Commands*

Task	Command Syntax
Define an edge port.	Switch(config-if)# **spanning-tree portfast**
Override a port type.	Switch(config-if)# **spanning-tree link-type point-to-point**

Table 10-5   *MST Region Configuration Commands*

Task	Command Syntax
Enable MST on a switch.	Switch(config)# **spanning-tree mode mst**
Enter MST configuration mode.	Switch(config)# **spanning-tree mst configuration**
Name the MST region.	Switch(config-mst)# **name** *name*
Set the configuration revision number.	Switch(config-mst)# **revision** *version*

This chapter covers the following topics that you need to master for the CCNP SWITCH exam:

InterVLAN Routing—This section discusses how you can use a routing function with a switch to forward packets between VLANs.

Multilayer Switching with CEF—This section discusses Cisco Express Forwarding (CEF) and how it is implemented on Catalyst switches. CEF forwards or routes packets in hardware at a high throughput.

Verifying Multilayer Switching—This section provides a brief summary of the commands that can verify the configuration and operation of interVLAN routing, CEF, and fallback bridging.

Using DHCP with a Multilayer Switch—This section covers the basic configuration needed to make a switch act as a DHCP server or as a DHCP relay so that hosts can request addresses and learn their local default gateway addresses.

CHAPTER 11

Multilayer Switching

Chapter 2, "Switch Operation," presents a functional overview of how multilayer switching (MLS) is performed at Layers 3 and 4. The actual MLS process can take two forms: interVLAN routing and Cisco Express Forwarding (CEF). This chapter expands on multilayer switch operation by discussing both of these topics in greater detail.

"Do I Know This Already?" Quiz

The "Do I Know This Already?" quiz allows you to assess whether you should read this entire chapter thoroughly or jump to the "Exam Preparation Tasks" section. If you are in doubt based on your answers to these questions or your own assessment of your knowledge of the topics, read the entire chapter. Table 11-1 outlines the major headings in this chapter and the "Do I Know This Already?" quiz questions that go with them. You can find the answers in Appendix A, "Answers to the 'Do I Know This Already?' Quizzes."

Table 11-1 *"Do I Know This Already?" Section-to-Question Mapping*

Foundation Topics Section	Questions Covered in This Section
InterVLAN Routing	1–5
Multilayer Switching with CEF	6–10
Verifying Multilayer Switching	11
Using DHCP with a Multilayer Switch	12

1. Which of the following arrangements can be considered interVLAN routing?

    a. One switch, two VLANs, one connection to a router.

    b. One switch, two VLANs, two connections to a router.

    c. Two switches, two VLANs, two connections to a router.

    d. All of these answers are correct.

2. How many interfaces are needed in a "router on a stick" implementation for interVLAN routing among four VLANs?

    a. 1

    b. 2

    c. 4

    d. Cannot be determined

3. Which of the following commands configures a switch port for Layer 2 operation?

    a. switchport

    b. no switchport

    c. ip address 192.168.199.1 255.255.255.0

    d. no ip address

4. Which of the following commands configures a switch port for Layer 3 operation?

    a. switchport

    b. no switchport

    c. ip address 192.168.199.1 255.255.255.0

    d. no ip address

5. Which one of the following interfaces is an SVI?

    a. interface fastethernet 0/1

    b. interface gigabit 0/1

    c. interface vlan 1

    d. interface svi 1

6. What information must be learned before CEF can forward packets?

    a. The source and destination of the first packet in a traffic flow

    b. The MAC addresses of both the source and destination

    c. The contents of the routing table

    d. The outbound port of the first packet in a flow

7. Which of the following best defines an adjacency?

    a. Two switches connected by a common link.

    b. Two contiguous routes in the FIB.

    c. Two multilayer switches connected by a common link.

    d. The MAC address of a host is known.

8. Assume that CEF is active on a switch. What happens to a packet that arrives needing fragmentation?

    a. The packet is switched by CEF and kept intact.

    b. The packet is fragmented by CEF.

    c. The packet is dropped.

    d. The packet is sent to the Layer 3 engine.

9. Suppose that a host sends a packet to a destination IP address and that the CEF-based switch does not yet have a valid MAC address for the destination. How is the ARP entry (MAC address) of the next-hop destination in the FIB obtained?

   a. The sending host must send an ARP request for it.

   b. The Layer 3 forwarding engine (CEF hardware) must send an ARP request for it.

   c. CEF must wait until the Layer 3 engine sends an ARP request for it.

   d. All packets to the destination are dropped.

10. During a packet rewrite, what happens to the source MAC address?

    a. There is no change.

    b. It is changed to the destination MAC address.

    c. It is changed to the MAC address of the outbound Layer 3 switch interface.

    d. It is changed to the MAC address of the next-hop destination.

11. What command can you use to view the CEF FIB table contents?

    a. show fib

    b. show ip cef fib

    c. show ip cef

    d. show fib-table

12. Which one of the following answers represents configuration commands needed to implement a DHCP relay function?

    a. ```
       interface vlan 5
       ip address 10.1.1.1 255.255.255.0
       ip helper-address 10.1.1.10
       ```

    b. ```
       interface vlan 5
       ip address 10.1.1.1 255.255.255.0
       ip dhcp-relay
       ```

    c. ```
       ip dhcp pool staff
       network 10.1.1.0 255.255.255.0
       default-router 10.1.1.1
       exit
       ```

    d. ```
       hostname Switch
       ip helper-address 10.1.1.10
       ```

Foundation Topics

InterVLAN Routing

Recall that a Layer 2 network is defined as a broadcast domain. A Layer 2 network can also exist as a VLAN inside one or more switches. VLANs essentially are isolated from each other so that packets in one VLAN cannot cross into another VLAN.

Key Topic

To transport packets between VLANs, you must use a Layer 3 device. Traditionally, this has been a router's function. The router must have a physical or logical connection to each VLAN so that it can forward packets between them. This is known as *interVLAN routing*.

InterVLAN routing can be performed by an external router that connects to each of the VLANs on a switch. Separate physical connections can be used, or the router can access each of the VLANs through a single trunk link. Part A of Figure 11-1 illustrates this concept. The external router also can connect to the switch through a single trunk link, carrying all the necessary VLANs, as illustrated in Part B of Figure 11-1. Part B illustrates what commonly is referred to as a "router on a stick" or a "one-armed router" because the router needs only a single interface to do its job.

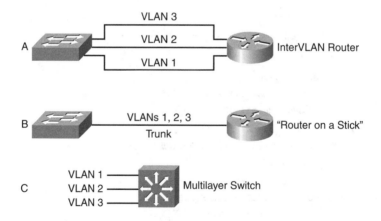

Figure 11-1   *Examples of InterVLAN Routing Connections*

Finally, Part C of Figure 11-1 shows how the routing and switching functions can be combined into one device: a multilayer switch. No external router is needed.

Types of Interfaces

Multilayer switches can perform both Layer 2 switching and interVLAN routing, as appropriate. Layer 2 switching occurs between interfaces that are assigned to Layer 2 VLANs or Layer 2 trunks. Layer 3 switching can occur between any type of interface, as long as the interface can have a Layer 3 address assigned to it.

As with a router, a multilayer switch can assign a Layer 3 address to a physical interface. It also can assign a Layer 3 address to a logical interface that represents an entire VLAN. This is known as a *switched virtual interface (SVI)*. Keep in mind that the Layer 3 address you configure becomes the default gateway for any hosts that are connected to the interface or VLAN. The hosts will use the Layer 3 interface to communicate outside of their local broadcast domains.

Configuring InterVLAN Routing

InterVLAN routing first requires that routing be enabled for the Layer 3 protocol. In the case of IP, you would enable IP routing. In addition, you must configure static routes or a dynamic routing protocol. These topics are covered fully in the CCNP ROUTE course. By default, every switch port on most Catalyst switch platforms is a Layer 2 interface, whereas every switch port on a Catalyst 6500 is a Layer 3 interface. If an interface needs to operate in a different mode, you must explicitly configure it.

An interface is either in Layer 2 or Layer 3 mode, depending on the use of the **switchport** interface configuration command. You can display a port's current mode with the following command:

```
Switch# show interface type mod/num switchport
```

If the **Switchport:** line in the command output is shown as enabled, the port is in Layer 2 mode. If this line is shown as disabled, as in the following example, the port is in Layer 3 mode:

```
Switch# show interface gigabitethernet 0/1 switchport
Name: Gi0/1
Switchport: Disabled
Switch#
```

Tip: Whenever you see the word *switchport*, think Layer 2. So if switchport is disabled, it must be Layer 3.

Figure 11-2 shows how the different types of interface modes can be used within a single switch.

Layer 2 Port Configuration

If an interface is in Layer 3 mode and you need to reconfigure it for Layer 2 functionality instead, use the following command sequence:

```
Switch(config)# interface type mod/num
Switch(config-if)# switchport
```

The **switchport** command puts the port in Layer 2 mode. Then you can use other **switchport** command keywords to configure trunking, access VLANs, and so on. As displayed in Figure 11-2, several Layer 2 ports exist, each assigned to a specific VLAN. A Layer 2 port also can act as a trunk, transporting multiple Layer 2 VLANs.

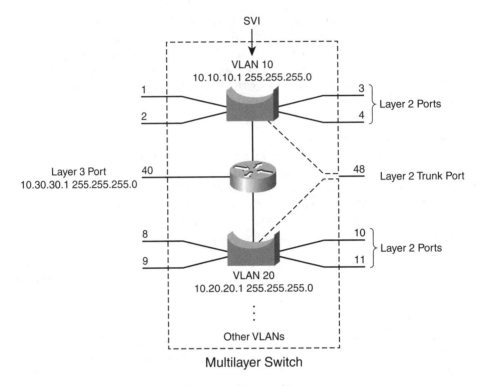

Figure 11-2 *Catalyst Switch with Various Types of Ports*

Layer 3 Port Configuration

Physical switch ports also can operate as Layer 3 interfaces, where a Layer 3 network address is assigned and routing can occur, as shown previously in Figure 11-2. For Layer 3 functionality, you must explicitly configure switch ports with the following command sequence:

```
Switch(config)# interface type mod/num
Switch(config-if)# no switchport
Switch(config-if)# ip address ip-address mask [secondary]
```

The **no switchport** command takes the port out of Layer 2 operation. You then can assign a network address to the port, as you would to a router interface.

Note: Keep in mind that a Layer 3 port assigns a network address to one specific physical interface. If several interfaces are bundled as an EtherChannel, the EtherChannel can also become a Layer 3 port. In that case, the network address is assigned to the port-channel interface—not to the individual physical links within the channel.

SVI Port Configuration

On a multilayer switch, you also can enable Layer 3 functionality for an entire VLAN on the switch. This allows a network address to be assigned to a logical interface—that of the VLAN itself. This is useful when the switch has many ports assigned to a common VLAN, and routing is needed in and out of that VLAN.

In Figure 11-2, you can see how an IP address is applied to the switched virtual interface called VLAN 10. Notice that the SVI itself has no physical connection to the outside world; to reach the outside, VLAN 10 must extend through a Layer 2 port or trunk to the outside.

The logical Layer 3 interface is known as an *SVI*. However, when it is configured, it uses the much more intuitive interface name **vlan** *vlan-id*, as if the VLAN itself is a physical interface. First, define or identify the VLAN interface; then assign any Layer 3 functionality to it with the following configuration commands:

```
Switch(config)# interface vlan vlan-id
Switch(config-if)# ip address ip-address mask [secondary]
```

The VLAN must be defined and active on the switch before the SVI can be used. Make sure that the new VLAN interface also is enabled with the **no shutdown** interface configuration command.

Note: The VLAN and the SVI are configured separately, even though they interoperate. Creating or configuring the SVI doesn't create or configure the VLAN; you still must define each one independently.

As an example, the following commands show how VLAN 100 is created and then defined as a Layer 3 SVI:

```
Switch(config)# vlan 100
Switch(config-vlan)# name Example_VLAN
Switch(config-vlan)# exit
Switch(config)# interface vlan 100
Switch(config-if)# ip address 192.168.100.1 255.255.255.0
Switch(config-if)# no shutdown
```

Multilayer Switching with CEF

Catalyst switches can use several methods to forward packets based on Layer 3 and Layer 4 information. The current generation of Catalyst multilayer switches uses the efficient Cisco Express Forwarding (CEF) method. This section describes the evolution of multilayer switching and discusses CEF in detail. Although CEF is easy to configure and use, the underlying switching mechanisms are more involved and should be understood.

Traditional MLS Overview

Multilayer switching began as a dual effort between a route processor (RP) and a switching engine (SE). The basic idea is to "route once and switch many." The RP receives the first packet of a new traffic flow between two hosts, as usual. A routing decision is made, and the packet is forwarded toward the destination.

To participate in multilayer switching, the SE must know the identity of each RP. The SE then can listen in to the first packet going to the router and also going away from the router. If the SE can switch the packet in both directions, it can learn a "shortcut path" so that subsequent packets of the same flow can be switched directly to the destination port without passing through the RP.

This technique also is known as *NetFlow switching* or *route cache switching*. Traditionally, NetFlow switching was performed on Cisco hardware, such as the Catalyst 6000 Supervisor 1/1a and Multilayer Switch Feature Card (MSFC), Catalyst 5500 with a Route Switch Module (RSM), Route Switch Feature Card (RSFC), or external router. Basically, the hardware consisted of an independent RP component and a NetFlow-capable SE component.

CEF Overview

NetFlow switching has given way to a more efficient form of multilayer switching: Cisco Express Forwarding. Cisco developed CEF for its line of routers, offering high-performance packet forwarding through the use of dynamic lookup tables.

CEF also has been carried over to the Catalyst switching platforms. The following platforms all perform CEF in hardware:

■   Catalyst 6500 Supervisor 720 (with an integrated MSFC3)

■   Catalyst 6500 Supervisor 2/MSFC2 combination

■   Catalyst 4500 Supervisor III, IV, V, and 6-E

■   Fixed-configuration switches, such as the Catalyst 3750, 3560, 3550, and 2950

CEF runs by default, taking advantage of the specialized hardware.

A CEF-based multilayer switch consists of two basic functional blocks, as shown in Figure 11-3: The Layer 3 engine is involved in building routing information that the Layer 3 forwarding engine can use to switch packets in hardware.

Forwarding Information Base

The Layer 3 engine (essentially a router) maintains routing information, whether from static routes or dynamic routing protocols. Basically, the routing table is reformatted into an ordered list with the most specific route first, for each IP destination subnet in the table. The new format is called a Forwarding Information Base (FIB) and contains routing or forwarding information that the network prefix can reference.

Key Topic

In other words, a route to 10.1.0.0/16 might be contained in the FIB along with routes to 10.1.1.0/24 and 10.1.1.128/25, if those exist. Notice that these examples are increasingly more specific subnets, as designated by the longer subnet masks. In the FIB, these would be ordered with the most specific, or longest match, first, followed by less specific subnets. When the switch receives a packet, it easily can examine the destination address and find the longest-match destination route entry in the FIB.

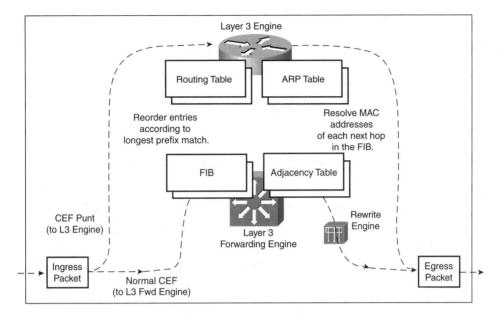

Figure 11-3 *Packet Flow Through a CEF-Based Multilayer Switch*

The FIB also contains the next-hop address for each entry. When a longest-match entry is found in the FIB, the Layer 3 next-hop address is found, too.

You might be surprised to know that the FIB also contains host route (subnet mask 255.255.255.255) entries. These normally are not found in the routing table unless they are advertised or manually configured. Host routes are maintained in the FIB for the most efficient routing lookup to directly connected or adjacent hosts.

As with a routing table, the FIB is dynamic in nature. When the Layer 3 engine sees a change in the routing topology, it sends an update to the FIB. Anytime the routing table receives a change to a route prefix or the next-hop address, the FIB receives the same change. Also, if a next-hop address is changed or aged out of the Address Resolution Protocol (ARP) table, the FIB must reflect the same change.

You can display FIB table entries related to a specific interface or VLAN with the following form of the **show ip cef** command:

```
Switch# show ip cef [type mod/num | vlan vlan-id] [detail]
```

The FIB entries corresponding to the VLAN 101 switched virtual interface might be shown as demonstrated in Example 11-1.

Example 11-1 *Displaying FIB Table Entries for a Specified VLAN*

```
Switch# show ip cef vlan 101
Prefix               Next Hop            Interface
10.1.1.0/24          attached            Vlan101
10.1.1.2/32          10.1.1.2            Vlan101
10.1.1.3/32          10.1.1.3            Vlan101
Switch#
```

You also can view FIB entries by specifying an IP prefix address and mask, using the following form of the **show ip cef** command:

```
Switch# show ip cef [prefix-ip prefix-mask] [longer-prefixes] [detail]
```

The output in Example 11-2 displays any subnet within 10.1.0.0/16 that is known by the switch, regardless of the prefix or mask length. Normally, only an exact match of the IP prefix and mask will be displayed if it exists in the CEF table. To see other longer match entries, you can add the **longer-prefixes** keyword.

Example 11-2 *Displaying FIB Table Entries for a Specified IP Prefix Address/Mask*

```
Switch# show ip cef 10.1.0.0 255.255.0.0 longer-prefixes
Prefix               Next Hop            Interface
10.1.1.0/24          attached            Vlan101
10.1.1.2/32          10.1.1.2            Vlan101
10.1.1.3/32          10.1.1.3            Vlan101
10.1.2.0/24          attached            Vlan102
10.1.3.0/26          192.168.1.2         Vlan99
                     192.168.1.3         Vlan99
10.1.3.64/26         192.168.1.2         Vlan99
                     192.168.1.3         Vlan99
10.1.3.128/26        192.168.1.4         Vlan99
                     192.168.1.3         Vlan99
[output omitted]
Switch#
```

Notice that the first three entries are the same ones listed in Example 11-1. Other subnets also are displayed, along with their next-hop router addresses and switch interfaces.

You can add the **detail** keyword to see more information about each FIB table entry for CEF, as demonstrated in Example 11-3.

Example 11-3 *Displaying Detailed CEF Entry Information*

```
Switch# show ip cef 10.1.3.0 255.255.255.192 detail
10.1.3.0/26, version 270, epoch 0, per-destination sharing
0 packets, 0 bytes
  via 192.168.1.2, Vlan99, 0 dependencies
```

```
    traffic share 1
    next hop 192.168.1.2, Vlan99
    valid adjacency
  via 192.168.1.3, Vlan99, 0 dependencies
    traffic share 1
    next hop 192.168.1.3, Vlan99
    valid adjacency
  0 packets, 0 bytes switched through the prefix
  tmstats: external 0 packets, 0 bytes
            internal 0 packets, 0 bytes
Switch#
```

The version number describes the number of times the CEF entry has been updated since the table was generated. The epoch number denotes the number of times the CEF table has been flushed and regenerated as a whole. The 10.1.3.0/26 subnet has two next-hop router addresses, so the local switch is using per-destination load sharing between the two routers.

After the FIB is built, packets can be forwarded along the bottom dashed path in Figure 11-3. This follows the hardware switching process, in which no "expensive" or time-consuming operations are needed. At times, however, a packet cannot be switched in hardware, according to the FIB. Packets then are marked as "CEF punt" and immediately are sent to the Layer 3 engine for further processing, as shown in the top dashed path in Figure 11-3. Some of the conditions that can cause this are as follows:

- An entry cannot be located in the FIB.

- The FIB table is full.

- The IP Time-To-Live (TTL) has expired.

- The maximum transmission unit (MTU) is exceeded, and the packet must be fragmented.

- An Internet Control Message Protocol (ICMP) redirect is involved.

- The encapsulation type is not supported.

- Packets are tunneled, requiring a compression or encryption operation.

- An access list with the **log** option is triggered.

- A Network Address Translation (NAT) operation must be performed (except on the Catalyst 6500 Supervisor 720, which can handle NAT in hardware).

CEF operations can be handled on a single hardware platform, such as the Catalyst 3560 and 3750 switches. The FIB is generated and contained centrally in the switch. CEF also can be optimized through the use of specialized forwarding hardware, using the following techniques:

- **Accelerated CEF (aCEF)**—CEF is distributed across multiple Layer 3 forwarding engines, typically located on Catalyst 6500 line cards. These engines do not have the capability to store and use the entire FIB, so only a portion of the FIB is downloaded to them at any time. This functions as an FIB "cache," containing entries that are likely to be used again. If FIB entries are not found in the cache, requests are sent to the Layer 3 engine for more FIB information. The net result is that CEF is accelerated on the line cards, but not necessarily at a sustained wire-speed rate.

- **Distributed CEF (dCEF)**—CEF can be distributed completely among multiple Layer 3 forwarding engines for even greater performance. Because the FIB is self-contained for complete Layer 3 forwarding, it can be replicated across any number of independent Layer 3 forwarding engines. The Catalyst 6500 has line cards that support dCEF, each with its own FIB table and forwarding engine. A central Layer 3 engine (the MSFC3, for example) maintains the routing table and generates the FIB, which is then dynamically downloaded in full to each of the line cards.

Adjacency Table

A router normally maintains a routing table containing Layer 3 network and next-hop information, and an ARP table containing Layer 3 to Layer 2 address mapping. These tables are kept independently.

Key Topic

Recall that the FIB keeps the Layer 3 next-hop address for each entry. To streamline packet forwarding even more, the FIB has corresponding Layer 2 information for every next-hop entry. This portion of the FIB is called the *adjacency table*, consisting of the MAC addresses of nodes that can be reached in a single Layer 2 hop.

You can display the adjacency table's contents with the following command:

```
Switch# show adjacency [type mod/num | vlan vlan-id] [summary | detail]
```

As an example, the total number of adjacencies known on each physical or VLAN interface can be displayed with the **show adjacency summary** command, as demonstrated in Example 11-4.

Example 11-4 *Displaying the Total Number of Known Adjacencies*

```
Switch# show adjacency summary
Adjacency Table has 106 adjacencies
  Table epoch: 0 (106 entries at this epoch)
  Interface                Adjacency Count
  Vlan99                   21
  Vlan101                  3
  Vlan102                  1
  Vlan103                  47
  Vlan104                  7
  Vlan105                  27
Switch#
```

Adjacencies are kept for each next-hop router and each host that is connected directly to the local switch. You can see more detailed information about the adjacencies by using the **detail** keyword, as demonstrated in Example 11-5.

Example 11-5 *Displaying Detailed Information About Adjacencies*

```
Switch# show adjacency vlan 99 detail
Protocol Interface            Address
IP       Vlan99               192.168.1.2(5)
                              0 packets, 0 bytes
                              000A5E45B145000E387D51000800
                              ARP          01:52:50
                              Epoch: 0
IP       Vlan99               192.168.1.3(5)
                              1 packets, 104 bytes
                              000CF1C909A0000E387D51000800
                              ARP          04:02:11
                          Epoch: 0
```

Notice that the adjacency entries include both the IP address (Layer 3) and the MAC address (Layer 2) of the directly attached host. The MAC address could be shown as the first
six octets of the long string of hex digits (as shaded in the previous output) or on a line by
itself. The remainder of the string of hex digits contains the MAC address of the Layer 3
engine's interface (six octets, corresponding to the Vlan99 interface in the example) and
the EtherType value (two octets, where 0800 denotes IP).

The adjacency table information is built from the ARP table. Example 11-5 shows adjacency with the age of its ARP entry. As a next-hop address receives a valid ARP entry, the
adjacency table is updated. If an ARP entry does not exist, the FIB entry is marked as
"CEF glean." This means that the Layer 3 forwarding engine can't forward the packet in
hardware because of the missing Layer 2 next-hop address. The packet is sent to the Layer
3 engine so that it can generate an ARP request and receive an ARP reply. This is known as
the *CEF glean* state, in which the Layer 3 engine must glean the next-hop destination's
MAC address.

The glean state can be demonstrated in several ways, as demonstrated in Example 11-6.

Example 11-6 *Displaying Adjacencies in the CEF Glean State*

```
Switch# show ip cef adjacency glean
Prefix                Next Hop          Interface
10.1.1.2/32           attached          Vlan101
127.0.0.0/8           attached          EOBC0/0
[output omitted]
Switch# show ip arp 10.1.1.2
Switch# show ip cef 10.1.1.2 255.255.255.255 detail
10.1.1.2/32, version 688, epoch 0, attached, connected
0 packets, 0 bytes
  via Vlan101, 0 dependencies
    valid glean adjacency
Switch#
```

Notice that the FIB entry for directly connected host 10.1.1.2/32 is present but listed in the glean state. The **show ip arp** command shows that there is no valid ARP entry for the IP address.

During the time that an FIB entry is in the CEF glean state waiting for the ARP resolution, subsequent packets to that host are immediately dropped so that the input queues do not fill and the Layer 3 engine does not become too busy worrying about the need for duplicate ARP requests. This is called *ARP throttling* or *throttling adjacency*. If an ARP reply is not received in 2 seconds, the throttling is released so that another ARP request can be triggered. Otherwise, after an ARP reply is received, the throttling is released, the FIB entry can be completed, and packets can be forwarded completely in hardware.

The adjacency table also can contain other types of entries so that packets can be handled efficiently. For example, you might see the following adjacency types listed:

- **Null adjacency**—Used to switch packets destined for the null interface. The null interface always is defined on a router or switch; it represents a logical interface that silently absorbs packets without actually forwarding them.

- **Drop adjacency**—Used to switch packets that can't be forwarded normally. In effect, these packets are dropped without being forwarded. Packets can be dropped because of an encapsulation failure, an unresolved address, an unsupported protocol, no valid route present, no valid adjacency, or a checksum error. You can gauge drop adjacency activity with the following command:

```
Switch# show cef drop
CEF Drop Statistics
Slot   Encap_fail   Unresolved   Unsupported    No_route     No_adj   ChkSum_Err
RP       8799327            1         45827      5089667         32            0
Switch#
```

- **Discard adjacency**—Used when packets must be discarded because of an access list or other policy action.

- **Punt adjacency**—Used when packets must be sent to the Layer 3 engine for further processing. You can gauge the CEF punt activity by looking at the various punt adjacency reasons listed by the **show cef not-cef-switched** command:

```
Switch# show cef not-cef-switched
CEF Packets passed on to next switching layer
Slot   No_adj   No_encap   Unsupp'ted   Redirect    Receive   Options   Access   Frag
RP    3579706          0            0          0   41258564         0        0      0
Switch#
```

The reasons shown are as follows:

- **No_adj**—An incomplete adjacency

- **No_encap**—An incomplete ARP resolution

- **Unsupp'ted**—Unsupported packet features

- **Redirect**—ICMP redirect

- **Receive**—Layer 3 engine interfaces; includes packets destined for IP addresses that are assigned to interfaces on the Layer 3 engine, IP network addresses, and IP broadcast addresses

- **Options**—IP options present

- **Access**—Access list evaluation failure

- **Frag**—Fragmentation failure

Packet Rewrite

When a multilayer switch finds valid entries in the FIB and adjacency tables, a packet is almost ready to be forwarded. One step remains: The packet header information must be rewritten. Keep in mind that multilayer switching occurs as quick table lookups to find the next-hop address and the outbound switch port. The packet is untouched and still has the original destination MAC address of the switch itself. The IP header also must be adjusted, as if a traditional router had done the forwarding.

The switch has an additional functional block that performs a packet rewrite in real time. The packet rewrite engine (shown in Figure 11-3) makes the following changes to the packet just before forwarding:

> **Key Topic**

- **Layer 2 destination address**—Changed to the next-hop device's MAC address

- **Layer 2 source address**—Changed to the outbound Layer 3 switch interface's MAC address

- **Layer 3 IP TTL**—Decremented by one because one router hop has just occurred

- **Layer 3 IP checksum**—Recalculated to include changes to the IP header

- **Layer 2 frame checksum**—Recalculated to include changes to the Layer 2 and Layer 3 headers

A traditional router normally would make the same changes to each packet. The multilayer switch must act as if a traditional router were being used, making identical changes. However, the multilayer switch can do this very efficiently with dedicated packet-rewrite hardware and address information obtained from table lookups.

Configuring CEF

CEF is enabled on all CEF-capable Catalyst switches by default. In fact, the Catalyst 6500 (with a Supervisor 720 and its integrated MSFC3, or a Supervisor 2 and MSFC2 combination) runs CEF inherently, so CEF never can be disabled.

Tip: Switches such as the Catalyst 3750 and 4500 run CEF by default, but you can disable CEF on a per-interface basis. You can use the **no ip route-cache cef** and **no ip cef** interface configuration commands to disable CEF on the Catalyst 3750 and 4500, respectively.

> You should always keep CEF enabled whenever possible, except when you need to disable it for debugging purposes.

Verifying Multilayer Switching

The multilayer switching topics presented in this chapter are not difficult to configure; however, you might need to verify how a switch is forwarding packets. In particular, the following sections discuss the commands that you can use to verify the operation of inter-VLAN routing and CEF.

Verifying InterVLAN Routing

To verify the configuration of a Layer 2 port, you can use the following EXEC command:

```
Switch# show interface type mod/num switchport
```

The output from this command displays the access VLAN or the trunking mode and native VLAN. The administrative modes reflect what has been configured for the port, whereas the operational modes show the port's active status.

You can use this same command to verify the configuration of a Layer 3 or routed port. In this case, you should see the switchport (Layer 2) mode disabled, as in Example 11-7.

Example 11-7 *Verifying Configuration of a Layer 3 Switch Port*

```
Switch# show interface fastethernet 0/16 switchport
Name: Fa0/16
Switchport: Disabled
Switch#
```

To verify the configuration of an SVI, you can use the following EXEC command:

```
Switch# show interface vlan vlan-id
```

The VLAN interface should be up, with the line protocol also up. If this is not true, either the interface is disabled with the **shutdown** command or the VLAN itself has not been defined on the switch. Use the **show vlan** command to see a list of configured VLANs.

Example 11-8 shows the output produced from the **show vlan** command. Notice that each defined VLAN is shown, along with the switch ports that are assigned to it.

Example 11-8 *Displaying a List of Configured VLANs*

```
Switch# show vlan


VLAN Name                             Status     Ports
---- -------------------------------- ---------- -------------------------------
1    default                          active     Fa0/5, Fa0/6,  Fa0/7,  Fa0/8
                                                 Fa0/9, Fa0/10, Fa0/11, Fa0/12
```

```
                                                    Fa0/13, Fa0/14, Fa0/15, Fa0/17
                                                    Fa0/18, Fa0/19, Fa0/20, Fa0/21
                                                    Fa0/22, Fa0/23, Fa0/24, Fa0/25
                                                    Fa0/26, Fa0/27, Fa0/28, Fa0/29
                                                    Fa0/30, Fa0/32, Fa0/33, Fa0/34
                                                    Fa0/36, Fa0/37, Fa0/38, Fa0/39
                                                    Fa0/41, Fa0/42, Fa0/43, Fa0/44
                                                    Fa0/45, Fa0/46, Fa0/47, Gi0/1
                                                    Gi0/2
2      VLAN0002                       active        Fa0/40
5      VLAN0005                       active
10     VLAN0010                       active
11     VLAN0011                       active        Fa0/31
12     VLAN0012                       active
99     VLAN0099                       active        Fa0/35
Switch#
```

You also can display the IP-related information about a switch interface with the **show ip interface** command, as demonstrated in Example 11-9.

Example 11-9 *Displaying IP-Related Information About a Switch Interface*

```
Switch# show ip interface vlan 101
Vlan101 is up, line protocol is up
  Internet address is 10.1.1.1/24
  Broadcast address is 255.255.255.255
  Address determined by setup command
  MTU is 1500 bytes
  Helper address is not set
  Directed broadcast forwarding is disabled
  Outgoing access list is not set
  Inbound  access list is not set
  Proxy ARP is enabled
  Local Proxy ARP is disabled
  Security level is default
  Split horizon is enabled
  ICMP redirects are always sent
  ICMP unreachables are always sent
  ICMP mask replies are never sent
  IP fast switching is enabled
  IP fast switching on the same interface is disabled
  IP Flow switching is disabled
  IP CEF switching is enabled
  IP Feature Fast switching turbo vector
  IP Feature CEF switching turbo vector
  IP multicast fast switching is enabled
```

```
      IP multicast distributed fast switching is disabled
      IP route-cache flags are Fast, Distributed, CEF
      Router Discovery is disabled
      IP output packet accounting is disabled
      IP access violation accounting is disabled
      TCP/IP header compression is disabled
      RTP/IP header compression is disabled
      Probe proxy name replies are disabled
      Policy routing is disabled
      Network address translation is disabled
      WCCP Redirect outbound is disabled
      WCCP Redirect inbound is disabled
      WCCP Redirect exclude is disabled
      BGP Policy Mapping is disabled
      Sampled Netflow is disabled
      IP multicast multilayer switching is disabled
Switch#
```

You can use the **show ip interface brief** command to see a summary listing of the Layer 3 interfaces involved in routing IP traffic, as demonstrated in Example 11-10.

Example 11-10 *Displaying a Summary Listing of Interfaces Routing IP Traffic*

```
Switch# show ip interface brief
Interface              IP-Address      OK? Method Status
Protocol
Vlan1                  unassigned      YES NVRAM  administratively down down
Vlan54                 10.3.1.6        YES manual up                    up
Vlan101                10.1.1.1        YES manual up                    up
GigabitEthernet1/1     10.1.5.1        YES manual up                    up
[output omitted]
Switch#
```

Verifying CEF

CEF operation depends on the correct routing information being generated and downloaded to the Layer 3 forwarding engine hardware. This information is contained in the FIB and is maintained dynamically. To view the entire FIB, use the following EXEC command:

```
Switch# show ip cef
```

Example 11-11 shows sample output from this command.

Example 11-11 *Displaying the FIB Contents for a Switch*

```
Switch# show ip cef
Prefix              Next Hop           Interface
0.0.0.0/32          receive
```

```
192.168.199.0/24      attached              Vlan1
192.168.199.0/32      receive
192.168.199.1/32      receive
192.168.199.2/32      192.168.199.2         Vlan1
192.168.199.255/32    receive
Switch#
```

On this switch, only VLAN 1 has been configured with the IP address 192.168.199.1 255.255.255.0. Notice several things about the FIB for such a small configuration:

- **0.0.0.0/32**—An FIB entry has been reserved for the default route. No next hop is defined, so the entry is marked "receive" so that packets will be sent to the Layer 3 engine for further processing.

- **192.168.199.0/24**—The subnet assigned to the VLAN 1 interface is given its own entry. This is marked "attached" because it is connected directly to an SVI, VLAN 1.

- **192.168.199.0/32**—An FIB entry has been reserved for the exact network address. This is used to contain an adjacency for packets sent to the network address, if the network is not directly connected. In this case, there is no adjacency, and the entry is marked "receive."

- **192.168.199.1/32**—An entry has been reserved for the VLAN 1 SVI's IP address. Notice that this is a host route (/32). Packets destined for the VLAN 1 interface must be dealt with internally, so the entry is marked "receive."

- **192.168.199.2/32**—This is an entry for a neighboring multilayer switch, found on the VLAN 1 interface. The next-hop field has been filled in with the same IP address, denoting that an adjacency is available.

- **192.168.199.255/32**—An FIB entry has been reserved for the 192.168.199.0 subnet's broadcast address. The route processor (Layer 3 engine) handles all directed broadcasts, so the entry is marked "receive."

To see complete FIB table information for a specific interface, use the following EXEC command:

```
Switch# show ip cef type mod/num [detail]
```

Using DHCP with a Multilayer Switch

When a switch is configured with a Layer 3 address on an interface, it becomes the router or default gateway that connected hosts will use to send traffic to and from their local VLAN or subnet. How do those hosts know to use the Layer 3 interface as their default gateway? As well, how do those hosts know what IP address to use for their own identities?

Hosts can be manually configured to use a static IP address, subnet mask, default gateway address, and so on. That might be appropriate for some devices, such as servers, which would need stable and reserved addresses. For the majority of end user devices, static address assignment can become a huge administrative chore.

Instead, the Dynamic Host Configuration Protocol (DHCP) is usually leveraged to provide a means for dynamic address assignment to any host that can use the protocol. DHCP is defined in RFC 2131 and is built around a client/server model—hosts requesting IP addresses use a DHCP client, whereas address assignment is handled by a DHCP server.

Suppose a host connects to the network, but doesn't yet have an IP address. It needs to request an address via DHCP. How can it send a packet to a DHCP server without having a valid IP address to use as a source address? The answer lies in the DHCP negotiation, which plays out in the following four steps:

Key Topic

1. **The client sends a "DHCP Discover" message as a broadcast**—Even without a valid source address, the client can send to the broadcast address to find any DHCP server that might be listening. The client's MAC address is included in the broadcast message.

2. **A DHCP server replies with a "DHCP Offer" message**—The offer contains an offer for the use of an IP address, subnet mask, default gateway, and some parameters for using the IP address.

   The server also includes its own IP address to identify who is making the offer. (There could be multiple addresses offered, if more than one DHCP server received the broadcast DHCP Discover message.) Because the client doesn't yet have a valid IP address, the server must broadcast the offer so the client can receive it.

3. **The client sends a "DHCP Request" message**—When it is satisfied with a DHCP offer, the client formally requests use of the offered address. A record of the offer is included so that only the server that sent the offer will set aside the requested IP address. Again, the request is sent as a broadcast because the client hasn't officially started using a valid address.

4. **The DHCP server replies with a "DHCP ACK" message**—The IP address and all parameters for its use are returned to the client as formal approval to begin using the address. The ACK message is sent as a broadcast.

Because DHCP is a dynamic mechanism, IP addresses are offered on a leased basis. Before the offered lease time expires, the client must try to renew its address; otherwise, that address may be offered up to a different client.

Notice that DHCP is designed to work within a broadcast domain. Most of the messages in a DHCP exchange are sent as broadcasts. On this basis, the DHCP server would need to be located in the same broadcast domain as the client. In this scenario, you might have a dedicated DHCP server connected to the network and located in the same VLAN as the client. You can also configure a multilayer switch to operate as a DHCP server if you have configured a Layer 3 address on the switch interface or SVI where the client is located.

This design would require one DHCP server for each broadcast domain or VLAN on the network—something that isn't always practical at all! You can get around this requirement by configuring a multilayer switch to relay the DHCP negotiation across VLAN boundaries.

The following sections explain how to configure a DHCP server on a multilayer switch within a VLAN and how to configure DHCP relay between VLANs.

Configuring an IOS DHCP Server

After you have configured a Layer 3 address on a switch interface, you can configure a DHCP server that runs natively on the switch itself. The switch will intercept DHCP broadcast packets from client machines within a VLAN. Use the following command sequence to configure a DHCP server:

```
Switch(config)# ip dhcp excluded-address start-ip end-ip
Switch(config)# ip dhcp pool pool-name
Switch(config-dhcp)# network ip-address subnet-mask
Switch(config-dhcp)# default-router ip-address [ip-address2] [ip-address3] ...
Switch(config-dhcp)# lease {infinite | {days [hours [minutes]]}}
Switch(config-dhcp)# exit
```

If there are addresses within the IP subnet that should be reserved and not offered to clients, use the **ip dhcp excluded-address** command. You can define a range of addresses or a single address to be excluded.

The **ip dhcp pool** command uses a text string *pool-name* to define the pool or scope of addresses that will be offered. The **network** command identifies the IP subnet and subnet mask of the address range. The subnet should be identical to the one configured on the Layer 3 interface. In fact, the switch uses the **network** command to bind its DHCP server to the matching Layer 3 interface. By definition, the network and broadcast addresses for the subnet won't be offered to any client. The **default-router** command identifies the default router address that will be offered to clients. Generally, the default router should be the IP address of the corresponding Layer 3 interface on the switch.

Finally, you can set the IP address lease duration with the **lease** command. By default, leases are offered with a 1 day limit.

You can monitor the DHCP server address leases with the **show ip dhcp binding** command.

> **Tip:** Many more commands are available for configuring the DHCP server. For the CCNP SWITCH exam, try to keep things simple and know the basic structure of DHCP pool configuration, as previously shown.

Configuring a DHCP Relay

If a DHCP server is centrally located in the network, you can configure the multilayer switch to relay DHCP messages between clients and the server, even if they are located on different VLANs or subnets.

First, configure a Layer 3 interface that joins the same VLAN as the client machines. This interface can be the default gateway for the clients and can act as a DHCP relay. Next, use the **ip helper-address** command to identify the IP address of the actual DHCP server, as in the following example:

```
Switch(config)# interface vlan5
Switch(config-if)# ip address 192.168.1.1 255.255.255.0
Switch(config-if)# ip helper-address 192.168.199.4
Switch(config-if)# exit
```

As a DHCP relay, the switch will intercept the broadcast DHCP messages from the client and will forward them on to the server address as unicast messages. The switch keeps track of the subnet where the client messages arrived so that it can relay the DHCP server responses back appropriately.

You can configure more than one helper address by repeating the **ip helper-address** command with different addresses. In this case, the switch will relay each DHCP request from a client to each of the helper addresses simultaneously. If more than one server replies, each reply will be relayed back to the client and the client will have to choose one acceptable response.

Exam Preparation Tasks

Review All Key Topics

Review the most important topics in the chapter, noted with the Key Topic icon in the outer margin of the page. Table 11-2 lists a reference of these key topics and the page numbers on which each is found.

**Key
Topic**

Table 11-2 *Key Topics for Chapter 11*

Key Topic Element	Description	Page Number
Paragraph	Describes InterVLAN routing	220
Paragraph	Describes SVIs	221
Paragraph	Explains Layer 2 interface mode configuration	221
Paragraph	Explains Layer 3 interface mode configuration	222
Paragraph	Explains how to configure an SVI	223
Paragraph	Discusses the FIB and its contents	224
Paragraph	Explains the CEF Adjacency table	228
List	Explains which IP packet fields are changed during the packet rewrite process	231
List	Explains DHCP address negotiation	236
Paragraph	Discusses how to configure a DHCP relay	237

Complete Tables and Lists from Memory

Print a copy of Appendix C, "Memory Tables," (found on the CD), or at least the section for this chapter, and complete the tables and lists from memory. Appendix D, "Memory Tables Answer Key," also on the CD, includes completed tables and lists to check your work.

Define Key Terms

Define the following key terms from this chapter, and check your answers in the glossary:

interVLAN routing, SVI, FIB, adjacency table, packet rewrite, DHCP, DHCP relay

Use Command Reference to Check Your Memory

This section includes the most important configuration and EXEC commands covered in this chapter. It might not be necessary to memorize the complete syntax of every command, but you should be able to remember the basic keywords that are needed.

To test your memory of the interVLAN routing and CEF configuration and verification commands, use a piece of paper to cover the right side of Tables 11-3 through 11-5, respectively. Read the description on the left side, and then see how much of the command you can remember. Remember that the CCNP exam focuses on practical or hands-on skills that are used by a networking professional.

Table 11-3 *InterVLAN Routing Configuration Commands*

Task	Command Syntax
Put a port into Layer 2 mode.	Switch(config-if)# **switchport**
Put a port into Layer 3 mode.	Switch(config-if)# **no switchport**
Define an SVI.	Switch(config)# **interface vlan** *vlan-id*

Table 11-4 *Multilayer Switching Verification Commands*

Task	Command Syntax
Show a Layer 2 port status.	Switch# **show interface** *type mod/num* **switchport**
Show a Layer 3 port status.	Switch# **show interface** *type mod/num*
Show an SVI status.	Switch# **show interface vlan** *vlan-id*
View the FIB contents.	Switch# **show ip cef**
View FIB information for an interface.	Switch# **show ip cef** [*type mod/num* | **vlan** *vlan-id*] [**detail**]
View FIB information for an IP prefix.	Switch# **show ip cef** [*prefix-ip prefix-mask*] [**longer-prefixes**] [**detail**]
View FIB adjacency information.	Switch# **show adjacency** [*type mod/num* | **vlan** *vlan-id*] [**summary** | **detail**]
View counters for packets not switched by CEF.	Switch# **show cef not-cef-switched**

Table 11-5 *DHCP-Related Commands*

Task	Command Syntax
Exclude addresses from a DHCP server scope.	Switch(config-if)# **ip dhcp excluded-address** *start-ip end-ip*
Define a DHCP server scope.	Switch(config-if)# **ip dhcp pool** *pool-name*
Identify the IP subnet for the server scope.	Switch(config-dhcp)# **network** *ip-address subnet-mask*
Identify the default router used in the server scope.	Switch(config-dhcp)# **default-router** *ip-address* [*ip-address2*] [*ip-address3*] ...
Define the DHCP server lease time.	Switch(config-dhcp)# **lease** {infinite	{*days* [*hours* [*minutes*]]}}
Enable DHCP relay on a Layer 3 interface.	Switch(config-if)# **ip helper-address** *ip-address*

Cisco Published SWITCH Exam Topics Covered in This Part

Implement high availability, given a network design and a set of requirements:

- Determine network resources needed for implementing high availability on a network

- Create a high-availability implementation plan

- Create a high-availability verification plan

- Implement first-hop redundancy protocols

- Implement switch supervisor redundancy

- Verify high-availability solution was implemented properly using show and debug commands

- Document results of high-availability implementation and verification

(Always check Cisco.com for the latest posted exam topics.)

Part III: Designing Campus Networks

This chapter covers the following topics that you need to master for the CCNP SWITCH exam:

Hierarchical Network Design—This section details a three-layer, hierarchical structure of campus network designs.

Modular Network Design—This section covers the process of designing a campus network, based on breaking it into functional modules. You also learn how to size and scale the modules in a design.

CHAPTER 12

Enterprise Campus Network Design

This chapter presents a logical design process that you can use to build a new switched campus network or to modify and improve an existing network. Networks can be designed in layers using a set of building blocks that can organize and streamline even a large, complex campus network. These building blocks then can be placed using several campus design models to provide maximum efficiency, functionality, and scalability.

"Do I Know This Already?" Quiz

The "Do I Know This Already?" quiz allows you to assess whether you should read this entire chapter thoroughly or jump to the "Exam Preparation Tasks" section. If you are in doubt based on your answers to these questions or your own assessment of your knowledge of the topics, read the entire chapter. Table 12-1 outlines the major headings in this chapter and the "Do I Know This Already?" quiz questions that go with them. You can find the answers in Appendix A, "Answers to the 'Do I Know This Already?' Quizzes."

Table 12-1 *"Do I Know This Already?" Foundation Topics Section-to-Question Mapping*

Foundation Topics Section	Questions Covered in This Section
Hierarchical Network Design	1–10
Modular Network Design	11–17

1. Where does a collision domain exist in a switched network?

    a.   On a single switch port

    b.   Across all switch ports

    c.   On a single VLAN

    d.   Across all VLANs

2. Where does a broadcast domain exist in a switched network?

    a.   On a single switch port

    b.   Across all switch ports

    c.   On a single VLAN

    d.   Across all VLANs

3. What is a VLAN primarily used for?

    a. To segment a collision domain

    b. To segment a broadcast domain

    c. To segment an autonomous system

    d. To segment a spanning-tree domain

4. How many layers are recommended in the hierarchical campus network design model?

    a. 1

    b. 2

    c. 3

    d. 4

    e. 7

5. What is the purpose of breaking a campus network into a hierarchical design?

    a. To facilitate documentation

    b. To follow political or organizational policies

    c. To make the network predictable and scalable

    d. To make the network more redundant and secure

6. End-user PCs should be connected into which of the following hierarchical layers?

    a. Distribution layer

    b. Common layer

    c. Access layer

    d. Core layer

7. In which OSI layer should devices in the distribution layer typically operate?

    a. Layer 1

    b. Layer 2

    c. Layer 3

    d. Layer 4

8. A hierarchical network's distribution layer aggregates which of the following?

    a. Core switches

    b. Broadcast domains

    c. Routing updates

    d. Access-layer switches

9. In the core layer of a hierarchical network, which of the following are aggregated?

   a. Routing tables

   b. Packet filters

   c. Distribution switches

   d. Access-layer switches

10. In a properly designed hierarchical network, a broadcast from one PC is confined to what?

    a. One access-layer switch port

    b. One access-layer switch

    c. One switch block

    d. The entire campus network

11. Which one or more of the following are the components of a typical switch block?

    a. Access-layer switches

    b. Distribution-layer switches

    c. Core-layer switches

    d. E-commerce servers

    e. Service provider switches

12. What are two types of core, or backbone, designs?

    a. Collapsed core

    b. Loop-free core

    c. Dual core

    d. Layered core

13. What is the maximum number of access-layer switches that can connect into a single distribution-layer switch?

    a. 1

    b. 2

    c. Limited only by the number of ports on the access-layer switch

    d. Limited only by the number of ports on the distribution-layer switch

    e. Unlimited

14. A switch block should be sized according to which two of the following parameters?

    a. The number of access-layer users

    b. A maximum of 250 access-layer users

    c. A study of the traffic patterns and flows

    d. The amount of rack space available

    e. The number of servers accessed by users

15. What evidence can be seen when a switch block is too large? (Choose all that apply.)

   a. IP address space is exhausted.

   b. You run out of access-layer switch ports.

   c. Broadcast traffic becomes excessive.

   d. Traffic is throttled at the distribution-layer switches.

   e. Network congestion occurs.

16. How many distribution switches should be built into each switch block?

   a. 1

   b. 2

   c. 4

   d. 8

17. What are the most important aspects to consider when designing the core layer in a large network? (Choose all that apply.)

   a. Low cost

   b. Switches that can efficiently forward traffic, even when every uplink is at 100 percent capacity

   c. High port density of high-speed ports

   d. A low number of Layer 3 routing peers

Foundation Topics

Hierarchical Network Design

A campus network is an enterprise network consisting of many LANs in one or more buildings, all connected and all usually in the same geographic area. A company typically owns the entire campus network and the physical wiring. Campus networks commonly consist of wired Ethernet LANs running at speeds of up to 10 Gbps and shared wireless LANs.

An understanding of traffic flow is a vital part of the campus network design. You might be able to leverage high-speed LAN technologies and "throw bandwidth" at a network to improve traffic movement. However, the emphasis should be on providing an overall design that is tuned to known, studied, or predicted traffic flows. The network traffic then can be effectively moved and managed, and you can scale the campus network to support future needs.

As a starting point, consider the simple network shown in Figure 12-1. A collection of PCs, printers, and servers are all connected to the same network segment and use the 192.168.1.0 subnet. All devices on this network segment must share the available bandwidth, and all are members of the same broadcast and collision domains.

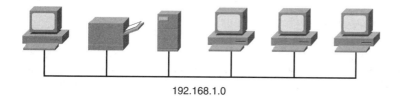

192.168.1.0

Figure 12-1 *Simple Shared Ethernet Network*

A network segment with six hosts might not seem crowded. Suppose the segment contains hundreds of hosts instead. Now the network might not perform very well. Through network segmentation, you can reduce the number of stations on a segment, which will help prevent collisions and broadcasts from reducing any one network segment's performance. By reducing the number of stations, the probability of a collision decreases because fewer stations can be transmitting at a given time. For broadcast containment, the idea is to provide a barrier at the edge of a LAN segment so that broadcasts cannot pass outward or be forwarded.

You can provide segmentation at Layer 3 by using either a router or a multilayer switch, as shown in Figure 12-2. The simple network of Figure 12-1 now has two segments or VLANs interconnected by Switch A, a multilayer switch. A Layer 3 device cannot propagate a collision condition from one segment to another, and it will not forward broadcasts between segments.

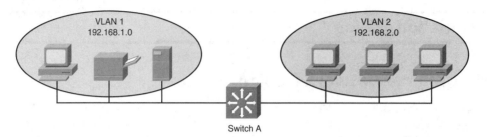

Figure 12-2 *Example of Network Segmentation*

The network might continue to grow as more users and devices are added to it. Switch A has a limited number of ports, so it cannot directly connect to every device. Instead, the network segments can be grown by adding a new switch to each, as shown in Figure 12-3.

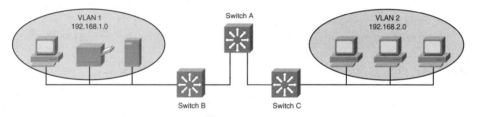

Figure 12-3 *Expanding a Segmented Network*

Switch B aggregates traffic to and from VLAN 1, while Switch C aggregates VLAN 2. As the network continues to grow, more VLANs can be added to support additional applications or user communities. As an example, Figure 12-4 shows how Voice over IP (VoIP) has been implemented by placing IP Phones into two new VLANs (10 and 20). The same two aggregating switches can easily support the new VLANs.

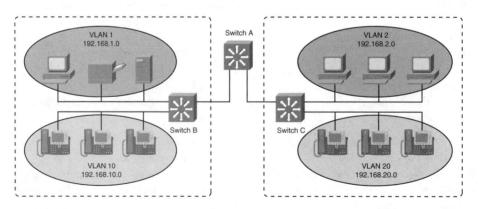

Figure 12-4 *Network Growth Through New VLANs*

Predictable Network Model

Ideally, you should design a network with a predictable behavior in mind to offer low maintenance and high availability. For example, a campus network needs to recover from failures and topology changes quickly and in a predetermined manner. You should scale the network to easily support future expansions and upgrades. With a wide variety of multiprotocol and multicast traffic, the network should be capable of efficiently connecting users with the resources they need, regardless of location.

In other words, design the network around traffic flows rather than a particular type of traffic. Ideally, the network should be arranged so that all end users are located at a consistent distance from the resources they need to use. If one user at one corner of the network passes through two switches to reach an email server, any other user at any other location in the network should also require two switch hops for email service.

Cisco has refined a hierarchical approach to network design that enables network designers to organize the network into distinct layers of devices. The resulting network is efficient, intelligent, scalable, and easily managed.

> **Key Topic**

Figure 12-4 can be redrawn to emphasize the hierarchy that is emerging. In Figure 12-5, two layers become apparent: the access layer, where switches are placed closest to the end users; and the distribution layer, where access layer switches are aggregated.

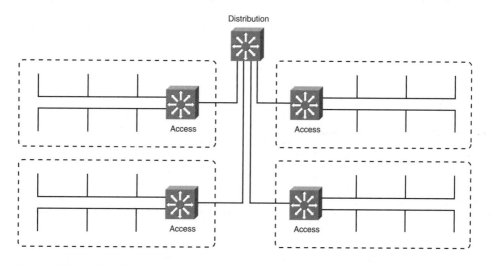

Figure 12-5 *Two-Layer Network Hierarchy Emerges*

As the network continues to grow, with more buildings, more floors, and larger groups of users, the number of access switches increases. As a result, the number of distribution switches increases. Now things have scaled to the point where the distribution switches need to be aggregated. This is done by adding a third layer to the hierarchy, the *core layer*, as shown in Figure 12-6.

Traffic flows in a campus network can be classified as three types, based on where the network service or resource is located in relation to the end user. Table 12-2 lists these types, along with the extent of the campus network that is crossed going from any user to the service.

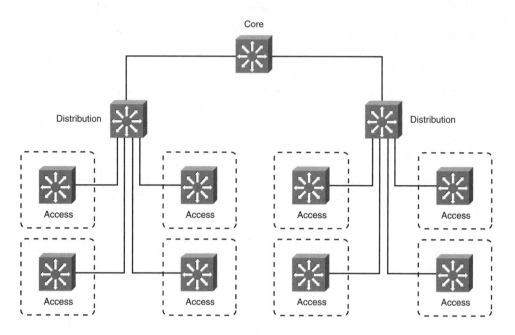

Figure 12-6 *Core Layer Emerges*

Table 12-2 *Types of Network Services*

Service Type	Location of Service	Extent of Traffic Flow
Local	Same segment/VLAN as user	Access layer only
Remote	Different segment/VLAN as user	Access to distribution layers
Enterprise	Central to all campus users	Access to distribution to core layers

Notice how easily the traffic paths can be described. Regardless of where the user is located, the traffic path always begins at the access layer and progresses into the distribution and perhaps into the core layers. Even a path between two users at opposite ends of the network becomes a consistent and predictable access > distribution > core > distribution > access layer.

Each layer has attributes that provide both physical and logical network functions at the appropriate point in the campus network. Understanding each layer and its functions or limitations is important to properly apply the layer in the design process.

Access Layer

The access layer is present where the end users are connected to the network. Access switches usually provide Layer 2 (VLAN) connectivity between users. Devices in this layer, sometimes called building access switches, should have the following capabilities:

- Low cost per switch port

- High port density

- Scalable uplinks to higher layers

- User access functions such as VLAN membership, traffic and protocol filtering, and quality of service (QoS)

- Resiliency through multiple uplinks

Distribution Layer

The distribution layer provides interconnection between the campus network's access and core layers. Devices in this layer, sometimes called building distribution switches, should have the following capabilities:

- Aggregation of multiple access-layer devices

- High Layer 3 throughput for packet handling

- Security and policy-based connectivity functions through access lists or packet filters

- QoS features

- Scalable and resilient high-speed links to the core and access layers

In the distribution layer, uplinks from all access-layer devices are aggregated, or come together. The distribution-layer switches must be capable of processing the total volume of traffic from all the connected devices. These switches should have a high port density of high-speed links to support the collection of access-layer switches.

VLANs and broadcast domains converge at the distribution layer, requiring routing, filtering, and security. The switches at this layer also must be capable of performing multilayer switching with high throughput.

Notice that the distribution layer usually is a Layer 3 boundary, where routing meets the VLANs of the access layer.

Core Layer

A campus network's core layer provides connectivity of all distribution-layer devices. The core, sometimes referred to as the backbone, must be capable of switching traffic as efficiently as possible. Core devices, sometimes called campus backbone switches, should have the following attributes:

- Very high throughput at Layer 3

- No costly or unnecessary packet manipulations (access lists, packet filtering)

■   Redundancy and resilience for high availability

■   Advanced QoS functions

Devices in a campus network's core layer or backbone should be optimized for high-performance switching. Because the core layer must handle large amounts of campuswide data, the core layer should be designed with simplicity and efficiency in mind.

Although campus network design is presented as a three-layer approach (access, distribution, and core layers), the hierarchy can be collapsed or simplified in certain cases. For example, small or medium-size campus networks might not have the size, multilayer switching, or volume requirements that would require the functions of all three layers. Here, you could combine the distribution and core layers for simplicity and cost savings. When the distribution and core layers are combined into a single layer of switches, a *collapsed core* network results.

Modular Network Design

Designing a new network that has a hierarchy with three layers is fairly straightforward. You can also migrate an existing network into a hierarchical design. The resulting network is organized, efficient, and predictable. However, a simple hierarchical design does not address other best practices like redundancy, in the case where a switch or a link fails, or scalability, when large additions to the network need to be added.

Consider the hierarchical network shown in the left portion of Figure 12-7. Each layer of the network is connected to the adjacent layer by single links. If a link fails, a significant portion of the network will become isolated. In addition, the access layer switches are aggregated into a single distribution layer switch. If that switch fails, all the users will become isolated.

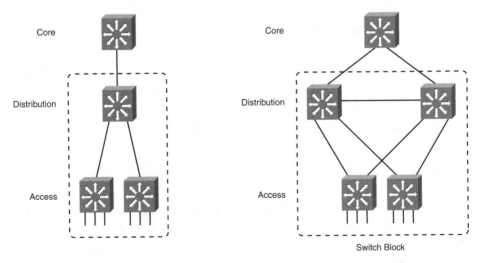

Figure 12-7   *Improving Availability in the Distribution and Access Layers*

To mitigate a potential distribution switch failure, you can add a second, redundant distribution switch. To mitigate a potential link failure, you can add redundant links from each access layer switch to each distribution switch. These improvements are shown in the right portion of Figure 12-7.

One weakness is still present in the redundant design of Figure 12-7: The core layer has only one switch. If that core switch fails, users in the access layer will still be able to communicate. However, they will not be able to reach other areas of the network, such as a data center, the Internet, and so on. To mitigate the effects of a core switch failure, you can add a second, redundant core switch, as shown in Figure 12-8. Now redundant links should be added between each distribution layer switch and each core layer switch.

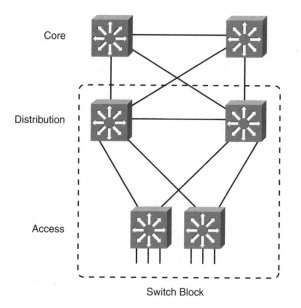

Figure 12-8   *Fully Redundant Hierarchical Network Design*

When the redundant switches and redundant links are added into the design, network growth can become confusing. For example, suppose many more access layer switches need to be added to the network of Figure 12-8 because several departments of users have moved into the building. Or perhaps they have moved into an adjacent building. Should the new access layer switches be dual-connected into the same two distribution switches? Should new distribution switches be added, too? If so, should each of the distribution switches be connected to every other distribution *and* every other core switch, creating a fully meshed network?

Figure 12-9 shows one possible network design that might result. There are so many interconnecting links between switches that it becomes a "brain-buster" exercise to figure out where VLANs are trunked, what the spanning-tree topologies look like, which links should have Layer 3 connectivity, and so on. Users might have connectivity through this network, but it might not be clear how they are actually working or what has gone wrong if they are not working. This network looks more like a spider web than an organized, streamlined design.

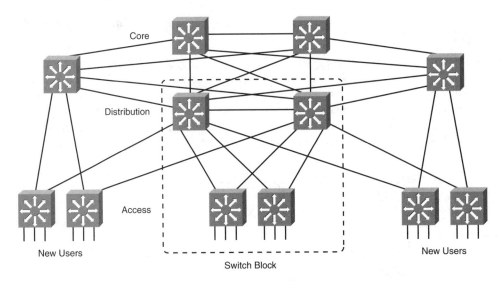

Figure 12-9 *Network Growth in a Disorganized Fashion*

To maintain organization, simplicity, and predictability, you can design a campus network in a logical manner, using a modular approach. In this approach, each layer of the hierarchical network model can be broken into basic functional units. These units, or *modules*, can then be sized appropriately and connected, while allowing for future scalability and expansion.

You can divide enterprise campus networks into the following basic elements:

■ **Switch block**—A group of access-layer switches, together with their distribution switches. The dashed rectangle in Figures 12-4 through 12-9 represents a switch block.

■ **Core block**—The campus network's backbone.

Other related elements can exist. Although these elements do not contribute to the campus network's overall function, they can be designed separately and added to the network design. For example, a data center can have its own access and distribution layer switches, forming a switch block that connects into the core layer. In fact, if the data center is very large, it might have its own core switches, too, which connect into the normal campus core.

Switch Block

Recall how a campus network is divided into access, distribution, and core layers. The switch block contains switching devices from the access and distribution layers. All switch blocks then connect into the core block, providing end-to-end connectivity across the campus.

Switch blocks contain a balanced mix of Layer 2 and Layer 3 functionality, as might be present in the access and distribution layers. Layer 2 switches located in wiring closets (access layer) connect end users to the campus network. With one end user per switch port, each user receives dedicated bandwidth access.

Upstream, each access-layer switch connects to devices in the distribution layer. Here, Layer 2 functionality transports data among all connected access switches at a central connection point. Layer 3 functionality also can be provided in the form of routing and other networking services (security, QoS, and so on). Therefore, a distribution-layer device should be a multilayer switch.

The distribution layer also shields the switch block from certain failures or conditions in other parts of the network. For example, broadcasts are not propagated from the switch block into the core and other switch blocks. Therefore, the Spanning Tree Protocol (STP) is confined to each switch block, where a VLAN is bounded, keeping the spanning-tree domain well defined and controlled.

Access-layer switches can support VLANs by assigning individual ports to specific VLAN numbers. In this way, stations connected to the ports configured for the same VLAN can share the same Layer 3 subnet. However, be aware that a single VLAN can support multiple subnets. Because the switch ports are configured for a VLAN number only (and not a network address), any station connected to a port can present any subnet address range. The VLAN functions as traditional network media and allows any network address to connect.

In this network design model, you should not extend VLANs beyond distribution switches. The distribution layer always should be the boundary of VLANs, subnets, and broadcasts. Although Layer 2 switches can extend VLANs to other switches and other layers of the hierarchy, this activity is discouraged. VLAN traffic should not traverse the network core.

Sizing a Switch Block

Containing access- and distribution-layer devices, the switch block is simple in concept. You should consider several factors, however, to determine an appropriate size for the switch block. The range of available switch devices makes the switch block size very flexible. At the access layer, switch selection usually is based on port density or the number of connected users.

The distribution layer must be sized according to the number of access-layer switches that are collapsed or brought into a distribution device. Consider the following factors:

- Traffic types and patterns

- Amount of Layer 3 switching capacity at the distribution layer

- Number of users connected to the access-layer switches

- Geographic boundaries of subnets or VLANs

- Size of spanning-tree domains

Designing a switch block based solely on the number of users or stations contained within the block is usually inaccurate. Usually, no more than 2000 users should be placed within a single switch block. Although this is useful for initially estimating a switch block's size, this idea doesn't take into account the many dynamic processes that occur on a functioning network.

Instead, switch block size should be based primarily on the following:

- Traffic types and behavior

- Size and number of common workgroups

Because of the dynamic nature of networks, you can size a switch block too large to handle the load that is placed on it. Also, the number of users and applications on a network tends to grow over time. A provision to break up or downsize a switch block is necessary. Again, base these decisions on the actual traffic flows and patterns present in the switch block. You can estimate, model, or measure these parameters with network-analysis applications and tools.

> **Note:** The actual network-analysis process is beyond the scope of this book. Traffic estimation, modeling, and measurement are complex procedures, each requiring its own dedicated analysis tool.

Generally, a switch block is too large if the following conditions are observed:

- The routers (multilayer switches) at the distribution layer become traffic bottlenecks. This congestion could be because of the volume of interVLAN traffic, intensive CPU processing, or switching times required by policy or security functions (access lists, queuing, and so on).

- Broadcast or multicast traffic slows the switches in the switch block. Broadcast and multicast traffic must be replicated and forwarded out many ports. This process requires some overhead in the multilayer switch, which can become too great if significant traffic volumes are present.

Access switches can have one or more redundant links to distribution-layer devices. This situation provides a fault-tolerant environment in which access layer connectivity is preserved on a secondary link if the primary link fails. Because Layer 3 devices are used in the distribution layer, traffic can be load-balanced across both redundant links using redundant gateways.

Generally, you should provide two distribution switches in each switch block for redundancy, with each access-layer switch connecting to the two distribution switches. Then, each Layer 3 distribution switch can load-balance traffic over its redundant links into the core layer (also Layer 3 switches) using routing protocols.

Figure 12-10 shows a typical switch block design. At Layer 3, the two distribution switches can use one of several redundant gateway protocols to provide an active IP gateway and a standby gateway at all times. These protocols are discussed in Chapter 13, "Layer 3 High Availability."

Switch Block Redundancy

A switch block consists of two distribution switches that aggregate one or more access layer switches. Each access layer switch should have a pair of uplinks—one connecting to each distribution switch. The physical cabling is easy to draw, but the logical connectivity is not always obvious. For example, the left portion of Figure 12-11 shows a switch block that has a single VLAN that spans multiple access switches. You might find this where there are several separate physical switch chassis in an access layer room, or where two nearby communications rooms share a common VLAN. Notice how the single VLAN spans across every switch (both access and distribution) and across every link connecting the switches. This is necessary for the VLAN to be present on both access switches and to have redundant uplinks for high availability.

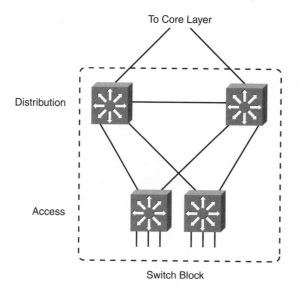

Figure 12-10   *Typical Switch Block Design*

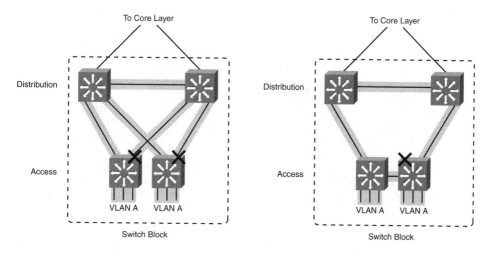

Figure 12-11   *Switch Block Redundancy Considerations*

Although this design works, it is not optimal and comes with the following consequences:

■   The switch block becomes fully dependent on spanning-tree convergence to keep the connections loop free. RSTP should be used on all the switches to improve the convergence time.

■ The link between the two distribution switches must be a Layer 2 link. The access VLAN must extend across this link so that users on either access switch can reach the Layer 3 gateway.

Some people prefer to simplify the redundant connections by daisy chaining access layer switches, as shown in the rightmost portion of Figure 12-11. Each access switch has a single uplink to one of the distribution switches, so that the daisy chain of access switches has two redundant links as a whole. This design is not optimal, either; its consequences are as follows:

■ The switch block depends on STP convergence; Rapid STP (RSTP) should be used whenever possible.

■ The link between the two distribution switches must be a Layer 2 link that carries the access VLAN.

■ The access layer switches must be connected by Layer 2 links along the daisy chain. Without these links, the access switches will not have a redundant path upward.

■ When a link between two access switches fails, the users can become isolated from the Layer 3 gateway in the distribution layer. This can create strange behavior from the user's perspective.

Key Topic

As a best practice, all Layer 2 connectivity should be contained within the access layer. The distribution layer should have only Layer 3 links. Figure 12-12 shows two of the most common and best practice designs.

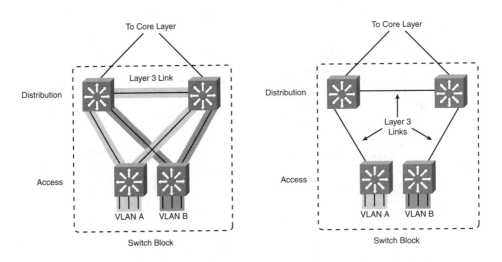

Figure 12-12 *Best Practice Designs for Switch Block Redundancy*

In the leftmost portion of Figure 12-12, VLANs do not span across switches at all. Each VLAN is contained within a single access-layer switch, switch chassis, or stacked switch, and extends across Layer 2 uplinks from each access-layer switch to each distribution switch. This best practice design offers the following attributes:

■ No dependence on STP convergence; each VLAN extends to the distributions switches, but no further. Therefore, the STP topology is always converged.

■ A Layer 3 link is needed between the distribution switches to carry routing updates.

It is also possible to keep Layer 2 VLANs limited to the access-layer switches. This design is shown in the rightmost portion of Figure 12-12 and is possible only if the access switches are Layer 3-capable. This best practice design offers the following attributes:

■ No dependence on STP convergence; each VLAN extends to the distributions switches, but no further. Therefore, the STP topology is always converged.

■ Layer 3 links between the access and distribution switches carry routing updates. Network stability is offered through the fast convergence of the routing protocol.

Core Block

A core block is required to connect two or more switch blocks in a campus network. Because all traffic passing to and from all switch blocks, data center blocks, and the enterprise edge block must cross the core block, the core must be as efficient and resilient as possible. The core is the campus network's basic foundation and carries much more traffic than any other block.

Recall that both the distribution and core layers provide Layer 3 functionality. The links between distribution and core layer switches can be Layer 3 routed interfaces. You can also use Layer 2 links that carry a small VLAN bounded by the two switches. In the latter case, a Layer 3 SVI is used to provide routing within each small VLAN.

The links between layers also should be designed to carry at least the amount of traffic load handled by the distribution switches. The links between core switches in the same core subnet should be of sufficient size to carry the aggregate amount of traffic coming into the core switch. Consider the average link utilization, but allow for future growth. An Ethernet core allows simple and scalable upgrades of magnitude; consider the progression from Ethernet to Fast Ethernet to Fast EtherChannel to Gigabit Ethernet to Gigabit Ether-Channel, and so on.

Two basic core block designs are presented in the following sections, each designed around a campus network's size:

■ Collapsed core

■ Dual core

Collapsed Core

A *collapsed core block* is one in which the hierarchy's core layer is collapsed into the distribution layer. Here, both distribution and core functions are provided within the same switch devices. This situation usually is found in smaller campus networks, where a separate core layer (and additional cost or performance) is not warranted.

Key Topic

Figure 12-13 shows the basic collapsed core design. Although the distribution- and core-layer functions are performed in the same device, keeping these functions distinct and properly designed is important. Note also that the collapsed core is not an independent building block but is integrated into the distribution layer of the individual standalone switch blocks.

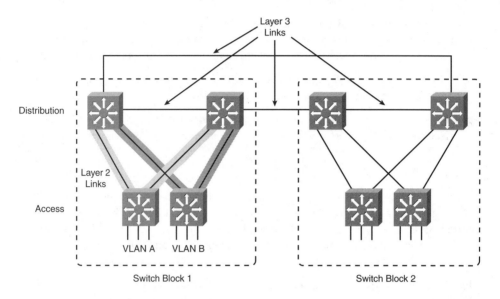

Figure 12-13   *Collapsed Core Design*

In the collapsed core design, each access-layer switch has a redundant link to each distribution- and core-layer switch. All Layer 3 subnets present in the access layer terminate at the distribution switches' Layer 3 ports, as in the basic switch block design. The distribution and core switches connect to each other by one or more links, completing a path to use during a redundancy failover.

Connectivity between the distribution and core switches is accomplished using Layer 3 links (Layer 3 switch interfaces, with no inherent VLANs). The Layer 3 switches route traffic to and from each other directly. Figure 2-3 shows the extent of two VLANs. Notice that VLAN A and VLAN B each extend only from the access-layer switches, where their respective users are located, down to the distribution layer over the Layer 2 uplinks. The VLANs terminate there because the distribution layer uses Layer 3 switching. This is good because it limits the broadcast domains, removes the possibility of Layer 2 bridging loops, and provides fast failover if one uplink fails.

At Layer 3, redundancy is provided through a redundant gateway protocol for IP (covered in Chapter 13). In some of the protocols, the two distribution switches provide a common default gateway address to the access-layer switches, but only one is active at any time. In other protocols, the two switches can both be active, load balancing traffic. If a distribution and core switch failure occurs, connectivity to the core is maintained because the redundant Layer 3 switch is always available.

Dual Core

A *dual core* connects two or more switch blocks in a redundant fashion. Althoug
lapsed core can connect two switch blocks with some redundancy, the core is no
when more switch blocks are added. Figure 12-14 illustrates the dual core. Notic
core appears as an independent module and is not merged into any other block or layer.

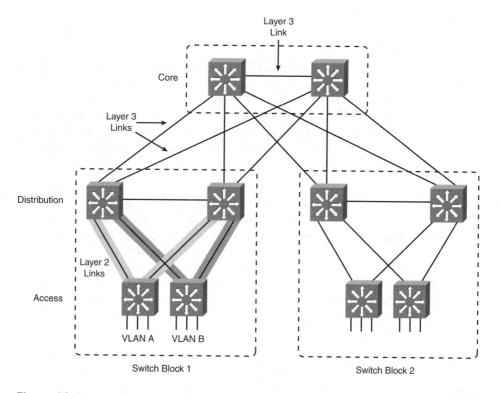

Figure 12-14 *Dual Core Design*

In the past, the dual core usually was built with Layer 2 switches to provide the simplest
and most efficient throughput. Layer 3 switching was provided in the distribution layer.
Multilayer switches now have become cost-effective and offer high switching performance. Building a dual core with multilayer switches is both possible and recommended.
The dual core uses two identical switches to provide redundancy. Redundant links connect each switch block's distribution-layer portion to each of the dual core switches. The
two core switches connect by a common link. In a Layer 2 core, the switches cannot be
linked to avoid any bridging loops. A Layer 3 core uses routing rather than bridging, so
bridging loops are not an issue.

In the dual core, each distribution switch has two equal-cost paths to the core, allowing
the available bandwidth of both paths to be used simultaneously. Both paths remain active
because the distribution and core layers use Layer 3 devices that can manage equal-cost
paths in routing tables. The routing protocol in use determines the availability or loss of a

neighboring Layer 3 device. If one switch fails, the routing protocol reroutes traffic using an alternative path through the remaining redundant switch.

Notice again in Figure 12-12 the extent of the access VLANs. Although Layer 3 devices have been added into a separate core layer, VLANs A and B still extend only from the Layer 2 access-layer switches down to the distribution layer. Although the distribution-layer switches use Layer 3 switch interfaces to provide Layer 3 functionality to the access layer, these links actually pass traffic only at Layer 2.

Core Size in a Campus Network

The dual core is made up of redundant switches and is bounded and isolated by Layer 3 devices. Routing protocols determine paths and maintain the core's operation. As with any network, you must pay some attention to the overall design of the routers and routing protocols in the network. Because routing protocols propagate updates throughout the network, network topologies might be undergoing change. The network's size (the number of routers) then affects routing protocol performance as updates are exchanged and network convergence takes place.

Although the network shown previously in Figure 12-14 might look small, with only two switch blocks of two Layer 3 switches (route processors within the distribution-layer switches) each, large campus networks can have many switch blocks connected into the core block. If you think of each multilayer switch as a router, you will recall that each route processor must communicate with and keep information about each of its directly connected peers. Most routing protocols have practical limits on the number of peer routers that can be directly connected on a point-to-point or multiaccess link. In a network with a large number of switch blocks, the number of connected routers can grow quite large. Should you be concerned about a core switch peering with too many distribution switches?

No, because the actual number of directly connected peers is quite small, regardless of the campus network size. Access-layer VLANs terminate at the distribution-layer switches. The only peering routers at that boundary are pairs of distribution switches, each providing routing redundancy for each of the access-layer VLAN subnets. At the distribution and core boundary, each distribution switch connects to only two core switches over Layer 3 switch interfaces. Therefore, only pairs of router peers are formed.

When multilayer switches are used in the distribution and core layers, the routing protocols running in both layers regard each pair of redundant links between layers as equal-cost paths. Traffic is routed across both links in a load-sharing fashion, utilizing the bandwidth of both.

One final core-layer design point is to scale the core switches to match the incoming load. At a minimum, each core switch must handle switching each of its incoming distribution links at 100 percent capacity.

Exam Preparation Tasks

Review All Key Topics

Review the most important topics in the chapter, noted with the Key Topic icon in the outer margin of the page. Table 12-3 lists a reference of these key topics and the page numbers on which each is found.

Key Topic

Table 12-3 *Key Topics for Chapter 12*

Key Topic Element	Description	Page Number
Paragraph	Describes the Cisco hierarchical network design principles	251
Paragraph	Describes the access layer	253
Paragraph	Describes the distribution layer	253
Paragraph	Describes the core layer	253
Paragraph	Explains modular network design using switch blocks	256
Paragraph	Discusses the pitfalls of letting VLANs span access layer switches	258
Paragraph	Discusses two best practice designs for switch block redundancy	260
Paragraph	Explains a collapsed core design	261
Paragraph	Discusses a dual core design	263

Complete Tables and Lists from Memory

Print a copy of Appendix C, "Memory Tables," (found on the CD), or at least the section for this chapter, and complete the tables and lists from memory. Appendix D, "Memory Tables Answer Key," also on the CD, includes completed tables and lists to check your work.

Define Key Terms

Define the following key terms from this chapter, and check your answers in the glossary:

hierarchical network design, access layer, distribution layer, core layer, switch block, collapsed core, dual core

This chapter covers the following topics that you need to master for the CCNP SWITCH exam:

Router Redundancy in Multilayer Switching—This section discusses three protocols that are available on Catalyst switches to provide redundant router or gateway addresses. The protocols include Hot Standby Routing Protocol (HSRP), Virtual Router Redundancy Protocol (VRRP), and Gateway Load Balancing Protocol (GLBP).

Supervisor and Route Processor Redundancy—This section covers the methods that can be used on some Catalyst switch platforms to operate an active-standby pair of hardware modules in one chassis. The redundancy modes include route processor redundancy (RPR), RPR+, stateful switchover (SSO), and nonstop forwarding (NSF).

CHAPTER 13

Layer 3 High Availability

A multilayer switch can provide routing functions for devices on a network, as described in Chapter 11, "Multilayer Switching." If that switch happens to fail, clients have no way of having their traffic forwarded; their gateway has gone away.

Other multilayer switches can be added into the network to provide redundancy in the form of redundant router or gateway addresses. This chapter describes the protocols that can be used for redundant router addresses, load balancing across multiple routers, and load balancing into a server farm.

This chapter also describes the features that support redundancy in hardware. Within a single multilayer switch chassis, two supervisor modules with integrated route processors can be used to provide hardware redundancy. If an entire supervisor module fails, the other module can pick up the pieces and continue operating the switch.

"Do I Know This Already?" Quiz

The "Do I Know This Already?" quiz allows you to assess whether you should read this entire chapter thoroughly or jump to the "Exam Preparation Tasks" section. If you are in doubt based on your answers to these questions or your own assessment of your knowledge of the topics, read the entire chapter. Table 13-1 outlines the major headings in this chapter and the "Do I Know This Already?" quiz questions that go with them. You can find the answers in Appendix A, "Answers to the 'Do I Know This Already?' Quizzes."

Table 13-1 *"Do I Know This Already?" Foundation Topics Section-to-Question Mapping*

Foundation Topics Section	Questions Covered in This Section
Router Redundancy in Multilayer Switching	1–10
Supervisor and Route Processor Redundancy	11–12

1. Which one of the following do multilayer switches share when running HSRP?

    a. Routing tables

    b. ARP cache

    c. CAM table

    d. IP address

2. What HSRP group uses the MAC address 0000.0c07.ac11?

   a.   Group 0

   b.   Group 7

   c.   Group 11

   d.   Group 17

3. Two routers are configured for an HSRP group. One router uses the default HSRP priority. What priority should be assigned to the other router to make it more likely to be the active router?

   a.   1

   b.   100

   c.   200

   d.   500

4. How many routers are in the Standby state in an HSRP group?

   a.   0

   b.   1

   c.   2

   d.   All but the active router

5. A multilayer switch is configured as follows:

```
interface fastethernet 1/1
no switchport
ip address 192.168.199.3 255.255.255.0
standby 1 ip 192.168.199.2
```

Which IP address should a client PC use as its default gateway?

   a.   192.168.199.1

   b.   192.168.199.2

   c.   192.168.199.3

   d.   Any of these

6. Which one of the following is based on an IETF RFC standard?

   a.   HSRP

   b.   VRRP

   c.   GLBP

   d.   STP

7. What VRRP group uses the virtual MAC address 0000.5e00.01ff?

   a. Group 0

   b. Group 1

   c. Group 255

   d. Group 94

8. Which one of the following protocols is the best choice for load balancing redundant gateways?

   a. HSRP

   b. VRRP

   c. GLBP

   d. GVRP

9. Which one of the following GLBP functions answers ARP requests?

   a. AVF

   b. VARP

   c. AVG

   d. MVR

10. By default, which of the following virtual MAC addresses will be sent to the next client that looks for the GLBP virtual gateway?

   a. The GLBP interface's MAC address

   b. The next virtual MAC address in the sequence

   c. The virtual MAC address of the least-used router

   d. 0000.0c07.ac00

11. Which one of these features is used to reduce the amount of time needed to rebuild the routing information after a supervisor module failure?

   a. NFS

   b. NSF

   c. RPR+

   d. SSO

12. Which one of the following features provides the fastest failover for supervisor or route processor redundancy?

   a. SSL

   b. SSO

   c. RPR+

   d. RPR

Foundation Topics

Router Redundancy in Multilayer Switching

Multilayer switches can act as IP gateways for connected hosts by providing gateway addresses at VLAN SVIs and Layer 3 physical interfaces. These switches can also participate in routing protocols, just as traditional routers do.

For high availability, multilayer switches should offer a means of preventing one switch (gateway) failure from isolating an entire VLAN. This chapter discusses several approaches to providing router redundancy, including the following:

- Hot Standby Router Protocol (HSRP)

- Virtual Router Redundancy Protocol (VRRP)

- Gateway Load Balancing Protocol (GLBP)

These are also commonly called first-hop redundancy protocols (FHRP) because the first router hop is given high availability.

Packet-Forwarding Review

When a host must communicate with a device on its local subnet, it can generate an Address Resolution Protocol (ARP) request, wait for the ARP reply, and exchange packets directly. However, if the far end is located on a different subnet, the host must rely on an intermediate system (a router, for example) to relay packets to and from that subnet.

A host identifies its nearest router, also known as the *default gateway* or *next hop*, by its IP address. If the host understands something about routing, it recognizes that all packets destined off-net must be sent to the gateway's MAC address rather than the far end's MAC address. Therefore, the host first sends an ARP request to find the gateway's MAC address. Then packets can be relayed to the gateway directly without having to look for ARP entries for individual destinations.

If the host is not so savvy about routing, it might still generate ARP requests for every off-net destination, hoping that someone will answer. Obviously, the off-net destinations cannot answer because they never receive the ARP request broadcasts; these requests are not forwarded across subnets. Instead, you can configure the gateway to provide a proxy ARP function so that it will reply to ARP requests with its own MAC address, as if the destination itself had responded.

Now the issue of gateway availability becomes important. If the gateway router for a subnet or VLAN goes down, packets have no way of being forwarded off the local subnet. Several protocols are available that allow multiple routing devices to share a common gateway address so that if one goes down, another automatically can pick up the active gateway role. The sections that follow describe these protocols.

Hot Standby Router Protocol

HSRP is a Cisco-proprietary protocol developed to allow several routers (or multilayer switches) to appear as a single gateway IP address. RFC 2281 describes this protocol in more detail.

Basically, each of the routers that provides redundancy for a given gateway address is assigned to a common HSRP group. One router is elected as the primary, or *active*, HSRP router; another is elected as the *standby* HSRP router; and all the others remain in the *listen* HSRP state. The routers exchange HSRP hello messages at regular intervals so that they can remain aware of each other's existence and that of the active router.

Key
Topic

Note: HSRP sends its hello messages to the multicast destination 224.0.0.2 ("all routers") using UDP port 1985.

An HSRP group can be assigned an arbitrary group number, from 0 to 255. If you configure HSRP groups on several VLAN interfaces, it can be handy to make the group number the same as the VLAN number. However, most Catalyst switches support only up to 16 unique HSRP group numbers. If you have more than 16 VLANs, you will quickly run out of group numbers. An alternative is to make the group number the same (that is, 1) for every VLAN interface. This is perfectly valid because the HSRP groups are locally significant only on an interface. In other words, HSRP Group 1 on interface VLAN 10 is unique and independent from HSRP Group 1 on interface VLAN 11.

HSRP Router Election

HSRP election is based on a priority value (0 to 255) that is configured on each router in the group. By default, the priority is 100. The router with the highest priority value (255 is highest) becomes the active router for the group. If all router priorities are equal or set to the default value, the router with the highest IP address on the HSRP interface becomes the active router. To set the priority, use the following interface configuration command:

```
Switch(config-if)# standby group priority priority
```

For example, suppose that one switch is left at its default priority of 100, while the local switch is intended to win the active role election. You can use the following command to set the HSRP priority to 200:

```
Switch(config-if)# standby 1 priority 200
```

When HSRP is configured on an interface, the router progresses through a series of states before becoming active. This forces a router to listen for others in a group and see where it fits into the pecking order. Devices participating in HSRP must progress their interfaces through the following state sequence:

1. Disabled

2. Init

3. Listen

4. Speak

5. Standby

6. Active

Only the standby (the one with the second-highest priority) router monitors the hello messages from the active router. By default, hellos are sent every 3 seconds. If hellos are missed for the duration of the holdtime timer (default 10 seconds, or three times the hello timer), the active router is presumed to be down. The standby router is then clear to assume the active role.

At that point, if other routers are sitting in the Listen state, the next-highest priority router is allowed to become the new standby router.

If you need to change the timer values, use the following interface configuration command. If you decide to change the timers on a router, you should change them identically on all routers in the HSRP group.

```
Switch(config-if)# standby group timers [msec] hello [msec] holdtime
```

The hello and holdtime values can be given in seconds or in milliseconds, if the **msec** keyword precedes a value. The hello time can range from 1 to 254 seconds or from 15 to 999 milliseconds. The holdtime always should be at least three times the hello timer and can range from 1 to 255 seconds or 50 to 3000 milliseconds.

As an example, the following command can be used to set the hello time at 100 milliseconds and the holdtime to 300 milliseconds:

```
Switch(config-if)# standby 1 timers msec 100 msec 300
```

Note: Be aware that decreasing the HSRP hello time allows a router failure to be detected more quickly. At the same time, HSRP hellos will be sent more often, increasing the amount of traffic on the interface.

Normally, after the active router fails and the standby becomes active, the original active router cannot immediately become active when it is restored. In other words, if a router is not already active, it cannot become active again until the current active router fails—even if its priority is higher than that of the active router. An interesting case arises when routers are just being powered up or added to a network. The first router to bring up its interface becomes the HSRP active router, even if it has the lowest priority of all.

You can configure a router to preempt or immediately take over the active role if its priority is the highest *at any time*. Use the following interface configuration command to allow preemption:

```
Switch(config-if)# standby group preempt [delay [minimum seconds] [reload
    seconds]]
```

By default, the local router immediately can preempt another router that has the a
role. To delay the preemption, use the **delay** keyword followed by one or both of the
lowing parameters:

- Add the **minimum** keyword to force the router to wait for *seconds* (0 to 3600 seconds) before attempting to overthrow an active router with a lower priority. This delay
  time begins as soon as the router is capable of assuming the active role, such as after
  an interface comes up or after HSRP is configured.

- Add the **reload** keyword to force the router to wait for *seconds* (0 to 3600 seconds)
  after it has been reloaded or restarted. This is handy if there are routing protocols that
  need time to converge. The local router should not become the active gateway before
  its routing table is fully populated; otherwise, it might not be capable of routing traffic properly.

- HSRP also can use an authentication method to prevent unexpected devices from
  spoofing or participating in HSRP. All routers in the same standby group must have
  an identical authentication method and key. You can use either plain-text or MD5 authentication, as described in the following sections.

Plain-Text HSRP Authentication

HSRP messages are sent with a plain-text key string (up to eight characters) as a simple
method to authenticate HSRP peers. If the key string in a message matches the key configured on an HSRP peer, the message is accepted.

When keys are sent in the clear, they can be easily intercepted and used to impersonate legitimate peers. Plain-text authentication is intended only to prevent peers with a default
configuration from participating in HSRP. Cisco devices use cisco as the default key string.

You can configure a plain-text authentication key for an HSRP group with the following
interface configuration command:

```
Switch(config-if)# standby group authentication string
```

MD5 Authentication

A Message Digest 5 (MD5) hash is computed on a portion of each HSRP message and a
secret key known only to legitimate HSRP group peers. The MD5 hash value is sent along
with HSRP messages. As a message is received, the peer recomputes the hash of the expected message contents and its own secret key; if the hash values are identical, the message is accepted.

MD5 authentication is more secure than plain-text authentication because the hash value
contained in the HSRP messages is extremely difficult (if not impossible) to reverse. The
hash value itself is not used as a key; instead, the hash is used to validate the message
contents.

You can configure MD5 authentication by associating a key string with an interface, using
the following interface configuration command:

```
Switch(config-if)# standby group authentication md5 key-string [0 | 7] string
```

By default, the key *string* (up to 64 characters) is given as plain text. This is the same as specifying the **0** keyword. After the key string is entered, it is shown as an encrypted value in the switch configuration. You also can copy and paste an encrypted key string value into this command by preceding the string with the **7** keyword.

Alternatively, you can define an MD5 key string as a key on a key chain. This method is more flexible, enabling you to define more than one key on the switch. Any of the keys then can be associated with HSRP on any interface. If a key needs to be changed, you simply add a new key to the key chain and retire (delete) an old key.

First define the key chain globally with the **key chain** command; then add one key at a time with the **key** and **key-string** commands. The *key-number* index is arbitrary, but keys are tried in sequential order. Finally, associate the key chain with HSRP on an interface by referencing its *chain-name*. You can use the following commands to configure HSRP MD5 authentication:

```
Switch(config)# key chain chain-name
Switch(config-keychain)# key key-number
Switch(config-keychain-key)# key-string [0 | 7] string
Switch(config)# interface type mod/num
Switch(config-if)# standby group authentication md5 key-chain chain-name
```

Tip: HSRP MD5 authentication was introduced into some Catalyst switch platforms with Cisco IOS Software Release 12.2(25)S. At the time of this writing, this feature is available only on the Catalyst 3560 and 3750.

Conceding the Election

Consider an active router in an HSRP group: A group of clients sends packets to it for forwarding, and it has one or more links to the rest of the world. If one of those links fails, the router remains active. If all of those links fail, the router still remains active. But sooner or later, the path to the rest of the world is either crippled or removed, and packets from the clients no longer can be forwarded.

HSRP has a mechanism for detecting link failures and swaying the election, giving another router an opportunity to take over the active role. When a specific interface is tracked, HSRP reduces the router's priority by a configurable amount as soon as the interface goes down. If more than one interface is tracked, the priority is reduced even more with each failed interface. The priority is incremented by the same amount as interfaces come back up.

This is particularly useful when a switch has several paths out of a VLAN or subnet; as more interfaces fail and remove the possible paths, other HSRP peers should appear to be more desirable and take over the active role. To configure interface tracking, use the following interface configuration command:

```
Switch(config-if)# standby group track type mod/num [decrementvalue]
```

By default, the *decrementvalue* for an interface is 10. Keep in mind that interface tracking does not involve the state of the HSRP interface itself. Instead, the state of other specific interfaces affects the usefulness of the local router as a gateway. You also should be aware that the only way another router can take over the active role after interface tracking reduces the priority is if the following two conditions are met:

■   Another router now has a higher HSRP priority.

■   That same router is using **preempt** in its HSRP configuration.

Without preemption, the active role cannot be given to any other router.

HSRP Gateway Addressing

Each router in an HSRP group has its own unique IP address assigned to an interface. This address is used for all routing protocol and management traffic initiated by or destined to the router. In addition, each router has a common gateway IP address, the virtual router address, which is kept alive by HSRP. This address also is referred to as the *HSRP address* or the *standby address*. Clients can point to that virtual router address as their default gateway, knowing that a router always keeps that address active. Keep in mind that the actual interface address and the virtual (standby) address must be configured to be in the same IP subnet.

You can assign the HSRP address with the following interface command:

```
Switch(config-if)# standby group ip ip-address [secondary]
```

When HSRP is used on an interface that has secondary IP addresses, you can add the **secondary** keyword so that HSRP can provide a redundant secondary gateway address.

Naturally, each router keeps a unique MAC address for its interface. This MAC address is always associated with the unique IP address configured on the interface. For the virtual router address, HSRP defines a special MAC address of the form 0000.0c07.ac*xx*, where *xx* represents the HSRP group number as a two-digit hex value. For example, HSRP Group 1 appears as 0000.0c07.ac01, HSRP Group 16 appears as 0000.0c07.ac10, and so on.

> **Key Topic**

Figure 13-1 shows a simple network in which two multilayer switches use HSRP Group 1 to provide the redundant gateway address 192.168.1.1. CatalystA is the active router, with priority 200, and answers the ARP request for the gateway address. Because CatalystB is in the Standby state, it never is used for traffic sent to 192.168.1.1. Instead, only CatalystA performs the gateway routing function, and only its uplink to the access layer is utilized.

Example 13-1 shows the configuration commands you can use on CatalystA. CatalystB would be configured similarly, except that its HSRP priority would use the default value of 100.

Example 13-1   *Configuring an HSRP Group on a Switch*

```
CatalystA(config)# interface vlan 50
CatalystA(config-if)# ip address 192.168.1.10 255.255.255.0
CatalystA(config-if)# standby 1 priority 200
CatalystA(config-if)# standby 1 preempt
CatalystA(config-if)# standby 1 ip 192.168.1.1
```

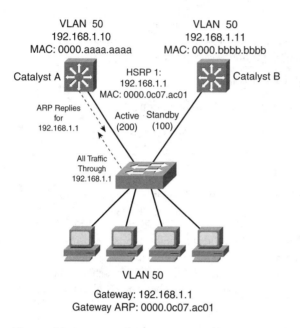

VLAN 50
192.168.1.10
MAC: 0000.aaaa.aaaa

VLAN 50
192.168.1.11
MAC: 0000.bbbb.bbbb

Catalyst A

HSRP 1:
192.168.1.1
MAC: 0000.0c07.ac01

Catalyst B

ARP Replies
for
192.168.1.1

Active
(200)

Standby
(100)

All Traffic
Through
192.168.1.1

VLAN 50

Gateway: 192.168.1.1
Gateway ARP: 0000.0c07.ac01

Figure 13-1 *Typical HSRP Scenario with One HSRP Group*

Load Balancing with HSRP

Consider a network in which HSRP is used on two distribution switches to provide a re-dundant gateway address for access-layer users. Only one of the two becomes the active HSRP router; the other remains in standby. All the users send their traffic to the active router over the uplink to the active router. The standby router and its uplink essentially sit idle until a router failure occurs.

Load balancing traffic across two uplinks to two HSRP routers with a single HSRP group is not possible. Then how is it possible to load balance with HSRP? The trick is to use two HSRP groups:

■ One group assigns an active router to one switch.

■ The other group assigns another active router to the other switch.

In this way, two different virtual router or gateway addresses can be used simultaneously. The rest of the trick is to make each switch function as the standby router for its partner's HSRP group. In other words, each router is active for one group and standby for the other group. The clients or end users also must have their default gateway addresses configured as one of the two virtual HSRP group addresses.

Figure 13-2 presents this scenario. Now, CatalystA is not only the active router for HSRP Group 1 (192.168.1.1), but it is also the standby router for HSRP Group 2 (192.168.1.2). CatalystB is configured similarly, but with its roles reversed. The remaining step is to con-figure half of the client PCs with the HSRP Group 1 virtual router address and the other half with the Group 2 address. This makes load balancing possible and effective. Each half of the hosts uses one switch as its gateway over one uplink.

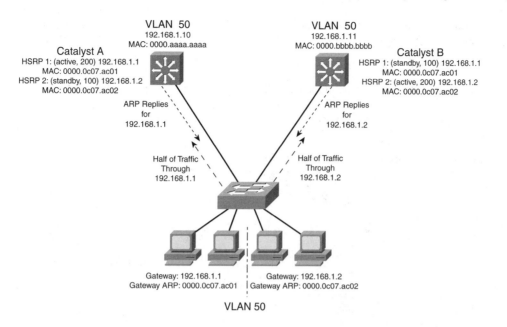

Figure 13-2   *Load Balancing with Two HSRP Groups*

Example 13-2 shows the configuration commands you can use for the scenario shown in Figure 13-2.

Example 13-2   *Configuring Load Balancing Between HSRP Groups*

```
CatalystA(config)# interface vlan 50
CatalystA(config-if)# ip address 192.168.1.10 255.255.255.0
CatalystA(config-if)# standby 1 priority 200
CatalystA(config-if)# standby 1 preempt
CatalystA(config-if)# standby 1 ip 192.168.1.1
CatalystA(config-if)# standby 1 authentication MyKey
CatalystA(config-if)# standby 2 priority 100
CatalystA(config-if)# standby 2 ip 192.168.1.2
CatalystA(config-if)# standby 2 authentication MyKey
CatalystB(config)# interface vlan 50
CatalystB(config-if)# ip address 192.168.1.11 255.255.255.0
CatalystB(config-if)# standby 1 priority 100
CatalystB(config-if)# standby 1 ip 192.168.1.1
CatalystB(config-if)# standby 1 authentication MyKey
CatalystB(config-if)# standby 2 priority 200
CatalystB(config-if)# standby 2 preempt
CatalystB(config-if)# standby 2 ip 192.168.1.2
CatalystB(config-if)# standby 2 authentication MyKey
```

You can use the following command to display information about the status of one or more HSRP groups and interfaces:

```
Router# show standby [brief] [vlan vlan-id | type mod/num]
```

Based on the configuration in Example 13-2, the output in Example 13-3 shows that the CatalystA switch is the active router for HSRP group 1 and the standby router for HSRP group 2 on interface VLAN 50.

Example 13-3   *Displaying the HSRP Router Role of a Switch: CatalystA*

```
CatalystA# show standby vlan 50 brief
                       P indicates configured to preempt.
                     |
Interface  Grp Prio P State   Active addr     Standby addr    Group addr
Vl50        1   200 P Active  local           192.168.1.11    192.168.1.1
Vl50        2   100   Standby 192.168.1.11    local           192.168.1.2
CatalystA#
CatalystA# show standby vlan 50
Vlan50 - Group 1

  Local state is Active, priority 200, may preempt
  Hellotime 3 sec, holdtime 10 sec
  Next hello sent in 2.248
  Virtual IP address is 192.168.1.1 configured
  Active router is local
  Standby router is 192.168.1.11 expires in 9.860
  Virtual mac address is 0000.0c07.ac01
  Authentication text "MyKey"
  2 state changes, last state change 00:11:58
  IP redundancy name is "hsrp-Vl50-1" (default)
Vlan50 - Group 2
  Local state is Standby, priority 100
  Hellotime 3 sec, holdtime 10 sec
  Next hello sent in 1.302
  Virtual IP address is 192.168.1.2 configured
  Active router is 192.168.1.11, priority 200 expires in 7.812
  Standby router is local
  Authentication text "MyKey"
  4 state changes, last state change 00:10:04
  IP redundancy name is "hsrp-Vl50-2" (default)
CatalystA#
```

The output from CatalystB in Example 13-4 shows that it has inverted roles from CatalystA for HSRP Groups 1 and 2.

Example 13-4 *Displaying the HSRP Router Role of a Switch: CatalystB*

```
CatalystB# show standby vlan 50 brief
                    P indicates configured to preempt.
                    |
Interface   Grp  Prio P State    Active addr      Standby addr    Group addr
Vl50         1   100    Standby  192.168.1.10     local           192.168.1.1
Vl50         2   200  P Active   local            192.168.1.10    192.168.1.2
CatalystB#
CatalystB# show standby vlan 50
Vlan50 - Group 1

  Local state is Standby, priority 100
  Hellotime 3 sec, holdtime 10 sec
  Next hello sent in 0.980
  Virtual IP address is 192.168.1.1 configured
  Active router is 192.168.1.10, priority 200 expires in 8.128
  Standby router is local
  Authentication text "MyKey"
  1 state changes, last state change 00:01:12
  IP redundancy name is "hsrp-Vl50-1" (default)
Vlan50 - Group 2
  Local state is Active, priority 200, may preempt
  Hellotime 3 sec, holdtime 10 sec
  Next hello sent in 2.888
  Virtual IP address is 192.168.1.2 configured
  Active router is local
  Standby router is 192.168.1.10 expires in 8.500
  Virtual mac address is 0000.0c07.ac02
  Authentication text "MyKey"
  1 state changes, last state change 00:01:16
CatalystB#
```

Virtual Router Redundancy Protocol

The Virtual Router Redundancy Protocol (VRRP) is a standards-based alternative to HSRP, defined in IETF standard RFC 2338. VRRP is so similar to HSRP that you need to learn only slightly different terminology and a couple of slight functional differences. When you understand HSRP operation and configuration, you will also understand VRRP. This section is brief, highlighting only the differences between HSRP and VRRP.

VRRP provides one redundant gateway address from a group of routers. The active router is called the *master router*, whereas all others are in the *backup state*. The master router is the one with the highest router priority in the VRRP group.

VRRP group numbers range from 0 to 255; router priorities range from 1 to 254. (254 is the highest, 100 is the default.)

The virtual router MAC address is of the form 0000.5e00.01*xx*, where *xx* is a two-digit hex VRRP group number.

VRRP advertisements are sent at 1-second intervals. Backup routers optionally can learn the advertisement interval from the master router.

By default, all VRRP routers are configured to preempt the current master router if their priorities are greater.

Note: VRRP sends its advertisements to the multicast destination address 224.0.0.18 (VRRP), using IP protocol 112. VRRP was introduced in Cisco IOS Software Release 12.0(18)ST for routers. At press time, VRRP is available only for the Catalyst 4500 (Cisco IOS Release 12.2[31]SG), Catalyst 6500 Supervisor 2 (Cisco IOS Software Release 12.2[9]ZA or later) and Catalyst 6500 Supervisor 720 (Cisco IOS Software Release 12.2[17a]SX4 or later).

To configure VRRP, use the interface configuration commands documented in Table 13-2.

Table 13-2 *VRRP Configuration Commands*

Task	Command Syntax
Assign a VRRP router priority (default 100).	**vrrp** *group* **priority** *level*
Alter the advertisement timer (default 1 second).	**vrrp** *group* **timers advertise** [*msec*] *interval*
Learn the advertisement interval from the master router.	**vrrp** *group* **timers learn**
Disable preempting (default is to preempt).	**no vrrp** *group* **preempt**
Change the preempt delay (default 0 seconds).	**vrrp** *group* **preempt** [**delay** *seconds*]
Use authentication for advertisements.	**vrrp** *group* **authentication** *string*
Assign a virtual IP address.	**vrrp** *group* **ip** *ip-address* [**secondary**]
Track an object.	**vrrp** *group* **track** *object-number* [**decrement** *priority*]

As an example, the load-balancing scenario shown in Figure 13-2 is implemented using VRRP. You would use the configuration commands in Example 13-5 on the two Catalyst switches.

Example 13-5 *Configuring Load Balancing with VRRP*

```
CatalystA(config)# interface vlan 50
CatalystA(config-if)# ip address 192.168.1.10 255.255.255.0
CatalystA(config-if)# vrrp 1 priority 200
CatalystA(config-if)# vrrp 1 ip 192.168.1.1
```

```
CatalystA(config-if)# vrrp 2 priority 100
CatalystA(config-if)# no vrrp 2 preempt
CatalystA(config-if)# vrrp 2 ip 192.168.1.2
CatalystB(config)# interface vlan 50
CatalystB(config-if)# ip address 192.168.1.11 255.255.255.0
CatalystB(config-if)# vrrp 1 priority 100
CatalystB(config-if)# no vrrp 1 preempt
CatalystB(config-if)# vrrp 1 ip 192.168.1.1
CatalystB(config-if)# vrrp 2 priority 200
CatalystB(config-if)# vrrp 2 ip 192.168.1.2
```

You can use the following command to display information about VRRP status on one or more interfaces:

```
Switch# show vrrp [brief]
```

Example 13-6 shows this command executed on both CatalystA and CatalystB, with the output showing the alternating roles for the two VRRP groups configured in Example 13-5.

Example 13-6   *Displaying Switch Roles for VRRP Load Balancing*

```
CatalystA# show vrrp brief
Interface        Grp Pri Time  Own Pre State   Master addr     Group addr
Vlan50            1   200 3218      Y   Master  192.168.1.10    192.168.1.1
Vlan50            2   100 3609          Backup  192.168.1.11    192.168.1.2
CatalystA#
CatalystB# show vrrp brief
Interface        Grp Pri Time  Own Pre State   Master addr     Group addr
Vlan50            1   100 3609          Backup  192.168.1.10    192.168.1.1
Vlan50            2   200 3218      Y   Master  192.168.1.11    192.168.1.2
CatalystB#
```

Table 13-3 compares the detailed VRRP status between the CatalystA and CatalystB switches.

Table 13-3   *Verifying VRRP Status for Multiple VRRP Groups*

CatalystA	CatalystB
CatalystA# **show vrrp**	CatalystB# **show vrrp**
Vlan50 - Group 1	Vlan50 - Group 1
State is Master	State is Backup
Virtual IP address is 192.168.1.1	Virtual IP address is 192.168.1.1
Virtual MAC address is 0000.5e00.0101	Virtual MAC address is 0000.5e00.0101
Advertisement interval is 1.000 sec	Advertisement interval is 1.000 sec
Preemption is enabled	Preemption is disabled
min delay is 0.000 sec	Priority is 100
Priority is 200	Authentication is enabled
Authentication is enabled	Master Router is 192.168.1.10, priority
Master Router is 192.168.1.10 (local),	is 200
priority is 200	Master Advertisement interval is 1.000
Master Advertisement interval is 1.000	sec
sec	Master Down interval is 3.609 sec
Master Down interval is 3.218 sec	(expires in 2.833 sec)
Vlan50 - Group 2	Vlan50 - Group 2
State is Backup	State is Master
Virtual IP address is 192.168.1.2	Virtual IP address is 192.168.1.2
Virtual MAC address is 0000.5e00.0102	Virtual MAC address is 0000.5e00.0102
Advertisement interval is 1.000 sec	Advertisement interval is 1.000 sec
Preemption is disabled	Preemption is enabled
Priority is 100	min delay is 0.000 sec
Authentication is enabled	Priority is 200
Master Router is 192.168.1.11, priority	Authentication is enabled
is 200	Master Router is 192.168.1.11 (local),
Master Advertisement interval is 1.000	priority is 200
sec	Master Advertisement interval is 1.000
Master Down interval is 3.609 sec	sec
(expires in 2.977 sec)	Master Down interval is 3.218 sec
CatalystA#	CatalystB#

Gateway Load Balancing Protocol

You should now know how both HSRP and VRRP can effectively provide a redundant gateway (virtual router) address. You can accomplish load balancing by configuring only multiple HSRP/VRRP groups to have multiple virtual router addresses. More manual configuration is needed so that the client machines are divided among the virtual routers. Each group of clients must point to the appropriate virtual router. This makes load balancing somewhat labor-intensive, having a more or less fixed, or static, behavior.

The Gateway Load Balancing Protocol (GLBP) is a Cisco-proprietary protocol designed to overcome the limitations of existing redundant router protocols. Some of the concepts are the same as with HSRP/VRRP, but the terminology is different, and the behavior is much more dynamic and robust.

> **Note:**   GLBP was introduced in Cisco IOS Software Release 12.2(14)S for routers. At the
> time of this writing, GLBP is available only for the Catalyst 6500 Supervisor 2 with IOS
> Release 12.2(14)SY4 or later and Supervisor 720 with IOS Release 12.2(17a)SX4 switch plat-
> forms.

To provide a virtual router, multiple switches (routers) are assigned to a common GLBP
group. Instead of having just one active router performing forwarding for the virtual router
address, *all* routers in the group can participate and offer load balancing by forwarding a
portion of the overall traffic.

The advantage is that none of the clients has to be pointed toward a specific gateway address; they can all have the same default gateway set to the virtual router IP address. The
load balancing is provided completely through the use of virtual router MAC addresses in
ARP replies returned to the clients. As a client sends an ARP request looking for the virtual router address, GLBP sends back an ARP reply with the virtual MAC address of a selected router in the group. The result is that all clients use the same gateway address but
have differing MAC addresses for it.

Active Virtual Gateway

The trick behind this load balancing lies in the GLBP group. One router is elected the
active virtual gateway (AVG). This router has the highest priority value, or the highest IP
address in the group, if there is no highest priority. The AVG answers all ARP requests for
the virtual router address. Which MAC address it returns depends on which load-balancing algorithm it is configured to use. In any event, the virtual MAC address supported by
one of the routers in the group is returned.

> **Key
> Topic**

The AVG also assigns the necessary virtual MAC addresses to each of the routers participating in the GLBP group. Up to four virtual MAC addresses can be used in any group.
Each of these routers is referred to as an *active virtual forwarder* (AVF), forwarding traffic received on its virtual MAC address. Other routers in the group serve as backup or secondary virtual forwarders, in case the AVF fails. The AVG also assigns secondary roles.

Assign the GLBP priority to a router with the following interface configuration command:

```
Switch(config-if)# glbp group priority level
```

GLBP group numbers range from 0 to 1023. The router priority can be 1 to 255 (255 is the
highest priority), defaulting to 100.

As with HSRP, another router cannot take over an active role until the current active router
fails. GLBP does allow a router to preempt and become the AVG if it has a higher priority
than the current AVG. Use the following command to enable preempting and to set a time
delay before preempting begins:

```
Switch(config-if)# glbp group preempt [delay minimum seconds]
```

Routers participating in GLBP must monitor each other's presence so that another router
can assume the role of a failed router. To do this, the AVG sends periodic hello messages

to each of the other GLBP peers. In addition, it expects to receive hello messages from each of them.

Hello messages are sent at *hellotime* intervals, with a default of 3 seconds. If hellos are not received from a peer within a *holdtime*, defaulting to 10 seconds, that peer is presumed to have failed. You can adjust the GLBP timers with the following interface configuration command:

```
Switch(config-if)# glbp group timers [msec] hellotime [msec] holdtime
```

The timer values normally are given in seconds, unless they are preceded by the **msec** keyword, to indicate milliseconds. The *hellotime* can range from 1 to 60 seconds or from 50 to 60,000 milliseconds. The *holdtime* must be greater than the *hellotime* and can go up to 180 seconds or 180,000 milliseconds. You always should make the *holdtime* at least three times greater than the *hellotime* to give some tolerance to missed or delayed hellos from a functional peer.

Tip: Although you can use the previous command to configure the GLBP timers on each peer router, it is not necessary. Instead, just configure the timers on the router you have identified as the AVG. The AVG will advertise the timer values it is using, and every other peer will learn those values if they have not already been explicitly set.

Active Virtual Forwarder

Each router participating in the GLBP group can become an AVF, if the AVG assigns it that role, along with a virtual MAC address. The virtual MAC addresses always have the form 0007.b4xx.xxyy. The 16-bit value denoted by xx.xx represents six zero bits followed by a 10-bit GLBP group number. The 8-bit yy value is the virtual forwarder number.

By default, GLBP uses the periodic hello messages to detect AVF failures, too. Each router within a GLBP group must send hellos to every other GLBP peer. Hellos also are expected from every other peer. For example, if hellos from the AVF are not received by the AVG before its holdtime timer expires, the AVG assumes that the current AVF has failed. The AVG then assigns the AVF role to another router.

Naturally, the router that is given the new AVF role might already be an AVF for a different virtual MAC address. Although a router can masquerade as two different virtual MAC addresses to support the two AVF functions, it does not make much sense to continue doing that for a long period of time. The AVG maintains two timers that help resolve this condition.

The *redirect* timer is used to determine when the AVG will stop using the old virtual MAC address in ARP replies. The AVF corresponding to the old address continues to act as a gateway for any clients that try to use it.

When the *timeout* timer expires, the old MAC address and the virtual forwarder using it are flushed from all the GLBP peers. The AVG assumes that the previously failed AVF will not return to service, so the resources assigned to it must be reclaimed. At this point, clients still using the old MAC address in their ARP caches must refresh the entry to obtain the new virtual MAC address.

The *redirect* timer defaults to 600 seconds (10 minutes) and can range from 0 to 3600 seconds (1 hour). The *timeout* timer defaults to 14,400 seconds (4 hours) and can range from 700 to 64,800 seconds (18 hours). You can adjust these timers with the following interface configuration command:

```
Switch(config-if)# glbp group timers redirect redirect timeout
```

GLBP also can use a weighting function to determine which router becomes the AVF for a virtual MAC address in a group. Each router begins with a maximum weight value (1 to 254). As specific interfaces go down, the weight is decreased by a configured amount. GLBP uses thresholds to determine when a router can and cannot be the AVF. If the weight falls below the lower threshold, the router must give up its AVF role. When the weight rises above the upper threshold, the router can resume its AVF role.

By default, a router receives a maximum weight of 100. If you want to make a dynamic weighting adjustment, GLBP must know which interfaces to track and how to adjust the weight. You first must define an interface as a tracked object with the following global configuration command:

```
Switch(config)# track object-number interface type mod/num {line-protocol | ip
  routing}
```

The *object-number* is an arbitrary index (1 to 500) that is used for weight adjustment. The condition that triggers an adjustment can be **line-protocol** (the interface line protocol is up) or **ip routing**. (IP routing is enabled, the interface has an IP address, and the interface is up.)

Next, you must define the weighting thresholds for the interface with the following interface configuration command:

```
Switch(config-if)# glbp group weighting maximum [lower lower] [upper upper]
```

The maximum weight can range from 1 to 254 (default 100). The upper (default *maximum*) and lower (default 1) thresholds define when the router can and cannot be the AVF, respectively.

Finally, you must configure GLBP to know which objects to track so that the weighting can be adjusted with the following interface configuration command:

```
Switch(config-if)# glbp group weighting track object-number [decrement value]
```

When the tracked object fails, the weighting is decremented by *value* (1 to 254, default 10).

Likewise, a router that might serve as an AVF cannot preempt another when it has a higher weight value.

GLBP Load Balancing

The AVG establishes load balancing by handing out virtual router MAC addresses to clients in a deterministic fashion. Naturally, the AVG first must inform the AVFs in the group of the virtual MAC address that each should use. Up to four virtual MAC addresses, assigned in sequential order, can be used in a group.

You can use one of the following load-balancing methods in a GLBP group:

- **Round robin**—Each new ARP request for the virtual router address receives the next available virtual MAC address in reply. Traffic load is distributed evenly across all routers participating as AVFs in the group, assuming that each of the clients sends and receives the same amount of traffic. This is the default method used by GLBP.

- **Weighted**—The GLBP group interface's weighting value determines the proportion of traffic that should be sent to that AVF. A higher weighting results in more frequent ARP replies containing the virtual MAC address of that router. If interface tracking is not configured, the maximum weighting value configured is used to set the relative proportions among AVFs.

- **Host dependent**—Each client that generates an ARP request for the virtual router address always receives the same virtual MAC address in reply. This method is used if the clients have a need for a consistent gateway MAC address. (Otherwise, a client could receive replies with different MAC addresses for the router over time, depending on the load-balancing method in use.)

On the AVG router (or its successors), use the following interface configuration command to define the method:

```
Switch(config-if)# glbp group load-balancing [round-robin | weighted | host-
    dependent]
```

Enabling GLBP

To enable GLBP, you must assign a virtual IP address to the group by using the following interface configuration command:

```
Switch(config-if)# glbp group ip [ip-address [secondary]]
```

If the *ip-address* is not given in the command, it is learned from another router in the group. However, if this router is to be the AVG, you must explicitly configure the IP address; otherwise, no other router knows what the value should be.

Figure 13-3 shows a typical network in which three multilayer switches are participating in a common GLBP group. CatalystA is elected the AVG, so it coordinates the entire GLBP process. The AVG answers all ARP requests for the virtual router 192.168.1.1. It has identified itself, CatalystB, and CatalystC as AVFs for the group.

In this figure, round-robin load balancing is being used. Each of the client PCs sends an ARP request to look for the virtual router address (192.168.1.1) in turn, from left to right. Each time the AVG replies, the next sequential virtual MAC address is sent back to a client. After the fourth PC sends a request, all three virtual MAC addresses (and AVF routers) have been used, so the AVG cycles back to the first virtual MAC address.

Notice that only one GLBP group has been configured, and all clients know of only one gateway IP address: 192.168.1.1. However, all uplinks are being used, and all routers are proportionately forwarding traffic.

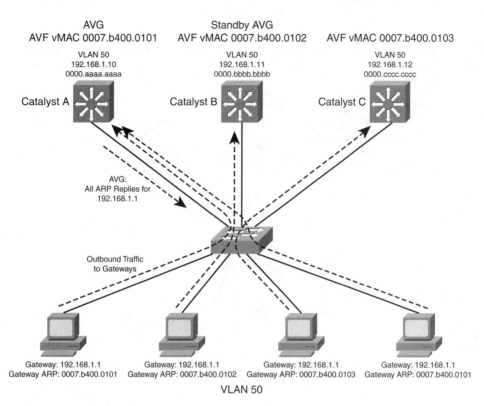

Figure 13-3 *Multilayer Switches in a GLBP Group*

Redundancy is also inherent in the GLBP group: CatalystA is the AVG, but the next-highest priority router can take over if the AVG fails. All routers have been given an AVF role for a unique virtual MAC address in the group. If one AVF fails, some clients remember the last-known virtual MAC address that was handed out. Therefore, another of the routers also takes over the AVF role for the failed router, causing the virtual MAC address to remain alive at all times.

Figure 13-4 shows how these redundancy features react when the current active AVG fails. Before its failure, CatalystA was the AVG because of its higher GLBP priority. After it failed, CatalystB became the AVG, answering ARP requests with the appropriate virtual MAC address for gateway 192.168.1.1. CatalystA also had been acting as an AVF, participating in the gateway load balancing. CatalystB also picks up this responsibility, using its virtual MAC address 0007.b400.0102 along with the one CatalystA had been using, 0007.b400.0101. Therefore, any hosts that know the gateway by any of its virtual MAC addresses still can reach a live gateway or AVF.

You can implement the scenario shown in Figures 13-3 and 13-4 with the configuration commands in Example 13-7 for CatalystA, CatalystB, and CatalystC, respectively.

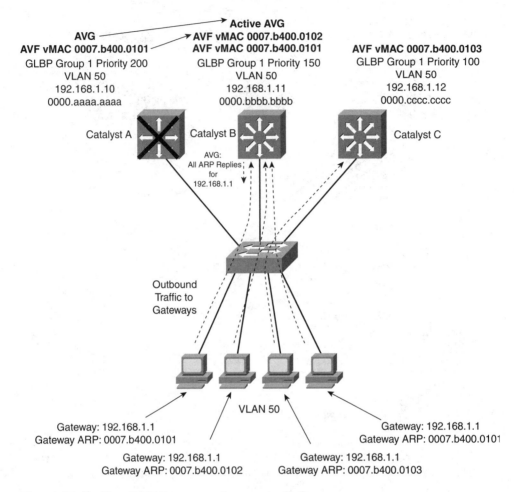

Figure 13-4   *How GLBP Reacts to a Component Failure*

Example 13-7   *Configuring GLBP Load Balancing*

```
CatalystA(config)# interface vlan 50
CatalystA(config-if)# ip address 192.168.1.10 255.255.255.0
CatalystA(config-if)# glbp 1 priority 200
CatalystA(config-if)# glbp 1 preempt
CatalystA(config-if)# glbp 1 ip 192.168.1.1
CatalystB(config)# interface vlan 50
CatalystB(config-if)# ip address 192.168.1.11 255.255.255.0
CatalystB(config-if)# glbp 1 priority 150
CatalystB(config-if)# glbp 1 preempt
CatalystB(config-if)# glbp 1 ip 192.168.1.1
CatalystC(config)# interface vlan 50
CatalystC(config-if)# ip address 192.168.1.12 255.255.255.0
CatalystC(config-if)# glbp 1 priority 100
CatalystC(config-if)# glbp 1 ip 192.168.1.1
```

You can verify GLBP operation with the **show glbp [brief]** command, as demonstrated in Example 13-8. With the **brief** keyword, the GLBP roles are summarized showing the interface, GLBP group number (Grp), virtual forwarder number (Fwd), GLBP priority (Pri), state, and addresses.

Example 13-8   *Verifying GLBP Operation*

```
CatalystA# show glbp brief
Interface   Grp   Fwd   Pri   State     Address          Active router    Standby router
V150        1     -     200   Active    192.168.1.1      local            192.168.1.11
V150        1     1     7     Active    0007.b400.0101   local            -
V150        1     2     7     Listen    0007.b400.0102   192.168.1.11     -
V150        1     3     7     Listen    0007.b400.0103   192.168.1.12     -
CatalystA#
```

```
CatalystB# show glbp brief
Interface   Grp   Fwd   Pri   State     Address          Active router    Standby router
V150        1     -     150   Standby   192.168.1.1      192.168.1.10     local
V150        1     1     7     Listen    0007.b400.0101   192.168.1.10     -
V150        1     2     7     Active    0007.b400.0102   local            -
V150        1     3     7     Listen    0007.b400.0103   192.168.1.12     -
CatalystB#
```

```
CatalystC# show glbp brief
Interface   Grp   Fwd   Pri   State     Address          Active router    Standby router

V150        1     -     100   Listen    192.168.1.1      192.168.1.10     192.168.1.11
V150        1     1     7     Listen    0007.b400.0101   192.168.1.10     -
V150        1     2     7     Listen    0007.b400.0102   192.168.1.11     -
V150        1     3     7     Active    0007.b400.0103   local            -
CatalystC#
```

Notice that CatalystA is shown to be the AVG because it has a dash in the Fwd column and is in the Active state. It also is acting as AVF for virtual forwarder number 1. Because the GLBP group has three routers, there are three virtual forwarders and virtual MAC addresses. CatalystA is in the Listen state for forwarders number 2 and 3, waiting to be given an active role in case one of those AVFs fails.

CatalystB is shown to have the Standby role, waiting to take over in case the AVG fails. It is the AVF for virtual forwarder number 2.

Finally, CatalystC has the lowest GLBP priority, so it stays in the Listen state, waiting for the active or standby AVG to fail. It is also the AVF for virtual forwarder number 3.

You also can display more detailed information about the GLBP configuration and status by omitting the **brief** keyword. Example 13-9 shows this output on the AVG router.

Because this is the AVG, the virtual forwarder roles it has assigned to each of the routers in the GLBP group also are shown.

Example 13-9 *Displaying Detailed GLBP Configuration and Status Information*

```
CatalystA# show glbp
Vlan50 - Group 1
  State is Active
    7 state changes, last state change 03:28:05
  Virtual IP address is 192.168.1.1
  Hello time 3 sec, hold time 10 sec
    Next hello sent in 1.672 secs
  Redirect time 600 sec, forwarder time-out 14400 sec
  Preemption enabled, min delay 0 sec
  Active is local
  Standby is 192.168.1.11, priority 150 (expires in 9.632 sec)
  Priority 200 (configured)
  Weighting 100 (default 100), thresholds: lower 1, upper 100
  Load balancing: round-robin
  There are 3 forwarders (1 active)
  Forwarder 1
    State is Active
      3 state changes, last state change 03:27:37
    MAC address is 0007.b400.0101 (default)
    Owner ID is 00d0.0229.b80a
    Redirection enabled
    Preemption enabled, min delay 30 sec
    Active is local, weighting 100
  Forwarder 2
    State is Listen
    MAC address is 0007.b400.0102 (learnt)
    Owner ID is 0007.b372.dc4a
    Redirection enabled, 598.308 sec remaining (maximum 600 sec)
    Time to live: 14398.308 sec (maximum 14400 sec)
    Preemption enabled, min delay 30 sec
    Active is 192.168.1.11 (primary), weighting 100 (expires in 8.308 sec)
  Forwarder 3
    State is Listen
    MAC address is 0007.b400.0103 (learnt)
    Owner ID is 00d0.ff8a.2c0a
    Redirection enabled, 599.892 sec remaining (maximum 600 sec)
    Time to live: 14399.892 sec (maximum 14400 sec)
    Preemption enabled, min delay 30 sec
    Active is 192.168.1.12 (primary), weighting 100 (expires in 9.892 sec)
CatalystA#
```

Verifying Gateway Redundancy

To verify the operation of the features discussed in this chapter, you can use the commands listed in Table 13-4. In particular, look for the active, standby, or backup routers in use.

Table 13-4   *Gateway Redundancy Verification Commands*

Task	Command Syntax
HSRP and VRRP	
Display HSRP status.	**show standby brief**
Display HSRP on an interface.	**show standby** *type mod/num*
Display VRRP status.	**show vrrp brief all**
Display VRRP on an interface.	**show vrrp interface** *type mod/num*
GLBP	
Display status of a GLBP group.	**show glbp** [*group*] [**brief**]

Supervisor and Route Processor Redundancy

The router or gateway redundancy protocols, such as HSRP, VRRP, and GLBP, can provide high availability only for the default gateway addresses. If one of the redundant gateway routers fails, another can pick up the pieces and appear to be the same gateway address.

But what happens to the devices that are connected directly to the router that fails? If the switching or routing engine fails, packets probably will not get routed and interfaces will go down. Some Cisco switches have the capability to provide redundancy for the supervisor engine itself. This is accomplished by having redundant hardware in place within a switch chassis, ready to take over during a failure.

You also should consider switch power as a vital part of achieving high availability. For example, if a switch has a single power supply and a single power cord, the whole switch will fail if the power supply fails or if the power cord is accidentally unplugged. Some switch platforms can have multiple power supplies; if one power supply fails, another immediately takes over the load.

Redundant Switch Supervisors

Modular switch platforms such as the Catalyst 4500R and 6500 can accept two supervisor modules installed in a single chassis. The first supervisor module to successfully boot becomes the active supervisor for the chassis. The other supervisor remains in a standby role, waiting for the active supervisor to fail.

The active supervisor always is allowed to boot up and become fully initialized and operational. All switching functions are provided by the active supervisor. The standby supervisor, however, is allowed to boot up and initialize only to a certain level. When the active module fails, the standby module can proceed to initialize any remaining functions and take over the active role.

Redundant supervisor modules can be configured in several modes. The redundancy mode affects how the two supervisors handshake and synchronize information. In addition, the mode limits the standby supervisor's state of readiness. The more ready the standby module is allowed to become, the less initialization and failover time will be required.

You can use the following redundancy modes on Catalyst switches:

Key Topic

- **Route processor redundancy (RPR)**—The redundant supervisor is only partially booted and initialized. When the active module fails, the standby module must reload every other module in the switch and then initialize all the supervisor functions.

- **Route processor redundancy plus (RPR+)**—The redundant supervisor is booted, allowing the supervisor and route engine to initialize. No Layer 2 or Layer 3 functions are started, however. When the active module fails, the standby module finishes initializing without reloading other switch modules. This allows switch ports to retain their state.

- **Stateful switchover (SSO)**—The redundant supervisor is fully booted and initialized. Both the startup and running configuration contents are synchronized between the supervisor modules. Layer 2 information is maintained on both supervisors so that hardware switching can continue during a failover. The state of the switch interfaces is also maintained on both supervisors so that links don't flap during a failover.

Tip: Sometimes the redundancy mode terminology can be confusing. In addition to the RPR, RPR+, and SSO terms, you might see single-router mode (SRM) and dual-router mode (DRM).

SRM simply means that two route processors (integrated into the supervisors) are being used, but only one of them is active at any time. In DRM, two route processors are active at all times. HSRP usually is used to provide redundancy in DRM.

Although RPR and RPR+ have only one active supervisor, the route processor portion is not initialized on the standby unit. Therefore, SRM is not compatible with RPR or RPR+.

SRM is inherent with SSO, which brings up the standby route processor. You usually will find the two redundancy terms together, as "SRM with SSO."

Configuring the Redundancy Mode

Table 13-5 details the redundancy modes you can configure on supported switch platforms.

Table 13-5 *Redundancy Modes, Platform Support, and Failover Time*

Redundancy Mode	Supported Platforms	Failover Time
RPR	Catalyst 6500 Supervisors 2 and 720, Catalyst 4500R Supervisors IV and V	Good (> 2 minutes)

continues

Table 13-5   *Redundancy Modes, Platform Support, and Failover Time (Continued)*

Redundancy Mode	Supported Platforms	Failover Time
RPR+	Catalyst 6500 Supervisors 2 and 720	Better (> 30 seconds)
SSO	Catalyst 6500 Supervisor 720, Catalyst 4500R Supervisors IV and V	Best (> 1 second)

Figure 13-5 shows how the supervisor redundancy modes compare with respect to the functions they perform. The shaded functions are performed as the standby supervisor initializes and then waits for the active supervisor to fail. When a failure is detected, the remaining functions must be performed in sequence before the standby supervisor can become fully active. Notice how the redundancy modes get progressively more initialized and ready to become active.

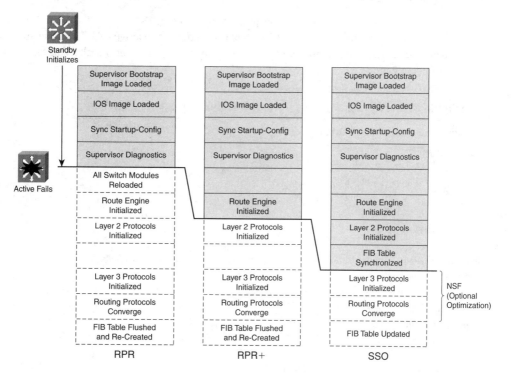

Figure 13-5   *Standby Supervisor Readiness as a Function of Redundancy Mode*

You can configure the supervisor redundancy mode by entering the redundancy configuration mode with the following command:

```
Router(config)# redundancy
```

Next, select the redundancy mode with one of the following commands:

```
Router(config-red)# mode {rpr | rpr-plus | sso}
```

If you are configuring redundancy for the first time on the switch, you must enter the previous commands on both supervisor modules. When the redundancy mode is enabled, you will make all configuration changes on the active supervisor only. The running configuration is synchronized automatically from the active to the standby module.

Tip: If you configure RPR+ with the **rpr-plus** keyword, the supervisor attempts to bring up RPR+ with its peer module. The IOS images must be of exactly the same release before RPR+ will work. If the images differ, the supervisor automatically falls back to RPR mode instead.

You can verify the redundancy mode and state of the supervisor modules by using the following command:

Router# **show redundancy states**

The output in Example 13-10 shows that the switch is using RPR+ and that the second supervisor module (denoted by unit ID 2 and "my state") holds the active role. The other supervisor module is in the standby state and is HOT, meaning that it has initialized as far as the redundancy mode will allow.

Example 13-10 *Verifying Supervisor Module Redundancy Mode and State*

```
Router# show redundancy states
       my state = 13 -ACTIVE
     peer state = 8  -STANDBY HOT
           Mode = Duplex
           Unit = Secondary

        Unit ID = 2

Redundancy Mode (Operational) = Route Processor Redundancy Plus
Redundancy Mode (Configured)  = Route Processor Redundancy Plus
      Split Mode = Disabled
   Manual Swact = Enabled
 Communications = Up

   client count = 11
 client_notification_TMR = 30000 milliseconds
         keep_alive TMR = 9000 milliseconds
       keep_alive count = 1
   keep_alive threshold = 18
         RF debug mask = 0x0
Router#
```

Configuring Supervisor Synchronization

By default, the active supervisor synchronizes its startup configuration and configuration register values with the standby supervisor. You also can specify other information that should be synchronized.

First, use the following commands to enter the main-cpu configuration mode:

```
Router(config)# redundancy
Router(config-red)# main-cpu
```

Then use the following command to specify the information that will be synchronized:

```
Router(config-r-mc)# auto-sync {startup-config | config-register | bootvar}
```

You can repeat the command if you need to use more than one of the keywords. To return to the default, use the **auto-sync standard** command.

Nonstop Forwarding

You can enable another redundancy feature along with SSO on the Catalyst 4500R and 6500 (Supervisor 720 only). Nonstop Forwarding (NSF) is an interactive method that focuses on quickly rebuilding the Routing Information Base (RIB) table after a supervisor switchover. The RIB is used to generate the FIB table for CEF, which is downloaded to any switch modules or hardware that can perform CEF.

Instead of waiting on any configured Layer 3 routing protocols to converge and rebuild the FIB, a router can use NSF to get assistance from other NSF-aware neighbors. The neighbors then can provide routing information to the standby supervisor, allowing the routing tables to be assembled quickly. In a nutshell, the Cisco-proprietary NSF functions must be built in to the routing protocols on both the router that will need assistance and the router that will provide assistance.

NSF is supported by the Border Gateway Protocol (BGP), Enhanced Interior Gateway Routing Protocol (EIGRP), Open Shortest path First (OSPF), and Intermediate System-to-Intermediate System (IS-IS) routing protocols. NSF is available on the Catalyst 6500 Supervisor 720 (with the integrated MSFC3) and on the Catalyst 4500R Supervisor III, IV, and V running IOS Software Release 12.2(20)EWA or later.

To configure NSF, you must add the commands in Table 13-6 to any routing protocol configuration on the switch.

Table 13-6 *Configuring NSF (by Routing Protocol)*

Routing Protocol	Configuration Commands
BGP	Router(config)# **router bgp** *as-number*
	Router(config-router)# **bgp graceful-restart**
EIGRP	Router(config)# **router eigrp** *as-number*
	Router(config-router)# **nsf**

continues

Table 13-6 *Configuring NSF (by Routing Protocol) (Continued)*

Routing Protocol	Configuration Commands
OSPF	Router(config)# **router ospf** *process-id*
	Router(config-router)# **nsf**
IS-IS	Router(config)# **router isis** [*tag*]
	Router(config-router)# **nsf** [**cisco** | **ietf**]
	Router(config-router)# **nsf interval** [*minutes*]
	Router(config-router)# **nsf t3** {**manual** [*seconds*] | **adjacency**}
	Router(config-router)# **nsf interface wait** *seconds*

Exam Preparation Tasks

Review All Key Topics

Review the most important topics in the chapter, noted with the Key Topic icon in the outer margin of the page. Table 13-7 lists a reference of these key topics and the page numbers on which each is found.

Key Topic

Table 13-7 *Key Topics for Chapter 13*

Key Topic Element	Description	Page Number
Paragraph	Explains HSRP active and standby routers	271
Paragraph	Describes the virtual MAC address used by HSRP	275
Paragraph	Discusses VRRP master and backup routers and the virtual MAC address	279
Paragraph	Describes the GLBP active virtual gateway and active virtual forwarder roles	283
List	Describes the methods GLBP uses for load balancing traffic within a GLBP group	286
List	Describes Catalyst supervisor redundancy modes	292
Paragraph	Describes nonstop forwarding	295

Define Key Terms

Define the following key terms from this chapter, and check your answers in the glossary:

HSRP active router, HSRP standby router, VRRP master router, VRRP backup router, active virtual gateway (AVG), active virtual forwarder (AVF), Route Processor Redundancy (RPR), Route Processor Redundancy Plus (RPR+), Stateful Switchover (SSO), nonstop forwarding (NSF)

Use Command Reference to Check Your Memory

This section includes the most important configuration and EXEC commands covered in this chapter. It might not be necessary to memorize the complete syntax of every command, but you should remember the basic keywords that are needed.

To test your memory of the Layer 3 high-availability commands, cover the right side of Tables 13-8 through 13-10 with a piece of paper, read the description on the left side, and then see how much of the command you can remember.

Table 13-8 *HSRP Configuration Commands*

Task	Command Syntax
Set the HSRP priority.	**standby** *group* **priority** *priority*
Set the HSRP timers.	**standby** *group* **timers** *hello holdtime*
Allow router preemption.	**standby** *group* **preempt** [**delay** *seconds*]
Use group authentication.	**standby** *group* **authentication** *string*
Adjust priority by tracking an interface.	**standby** *group* **track** *type mod/num decrement-value*
Assign the virtual router address.	**standby** *group* **ip** *ip-address* [**secondary**]

Table 13-10 *GLBP Configuration Commands*

Task	Command Syntax
Assign a GLBP priority.	**glbp** *group* **priority** *level*
Allow GLBP preemption.	**glbp** *group* **preempt** [**delay minimum** *seconds*]
Define an object to be tracked.	**track** *object-number* **interface** *type mod/num* {**line-protocol** | **ip routing**}
Define the weighting thresholds.	**glbp** *group* **weighting** *maximum* [**lower** *lower*] [**upper** *upper*]
Track an object.	**glbp** *group* **weighting track** *object-number* [**decrement** *value*]
Choose the load-balancing method.	**glbp** *group* **load-balancing** [**round-robin** | **weighted** | **host-dependent**]
Assign a virtual router address.	**glbp** *group* **ip** [*ip-address* [**secondary**]]

Table 13-9   *VRRP Configuration Commands*

Task	Command Syntax
Assign a VRRP router priority (default 100).	**vrrp** *group* **priority** *level*
Alter the advertisement timer (default 1 second).	**vrrp** *group* **timers advertise** [msec] *interval*
Learn the advertisement interval from the master router.	**vrrp** *group* **timers learn**
Disable preempting (default is to preempt).	**no vrrp** *group* **preempt**
Change the preempt delay (default 0 seconds).	**vrrp** *group* **preempt** [**delay** *seconds*]
Use authentication for advertisements.	**vrrp** *group* **authentication** *string*
Assign a virtual IP address.	**vrrp** *group* **ip** *ip-address* [**secondary**]

Remember that the CCNP exam focuses on practical or hands-on skills that are used by a networking professional.

Cisco Published SWITCH Exam Topics Covered in This Part

Prepare infrastructure to support advanced services:

- Implement a wireless extension of a Layer 2 solution

- Implement a VoIP support solution

- Implement video support solution

(Always check Cisco.com for the latest posted exam topics.)

Part IV: Campus Network Services

This chapter covers the following topics that you need to master for the CCNP SWITCH exam:

Power over Ethernet (PoE)—This section discusses how a Catalyst switch can provide power to operate devices such as Cisco IP Phones.

Voice VLANs—This section explains how voice traffic can be carried over the links between an IP Phone and a Catalyst switch.

Voice QoS—This section provides an overview of the mechanisms that provide premium quality of service (QoS) for voice traffic.

CHAPTER 14

IP Telephony

In addition to carrying regular data, switched campus networks can carry packets that are related to telephone calls. Voice over IP (VoIP), otherwise known as *IP telephony* (IPT), uses IP Phones that are connected to switched Ethernet ports.

To properly and effectively carry the traffic for a successful phone call, a combination of many switching features must be used. For example, the Catalyst switches can provide power to IP Phones, form trunk links with IP Phones, and provide the proper level of QoS for voice packet delivery. This chapter covers all these topics as related to the Cisco IP Phone.

"Do I Know This Already?" Quiz

The "Do I Know This Already?" quiz allows you to assess whether you should read this entire chapter thoroughly or jump to the "Exam Preparation Tasks" section. If you are in doubt based on your answers to these questions or your own assessment of your knowledge of the topics, read the entire chapter. Table 14-1 outlines the major headings in this chapter and the "Do I Know This Already?" quiz questions that go with them. You can find the answers in Appendix A, "Answers to the 'Do I Know This Already?' Quizzes."

Table 14-1 *"Do I Know This Already?" Foundation Topics Section-to-Question Mapping*

Foundation Topics Section	Questions Covered in This Section
Power over Ethernet (PoE)	1–2
Voice VLANs	3–8
Voice QoS	9–12

1. For a Catalyst switch to offer Power over Ethernet to a device, what must occur?

    a. Nothing; power always is enabled on a port.

    b. The switch must detect that the device needs inline power.

    c. The device must send a CDP message asking for power.

    d. The switch is configured to turn on power to the port.

2. Which one of these commands can enable Power over Ethernet to a switch interface?

    a. inline power enable

    b. inline power on

    c. power inline on

    d. power inline auto

3. What does a Cisco IP Phone contain to allow it to pass both voice and data packets?

    a. An internal Ethernet hub

    b. An internal two-port switch

    c. An internal three-port switch

    d. An internal four-port switch

4. How can voice traffic be kept separate from any other data traffic through an IP Phone?

    a. Voice and data travel over separate links.

    b. A special-case 802.1Q trunk is used to connect to the switch.

    c. Voice and data can't be separated; they must intermingle on the link.

    d. Voice and data packets both are encapsulated over an ISL trunk.

5. What command configures an IP Phone to use VLAN 9 for voice traffic?

    a. switchport voice vlan 9

    b. switchport voice-vlan 9

    c. switchport voice 9

    d. switchport voip 9

6. What is the default voice VLAN condition for a switch port?

    a. switchport voice vlan 1

    b. switchport voice vlan dot1p

    c. switchport voice vlan untagged

    d. switchport voice vlan none

7. If the following interface configuration commands have been used, what VLAN numbers will the voice and PC data be carried over, respectively?

```
interface gigabitethernet1/0/1
    switchport access vlan 10
    switchport trunk native vlan 20
    switchport voice vlan 50
    switchport mode access
```

    a. VLAN 50, VLAN 20

    b. VLAN 50, VLAN 1

    c. VLAN 1, VLAN 50

    d. VLAN 20, VLAN 50

    e. VLAN 50, VLAN 10

8. What command can verify the voice VLAN used by a Cisco IP Phone?

    a.   show cdp neighbor

    b.   show interface switchport

    c.   show vlan

    d.   show trunk

9. When a PC is connected to the PC switch port on an IP Phone, how is QoS trust handled?

    a.   The IP Phone always trusts the class of service (CoS) information coming from the PC.

    b.   The IP Phone never trusts the PC and always overwrites the CoS bits.

    c.   QoS trust for the PC data is handled at the Catalyst switch port, not the IP Phone.

    d.   The Catalyst switch instructs the IP Phone how to trust the PC QoS information.

10. An IP Phone should mark all incoming traffic from an attached PC to have CoS 1. Complete the following switch command to make that happen:

```
switchport priority extend _____
```

    a.   untrusted

    b.   1

    c.   cos 1

    d.   overwrite 1

11. What command can verify the Power over Ethernet status of each switch port?

    a.   show inline power

    b.   show power inline

    c.   show interface

    d.   show running-config

12. Which DSCP codepoint name usually is used for time-critical packets containing voice data?

    a.   7

    b.   Critical

    c.   AF

    d.   EF

Foundation Topics

Power over Ethernet

A Cisco IP Phone is like any other node on the network—it must have power to operate. Power can come from two sources:

■   An external AC adapter

■   Power over Ethernet (DC) over the network data cable

The external AC adapter plugs into a normal AC wall outlet and provides 48V DC to the phone. These adapters, commonly called *wall warts*, are handy if no other power source is available. However, if a power failure occurs to the room or outlet where the adapter is located, the IP Phone will fail.

A more elegant solution is available as *inline power* or *Power over Ethernet* (PoE). Here, the same 48V DC supply is provided to an IP Phone over the same unshielded twisted-pair cable that is used for Ethernet connectivity. The DC power's source is the Catalyst switch itself. No other power source is needed, unless an AC adapter is required as a redundant source.

PoE has the benefit that it can be managed, monitored, and offered only to an IP Phone. In fact, this capability is not limited to Cisco IP Phones—any device that can request and use inline power in a compatible manner can be used. Otherwise, if a nonpowered device such as a normal PC is plugged into the same switch port, the switch will not offer power to it.

In a best practice design, the Catalyst switch should be connected to an uninterruptible power supply (UPS) so that it continues to receive and offer power even if the regular AC source fails. This allows an IP Phone or other powered device to be available for use even across a power failure.

How PoE Works

A Catalyst switch can offer power over its Ethernet ports only if it is designed to do so. It must have one or more power supplies that are rated for the additional load that will be offered to the connected devices. PoE is available on many platforms, including the Catalyst 3750, Catalyst 4500, and Catalyst 6500.

Two methods provide PoE to connected devices:

■   **Cisco Inline Power (ILP)**—A Cisco-proprietary method developed before the IEEE 802.3af standard

■   **IEEE 802.3af**—A standards-based method that offers vendor interoperability (see http://standards.ieee.org/getieee802/download/802.3af-2003.pdf)

Detecting a Powered Device

The switch always keeps the power disabled when a switch port is down. However, the switch must continually try to detect whether a powered device is connected to a port. If it is, the switch must begin providing power so that the device can initialize and become operational. Only then will the Ethernet link be established.

Because there are two PoE methods, a Catalyst switch tries both to detect a powered device. For IEEE 802.3af, the switch begins by supplying a small voltage across the transmit and receive pairs of the copper twisted-pair connection. It then can measure the resistance across the pairs to detect whether current is being drawn by the device. If 25K ohm resistance is measured, a powered device is indeed present.

The switch also can apply several predetermined voltages to test for corresponding resistance values. These values are applied by the powered device to indicate which of the five IEEE 802.3af power classes it belongs to. Knowing this, the switch can begin allocating the appropriate maximum power needed by the device. Table 14-2 defines the power classes.

Table 14-2 *IEEE 802.3af Power Classes*

Power Class	Maximum Power Offered at 48V DC	Notes
0	15.4 W	Default class
1	4.0 W	Optional class
2	7.0 W	Optional class
3	15.4 W	Optional class
4	Up to 50 W	Optional class (802.3at)

The default class 0 is used if either the switch or the powered device does not support or doesn't attempt the optional power class discovery. While class 4 was reserved under IEEE 802.3af, it is available under IEEE 802.3at, also called PoE Plus, as up to 50 W per connected device. Some Cisco Catalyst switches, such as the Catalyst 3750-E series, also offer up to 20 W of "enhanced PoE" power.

Cisco inline power device discovery takes a totally different approach than IEEE 802.3af. Instead of offering voltage and checking resistance, the switch sends out a 340 kHz test tone on the transmit pair of the twisted-pair Ethernet cable. A tone is transmitted instead of DC power because the switch first must detect an inline power-capable device before offering it power. Otherwise, other types of devices (normal PCs, for example) could be damaged.

A powered device such as a Cisco IP Phone loops the transmit and receives pairs of its Ethernet connection while it is powered off. When it is connected to an inline power switch port, the switch can "hear" its test tone looped back. Then it safely assumes that a known powered device is present, and power can be applied to it.

Supplying Power to a Device

A switch first offers a default power allocation to the powered device. On a Catalyst 3750-24-PWR, for example, an IP Phone first receives 15.4 W (0.32 amps at 48 V DC).

Power can be supplied in two ways:

- For Cisco ILP, inline power is provided over data pairs 2 and 3 (RJ-45 pins 1,2 and 3,6) at 48 V DC.

- For IEEE 802.3af, power can be supplied in the same fashion (pins 1,2 and 3,6) or over pairs 1 and 4 (RJ-45 pins 4,5 and 7,8).

Now the device has a chance to power up and bring up its Ethernet link, too. The power budget offered to the device can be changed from the default to a more appropriate value. This can help prevent the switch from wasting its total power budget on devices that use far less power than the per-port default. With IEEE 802.3af, the power budget can be changed by detecting the device's power class.

For Cisco ILP, the switch can attempt a Cisco Discovery Protocol (CDP) message exchange with the device. If CDP information is returned, the switch can discover the device type (Cisco IP Phone, for example) and the device's actual power requirements. The switch then can reduce the inline power to the amount requested by the device.

To see this in operation, look at Example 14-1. Here, the power was reduced from 15,000 mW to 6300 mW. This output was produced by the **debug ilpower controller** and **debug cdp packets** commands.

Example 14-1 *Displaying Inline Power Adjustment*

```
00:58:46: ILP uses AC Disconnect(Fa1/0/47): state= ILP_DETECTING_S, event=
  PHY_CSCO_DETECTED_EV
00:58:46: %ILPOWER-7-DETECT: Interface Fa1/0/47: Power Device detected: Cisco PD
00:58:46: Ilpower PD device 1 class 2 from interface (Fa1/0/47)
00:58:46: ilpower new power from pd discovery Fa1/0/47, power_status ok
00:58:46: Ilpower interface (Fa1/0/47) power status change, allocated power 15400
00:58:46: ILP Power apply to ( Fa1/0/47 ) Okay
00:58:46: ILP Start PHY Cisco IP phone detection ( Fa1/0/47 ) Okay
00:58:46: %ILPOWER-5-POWER_GRANTED: Interface Fa1/0/47: Power granted
00:58:46: ILP uses AC Disconnect(Fa1/0/47): state= ILP_CSCO_PD_DETECTED_S, event=
  IEEE_PWR_GOOD_EV
00:58:48: ILP State_Machine ( Fa1/0/47 ): State= ILP_PWR_GOOD_USE_IEEE_DISC_S,
  Event= PHY_LINK_UP_EV
00:58:48: ILP uses AC Disconnect(Fa1/0/47): state= ILP_PWR_GOOD_USE_IEEE_DISC_S,
  event= PHY_LINK_UP_EV
00:58:50: %LINK-3-UPDOWN: Interface FastEthernet1/0/47, changed state to up
00:58:50: CDP-AD: Interface FastEthernet1/0/47 coming up
00:58:50: ilpower_powerman_power_available_tlv: about sending patlv on Fa1/0/47
00:58:50:     req id 0, man id 1, pwr avail 15400, pwr man -1
00:58:50: CDP-PA: version 2 packet sent out on FastEthernet1/0/47
00:58:51: %LINEPROTO-5-UPDOWN: Line protocol on Interface FastEthernet1/0/47,
  changed state to up
00:58:54: CDP-PA: Packet received from SIP0012435D594D on interface
  FastEthernet1/0/47
00:58:54: **Entry NOT found in cache**
```

```
00:58:54: Interface(Fa1/0/47) - processing old tlv from cdp, request 6300,
   current
allocated 15400
00:58:54: Interface (Fa1/0/47) efficiency is 100
00:58:54: ilpower_powerman_power_available_tlv: about sending patlv on Fa1/0/47
00:58:54:     req id 0, man id 1, pwr avail 6300, pwr man -1
00:58:54: CDP-PA: version 2 packet sent out on FastEthernet1/0/47
```

Configuring PoE

PoE or inline power configuration is simple. Each switch port can automatically detect the presence of an inline power-capable device before applying power, or the feature can be disabled to ensure that the port can never detect or offer inline power. By default, every switch port attempts to discover an inline-powered device. To change this behavior, use the following interface-configuration commands:

```
Switch(config)# interface type mod/num
Switch(config-if)# power inline {auto [max milli-watts] | static [max
   milli-watts] | never}
```

By default, every switch interface is configured for auto mode, where the device and power budget automatically is discovered. In addition, the default power budget is 15.4 W. You can change the maximum power offered as **max** *milli-watts* (4000 to 15400).

You can configure a **static** power budget for a switch port if you have a device that cannot interact with either of the powered device-discovery methods. Again, you can set the maximum power offered to the device with **max** *milli-watts*. Otherwise, the default value of 15.4 W is used.

If you want to disable PoE on a switch port, use the **never** keyword. Power never will be offered and powered devices never will be detected on that port.

Verifying PoE

You can verify the power status for a switch port with the following EXEC command:

```
Switch# show power inline [type mod/num]
```

Example 14-2 provides some sample output from this command. If the class is shown as **n/a**, Cisco ILP has been used to supply power. Otherwise, the IEEE 802.3af power class (0 through 4) is shown.

Example 14-2 *Displaying PoE Status for Switch Ports*

```
Switch# show power inline
Module   Available    Used     Remaining
          (Watts)    (Watts)    (Watts)
------   ---------   --------   ---------
1           370.0      39.0       331.0
Interface Admin   Oper        Power   Device              Class Max
                              (Watts)
```

```
. . . . . . . . . .   . . . . . .   . . . . . . . . . .   . . . . . . .   . . . . . . . . . . . . . . . . . . . . .   . . . . .   . . . .
Fa1/0/1    auto    on              6.5       AIR-AP1231G-A-K9       n/a     15.4
Fa1/0/2    auto    on              6.3       IP Phone 7940          n/a     15.4
Fa1/0/3    auto    on              6.3       IP Phone 7960          n/a     15.4
Fa1/0/4    auto    on             15.4       Ieee PD                0       15.4
Fa1/0/5    auto    on              4.5       Ieee PD                1       15.4
Fa1/0/6    static  on             15.4       n/a                    n/a     15.4
Fa1/0/7    auto    off             0.0       n/a                    n/a     15.4
[output omitted]
```

Tip: As you plan and implement PoE for IP Phones and wireless access points, be aware of the switch power budget—the total amount of power that a switch can offer end devices. In Example 14-2, the switch has 370 W total available. When power is offered to the connected devices, the switch has no more than 331 W remaining for other powered devices.

Voice VLANs

A Cisco IP Phone provides a data connection for a user's PC, in addition to its own voice data stream. This allows a single Ethernet drop to be installed per user. The IP Phone also can control some aspects of how the packets (both voice and user data) are presented to the switch.

Most Cisco IP Phone models contain a three-port switch, connecting to the upstream switch, the user's PC, and the internal VoIP data stream, as illustrated in Figure 14-1. The voice and user PC ports always function as access-mode switch ports. The port that connects to the upstream switch, however, can operate as an 802.1Q trunk or as an access-mode (single VLAN) port.

The link mode between the IP Phone and the switch is negotiated; you can configure the switch to instruct the phone to use a special-case 802.1Q trunk or a single VLAN access link. With a trunk, the voice traffic can be isolated from other user data, providing security and QoS capabilities.

As an access link, both voice and data must be combined over the single VLAN. This simplifies other aspects of the switch configuration because a separate voice VLAN is not needed, but it could compromise the voice quality, depending on the PC application mix and traffic load.

Voice VLAN Configuration

Although you can configure the IP Phone uplink as a trunk or nontrunk, the real consideration pertains to how the voice traffic will be encapsulated. The voice packets must be carried over a unique voice VLAN (known as the *voice VLAN ID* or *VVID*) or over the regular data VLAN (known as the *native VLAN* or the *port VLAN ID*, *PVID*). The QoS information from the voice packets also must be carried.

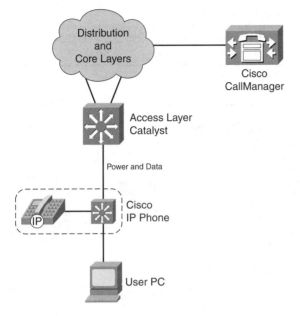

Figure 14-1 *Basic Connections to a Cisco IP Phone*

To configure the IP Phone uplink, just configure the switch port where it connects. The switch instructs the phone to follow the mode that is selected. In addition, the switch port does not need any special trunking configuration commands if a trunk is wanted. If an 802.1Q trunk is needed, a special-case trunk automatically is negotiated by the Dynamic Trunking Protocol (DTP) and CDP.

Use the following interface configuration command to select the voice VLAN mode that will be used:

```
Switch(config-if)# switchport voice vlan {vlan-id | dot1p | untagged | none}
```

Figure 14-2 shows the four different voice VLAN configurations. Pay particular attention to the link between the IP Phone and the switch.

Table 14-3 documents the four different voice VLAN configurations.

Table 14-3 *Trunking Modes with a Cisco IP Phone*

Keyword	Representation in Figure 14-2	Native VLAN (Untagged)	Voice VLAN	Voice QoS (CoS Bits)
vlan-id	A	PC data	VLAN *vlan-id*	802.1p
dot1p	B	PC data	VLAN 0	802.1p
untagged	C	PC data/voice	—	—

continues

Table 14-3   *Trunking Modes with a Cisco IP Phone (Continued)*

Keyword	Representation in Figure 14-2	Native VLAN (Untagged)	Voice VLAN	Voice QoS (CoS Bits)
none (default)	D	PC data/voice	—	—

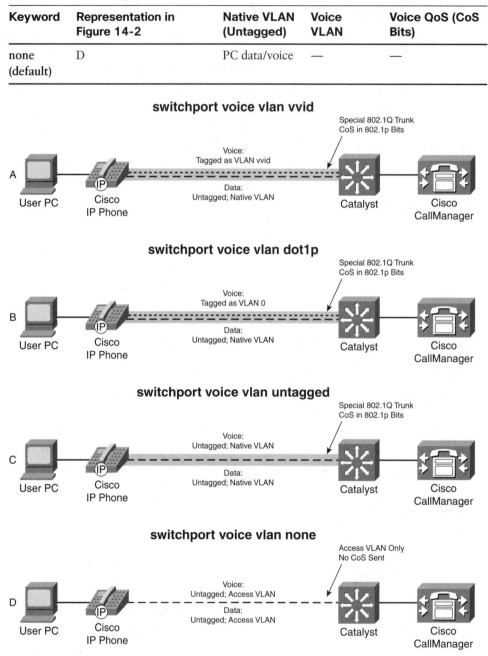

Figure 14-2   *Trunking Modes for Voice VLANs with a Cisco IP Phone*

The default condition for every switch port is **none**, where a trunk is not used. All modes except for **none** use the special-case 802.1Q trunk. The only difference between the **dot1p** and **untagged** modes is the encapsulation of voice traffic. The **dot1p** mode puts the voice packets on VLAN 0, which requires a VLAN ID (not the native VLAN) but doesn't require a unique voice VLAN to be created. The **untagged** mode puts voice packets in the native VLAN, requiring neither a VLAN ID nor a unique voice VLAN.

The most versatile mode uses the *vlan-id*, as shown in case A in Figure 14-2. Here, voice and user data are carried over separate VLANs. VoIP packets in the voice VLAN also carry the CoS bits in the 802.1p trunk encapsulation field.

Be aware that the special-case 802.1Q trunk automatically is enabled through a CDP information exchange between the switch and the IP Phone. The trunk contains only two VLANs—a voice VLAN (tagged VVID) and the data VLAN. The switch port's access VLAN is used as the data VLAN that carries packets to and from a PC that is connected to the phone's PC port.

If an IP Phone is removed and a PC is connected to the same switch port, the PC still will be capable of operating because the data VLAN still will appear as the access VLAN—even though the special trunk no longer is enabled.

Verifying Voice VLAN Operation

You can verify the switch port mode (access or trunk) and the voice VLAN by using the **show interface switchport** command. As demonstrated in Example 14-3, the port is in access mode and uses access VLAN 10 and voice VLAN 110.

Example 14-3 *Verifying Switch Port Mode and Voice VLAN*

```
Switch# show interfaces fastEthernet 1/0/1 switchport
Name: Fa1/0/1
Switchport: Enabled
Administrative Mode: dynamic auto
Operational Mode: static access
Administrative Trunking Encapsulation: negotiate
Operational Trunking Encapsulation: native
Negotiation of Trunking: On
Access Mode VLAN: 10 (VLAN0010)
Trunking Native Mode VLAN: 1 (default)
Administrative Native VLAN tagging: enabled
Voice VLAN: 110 (VoIP)
Administrative private-vlan host-association: none
Administrative private-vlan mapping: none
Administrative private-vlan trunk native VLAN: none
Administrative private-vlan trunk Native VLAN tagging: enabled
Administrative private-vlan trunk encapsulation: dot1q
Administrative private-vlan trunk normal VLANs: none
Administrative private-vlan trunk private VLANs: none
Operational private-vlan: none
```

```
Trunking VLANs Enabled: ALL
Pruning VLANs Enabled: 2-1001
Capture Mode Disabled
Capture VLANs Allowed: ALL
Protected: false
Unknown unicast blocked: disabled
Unknown multicast blocked: disabled
Appliance trust: none
Switch#
```

When the IP Phone trunk is active, it is not shown in the trunking mode from any Cisco IOS Software **show** command. However, you can verify the VLANs being carried over the trunk link by looking at the Spanning Tree Protocol (STP) activity. STP runs with two instances—one for the voice VLAN and one for the data VLAN, which can be seen with the **show spanning-tree interface** command.

For example, suppose that a switch port is configured with access VLAN 10, voice VLAN 110, and native VLAN 99. Example 14-4 shows the switch port configuration and STP information when the switch port is in access mode.

Example 14-4   *IP Phone Trunk Configuration and STP Information*

```
Switch# show running-config interface fastethernet 1/0/1
interface FastEthernet1/0/1
 switchport trunk native vlan 99
 switchport access vlan 10
 switchport voice vlan 110
Switch# show spanning-tree interface fastethernet 1/0/1
Vlan              Role Sts Cost       Prio.Nbr Type
---------------- ---- --- ---------- -------- --------------------------------
VLAN0010          Desg FWD 19         128.51   P2p
VLAN0110          Desg FWD 19         128.51   P2p
Switch#
```

The access VLAN (10) is being used as the data VLAN from the IP Phone.

Voice QoS

On a quiet, underutilized network, a switch generally can forward packets as soon as they are received. However, if a network is congested, packets cannot always be delivered in a timely manner. Traditionally, network congestion has been handled by increasing link bandwidths and switching hardware performance. This does little to address how one type of traffic can be preferred or delivered ahead of another.

Quality of service (QoS) is the overall method used in a network to protect and prioritize time-critical or important traffic. The most important aspect of transporting voice traffic across a switched campus network is maintaining the proper QoS level. Voice packets must be delivered in the most timely fashion possible, with little jitter, little loss, and little delay.

Remember, a user expects to receive a dial tone, a call to go through, and a good-quality audio connection with the far end when an IP Phone is used. Above that, any call that is made could be an emergency 911 call. It is then very important that QoS be implemented properly.

QoS Overview

The majority of this book has discussed how Layer 2 and Layer 3 Catalyst switches forward packets from one switch port to another. On the surface, it might seem that there is only one way to forward packets—just look up the next packet's destination in a content-addressable memory (CAM) or Cisco Express Forwarding (CEF) table and send it on its way. But that addresses only *whether* the packet can be forwarded, not *how* it can be forwarded.

Different types of applications have different requirements for how their data should be sent end to end. For example, it might be acceptable to wait a short time for a web page to be displayed after a user requests it. That same user probably cannot tolerate the same delays in receiving packets that belong to a streaming video presentation or an audio telephone call. Any loss or delay in packet delivery could ruin the purpose of the application.

Three basic things can happen to packets as they are sent from one host to another across a network:

- **Delay**—As a packet is sent from one network device to another, its delivery is delayed by some amount of time. This can be caused by the time required to send the packet serially across a wire, the time required for a router or switch to perform table lookups or make decisions, the time required for the data to travel over a geographically long path, and so on. The total delay from start to finish is called the *latency*. This is seen most easily as the time from when a user presses a key until the time the character is echoed and displayed in a terminal session.

- **Jitter**—Some applications involve the delivery of a stream of related data. As these packets are delivered, variations can occur in the amount of delay so that they do not all arrive at predictable times. The variation in delay is called *jitter*. Audio streams are particularly susceptible to jitter; if the audio data is not played back at a constant rate, the resulting speech or music sounds choppy.

- **Loss**—In extreme cases, packets that enter a congested or error-prone part of the network are simply dropped without delivery. Some amount of packet loss is acceptable and recoverable by applications that use a reliable, connection-oriented protocol such as TCP. Other application protocols are not as tolerant, and dropped packets mean data is missing.

To address and alleviate these conditions, a network can employ three basic types of QoS:

- Best-effort delivery

- Integrated services model

- Differentiated services model

Keep in mind that QoS works toward making policies or promises to improve packet delivery from a sender to a receiver. The same QoS policies should be used on *every* network device that connects the sender to the receiver. QoS must be implemented end to end before it can be totally effective.

Best-Effort Delivery

Key Topic

A network that just forwards packets in the order they were received has no real QoS. Switches and routers then make their "best effort" to deliver packets as quickly as possible, with no regard for the type of traffic or the need for priority service.

To get an idea of how QoS operates in a network, consider a fire truck or an ambulance trying to quickly work its way through a crowded city. The lights are flashing and the siren is sounding to signal that this is a "priority" vehicle needing to get through ahead of everyone else. The priority vehicle does not need to obey normal traffic rules.

However, the best effort scenario says that the fire truck must stay within the normal flow of traffic. At an intersection, it must wait in the line or queue of traffic like any other vehicle—even if its lights and siren are on. It might arrive on time or too late to help, depending on the conditions along the road.

Integrated Services Model

One approach to QoS is the integrated services (IntServ) model. The basic idea is to prearrange a path for priority data along the complete path, from source to destination. Beginning with RFC 1633, the Resource Reservation Protocol (RSVP) was developed as the mechanism for scheduling and reserving adequate path bandwidth for an application.

The source application itself is involved by requesting QoS parameters through RSVP. Each network device along the way must check to see whether it can support the request. When a complete path meeting the minimum requirements is made, the source is signaled with a confirmation. Then the source application can begin using the path.

Applying the fire truck example to the IntServ model, a fire truck would radio ahead to the nearest intersection before it left the firehouse. Police stationed at each intersection would contact each other in turn to announce that the fire truck was coming and to assess the traffic conditions. The police might reserve a special lane so that the fire truck could move at full speed toward the destination, regardless of what other traffic might be present.

Differentiated Services Model

As you might imagine, the IntServ model does not scale very well when many sources are trying to compete with each other to reserve end-to-end bandwidth. Another approach is the differentiated services (DiffServ) model, which permits each network device to handle packets on an individual basis. Each router or switch can be configured with QoS policies to follow, and forwarding decisions are made accordingly.

Key Topic

DiffServ requires no advance reservations; QoS is handled dynamically, in a distributed fashion. In other words, whereas IntServ applies QoS on a per-flow basis, DiffServ applies it on a per-hop basis to a whole group of similar flows. DiffServ also bases its QoS decisions on information contained in each packet header.

Continuing with the emergency vehicle analogy, here police are stationed at every inter-section, as before. However, none of them knows a fire truck is coming until they see the lights or hear the siren. At each intersection, a decision is made as to how to handle the ap-proaching fire truck. Other traffic can be held back, if needed, so that the fire truck can go right through.

Giving premium service to voice traffic focuses almost entirely on the DiffServ model. QoS is a complex and intricate topic in itself. The CCNP SWITCH course and exam cover only the theory behind DiffServ QoS, along with the features and commands that address voice QoS specifically.

DiffServ QoS

DiffServ is a per-hop behavior, with each router or switch inspecting each packet's header to decide how to go about forwarding that packet. All the information needed for this de-cision is carried along with each packet in the header. The packet itself cannot affect how it will be handled. Instead, it merely presents some flags, classifications, or markings that can be used to make a forwarding decision based on QoS policies that are configured into each switch or router along the path.

Layer 2 QoS Classification

Layer 2 frames themselves have no mechanism to indicate the priority or importance of their contents. One frame looks just as important as another. Therefore, a Layer 2 switch can forward frames only according to a best-effort delivery.

When frames are carried from switch to switch, however, an opportunity for classification occurs. Recall that a trunk is used to carry frames from multiple VLANs between switches. The trunk does this by encapsulating the frames and adding a tag indicating the source VLAN number. The encapsulation also includes a field that can mark the class of service (CoS) of each frame. This can be used at switch boundaries to make some QoS de-cisions. After a trunk is unencapsulated at the far-end switch, the CoS information is re-moved and lost.

Key Topic

The two trunk encapsulations handle CoS differently:

- **IEEE 802.1Q**—Each frame is tagged with a 12-bit VLAN ID and a User field. The User field contains three 802.1p priority bits that indicate the frame CoS, a unitless value ranging from 0 (lowest-priority delivery) to 7 (highest-priority delivery). Frames from the native VLAN are not tagged (no VLAN ID or User field), so they receive a default CoS that is configured on the receiving switch.

- **Inter-Switch Link (ISL)**—Each frame is tagged with a 15-bit VLAN ID. In addition, next to the frame Type field is a 4-bit User field. The lower 3 bits of the User field are used as a CoS value. Although ISL is not standards-based, Catalyst switches make CoS seamless by copying the 802.1p CoS bits from an 802.1Q trunk into the User CoS bits of an ISL trunk. This allows CoS information to propagate along trunks of differing encapsulations.

Layer 3 QoS Classification with DSCP

From the beginning, IP packets have always had a type of service (ToS) byte that can be used to mark packets. This byte is divided into a 3-bit IP Precedence value and a 4-bit ToS value. This offers a rather limited mechanism for QoS because only the 3 bits of IP Precedence are used to describe the per-hop QoS behavior.

The DiffServ model keeps the existing IP ToS byte but uses it in a more scalable fashion. This byte also is referred to as the Differentiated Services (DS) field, with a different format, as shown in Figure 14-3. The 6-bit DS value is known as the differentiated service codepoint (DSCP) and is the one value that is examined by any DiffServ network device.

ToS Byte:	P2	P1	P0	T3	T2	T1	T0	Zero
DS Byte:	DS5	DS4	DS3	DS2	DS1	DS0	ECN1	ECN0
	(Class Selector)			(Drop Precedence)				

Figure 14-3 *ToS and DSCP Byte Formats*

Do not be confused by the dual QoS terminology—the ToS and DS bytes are the same, occupying the same location in the IP header. Only the names are different, along with the way the value is interpreted. In fact, the DSCP bits have been arranged to be backward compatible with the IP precedence bits so that a non-DiffServ device still can interpret some QoS information.

The DSCP value is divided into a 3-bit class selector and a 3-bit Drop Precedence value. Table 14-4 shows how the IP precedence, DSCP per-hop behavior, and DSCP codepoint names and numbers relate.

Table 14-4 *Mapping of IP Precedence and DSCP Fields*

IP Precedence (3 Bits)			DSCP (6 Bits)				
Name	Value	Bits	Per-Hop Behavior	Class Selector	Drop Precedence	Codepoint Name	DSCP Bits (Decimal)
Routine	0	000	Default			Default	000 000 (0)
Priority	1	001	AF	1	1: Low	AF11	001 010 (10)
					2: Medium	AF12	001 100 (12)
					3: High	AF13	001 110 (14)
Immediate	2	010	AF	2	1: Low	AF21	010 010 (18)
					2: Medium	AF22	010 100 (20)
					3: High	AF23	010 110 (22)

Table 14-4 *Mapping of IP Precedence and DSCP Fields*

IP Precedence (3 Bits)			DSCP (6 Bits)				
Name	Value	Bits	Per-Hop Behavior	Class Selector	Drop Pre-cedence	Code-point Name	DSCP Bits (Decimal)
Flash	3	011	AF	3	1: Low	AF31	011 010 (26)
					2: Medium	AF32	011 100 (28)
					3: High	AF33	011 110 (30)
Flash Override	4	100	AF	4	1: Low	AF41	100 010 (34)
					2: Medium	AF42	100 100 (36)
					3: High	AF43	100 110 (38)
Critical	5	101	EF			EF	101 110 (46)*
Internet-work Control	6	110					(48–55)
Network Control	7	111					(56–63)

*IP precedence value 5 (DSCP EF) corresponds to the range of DSCP bits 101000 through 101111, or 40–47. However, only the value 101110 or 46 is commonly used and is given the EF designation.

The three class selector bits (DS5 through DS3) coarsely classify packets into one of eight classes:

- Class 0, the default class, offers only best-effort forwarding.

- Classes 1 through 4 are called assured forwarding (AF) service levels. Higher AF class numbers indicate the presence of higher-priority traffic.

  Packets in the AF classes can be dropped, if necessary, with the lower-class numbers the most likely to be dropped. For example, packets with AF Class 4 will be delivered in preference to packets with AF Class 3.

- Class 5 is known as expedited forwarding (EF), with those packets given premium service. EF is the least likely to be dropped, so it always is reserved for time-critical data such as voice traffic.

- Classes 6 and 7 are called internetwork control and network control, respectively, and are set aside for network control traffic. Usually, routers and switches use these classes for things such as the Spanning Tree Protocol and routing protocols. This ensures timely delivery of the packets that keep the network stable and operational.

Key Topic

Each class represented in the DSCP also has three levels of drop precedence, contained in bits DS2 through DS0 (DS0 is always zero):

■   Low (1)

■   Medium (2)

■   High (3)

Within a class, packets marked with a higher drop precedence have the potential for being dropped before those with a lower value. In other words, a lower drop precedence value gives better service. This gives finer granularity to the decision of what packets to drop when necessary.

Tip: The DSCP value can be given as a codepoint name, with the class selector providing the two letters and a number followed by the drop precedence number. For example, class AF Level 2 with drop precedence 1 (low) is written as AF21. The DSCP commonly is given as a decimal value. For AF21, the decimal value is 18. The relationship is confusing, and Table 14-2 should be a handy aid.

You should try to remember a few codepoint names and numbers. Some common values are EF (46) and most of the classes with low drop precedences: AF41 (34), AF31 (26), AF21 (18), and AF11 (10). Naturally, the default DSCP has no name (0).

Implementing QoS for Voice

To manipulate packets according to QoS policies, a switch somehow must identify which level of service each packet should receive. This process is known as *classification*. Each packet is classified according to the type of traffic (UDP or TCP port number, for example), according to parameters matched by an access list or something more complex, such as by stateful inspection of a traffic flow.

Recall that IP packets carry a ToS or DSCP value within their headers as they travel around a network. Frames on a trunk also can have CoS values associated with them. A switch then can decide whether to trust the ToS, DSCP, or CoS values already assigned to inbound packets. If it trusts any of these values, the values are carried over and used to make QoS decisions inside the switch.

If the QoS values are not trusted, they can be reassigned or overruled. This way, a switch can set the values to something known and trusted, and something that falls within the QoS policies that must be met. This prevents nonpriority users in the network from falsely setting the ToS or DSCP values of their packets to inflated levels so that they receive priority service.

Every switch must decide whether to trust incoming QoS values. Generally, an organization should be able to trust QoS parameters anywhere inside its own network. At the boundary with another organization or service provider, QoS typically should not be trusted. It is also prudent to trust only QoS values that have been assigned by the network devices themselves. Therefore, the QoS values produced by the end users should not be trusted until the network can verify or override them.

The perimeter formed by switches that do not trust incoming QoS is called the *trust boundary*. Usually, the trust boundary exists at the farthest reaches of the enterprise network (access-layer switches and WAN or ISP demarcation points). When the trust boundary has been identified and the switches there are configured with untrusted ports, everything else inside the perimeter can be configured to blindly trust incoming QoS values.

Key Topic

> **Tip:** Every switch and router within a network must be configured with the appropriate QoS features and policies so that a trust boundary is completely formed. The SWITCH exam limits QoS coverage to basic QoS configuration using the Auto-QoS feature. You can find more information about advanced QoS topics in the Implementing Cisco Quality of Service (QoS) course

Figure 14-4 shows a simple network in which the trust boundary is defined at the edges, where the network connects to end users and public networks. On Catalyst A, port Gigabit Ethernet2/1 is configured to consider inbound data as untrusted. Catalyst B's port Fast Ethernet0/2 connects to a PC that also is untrusted. The Cisco IP Phone on Catalyst B port Fast Ethernet0/1 is a special case because it supports its own voice traffic and an end user's PC. Therefore, the trust boundary cannot be clearly defined on that switch port.

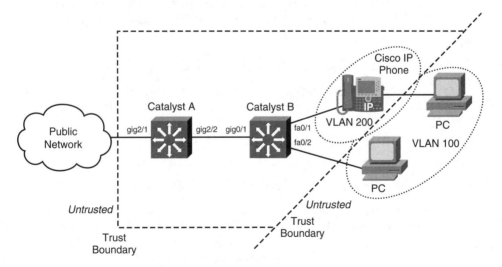

Figure 14-4 *QoS Trust Boundary Example*

Configuring a Trust Boundary

When a Cisco IP Phone is connected to a switch port, think of the phone as another switch (which it is). If you install the phone as a part of your network, you probably can trust the QoS information relayed by the phone.

However, remember that the phone also has two sources of data:

- **The VoIP packets native to the phone—** The phone can control precisely what QoS information is included in the voice packets because it produces those packets.

- **The user PC data switch port—** Packets from the PC data port are generated elsewhere, so the QoS information cannot necessarily be trusted to be correct or fair.

A switch instructs an attached IP Phone through CDP messages on how it should extend QoS trust to its own user data switch port. To configure the trust extension, use the following configuration steps:

Step 1. Enable QoS on the switch:

```
Switch(config)# mls qos
```

By default, QoS is disabled globally on a switch and all QoS information is allowed to pass from one switch port to another. When you enable QoS, all switch ports are configured as untrusted, by default.

Step 2. Define the QoS parameter that will be trusted:

```
Switch(config)# interface type mod/num
Switch(config-if)# mls qos trust {cos | ip-precedence | dscp}
```

You can choose to trust the CoS, IP precedence, or DSCP values of incoming packets on the switch port. Only one of these parameters can be selected. Generally, for Cisco IP Phones, you should use the **cos** keyword because the phone can control the CoS values on its two-VLAN trunk with the switch.

Step 3. Make the trust conditional:

```
Switch(config-if)# mls qos trust device cisco-phone
```

You also can make the QoS trust conditional if a Cisco IP Phone is present. If this command is used, the QoS parameter defined in Step 2 is trusted only if a Cisco IP Phone is detected through CDP. If a phone is not detected, the QoS parameter is not trusted.

Step 4. Instruct the IP Phone on how to extend the trust boundary:

```
Switch(config-if)# switchport priority extend {cos value | trust}
```

Normally, the QoS information from a PC connected to an IP Phone should not be trusted. This is because the PC's applications might try to spoof CoS or DSCP settings to gain premium network service. In this case, use the **cos** keyword so that the CoS bits are overwritten to *value* by the IP Phone as packets are forwarded to the switch. If CoS values from the PC cannot be trusted, they should be overwritten to a value of 0.

In some cases, the PC might be running trusted applications that are allowed to request specific QoS or levels of service. Here, the IP Phone can extend complete QoS trust to the PC, allowing the CoS bits to be forwarded through the phone unmodified. This is done with the **trust** keyword.

By default, a switch instructs an attached IP Phone to consider the PC port as untrusted. The phone will overwrite the CoS values to 0.

What about switch ports that don't connect to end-user or phone devices? Switch uplinks always should be considered as trusted ports—as long as they connect to other trusted devices that are within the QoS boundary. QoS parameters are trusted or overwritten at the network edge, as packets enter the trusted domain. After that, every switch inside the trusted boundary can implicitly trust and use the QoS parameters in any packet passing through.

You can configure a switch uplink port to be trusted with the following commands:

```
Switch(config)# interface type mod/num
Switch(config-if)# mls qos trust cos
```

Here, the trust is not conditional. The switch will trust only the CoS values that are found in the incoming packets.

Tip: A Cisco switch also has a CoS-to-DSCP map that is used to convert inbound CoS values to DSCP values. The CoS information is useful only on trunk interfaces because it can be carried within the trunk encapsulation. CoS must be converted to DSCP or IP precedence, which can be carried along in the IP packet headers on any type of connection.

Switches use a default CoS-to-DSCP mapping, which can be configured or changed. However, this is beyond the scope of the CCNP SWITCH course and exam.

Using Auto-QoS to Simplify a Configuration

You can also configure Cisco switches to support a variety of other QoS mechanisms and parameters. The list of features and configuration commands can be overwhelming, and the actual configuration can be quite complex. This is one reason why the bulk of QoS topics are no longer covered on the SWITCH exam.

Courses and testing aside, you will sometimes need to configure some advanced QoS features on a switch. To reduce the complexity, Cisco introduced the Auto-QoS feature on most switch platforms. By entering only a couple of configuration commands, you can enable the switch to automatically configure a variety of QoS parameters.

Auto-QoS is actually handled by a macro command, which in turn enters many other configuration commands as if they were entered from the command-line interface. Because of this, Auto-QoS is best used on a switch that still has the default QoS configuration. Otherwise, any existing QoS commands could be overwritten or could interfere with the commands produced by the Auto-QoS macro.

Tip: The Auto-QoS feature is designed to automatically configure many more advanced QoS parameters in specific applications. For example, Auto-QoS can be used on switch interfaces where Cisco IP Phones are connected. Auto-QoS is not meant to be used on all switches in a network. Therefore, you should consider using it in access layer switches and not necessarily the network core.

The configuration commands resulting from Auto-QoS were developed from rigorous testing and Cisco best practices. Auto-QoS handles the following types of QoS configuration:

- Enabling QoS

- CoS-to-DSCP mapping for QoS marking

- Ingress and egress queue tuning

- Strict priority queues for egress voice traffic

- Establishing an interface QoS trust boundary

Key Topic

Use the following steps to configure Auto-QoS:

Step 1. Select an interface at the QoS boundary:

```
Switch(config)# interface type mod/num
```

Step 2. Enable Auto-QoS with the appropriate trust:

```
Switch(config-if)# auto qos voip {cisco-phone | cisco-softphone | trust}
```

If the switch port is connected to a Cisco IP Phone, you should use the **cisco-phone** keyword. After that has been enabled, the switch will trust the class of service information presented by the phone, if a phone is detected by CDP. If no phone is connected, the port is considered untrusted.

If a PC running the Cisco SoftPhone application is connected, choose the **cisco-softphone** keyword. Packets that are received with DSCP values of 24, 26, or 46 will be trusted; packets with any other value will have their DSCP values set to 0.

On a switch port acting as an uplink to another switch or router, you should use the **trust** keyword. All packets received on that port will be trusted, and the QoS information will be left intact.

Tip: If you have already configured Auto-QoS on an interface by using the **cisco-phone**, **cisco-softphone**, or **trust** keyword, you won't be allowed to use the **auto qos voip** command again on the same interface. Instead, first remove any existing Auto-QoS by entering the **no auto qos voip** command. Then use the **auto qos voip** command with the desired keyword to enable Auto-QoS.

Remember that the **auto qos voip** command is actually a macro that executes many other configuration commands for you. The **auto qos voip** command will appear in the switch configuration, along with the other commands it enters. You won't see the additional commands until you show the running configuration. However, using the **debug auto qos** EXEC command displays the additional commands in the resulting debug messages. (Do not forget to disable the debugging with **no debug auto qos** when you finish with it.)

Example 14-5 shows what Auto-QoS is doing behind the scenes. By entering one interface configuration command, you can effectively configure many QoS parameters—even if you do not understand their functions. The commands are shown here as a demonstration; the CCNP SWITCH course and exam do not cover their meaning or use.

Interface Fast Ethernet 0/37 normally has a Cisco IP Phone connected to it. Therefore, the **auto qos voip cisco-phone** command is used. Notice that among the many **mls qos** and **wrr-queue** QoS-related commands are two shaded commands that enable trust for CoS values coming from a Cisco phone. Interface Gigabit Ethernet 0/1 is an uplink to another trusted switch, so the **auto qos voip trust** command is used on it. The shaded **mls qos trust cos** command causes the CoS information to be implicitly trusted.

Example 14-5 *Auto-QoS Commands Revealed*

```
Switch# debug auto qos
AutoQoS debugging is on

Switch# config term
Enter configuration commands, one per line.  End with CNTL/Z.

Switch(config)# interface fastethernet 0/37
Switch(config-if)# auto qos voip cisco-phone
Switch(config-if)#

*Sep  7 04:14:41.618 EDT: mls qos map cos-dscp 0 8 16 26 32 46 48 56
*Sep  7 04:14:41.622 EDT: mls qos min-reserve 5 170
*Sep  7 04:14:41.622 EDT: mls qos min-reserve 6 85
*Sep  7 04:14:41.622 EDT: mls qos min-reserve 7 51
*Sep  7 04:14:41.626 EDT: mls qos min-reserve 8 34
*Sep  7 04:14:41.626 EDT: mls qos
*Sep  7 04:14:42.598 EDT: interface FastEthernet0/37
*Sep  7 04:14:42.598 EDT:   mls qos trust device cisco-phone
*Sep  7 04:14:42.602 EDT:   mls qos trust cos
*Sep  7 04:14:42.606 EDT:   wrr-queue bandwidth 10 20 70 1
*Sep  7 04:14:42.610 EDT:   wrr-queue min-reserve 1 5
*Sep  7 04:14:42.618 EDT:   wrr-queue min-reserve 2 6
*Sep  7 04:14:42.626 EDT:   wrr-queue min-reserve 3 7
*Sep  7 04:14:42.634 EDT:   wrr-queue min-reserve 4 8
*Sep  7 04:14:42.642 EDT:   no wrr-queue cos-map
*Sep  7 04:14:42.646 EDT:   wrr-queue cos-map 1   0 1
*Sep  7 04:14:42.650 EDT:   wrr-queue cos-map 2   2 4
*Sep  7 04:14:42.654 EDT:   wrr-queue cos-map 3   3 6 7
*Sep  7 04:14:42.658 EDT:   wrr-queue cos-map 4   5
*Sep  7 04:14:42.662 EDT:   priority-queue out

Switch(config-if)# interface gigabitethernet 0/1
Switch(config-if)# auto qos voip trust
Switch(config-if)#
*Sep  7 15:05:50.943 EDT: interface GigabitEthernet0/1
```

```
*Sep  7 15:05:50.947 EDT:  mls qos trust cos
*Sep  7 15:05:50.951 EDT:  wrr-queue bandwidth 10 20 70 1
*Sep  7 15:05:50.955 EDT:  wrr-queue queue-limit 50 25 15 10
*Sep  7 15:05:50.959 EDT:  no wrr-queue cos-map
*Sep  7 15:05:50.963 EDT:  wrr-queue cos-map 1  0 1
*Sep  7 15:05:50.967 EDT:  wrr-queue cos-map 2  2 4
*Sep  7 15:05:50.971 EDT:  wrr-queue cos-map 3  3 6 7
*Sep  7 15:05:50.975 EDT:  wrr-queue cos-map 4  5
*Sep  7 15:05:50.979 EDT:  priority-queue out
```

Verifying Voice QoS

A switch port can be configured with a QoS trust state with the connected device. If that device is an IP Phone, the switch can instruct the phone on whether to extend QoS trust to an attached PC.

To verify how QoS trust has been extended to the IP Phone itself, use the following EXEC command:

Switch# **show mls qos interface** *type mod/num*

Key Topic

If the port is trusted, all traffic forwarded by the IP Phone is accepted with the QoS information left intact. If the port is not trusted, even the voice packets can have their QoS information overwritten by the switch. Example 14-6 demonstrates some sample output from the **show mls qos interface** command, where the switch port is trusting CoS information from the attached IP Phone.

Example 14-6   *Verifying QoS Trust to the IP Phone*

```
Switch# show mls qos interface fastethernet 0/1
FastEthernet0/1
trust state: trust cos
trust mode: trust cos
trust enabled flag: ena
COS override: dis
default COS: 0
DSCP Mutation Map: Default DSCP Mutation Map
Trust device: none
```

Next, you can verify how the IP Phone has been instructed to treat incoming QoS information from its attached PC or other device. This is shown in the **trust device:** line in Example 14-6, where the device is the IP Phone's device. You also can use the following EXEC command:

Switch# **show interface** *type mod/num* **switchport**

Here, the device trust is called *appliance trust*, as shown in Example 14-7.

Example 14-7   *Alternative Method for Verifying QoS Trust to an IP Phone*

```
Switch# show interface fastethernet 0/1 switchport
Name: Fa0/1
Switchport: Enabled
[output deleted...]
Voice VLAN: 2 (VLAN0002)
Appliance trust: none
```

Again, the IP Phone's device is not being trusted. If the switch port were configured with the **switchport priority extend trust** command, the appliance trust would show *trusted*. Example 14-8 shows the configuration commands that have been added to a switch interface where a Cisco IP Phone is connected.

Example 14-8   *Switch Port Configuration Commands to Support a Cisco IP Phone*

```
Switch# show running-config interface fastethernet 0/47
Building configuration...
Current configuration : 219 bytes
!
interface FastEthernet0/47
 switchport access vlan 10
 switchport trunk encapsulation dot1q
 switchport mode access
switchport voice vlan 100
 mls qos trust device cisco-phone
 mls qos trust cos
 no mdix auto
end
Switch#
```

If the IP Phone is not connected to the switch port, it is not detected and the trust parameter is not enabled, as Example 14-9 demonstrates.

Example 14-9   *Displaying IP Phone Connection and Trust Status*

```
Switch# show mls qos interface fastethernet 0/1
FastEthernet0/1
trust state: not trusted
trust mode: trust cos
trust enabled flag: dis
COS override: dis
default COS: 0
DSCP Mutation Map: Default DSCP Mutation Map
Trust device: cisco-phone
Switch#
```

When a Cisco IP Phone is connected, power is applied and the phone is detected. Then the conditional QoS trust (CoS, in this case) is enabled, as demonstrated in Example 14-10.

Example 14-10   *Conditional Trust (CoS) Enabled on a Cisco IP Phone*

```
6d18h: %ILPOWER-7-DETECT: Interface Fa1/0/1: Power Device detected: Cisco PD
6d18h: %ILPOWER-5-POWER_GRANTED: Interface Fa1/0/1: Power granted
6d18h: %LINK-3-UPDOWN: Interface FastEthernet1/0/1, changed state to up
6d18h: %LINEPROTO-5-UPDOWN: Line protocol on Interface FastEthernet1/0/1, changed
   state to up
6d18h: %SWITCH_QOS_TB-5-TRUST_DEVICE_DETECTED: cisco-phone detected on port Fa1/
   0/1, port trust enabled.
Switch# show mls qos interface fastethernet 1/0/1
FastEthernet1/0/1
trust state: trust cos
trust mode: trust cos
trust enabled flag: ena
COS override: dis
default COS: 0
DSCP Mutation Map: Default DSCP Mutation Map
Trust device: cisco-phone
Switch#
```

If you have used Auto-QoS to configure an interface, you can use the **show auto qos** [**interface** *type mod/num*] command to view the configuration status as demonstrated in Example 14-11.

Example 14-11   *Verifying Auto-Qos Interface Configuration*

```
Switch# show auto qos interface fastethernet 0/37
FastEthernet0/37
auto qos voip cisco-phone
```

Exam Preparation Tasks

Review All Key Topics

Review the most important topics in the chapter, noted with the Key Topic icon in the outer margin of the page. Table 14-5 lists a reference of these key topics and the page numbers on which each is found.

Key
Topic

Table 14-5   *Key Topics for Chapter 14*

Key Topic Element	Description	Page Number
Paragraph	Describes Power over Ethernet for Cisco IP Phones	306
Table	Lists IEEE 802.3af PoE device classes	307
Paragraph	Explains voice VLANs	310
List	Describes delay, jitter, and packet loss—things that can affect packet delivery.	315
Paragraph	Describes best-effort packet delivery	316
Paragraph	Describes the differentiated services QoS model	316
Paragraph	Explains CoS marking on a trunk link	317
List	Describes the DSCP class breakdown, including EF	319
Paragraph	Describes a QoS trust boundary	321
List	Explains how to configure QoS trust on a switch interface	322
List	Explains how to configure Auto-QoS on a switch interface	324
Paragraph	Describes how to verify QoS configuration on a switch interface	326

Complete Tables and Lists from Memory

Print a copy of Appendix C, "Memory Tables," (found on the CD), or at least the section for this chapter, and complete the tables and lists from memory. Appendix D, "Memory Tables Answer Key," also on the CD, includes completed tables and lists to check your work.

Define Key Terms

Define the following key terms from this chapter, and check your answers in the glossary:

Power over Ethernet (PoE), power class, voice VLAN, quality of service (QoS), delay, jitter, packet loss, best effort delivery, differentiated services (DiffServ) model, CoS marking, expedited forwarding (EF), trust boundary, Auto-QoS

Use Command Reference to Check Your Memory

This section includes the most important configuration and EXEC commands covered in this chapter. It might not be necessary to memorize the complete syntax of every command, but you should remember the basic keywords that are needed.

To test your memory of the telephony and voice configuration commands, cover the right side of Tables 14-6 and 14-7 with a piece of paper, read the description on the left side, and then see how much of the command you can remember.

Remember that the CCNP exam focuses on practical or hands-on skills that are used by a networking professional.

Table 14-6 *IP Telephony Configuration Commands*

Task	Command Syntax
Set power over Ethernet behavior.	Switch(config-if)# **power inline** {**auto**	**never**}
Enable QoS globally.	Switch(config)# **mls qos**
Define QoS parameter that will be trusted on an interface.	Switch(config-if)# **mls qos trust** {**cos**	**ip-precedence**	**dscp**}
Conditionally trust a Cisco IP Phone.	Switch(config-if)# **mls qos trust device cisco-phone**
Define the trunking on a port to a Cisco IP Phone.	Switch(config-if)# **switchport voice vlan** {*vlan-id*	**dot1p**	**untagged**	**none**}
Define the trust relationship of the IP Phone.	Switch(config-if)# **switchport priority extend** {**cos** *value*	**trust**}
Enable Auto-QoS on an interface.	Switch(config-if)# **auto qos voip** {**cisco-phone**	**cisco-softphone**	**trust**}

Table 14-7 *IP Telephony Verification Commands*

Task	Command Syntax
Display Power over Ethernet status.	Switch# **show power inline** [*type mod/num*]
Verify the voice VLAN	Switch# **show interface** *type mod/num* **switchport**
Display how QoS trust is extended to the phone.	Switch# **show mls qos interface** *type mod/num*
Verify Auto-QoS settings.	Switch# **show auto qos** [**interface** *type mod/num*]

This chapter covers the following topics that you need to master for the CCNP SWITCH exam:

Wireless LAN Basics—This section discusses wireless networks as they compare to wired Ethernet networks.

WLAN Building Blocks—This section covers wireless service sets in addition to wireless access points and their coverage areas.

WLAN Architecture—This section explores the design and operation of traditional WLANs and the Cisco Unified Wireless network architectures.

Roaming in a Cisco Unified Wireless Network—This section explains various roaming scenarios as a client moves between lightweight APs and controllers.

Configuring Switch Ports for WLAN Use—This section covers the tasks necessary to provide connectivity to WLAN components.

CHAPTER 15

Integrating Wireless LANs

Switched networks generally form the foundation of an enterprise network. Connectivity is offered from the core layer downward to reach end users located at the access layer. Traditionally, these end users have used wires to connect to the access layer.

Wireless networks allow the access layer to be extended to end users without wires. By designing and placing wireless LAN devices across an entire area of the network, end users can even become mobile and move around without losing their network connections.

This chapter presents an overview of the technologies used in wireless LANs. By becoming familiar with these topics, you can understand, design, and use wireless LAN devices to expand your switched network to reach wireless users.

"Do I Know This Already?" Quiz

The "Do I Know This Already?" quiz allows you to assess whether you should read this entire chapter thoroughly or jump to the "Exam Preparation Tasks" section. If you are in doubt based on your answers to these questions or your own assessment of your knowledge of the topics, read the entire chapter. Table 15-1 outlines the major headings in this chapter and the "Do I Know This Already?" quiz questions that go with them. You can find the answers in Appendix A, "Answers to the 'Do I Know This Already?' Quizzes."

Table 15-1 *"Do I Know This Already?" Foundation Topics Section-to-Question Mapping*

Foundation Topics Section	Questions Covered In This Section
Wireless LAN Basics	1–2
WLAN Building Blocks	3–4
WLAN Architecture	5–10
Roaming in a Cisco Unified Wireless Network	11–12
Configuring Switch Ports for WLAN Use	13–16

1. Which one of the following standard sets is used in wireless LANs?

    a. IEEE 802.1

    b. IEEE 802.3

    c. IEEE 802.5

    d. IEEE 802.11

2. Which one of the following methods is used to minimize collisions in a wireless LAN?

    a. CSMA/CD

    b. CSMA/CA

    c. LWAPP

    d. LACP

3. A wireless scenario is made up of five wireless clients and two APs connected by a switch. Which one of the following correctly describes the wireless network?

    a. BSS

    b. ESS

    c. IBSS

    d. CBS

4. If a wireless access point is connected to a switch by a trunk port, which one of the following is mapped to a VLAN?

    a. Channel

    b. Frequency

    c. BSS

    d. SSID

5. Which of the following terms represents a Cisco wireless access point that cannot operate independently?

    a. Autonomous AP

    b. Roaming AP

    c. Lightweight AP

    d. Dependent AP

6. Suppose that an autonomous AP is used to support wireless clients. Which one of the following answers lists the devices that traffic must take when passing from one wireless client to another?

    a. Through the AP only.

    b. Through the AP and its controller.

    c. Through the controller only.

    d. None of these answers is correct; traffic can go directly over the air.

7. Suppose that a lightweight AP is used to support wireless clients. Which one of the following answers lists the device path that traffic must take when passing from one wireless client to another?

    a. Through the AP only.

    b. Through the AP and its controller.

    c. Through the controller only.

    d. None of these answers is correct; traffic can go directly over the air.

8. A lightweight access point is said to have which one of the following architectures?

   a. Proxy MAC

   b. Tunnel MAC

   c. Split-MAC

   d. Fat MAC

9. How does a lightweight access point communicate with a wireless LAN controller?

   a. Through an IPsec tunnel

   b. Through an LWAPP or CAPWAP tunnel

   c. Through a GRE tunnel

   d. Directly over Layer 2

10. Which one of the following types of traffic is sent securely over an LWAPP tunnel?

   a. Control messages

   b. User data

   c. DHCP requests

   d. 802.11 beacons

11. Which one of the following must be consistent for a wireless client to roam between lightweight APs that are managed by the same WLC?

   a. SSID

   b. Mobility group

   c. VLAN ID

   d. AP management VLAN

12. Which one of the following must be consistent for a wireless client to roam between lightweight APs that are managed by two different WLCs?

   a. VLAN ID

   b. SSID

   c. AP management VLAN

   d. Mobility group

13. Which one of the following locations is appropriate for an LAP?

   a. Access-layer switch port

   b. Distribution-layer switch port

   c. Core-layer switch port

   d. Data center switch port

14. Which one of the following locations is appropriate for a WLC?

    a. Access-layer switch port

    b. Distribution-layer switch port

    c. Core-layer switch port

    d. Data center switch port

15. Which one of the following is the correct switch configuration for a port connected to an LAP?

    a. switchport mode trunk

    b. switchport mode lap

    c. switchport mode access

    d. switchport mode transparent

16. Suppose an LAP/WLC combination is used to provide connectivity from SSID "staff" to VLAN 17. Which one of the following is the correct extent for the VLAN?

    a. VLAN 17 exists on the LAP only.

    b. VLAN 17 extends from the LAP to the access switch only.

    c. VLAN 17 extends from the LAP to the WLC.

    d. VLAN 17 extends from the distribution switch to the WLC.

Foundation Topics

Wireless LAN Basics

This chapter presents wireless LAN (WLAN) operation from a practical viewpoint, building on the knowledge you've gained from the switched LAN topics. After all, this is a book (and exam) about switching technology, so you should know enough about wireless LANs to be able to integrate them into your switched network.

Comparing Wireless and Wired LANs

How exactly does a wireless LAN get integrated with a wired LAN? Where does switching fit into a wireless LAN? Before answering these questions, it might be helpful to see how the two technologies compare.

At the most basic level, switched networks involve wires, and wireless networks don't. That might seem silly, but it points out some major differences in the physical layer.

A traditional Ethernet network is defined by the IEEE 802.3 standards. Every Ethernet connection must operate under tightly controlled conditions, especially regarding the physical link itself. For example, the link status, link speed, and duplex mode must all operate like the standards describe. Wireless LANs have a similar arrangement but are defined by the IEEE 802.11 standards.

Wired Ethernet devices have to transmit and receive Ethernet frames according to the carrier sense multiple access/collision detect (CSMA/CD) method. On a shared Ethernet segment, where PCs communicate in half-duplex mode, each PC can freely "talk" first, and then listen for collisions with other devices that are also talking. The whole process of detecting collisions is based on having wired connections of a certain maximum length, with a certain maximum latency as a frame travels from one end of the segment to another before being detected at the far end.

Full-duplex or switched Ethernet links are not plagued with collisions or contention for the bandwidth. They do have to abide by the same specifications, though. For example, Ethernet frames must still be transmitted and received within an expected amount of time on a full-duplex link. This forces the maximum length of full-duplex, twisted-pair cabling to be the same as that of a half-duplex link.

Even though wireless LANs are also based on a set of stringent standards, the wireless medium itself is challenging to control. Generally speaking, when a PC attaches to a wired Ethernet network, it shares that network connection with a known number of other devices that are also connected. When the same PC uses a wireless network, it does so over the air. No wires or outlets exist at the access layer, as other end users are free to use the same air.

A wireless LAN then becomes a shared network, where a varying number of hosts contend for the use of the "air" at any time. Collisions are a fact of life in a wireless LAN because every wireless connection is in half-duplex mode.

> **Tip:**   IEEE 802.11 WLANs are always half duplex because transmitting and receiving stations use the same frequency. Only one station can transmit at any time; otherwise, collisions occur. To achieve full-duplex mode, all transmitting would have to occur on one frequency, and all receiving would occur over a different frequency—much like full-duplex Ethernet links work. Although this is certainly possible and practical, the 802.11 standards do not permit full-duplex operation.

Avoiding Collisions in a WLAN

When two or more wireless stations transmit at the same time, their signals become mixed. Receiving stations can see the result only as garbled data, noise, or errors.

No clear-cut way exists to determine whether a collision has occurred. Even the transmitting stations won't realize it because their receivers must be turned off while they are transmitting. As a basic feedback mechanism, whenever a wireless station transmits a frame, the receiving wireless station must send an acknowledgment back to confirm that the frame was received error-free.

Acknowledgment frames serve as a rudimentary collision detection tool; however, it does not work to prevent collisions from occurring in the first place.

The IEEE 802.11 standards use the CSMA/CA method. Notice that wired 802.3 networks detect collisions, whereas 802.11 networks try to avoid collisions.

Key Topic

Collision avoidance works by requiring all stations to listen before they transmit a frame. When a station has a frame that needs to be sent, one of the two following conditions occurs:

- **No other device is transmitting**—The station can transmit its frame immediately. The intended receiving station must send an acknowledgment frame to confirm that the original frame arrived intact and collision-free.

- **Another device is already transmitting a frame**—The station must wait until the frame in progress has completed; then it must wait a random amount of time before transmitting its own frame.

Wireless frames can vary in size. When a frame is transmitted, how can other stations know when the frame will be completed and the wireless medium is available for others to use? Obviously, stations could simply listen for silence, but doing so is not always efficient. Other stations can listen, too, and would likely decide to transmit at the same time. The 802.11 standards require all stations to wait a short amount of time, called the DCF interframe space (DIFS), before transmitting anything at all.

Transmitting stations can provide an estimate of the amount of time needed to send a frame by including a duration value within the 802.11 header. The duration contains the number of timeslots (typically in microseconds) needed for the size of frame being sent. Other wireless stations must look at the duration value and wait that length of time before considering their own transmissions.

Because every listening station receives and follows the same duration value found in a transmitted frame, every one of them might decide to transmit their own frames after the duration time has elapsed. This would result in a collision—the very condition that should be avoided.

In addition to the duration timer, every wireless station must also implement a random backoff timer. Before transmitting a frame, a station must select a random number of timeslots to wait. This number lies between zero and a maximum contention window value. The idea here is that stations ready to transmit will each wait a random amount of time, minimizing the number of stations that will try to transmit immediately.

This whole process is called the distributed coordination function (DCF) and is illustrated in Figure 15-1. Three wireless users have a frame to send at varying times. The following sequence of events occurs:

1. User A listens and determines that no other users are transmitting. User A transmits his frame and advertises the frame duration.

2. User B has a frame to transmit. He must wait until user A's frame is completed, and then wait until the DIFS period has expired.

3. B waits a random backoff time before attempting to transmit.

4. While user B is waiting, user C has a frame to transmit. He listens and detects that no one is transmitting. User C waits a random time, which is shorter than User B's random time.

5. User B transmits a frame and advertises the frame duration.

6. User C must now wait the duration of user B's frame plus the DIFS time before attempting to transmit again.

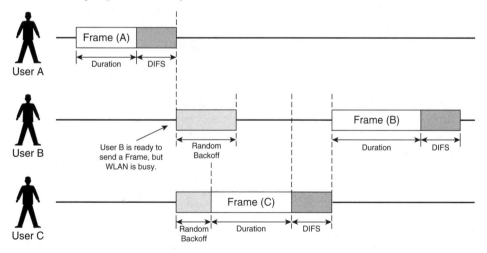

Figure 15-1   *Avoiding Collisions with the DCF Process*

Because the backoff timer is random, a chance still exists that two or more stations will choose the same value. Nothing else will prevent these stations from transmitting at the same time and causing a collision. This will simply be seen as an error over the wireless network; no acknowledgments will be returned, and the stations will have to reconsider sending their frames again.

Finally, what if a station waits until its random backoff timer expires and is ready to transmit, only to find that someone else is already transmitting? The waiting station must now wait the duration of the newly transmitted frame, followed by the DIFS time, and then the random backoff time.

WLAN Building Blocks

At the most basic level, a wireless medium has no inherent organization. For example, a PC with wireless capability can simply bring up its wireless adapter anywhere at any time. Naturally, there must be something else that can also send and receive over the wireless media before the PC can communicate.

Key Topic

Tip: In IEEE 802.11 terminology, any group of wireless devices is known as a service set. The devices must share a common service set identifier (SSID), which is a text string included in every frame sent. If the SSIDs match across the sender and receiver, the two devices can communicate.

The PC, as an end-user station, becomes a client of the wireless network. It must have a wireless network adapter and a supplicant, or software that interacts with the wireless protocols.

The 802.11 standards allow two or more wireless clients to communicate directly with each other, with no other means of network connectivity. This is known as an ad hoc wireless network, or an Independent basic service set (IBSS), as shown in part A of Figure 15-2.

No inherent control exists over the number of devices that can transmit and receive frames over a wireless medium. As well, many variables exist that can affect whether a wireless station can receive from or transmit to other stations. This makes providing reliable wireless access to all stations difficult.

An 802.11 BSS centralizes access and control over a group of wireless devices by placing an access point (AP) as the hub of the service set. Any wireless client attempting to use the wireless network must first arrange a membership with the AP. The AP can require any of the following criteria before allowing a client to join:

- A matching SSID

- A compatible wireless data rate

- Authentication credentials

Membership with the AP is called an *association*. The client must send an association request message, and the AP grants or denies the request by sending an association reply message. When associated, all communications to and from the client must pass through the AP, as shown in part B of Figure 15-2. Clients cannot communicate directly with each other as in an ad hoc network or IBSS.

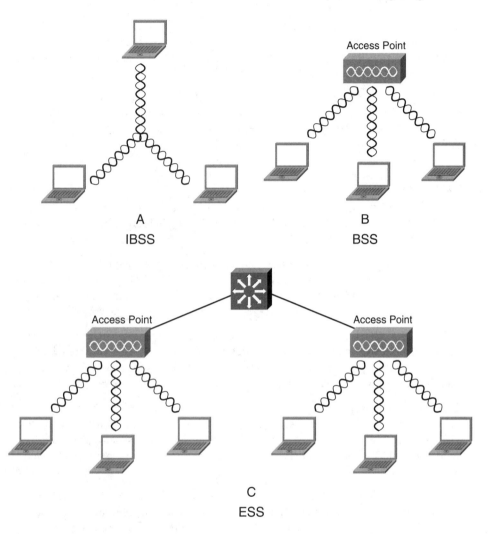

Figure 15-2 *Comparison of Wireless Service Sets*

Tip: Keep in mind that regardless of the association status, any PC is capable of listening to or receiving the frames that are sent over a wireless medium. Frames are freely available over the air to anyone who is within range to receive them.

A wireless AP is not a passive device like an Ethernet hub, however. An AP manages its wireless network, advertises its own existence so that clients can associate, and controls the communication process. For example, recall that every data frame sent successfully (without a collision) over a wireless medium must be acknowledged. The AP is responsible for sending the acknowledgment frames back to the sending stations.

Notice that a BSS involves a single AP and no explicit connection into a regular Ethernet network. In that setting, the AP and its associated clients make up a standalone network.

An AP can also uplink into an Ethernet network because it has both wireless and wired capabilities. If APs are placed at different geographic locations, they can all be interconnected by a switched infrastructure. This is called an 802.11 extended service set (ESS), as shown in part C of Figure 15-2.

In an ESS, a wireless client can associate with one AP while it is physically located near that AP. If the client later moves to a different location, it can associate with a different nearby AP. The 802.11 standards also define a method to allow the client to roam or to be passed from one AP to another as its location changes.

Access Point Operation

An AP's primary function is to bridge wireless data from the air to a normal wired network. An AP can accept "connections" from a number of wireless clients so that they become members of the LAN, as if the same clients were using wired connections.

An AP can also act as a bridge to form a single wireless link from one LAN to another over a long distance. In that case, an AP is needed on each end of the wireless link. AP-to-AP or line-of-sight links are commonly used for connectivity between buildings or between cities.

Cisco has developed an AP platform that can even bridge wireless LAN traffic from AP to AP in a daisy-chain fashion. This allows a large open outdoor area to be covered with a wireless LAN but without the use of network cabling. The APs form a mesh topology, much like an ESS where APs are interconnected by other wireless connections.

APs act as the central point of access (hence the AP name), controlling client access to the wireless LAN. Any client attempting to use the WLAN must first establish an association with an AP. The AP can allow open access so that any client can associate, or it can tighten control by requiring authentication credentials or other criteria before allowing associations.

The WLAN operation is tightly coupled to feedback from the far end of a wireless connection. For example, clients must handshake with an AP before they can associate and use the WLAN. At the most basic level, this assures a working two-way wireless connection because both client and AP must send and receive frames successfully. This process removes the possibility of one-way communication, where the client can hear the AP but the AP can't hear the client.

In addition, the AP can control many aspects of its WLAN by requiring conditions to be met before clients can associate. For example, the AP can require that clients support specific data rates, specific security measures, and specific credentials during client association.

You can think of an AP as a translational bridge, where frames from two dissimilar media are translated and then bridged at Layer 2. In simple terms, the AP is in charge of mapping a VLAN to an SSID. This is shown in the left portion of Figure 15-3, where VLAN 10 on the wired network is being extended to the AP over a switch port in access mode. The AP maps VLAN 10 to the wireless LAN using SSID Marketing. Users associated with the Marketing SSID will appear to be connected to VLAN 10.

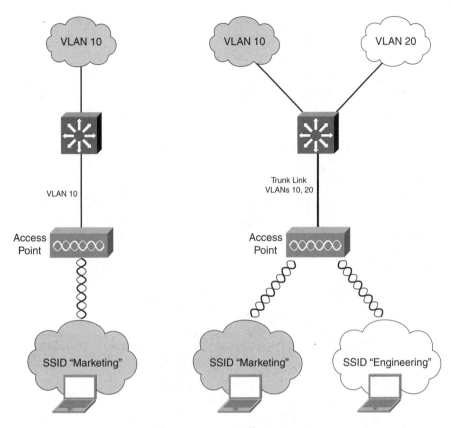

Figure 15-3   *Mapping VLANs to SSIDs*

This concept can be extended so that multiple VLANs are mapped to multiple SSIDs. To do this, the AP must be connected to the switch by a trunk link that carries the VLANs. In the right portion of Figure 15-3, VLAN 10 and VLAN 20 are both trunked to the AP. The AP uses the 802.1Q tag to map the VLAN numbers to SSIDs. For example, VLAN 10 is mapped to SSID Marketing, whereas VLAN 20 is mapped to SSID Engineering.

Key Topic

In effect, when an AP uses multiple SSIDs, it is trunking VLANs over the air to end users. The end users must use the appropriate SSID that has been mapped to their respective VLAN.

Wireless LAN Cells

An AP can provide WLAN connectivity to only the clients within its range. The signal range is roughly defined by the AP's antenna pattern. In an open-air setting, this might be a circular shape surrounding an omnidirectional antenna. At least the pattern will appear as a circle on a floor plan—keep in mind that the pattern is three-dimensional, also affecting floors above and below, in a multilevel building.

The AP's location must be carefully planned so that its range matches up with the coverage area that is needed. Even though you might design the AP's location according to a floor plan or an outdoor layout, the WLAN will operate under changing conditions.

Remember that although the AP's location will remain fixed, the wireless clients will change location quite frequently.

Roaming can make the AP's coverage turn out to be much different than you expect. After all, clients can move around and behind objects in a room, walls and doorways in a building, and so on. People will also be moving about, sometimes blocking the wireless signal.

The best approach to designing an AP's location and range or coverage area is to perform a site survey. A test AP is placed in a desirable spot while a test client moves about, taking live measurements of the signal strength and quality. The idea is to plot the AP's range using the actual environment into which it will be placed, with the actual obstacles that might interfere with the client's operation.

An AP's coverage area is called a cell. Clients within that cell can associate with the AP and use the wireless LAN. This concept is shown in Figure 15-4. One client is located outside the cell because it is beyond the AP's signal range.

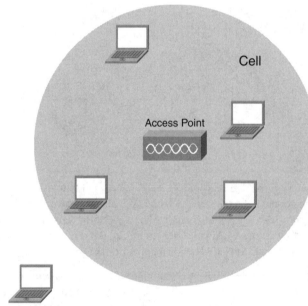

Figure 15-4   *Wireless Clients in an AP Cell*

Suppose that a typical indoor AP cell has a radius of 100 feet covering several rooms or part of a hallway. Clients can move around within that cell area and use the WLAN from any location. However, that one cell is rather limiting because clients might need to operate in other surrounding rooms or on other floors without losing their connectivity.

To expand the overall WLAN coverage area, other cells can be placed in surrounding areas simply by distributing other APs throughout the area. The idea is to place the APs so that their cells cover every area where a client is likely to be located. In fact, their cell areas should overlap each other by a small percentage, as shown in Figure 15-5.

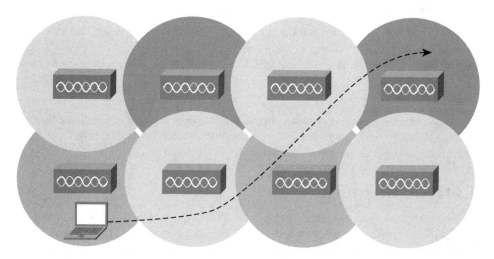

Figure 15-5   *AP Cells Arranged for Seamless Coverage*

Tip: When AP cells overlap, adjacent APs cannot use identical frequencies. If two neighboring APs did use the same frequency, they would only interfere with each other. Instead, AP frequencies must be alternated or staggered across the whole coverage area.

When a client associates with one AP, it can freely move about. As the client moves from one AP's cell into another, the client's association is also passed from one AP to another. Moving from one AP to another is called *roaming*. This movement is also shown in Figure 15-5 as the laptop PC moves along a path that passes through several AP cells.

When a client moves from one AP to another, its association must be established with the new AP. As well, any data that the client was sending just prior to the roaming condition is also relayed from the old AP to the new AP. In this way, any client connects to the WLAN through only one AP at a time. This also minimizes the chance that any data being sent or received while roaming is lost.

If the client maintains its same IP address as it roams between APs, it undergoes *Layer 2 roaming*. If the client roams between APs located in different IP subnets, it undergoes *Layer 3 roaming*.

When you design a wireless LAN, you might be tempted to try to cover the most area possible with each AP. You could run each AP at its maximum transmit power to make the most of its range. Doing so would also reduce the number of APs necessary to cover an area, which would in turn reduce the overall cost. However, you should consider some other factors.

When an AP is configured to provide a large coverage area, it also opens the potential for overcrowding. Remember that an AP cell is essentially a half-duplex shared medium that all clients must share. As the number of clients goes up, the amount of available bandwidth and airtime goes down.

Instead, consider reducing the cell size (by reducing the transmit power) so that only clients in close proximity to the AP can associate and use bandwidth. The AP can also assist in controlling the number of clients that associate at any given time. This becomes important for time-critical or bandwidth-intensive traffic such as voice, video, and medical applications.

When cell sizes are reduced, they are often called *microcells*. This concept can be further extended for extremely controlled environments like stock exchanges. In those cases, the AP power and cell size are minimized, and the cells are called *picocells*.

WLAN Architecture

Wireless networks have traditionally consisted of individually configured and individually operating access points scattered about. Monitoring and maintaining such a diverse network has become too much of an administrative chore. The following sections explore the traditional architecture as well as the Cisco technologies used to provide a unified and centrally managed wireless network.

Traditional WLAN Architecture

Traditional WLAN architecture centers around the wireless access point. Each AP serves as the central hub of its own BSS, where clients located with the AP cell gain an association. The traffic to and from each client has to pass through the AP to reach any other part of the network.

Notice that even though an AP is centrally positioned to support its clients, it is quite isolated and self-sufficient. Each AP must be configured individually, although many APs might be configured with identical network policies. Each AP also operates independently—the AP handles its own use of radio frequency (RF) channels, clients associate with the AP directly, the AP enforces any security policies unassisted, and so on.

Key Topic

In a nutshell, each AP is standalone or autonomous within the larger network. Cisco calls this an *autonomous mode AP* to distinguish it from other architectures.

Because each AP is autonomous, managing security over the wireless network can be difficult. Each autonomous AP handles its own security policies, with no central point of entry between the wireless and wired networks. That means no convenient place exists for monitoring traffic for things like intrusion detection and prevention, quality of service, bandwidth policing, and so on.

Finally, managing the RF operation of many autonomous APs can be quite difficult. As the network administrator, you are in charge of selecting and configuring AP channels and detecting and resolving rogue APs that might be interfering. You must also manage things such as AP output power, ensuring the wireless coverage is sufficient, that it does not overlap too much, and that no coverage holes exist—even when an AP's radio fails.

Cisco has realized the autonomous AP shortcomings and has offered a more unified approach. You should understand some important concepts about WLANs that are based on autonomous APs so that you can compare the traditional architecture to the unified architecture, as it is presented in the next section.

First, consider the traffic patterns in an autonomous AP architecture. Figure 15-6 shows two wireless clients associated with an autonomous AP. All traffic to and from the clients must pass through the AP. Notice how traffic from Client A to some other part of the network passes through the AP, where it is bridged onto the switched network. Even traffic between two wireless clients cannot travel directly over the air—it must first pass through the AP and back out to the other client.

Key Topic

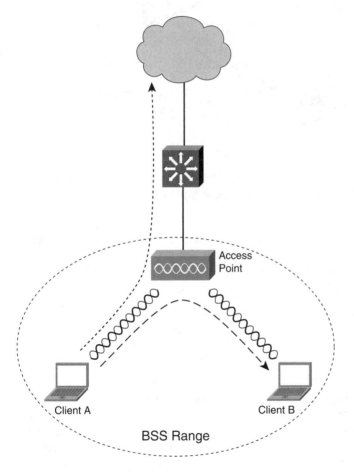

Figure 15-6 *Traffic Patterns Through an Autonomous AP*

Recall that an AP can support multiple SSIDs if multiple VLANs are extended to it over a trunk link. If you want to offer the same SSIDs from several autonomous APs, the VLANs must be extended to the APs in a contiguous fashion. This means that the switched network must carry the VLANs to each and every AP that needs them, as shown in Figure 15-7.

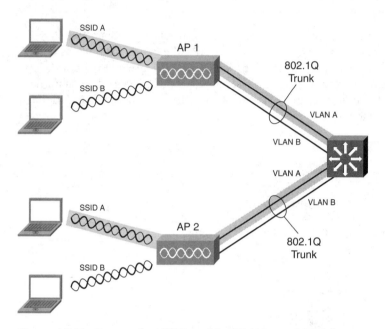

Figure 15-7   *Extent of an SSID and Its VLAN over Multiple Autonomous APs*

In the figure, SSID A and SSID B are offered on two APs. The two SSIDs correspond to VLAN A and VLAN B, respectively. The APs must be connected to a common switched network that extends VLANs A and B at Layer 2. This is done by carrying VLANs A and B over an 802.1Q trunk link to each AP.

Because SSIDs and their VLANs must be extended at Layer 2, you should consider how they are extended throughout the switched network. In Figure 15-7, SSID A and VLAN A have been shaded everywhere they appear. Naturally, they form a contiguous path that appears on both APs so that wireless clients can use SSID A in either location or while roaming between the two.

This concept becomes important when you think about extending SSIDs to many APs over a larger network. Perhaps you would like to offer an SSID on any AP served by your infrastructure so that wireless clients can roam anywhere in the area. To do that, the SSID and its VLAN would have to be extended everywhere that the user could possibly roam. This has the potential to look like an end-to-end or campuswide VLAN—something that goes against good network design practice, as presented in the early chapters of this book.

Cisco Unified Wireless Network Architecture

Cisco has collected a complete set of functions that are integral to wireless LANs and called them the Cisco Unified Wireless Network. This new architecture offers the following capabilities, which are centralized so that they affect wireless LAN devices located anywhere in the network:

■ WLAN security

■ WLAN deployment

■ WLAN management

■ WLAN control

To centralize these aspects of a WLAN, many of the functions found within autonomous APs have to be shifted toward some central location. The top portion of Figure 15-8 lists most of the activities performed by an autonomous AP. Notice that they have been grouped by real-time processes on the left and management processes on the right.

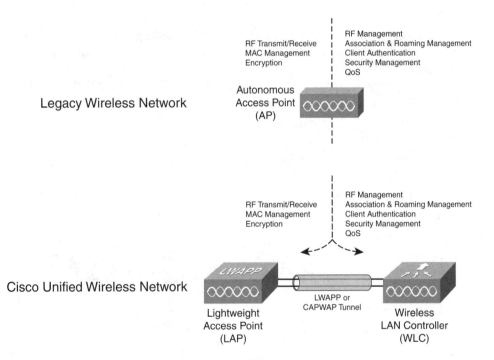

Figure 15-8 *Autonomous Versus Lightweight Access Points*

The real-time processes involve actually sending and receiving 802.11 frames, AP beacons, and probe messages. Data encryption is also handled in a real-time, per-packet basis. The AP must interact with wireless clients at the MAC layer. These functions must stay with the AP hardware, closest to the clients.

The management functions are not integral to handling frames over the RF channels but are things that should be centrally administered. Therefore, those functions are moved to a centrally located platform away from the AP.

In the Cisco unified wireless network, a lightweight access point (LAP) performs only the real-time 802.11 operation. The LAP gets its name because the code image and the local intelligence are stripped down, or lightweight, compared to the traditional autonomous AP.

The management functions are all performed on a wireless LAN controller (WLC), which is common to many LAPs. This is shown in the bottom portion of Figure 15-8. Notice that the LAP is left with duties in Layers 1 and 2, where frames are moved into and out of the RF domain. The LAP becomes totally dependent on the WLC for every other WLAN function, such as authenticating users, managing security policies, and even selecting RF channels and output power!

This division of labor is known as a *split-MAC architecture*, where the normal MAC operations are pulled apart into two distinct locations. This occurs for every LAP in the network—each one must bind itself to a WLC to boot up and support wireless clients. The WLC becomes the central hub that supports a number of LAPs scattered about in the switched network.

How does an LAP bind with a WLC to form a complete working access point? The two devices must bring up a tunnel between them to carry 802.11-related messages and also client data. Remember that the LAP and WLC can be located on the same VLAN or IP subnet, but they don't have to be. Instead, they can be located on two entirely different IP subnets in two entirely different locations.

The tunnel makes this all possible by encapsulating the data between the LAP and WLC within new IP packets. The tunneled data can then be switched or routed across the campus network, as shown in Figure 15-9.

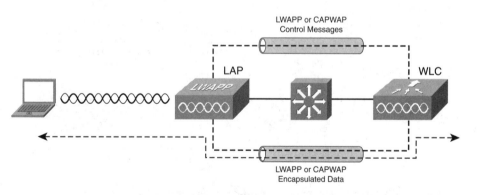

Figure 15-9 *Linking an LAP and WLC with LWAPP or CAPWAP*

The LAP and WLC pair uses either the Lightweight Access Point Protocol (LWAPP, developed by Cisco) or the Control and Provisioning Wireless Access Points protocol (CAPWAP, defined in RFC 4118) as the tunneling mechanism. Actually, these protocols consist of the two tunnels shown in Figure 15-9:

- **Control messages**—Exchanges that are used to configure the LAP and manage its operation. The control messages are authenticated and encrypted so that the LAP is securely controlled by only the WLC.

- **Data**—Packets to and from wireless clients associated with the LAP. The data is encapsulated within the LWAPP or CAPWAP protocol but is not encrypted or otherwise secured between the LAP and WLC.

Tip: Although Cisco developed LWAPP, it submitted the protocol as an IETF draft. The result is the CAPWAP standard in RFC 4118. LWAPP uses UDP destination ports 12222 and 12223 on the WLC end. Similarly, CAPWAP uses UDP ports 5246 and 5247.

Every LAP and WLC must also authenticate each other with digital certificates. An X.509 certificate is preinstalled in each device when it is purchased. By using certificates behind the scenes, every device is properly authenticated before becoming part of the Cisco Unified Wireless Network. This process helps ensure that no rogue LAP or WLC (or devices posing as an LAP or WLC) can be introduced into the network.

WLC Functions

When LWAPP or CAPWAP tunnels are built from a WLC to one or more LAPs, the WLC can begin offering a variety of additional functions. Think of all the puzzles and shortcomings that were discussed for the traditional WLAN architecture as you read over the following list of WLC activities:

- **Dynamic channel assignment**—The WLC chooses and configures the RF channel used by each LAP based on other active access points in the area.

- **Transmit power optimization**—The WLC sets the transmit power of each LAP based on the coverage area needed. Transmit power is also automatically adjusted periodically.

- **Self-healing wireless coverage**—If an LAP radio dies, the coverage hole is "healed" by turning up the transmit power of surrounding LAPs automatically.

- **Flexible client roaming**—Clients can roam at either Layer 2 or Layer 3 with very fast roaming times.

- **Dynamic client load balancing**—If two or more LAPs are positioned to cover the same geographic area, the WLC can associate clients with the least used LAP. This distributes the client load across the LAPs.

- **RF monitoring**—The WLC manages each LAP so that it scans channels to monitor the RF usage. By listening to a channel, the WLC can remotely gather information about RF interference, noise, signals from surrounding LAPs, and signals from rogue APs or ad-hoc clients.

- **Security management**—The WLC can require wireless clients to obtain an IP address from a trusted DHCP server before allowing them to associate and access the WLAN.

Cisco WLCs are available in several platforms, differing mainly in the number of managed LAPs. Table 15-2 lists some WLC platforms.

Table 15-2   *Cisco WLC Platforms and Capabilities*

Model	Interface	Attribute
2100	8 10/100TX	Handles up to 6, 12, or 25 LAPs
4402	2 GigE	Handles up to 12, 25, or 50 LAPs
4404	4 GigE	Handles up to 100 LAPs
5500	8 GigE	Handles up to 12, 25, 50, 100, or 250 LAPs
WiSM	4 GigE bundled in an Ether-Channel for each controller	Catalyst 6500 module with two WLCs; handles up to 300 LAPs (150 per controller); up to 5 WiSMs in a single chassis
WLC module for ISR routers	Can be integrated in 2800 and 3800 routers	Handles up to 6, 8, 12, or 25 LAPs
Catalyst 3750G integrated WLC	N/A (integrated in 24-port 10/100/1000TX switch)	Handles up to 50 LAPs per switch, up to 200 LAPs per switch stack

You can also deploy several WLCs in a network to handle a large number of LAPs. In addition, multiple WLCs offer some redundancy so that LAPs can recover from a WLC failure.

Managing several WLCs can require a significant effort, due to the number of LAPs and clients to be managed and monitored. The Cisco Wireless Control System (WCS) is an optional server platform that can be used as a single GUI front-end to all the WLCs in a network. From the WCS, you can perform any WLAN management or configuration task, as well as RF planning and wireless user tracking.

The WCS uses building floor plans to display dynamic representations of wireless coverage. It can also be fed information about the building construction to improve its concept of RF signal propagation. Once this is done, the WCS can locate a wireless client to within a few meters by triangulating the client's signal as received by multiple LAPs.

The WCS can be teamed with the Cisco Wireless Location Appliance to track the location of thousands of wireless clients. You can even deploy active 802.11 RFID tags to track objects as they move around in the wireless coverage area. Tracking objects by their MAC addresses can be handy when you need to locate a rogue or malicious wireless client, or when you need to track corporate assets that tend to move around within a building or complex.

Lightweight AP Operation

The LAP is designed to be a "zero-touch" configuration. The LAP must find a WLC and obtain all of its configuration parameters, so you never have to actually configure it through its console port or over the network.

The following sequence of steps detail the bootstrap process that an LAP must complete before it becomes active:

Step 1.   The LAP obtains an IP address from a DHCP server.

Step 2.   The LAP learns the IP addresses of any available WLCs.

Step 3.   The LAP sends a join request to the first WLC in its list of addresses. If that one fails to answer, the next WLC is tried. When a WLC accepts the LAP, it sends a join reply back to the LAP, effectively binding the two devices.

Step 4.   The WLC compares the LAP's code image release to the code release stored locally. If they differ, the LAP downloads the code image stored on the WLC and reboots itself.

Step 5.   The WLC and LAP build a secure LWAPP or CAPWAP tunnel for management traffic and an LWAPP or CAPWAP tunnel (not secured) for wireless client data.

You should notice a couple of things from this list. In Step 2, the LAP can find the WLC IP addresses using any of these methods:

■   A DHCP server that adds option 43 to its reply containing a list of WLC addresses.

■   With the IP subnet broadcast option, the LAP broadcasts a join request message, hoping that a WLC is also connected to the local subnet or VLAN. This method works only if the LAP and WLC are Layer 2-adjacent.

An LAP is always joined or bound to one WLC at any time. However, the LAP can maintain a list of up to three WLCs (primary, secondary, and tertiary). As the LAP boots, it tries to contact each WLC address in sequential order. If it cannot find a responding WLC at all, the LAP tries an IP subnet broadcast to find any available WLC.

Suppose that the LAP has booted up and has successfully joined a WLC. If that WLC fails for some reason, the LAP will no longer be able to forward traffic or to maintain client associations. Therefore, when the LAP realizes its WLC is no longer responding, it reboots and begins the process of searching for live WLCs again. This means any client associations will be dropped while the LAP reboots and joins a different controller.

Tip: When an LAP is cut off from a WLC, client associations are normally dropped and no data can pass over the WLAN between clients. Cisco Hybrid Remote Edge Access Point (HREAP) is a special case for remote sites where the LAPs are separated from the WLC by a WAN link. With HREAP, the remote LAPs can keep operating even while the WAN link is down and their WLC is not available, much like an autonomous AP would do. This allows wireless users to keep communicating within the remote site until the link (and WLC) is restored.

Traffic Patterns in a Cisco Unified Wireless Network

Because the LAPs connect to the wired network through logical LWAPP or CAPWAP tunnels, the traffic patterns into and out of the WLAN are different than traditional WLANs.

Consider the network shown in Figure 15-10. Two wireless clients are associated with the WLAN that is formed by the LAP and WLC combination. Traffic from Client A to a host somewhere on the network travels through the LAP, through the tunnel to the WLC, and then out onto the switched campus network.

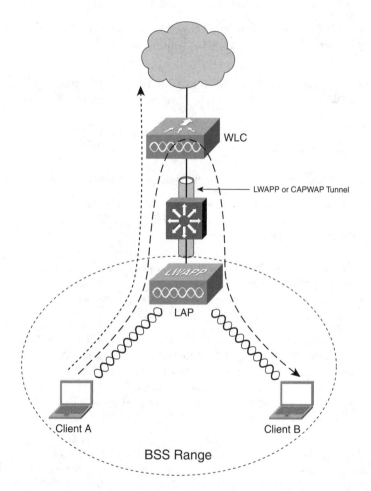

Figure 15-10 *Traffic Patterns Through an LAP*

Traffic between the two wireless clients, however, takes an interesting path. That traffic must go from Client A through the LAP, through the LWAPP or CAPWAP tunnel, into the WLC, back through the tunnel, through the LAP and on to Client B. This further illustrates what a vital role the WLC plays in the unified infrastructure.

Tip: Even though all traffic into and out of the WLAN must pass through the LWAPP or CAPWAP tunnel and the WLC, not all traffic operations are applied end-to-end across the tunnel.

For example, wireless encryption can still be used to secure data over the air, as with traditional WLANs. However, the encrypted data does not pass through the LWAPP or CAPWAP tunnel at all. Packets are encrypted as they leave the wireless client and unencrypted when they arrive on the LAP. The same is true for packet authentication, if it is used.

All the packet authentication and encryption functions remain within the LAP hardware and are not distributed to the WLC at all.

When autonomous APs are used in a network, the access VLANs serving the wireless clients must be extended or trunked all the way out to touch the APs. This is not true for LAPs.

First, consider the sample network shown in Figure 15-11. Two VLANs A and B are used to carry wireless client traffic that is associated to the respective SSIDs A and B. Notice that VLANs A and B exist on the trunk from switch SW2 to the WLC but go no further. Also notice that the WLC and the LAPs are connected by VLAN Z—something that is totally isolated from access VLANs A and B.

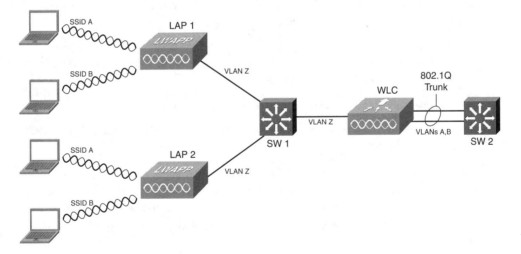

Figure 15-11 *Unified Wireless Network Supporting Multiple VLANs and SSIDs*

The access VLANs are actually carried over the LWAPP tunnel so that they logically touch the LAPs where the users reside. This is shown in Figure 15-12, where VLAN A is shaded as it extends to the two LAPs as SSID A.

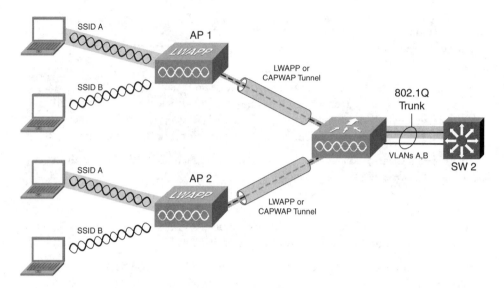

Figure 15-12 *VLAN A Extending over LWAPP/CAPWAP Tunnels*

Roaming in a Cisco Unified Wireless Network

Wireless clients must negotiate an association with LAPs, as with any 802.11 wireless network. However, the split-MAC architecture has an interesting effect on client associations.

Remember that the LAP handles mostly real-time wireless duties, so it will just pass the client's association requests on up to the WLC. In effect, the wireless clients negotiate their associations with the WLC directly. This is important for two reasons:

- All client associations can be managed in a central location.

- Client roaming becomes faster and easier; associations can be maintained or handed off at the controller level.

With autonomous APs, a client roams by moving its association from one AP to another. The client must negotiate the move with each AP independently, and the APs must also make sure any buffered data from the client is passed along to follow the association. Autonomous roaming occurs only at Layer 2; some other means must be added to support Layer 3 roaming.

With LAPs, a client still roams by moving its association. From the client's point of view, the association moves from AP to AP; actually it moves from WLC to WLC, according to the AP-WLC bindings.

Through the WLCs, LAPs can support both Layer 2 and Layer 3 roaming. Remember that the client's association is always contained within an LWAPP or CAPWAP tunnel. Moving to a new AP also moves the association into a new tunnel—the tunnel that connects the new AP to its WLC. The client's IP address can remain the same while roaming, no matter which tunnel the client passes through to reach the controllers.

The following sections discuss client roaming from the aspect of the WLC, where roaming and client associations are managed.

Intracontroller Roaming

In Figure 15-13, a wireless client has an active wireless association at location A. The association is with WLC1 through AP1. As you might expect, all traffic to and from the client passes through the LWAPP or CAPWAP tunnel between AP1 and WLC1.

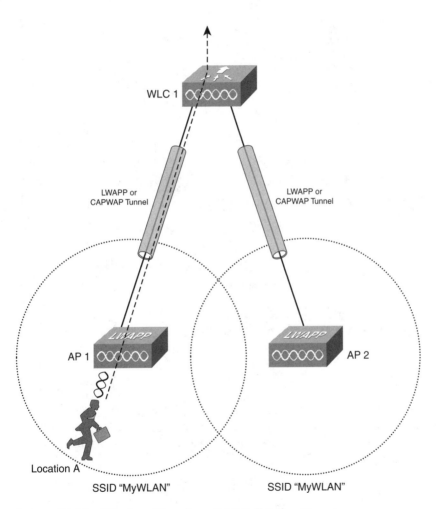

Figure 15-13 *Wireless Client in an LAP Cell Before Roaming*

The client begins moving in Figure 15-14 and roams into the area covered by AP2. For this example, notice two things: The cells provided by AP1 and AP2 both use the SSID MyWLAN, which enables the client to roam between them. In addition, both AP1 and AP2 are joined to a single controller, WC1.

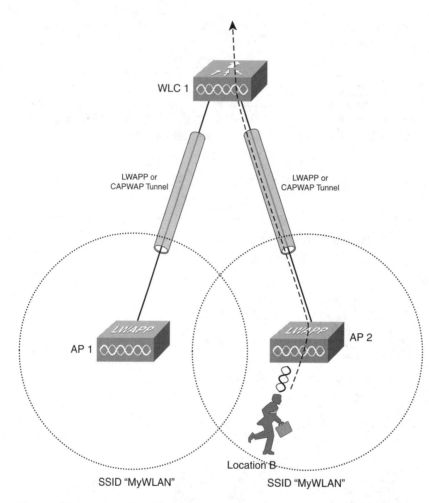

Figure 15-14 *Wireless Client After Roaming to a New LAP Cell*

In the figure, the client has moved its association to WLC1 through AP2. Although the AP has changed, the same controller is providing the association and the LWAPP or CAPWAP tunnel. This is known as an *intracontroller roam*, where the client's association stays within the same controller.

This type of roam is straightforward because controller WLC1 simply updates its tables to begin using the LWAPP or CAPWAP tunnel to AP2 to find the client. Any leftover data that was buffered from the old association is easily shifted over to the new association within the controller.

Intercontroller Roaming

In some cases, a client might roam from one controller to another. For example, a large wireless network might consist of too many LAPs to be supported by a single WLC. The

LAPs could also be distributed over several controllers for load balancing or redundancy purposes.

In Figure 15-15, a wireless client is using an association with WLC1 through AP1. This is similar to Figure 15-13, but now each of the adjacent LAP cells belongs to a different WLC. All the client's traffic passes through the tunnel from AP1 to WLC1.

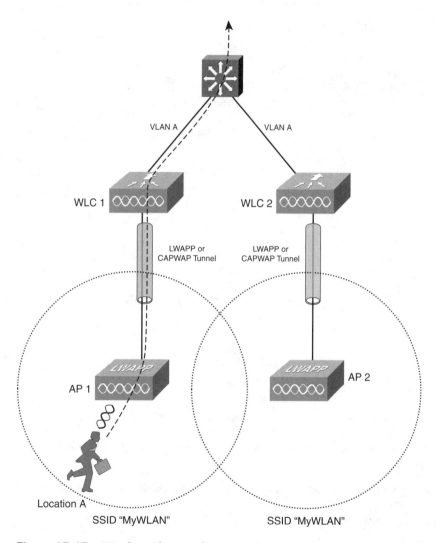

Figure 15-15 *Wireless Client Before Roaming to a Different Controller*

When the client moves into AP2's cell, the same SSID is found, and the client can move its association to WLC2. As long as the two controllers (WLC1 and WLC2) are located in the same IP subnet, they can easily hand off the client's association. This is done through a mobility message exchange where information about the client is transferred from one WLC to the other, as shown in Figure 15-16.

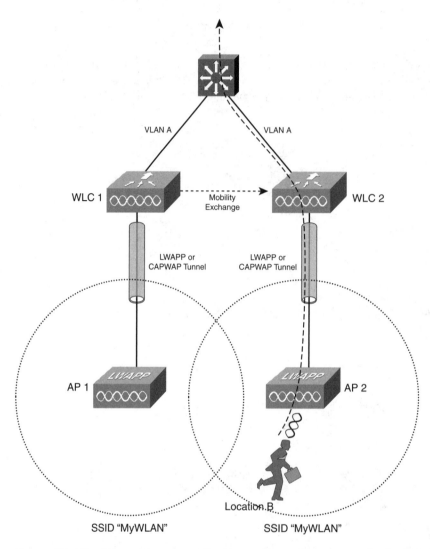

VLAN A   VLAN A

WLC 1   Mobility   WLC 2
              Exchange

LWAPP or   LWAPP or
CAPWAP Tunnel   CAPWAP Tunnel

AP 1   AP 2

Location B

SSID "MyWLAN"   SSID "MyWLAN"

Figure 15-16   *After an Intercontroller Roam, Controllers Are on the Same Subnet*

When the mobility exchange occurs, the client begins using the LWAPP or CAPWAP tunnel between AP2 and WLC2. The client's IP address has not changed; in fact, the roaming process was completely transparent to the client.

Now consider the scenario shown in Figure 15-17. The two controllers WLC1 and WLC2 are located in different IP subnets, shown as VLAN A and VLAN B. The wireless client begins in AP1's cell with an association to WLC1. The client obtains an IP address within VLAN A because AP1 offers VLAN A on its SSID. All the client's traffic passes through the LWAPP or CAPWAP tunnel between AP1 and WLC1 and onto VLAN A.

When the client travels into the cell provided by AP2, something interesting happens. In Figure 15-18, the client moves its association over to WLC2, through AP2, which offers access to VLAN B. The client's IP address has remained constant, but WLC1 and WLC2 are not located on the same subnet or VLAN. Therefore, the client's IP address has moved into a foreign subnet.

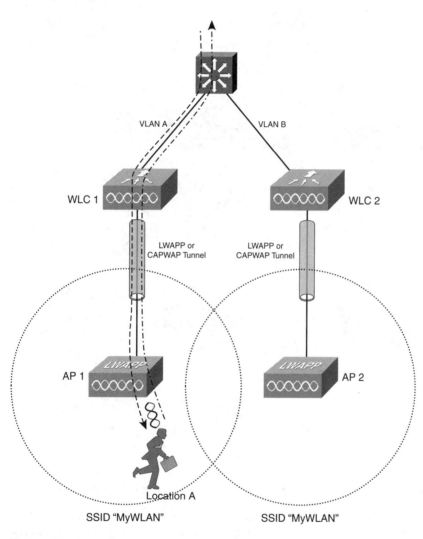

Figure 15-17 *Before an Intercontroller Roam, Controllers Are on Different Subnets*

The two controllers must begin working together to provide continuing service for the client, without requiring the client to obtain a new address. The two controllers bring up an Ether-IP tunnel between them for the specific purpose of carrying some of the client's traffic. The Ether-IP tunnel is simply a way that the controllers can encapsulate MAC-layer data inside an IP packet, using IP protocol 97. To move packets to and from the client, one controller encapsulates packets and sends them to the other controller. Packets received over the tunnel are unencapsulated by the other controller, where they reappear in their original form. (Ether-IP tunnels are defined in RFC 3378.)

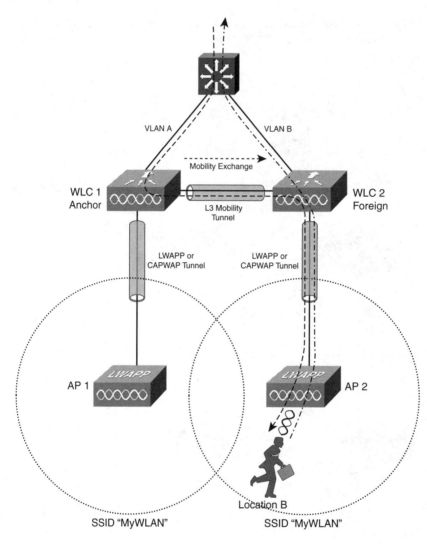

Figure 15-18 *After an Intercontroller Roam, Controllers Are on Different Subnets*

All the client's traffic will not be able to travel over the same path. Traffic leaving the client travels over the LWAPP or CAPWAP tunnel from AP2 to WLC2 and onto VLAN B, as you might expect. Even though the client has an IP address that is foreign to its new VLAN, it can still send packets onto the foreign VLAN.

Traffic coming toward the client takes a different path. In Figure 15-18, traffic enters the switch on VLAN A and is forwarded to WLC1. Why does it enter VLAN A and not VLAN B, where the client is now located? Remember that the client is still using an IP address it obtained on VLAN A, so it will continue to appear in VLAN A—no matter where it roams within the wireless network.

Traffic being sent to the client's destination address on VLAN A must be forwarded onto VLAN A. Therefore, WLC1 must accept that traffic and forward it onto the appropriate controller that has a current association with the client. WLC1 sends the traffic through the Ether-IP tunnel to WLC2, which in turn sends the traffic through the tunnel to AP2 and to the client.

Because the client originally joined the WLAN on WLC1, WLC1 will always refer to itself as the client's anchor point. Any controller that is serving the client from a different subnet is known as a foreign agent. As the client continues to roam, the anchor WLC will follow its movement by shifting the Ether-IP tunnel to connect with the client's foreign WLC.

Mobility Groups

For intercontroller roaming, a client must be able to roam from one LAP to another, where the LAPs are managed by different controllers. The controllers must be able to hand off a client's association information to each other during a roam.

To do this, the WLCs are configured into logical mobility groups. A client can roam to any LAP (and its associated WLC) as long as it stays within a mobility group.

A mobility group can have up to 24 WLCs of any type or platform. The number of LAPs contained in a mobility group can vary because the number of LAPs managed by any WLC can vary by platform.

Sometimes a wireless client might move across a mobility group boundary, where two adjacent LAPs are in two different mobility groups. In this case, the client can transfer its association into the new mobility group, but its IP address and all of its session information maintained in the WLCs will be dropped.

Configuring Switch Ports for WLAN Use

To implement a wireless LAN, both switches and access points must be configured. The CCNP SWITCH course and exam separate the configuration effort into two camps. The networking professional handles the design and configuration of the LAN switches to support the WLAN. The AP and WLC configuration is handled by a wireless LAN specialist. Therefore, the following sections cover only the configuration of switch ports where wireless devices are connected.

As you work through the remainder of this chapter, think about the steps you would need to execute to position and configure an AP and any WLC.

Configuring Support for Autonomous APs

Figure 15-19 shows a network scenario where one autonomous AP is connected into a campus network. Autonomous APs are normally positioned in the access layer of the network. Each SSID that is supported by the AP is mapped to a VLAN; when multiple SSIDs are offered, multiple VLANs must touch the AP. Therefore, you should configure the switch port connecting to the AP as a trunk link.

You can use the commands shown in Example 15-1 as a template to configure the switch port . In the scenario, interface Gigabit Ethernet 1/0/1 connects to the AP and acts as a trunk link, transporting VLANs 10, 20, and 30 to and from the AP. These VLANs correspond to the three SSIDs that are configured on the AP itself. You can optionally add the

spanning-tree portfast trunk command to shorten the time required for STP to bring the trunk link up into the forwarding state.

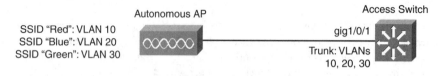

Figure 15-19   *Configuring a Switch to Support an Autonomous AP*

Example 15-1   *Switch Port Configuration for an Autonomous AP*

```
Switch(config)# interface gigabitethernet1/0/1
Switch(config-if)# switchport trunk encapsulation dot1q
Switch(config-if)# switchport trunk allowed vlan 10,20,30
Switch(config-if)# switchport mode trunk
Switch(config-if)# spanning-tree portfast trunk
```

Configuring Support for LAPs

Cisco LAPs are designed to be "zero-touch" devices, which can be installed and used with little or no manual intervention. The WLC can manage every aspect of LAP operation, including code image synchronization, so almost no information needs to be primed or preconfigured in the LAP itself.

Before you connect an LAP to a switch port, you should make sure that the port is properly configured. The LAP requires an access mode port—not a trunking port. The only VLAN needed at the LAP is one where the LAP can get an IP address and reach the WLC.

You can place the LAP on any VLAN that is convenient in a switch block. For example, the LAP can sit on the user access VLAN along with other end users in the area. Usually the best practice is to set aside a VLAN strictly for LAP management traffic. This VLAN contains one IP subnet reserved only for LAPs.

Any VLAN that is mapped to an SSID is transported over the LWAPP or CAPWAP tunnel from the LAP to the WLC. That means the LAP and WLC do not have to be connected with a Layer 2 VLAN or a trunk link at all.

Figure 15-20 shows a simple network scenario with an LAP and a WLC. The LAP should be located in the access layer, so it is connected to interface Gigabit Ethernet 1/0/10 on the access switch. The interface is configured for access mode using VLAN 100, which is set aside for LAP devices. The commands shown in Example 15-2 can be used as a template to configure the access switch port to connect to the LAP.

Example 15-2   *Switch Port Configuration for an LAP*

```
Switch(config)# vlan 100
Switch(config-vlan)# name ap-management
Switch(config-vlan)# exit
Switch(config)# interface gigabitethernet1/0/10
```

```
Switch(config-if)# switchport
Switch(config-if)# switchport access vlan 100
Switch(config-if)# switchport mode access
Switch(config-if)# spanning-tree portfast
Switch(config-if)# power inline auto
Switch(config-if)# exit
```

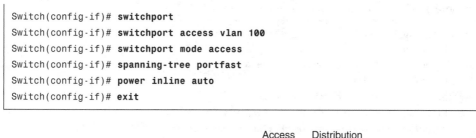

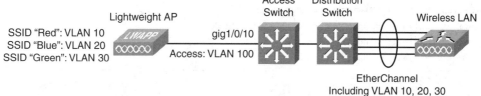

Figure 15-20 *Configuring a Switch to Support Cisco Unified Wireless Network Devices*

You can enable **spanning-tree portfast** on the access mode ports where LAPs connect. The LAP VLAN terminates on the LAPs and does not get extended any further. Therefore, no danger exists of that VLAN forming a loop somewhere in the wireless cloud.

When Power over Ethernet (PoE) is used to power an LAP from a switch interface, it is no different from using it to power a Cisco IP Phone. See Chapter 14, "IP Telephony," for PoE switch configuration information.

Configuring Support for WLCs

LAPs provide network access for wireless LAN users, whereas the WLCs aggregate WLAN traffic from the LAPs. Therefore, the WLCs should be located in the distribution layer of the campus network, as shown in Figure 15-20.

Cisco WLCs have a variety of interfaces that perform different functions. For the purposes of the CCNP SWITCH exam, you do not have to understand anything about those interfaces. Instead, you can assume that a wireless specialist will set the requirements for these interfaces and will work with you to come up with the appropriate switch configuration. Just be aware that the WLC needs direct connectivity to any VLANs that will be tunneled to the LAPs where the users are located.

The switch interfaces feeding a WLC should be configured as trunk links. Some WLCs need a single interface, others have several interfaces that should be bundled into a single EtherChannel. The WLC shown in Figure 15-20 has a four-interface Gigabit EtherChannel. The commands shown in Example 15-3 can be used as a template to configure the EtherChannel and its associated physical interfaces. The member interfaces should always be configured as an unconditional EtherChannel, because the WLC cannot negotiate one with the switch.

Example 15-3   *Configuring Switch Ports for a WLC*

```
Switch(config)# interface range gigabitethernet1/0/41 - 44
Switch(config-if)# switchport
Switch(config-if)# channel-group 1 mode on
Switch(config-if)# exit
Switch(config)# interface port-channel 1
Switch(config-if)# switchport trunk encapsulation dot1q
Switch(config-if)# switchport trunk allowed vlan 10,20,30
Switch(config-if)# switchport mode trunk
Switch(config-if)# spanning-tree portfast trunk
Switch(config-if)# no shutdown
Switch(config-if)# exit
```

Exam Preparation Tasks

Review All Key Topics

Review the most important topics in the chapter, noted with the Key Topic icon in the outer margin of the page. Table 15-3 lists a reference of these key topics and the page numbers on which each is found.

Table 15-3 *Key Topics for Chapter 15*

Key Topic Element	Description	Page Number
Paragraph	Explains the collision-avoidance mechanism	338
Tip	Defines an SSID as the common thread among WLAN clients that need to communicate with each other	340
Paragraph	Discusses how VLANs are mapped to SSIDs	343
Paragraph	Explains client roaming, Layer 2 roaming, and Layer 3 roaming	345
Paragraph	Discusses autonomous mode APs in traditional WLAN design	346
Paragraph	Explains how traffic between two WLAN clients must always pass through an AP	347
Paragraph	Discusses lightweight access points (LAP) and wireless LAN controllers (WLC)	350
Paragraph	Explains the split-MAC architecture	350
Paragraph	Explains the Lightweight Access Point Protocol (LWAPP) and Control and Provisioning Wireless Access Point tunnel protocols	350
Tip	Explains the HREAP functionality	353

Define Key Terms

Define the following key terms from this chapter, and check your answers in the glossary:

CSMA/CA, SSID, Layer 2 roaming, Layer 3 roaming, autonomous mode AP, lightweight access point (LAP), wireless LAN controller (WLC), split-MAC architecture, Lightweight Access Point Protocol (LWAPP), Control and Provisioning Wireless Access Point (CAP-WAP), Hybrid Remote Edge Access Point (HREAP)

Cisco Published SWITCH Exam Topics Covered in This Part

Implement a security extension of a Layer 2 solution, given a network design and a set of requirements:

- Determine network resources needed for implementing a security solution

- Create a implementation plan for the security solution

- Create a verification plan for the security solution

- Configure port security features

- Configure general switch security features

- Configure private VLANs

- Configure VACL and PACL

- Verify the security-based solution was implemented properly using show and debug commands

- Document results of security implementation and verification

(Always check Cisco.com for the latest posted exam topics.)

Part V: Securing Switched Networks

This chapter covers the following topics that you need to master for the CCNP SWITCH exam:

Port Security—This section explains how to configure switch ports to allow network access to only hosts with specific or learned MAC addresses.

Port-Based Authentication—This section discusses a method you can use to require user authentication before network access is offered to a client host.

Mitigating Spoofing Attacks—This section covers several types of attacks in which a malicious user generates spoofed information to become a man in the middle. When an attacker is wedged between other hosts and a router or gateway, for example, he can examine and exploit all traffic. DHCP snooping, IP Source Guard, and dynamic ARP inspection are three features that can be used to prevent these attacks.

Best Practices for Securing Switches—This section provides several guidelines for tightening control over Catalyst switches and the protocols they use for switch communication and maintenance.

CHAPTER 16

Securing Switch Access

Traditionally, users have been able to connect a PC to a switched network and gain immediate access to enterprise resources. As networks grow and as more confidential data and restricted resources become available, it is important to limit the access that users receive.

Catalyst switches have a variety of methods that can secure or control user access. Users can be authenticated as they connect to or through a switch and can be authorized to perform certain actions on a switch. User access can be recorded as switch accounting information. The physical switch port access also can be controlled based on the user's MAC address or authentication.

In addition, Catalyst switches can detect and prevent certain types of attacks. Several features can be used to validate information passing through a switch so that spoofed addresses can't be used to compromise hosts.

"Do I Know This Already?" Quiz

The "Do I Know This Already?" quiz allows you to assess whether you should read this entire chapter thoroughly or jump to the "Exam Preparation Tasks" section. If you are in doubt based on your answers to these questions or your own assessment of your knowledge of the topics, read the entire chapter. Table 16-1 outlines the major headings in this chapter and the "Do I Know This Already?" quiz questions that go with them. You can find the answers in Appendix A, "Answers to the 'Do I Know This Already?' Quizzes."

Table 16-1 *"Do I Know This Already?" Foundation Topics Section-to-Question Mapping*

Foundation Topics Section	Questions Covered in This Section
Port Security	1–4
Port-Based Authentication	5–9
Mitigating Spoofing Attacks	10–12
Best Practices for Securing Switches	13–14

1. Which switch feature can grant access through a port only if the host with MAC address 0005.0004.0003 is connected?

   a. SPAN

   b. MAC address ACL

   c. Port security

   d. Port-based authentication

2. Port security is being used to control access to a switch port. Which one of these commands will put the port into the errdisable state if an unauthorized station connects?

   a. switchport port-security violation protect

   b. switchport port-security violation restrict

   c. switchport port-security violation errdisable

   d. switchport port-security violation shutdown

3. If port security is left to its default configuration, how many different MAC addresses can be learned at one time on a switch port?

   a. 0

   b. 1

   c. 16

   d. 256

4. The following commands are configured on a Catalyst switch port. What happens when the host with MAC address 0001.0002.0003 tries to connect?
   ```
   switchport port-security
   switchport port-security maximum 3
   switchport port-security mac-address 0002.0002.0002
   switchport port-security violation shutdown
   ```

   a. The port shuts down.

   b. The host is allowed to connect.

   c. The host is denied a connection.

   d. The host can connect only when 0002.0002.0002 is not connected.

5. What protocol is used for port-based authentication?

   a. 802.1D

   b. 802.1Q

   c. 802.1x

   d. 802.1w

6. When 802.1x is used for a switch port, where must it be configured?

    a. Switch port and client PC

    b. Switch port only

    c. Client PC only

    d. Switch port and a RADIUS server

7. When port-based authentication is enabled globally, what is the default behavior for all switch ports?

    a. Authenticate users before enabling the port.

    b. Allow all connections without authentication.

    c. Do not allow any connections.

    d. There is no default behavior.

8. When port-based authentication is enabled, what method is available for a user to authenticate?

    a. Web browser

    b. Telnet session

    c. 802.1x client

    d. DHCP

9. The users in a department are using a variety of host platforms, some old and some new. All of them have been approved with a user ID in a RADIUS server database. Which one of these features should be used to restrict access to the switch ports in the building?

    a. AAA authentication

    b. AAA authorization

    c. Port security

    d. Port-based authentication

10. With DHCP snooping, an untrusted port filters out which one of the following?

    a. DHCP replies from legitimate DHCP servers

    b. DHCP replies from rogue DHCP servers

    c. DHCP requests from legitimate clients

    d. DHCP requests from rogue clients

11. Which two of the following methods does a switch use to detect spoofed addresses when IP Source Guard is enabled?

    a. ARP entries

    b. DHCP database

    c. DHCP snooping database

    d. Static IP source binding entries

    e. Reverse path-forwarding entries

12. Which one of the following should be configured as a trusted port for dynamic ARP inspection?

    a. The port where the ARP server is located.

    b. The port where an end-user host is located.

    c. The port where another switch is located.

    d. None; all ports are untrusted.

13. Which two of the following methods should you use to secure inbound CLI sessions to a switch?

    a. Disable all inbound CLI connections.

    b. Use SSH only.

    c. Use Telnet only.

    d. Apply an access list to the vty lines.

14. Suppose you need to disable CDP advertisements on a switch port so that untrusted devices cannot learn anything about your switch. Which one of the following interface configuration commands should be used?

    a. cdp disable

    b. no cdp

    c. no cdp enable

    d. no cdp trust

Foundation Topics

Port Security

In some environments, a network must be secured by controlling what stations can gain access to the network itself. Where user workstations are stationary, their MAC addresses always can be expected to connect to the same access-layer switch ports. If stations are mobile, their MAC addresses can be learned dynamically or added to a list of addresses to expect on a switch port.

Catalyst switches offer the port security feature to control port access based on MAC addresses. To configure port security on an access-layer switch port, begin by enabling it on a per-interface basis with the following interface-configuration command:

```
Switch(config-if)# switchport port-security
```

Next, you must identify a set of allowed MAC addresses so that the port can grant them access. You can explicitly configure addresses or they can be learned dynamically from port traffic. On each interface that uses port security, specify the maximum number of MAC addresses that will be allowed access using the following interface configuration command:

```
Switch(config-if)# switchport port-security maximum max-addr
```

By default, port security will make sure that only one MAC address will be allowed access on each switch port. You can set the maximum number of addresses in the range of 1 to 1024.

Each interface using port security dynamically learns MAC addresses by default and expects those addresses to appear on that interface in the future. These are called *sticky MAC addresses*. MAC addresses are learned as hosts transmit frames on an interface. The interface learns up to the maximum number of addresses allowed. Learned addresses also can be aged out of the table if those hosts are silent for a period of time. By default, no aging occurs.

Key Topic

For example, to set the maximum number of MAC addresses that can be active on a switch port at any time to two, you could use the following command:

```
Switch(config-if)# switchport port-security maximum 2
```

You also can statically define one or more MAC addresses on an interface. Any of these addresses are allowed to access the network through the port. Use the following interface configuration command to define a static address:

```
Switch(config-if)# switchport port-security mac-address mac-addr
```

The MAC address is given in dotted-triplet format. If the number of static addresses configured is less than the maximum number of addresses secured on a port, the remaining addresses are learned dynamically. Be sure to set the maximum number appropriately.

As an example, you could use the following command to configure a static address entry on an interface, so that 0006.5b02.a841 will be expected:

```
Switch(config-if)# switchport port-security mac-address 0006.5b02.a841
```

Finally, you must define how each interface using port security should react if a MAC address is in violation by using the following interface-configuration command:

```
Switch(config-if)# switchport port-security violation {shutdown | restrict |
  protect}
```

A violation occurs if more than the maximum number of MAC addresses are learned or if an unknown (not statically defined) MAC address attempts to transmit on the port. The switch port takes one of the following configured actions when a violation is detected:

- **Shutdown**—The port immediately is put into the Errdisable state, which effectively shuts it down. It must be reenabled manually or through errdisable recovery to be used again.

- **Restrict**—The port is allowed to stay up, but all packets from violating MAC addresses are dropped. The switch keeps a running count of the number of violating packets and can send an SNMP trap and a syslog message as an alert of the violation.

- **Protect**—The port is allowed to stay up, as in the restrict mode. Although packets from violating addresses are dropped, no record of the violation is kept.

As an example of the restrict mode, a switch interface has received the following configuration commands:

```
interface GigabitEthernet0/11
 switchport access vlan 991
 switchport mode access
 switchport port-security
 switchport port-security violation restrict
 spanning-tree portfast
```

When the default maximum of one MAC address is exceeded on this interface, the condition is logged but the interface stays up. This is shown by the following syslog message:

```
Jun  3 17:18:41.888 EDT: %PORT_SECURITY-2-PSECURE_VIOLATION: Security violation
  occurred, caused by MAC address 0000.5e00.0101 on port GigabitEthernet0/11.
```

Tip: If an interface is undergoing the restrict or protect condition, you might need to clear the learned MAC addresses so that a specific host can use the switch port. You can clear a MAC address or the complete port cache with the following command:

```
Switch# clear port-security dynamic [address mac-addr | interface type mod/num]
```

In the shutdown mode, the port security action is much more drastic. When the maximum number of MAC addresses is exceeded, the following syslog messages indicate that the port has been shut down in the Errdisable state:

```
Jun  3 17:14:19.018 EDT: %PM-4-ERR_DISABLE: psecure-violation error detected on
  Gi0/11, putting Gi0/11 in err-disable state
Jun  3 17:14:19.022 EDT: %PORT_SECURITY-2-PSECURE_VIOLATION: Security violation
  occurred, caused by MAC address 0003.a089.efc5 on port GigabitEthernet0/11.
Jun  3 17:14:20.022 EDT: %LINEPROTO-5-UPDOWN: Line protocol on Interface Gigabit
  Ethernet0/11, changed state to down
Jun  3 17:14:21.023 EDT: %LINK-3-UPDOWN: Interface GigabitEthernet0/11, changed
  state   to down
```

You also can show the port status with the **show port-security interface** command, as demonstrated in Example 16-1.

Example 16-1 *Displaying Port Security Port Status*

```
Switch# show port-security interface gigabitethernet 0/11
Port Security              : Enabled
Port Status                : Secure-shutdown

Violation Mode             : Shutdown
Aging Time                 : 0 mins
Aging Type                 : Absolute
SecureStatic Address Aging : Disabled
Maximum MAC Addresses      : 1
Total MAC Addresses        : 0
Configured MAC Addresses   : 0
Sticky MAC Addresses       : 0
Last Source Address        : 0003.a089.efc5
Security Violation Count   : 1
Switch#
```

To see a quick summary of only ports in the Errdisable state, along with the reason for errdisable, you can use the **show interfaces status err-disabled** command, as demonstrated in Example 16-2.

Example 16-2 *Displaying Summary Information for Ports in the Errdisable State*

```
Switch# show interfaces status err-disabled
Port      Name              Status       Reason
Gi0/11    Test port         err-disabled psecure-violation
Switch#
TIP
When a port is moved to the errdisable state, you must either manually cycle it
or configure the switch to automatically re-enable ports after a prescribed delay.
To manually cycle a port and return it to service, use the following commands:
Switch(config)# interface type mod/num
Switch(config-if)# shutdown
Switch(config-if)# no shutdown
```

Finally, you can display a summary of the port-security status with the **show port-security** command, as demonstrated in Example 16-3.

Example 16-3 *Displaying Port Security Status Summary Information*

```
Switch# show port-security
Secure Port  MaxSecureAddr  CurrentAddr  SecurityViolation  Security Action
              (Count)        (Count)       (Count)

------------------------------------------------------------------------

    Gi0/11          5              1                  0         Restrict
    Gi0/12          1              0                  0         Shutdown

------------------------------------------------------------------------

Total Addresses in System (excluding one mac per port)    : 0
Max Addresses limit in System (excluding one mac per port) : 6176
Switch#
```

Port-Based Authentication

Catalyst switches can support port-based authentication, a combination of AAA authentication and port security. This feature is based on the IEEE 802.1x standard. When it is enabled, a switch port will not pass any traffic until a user has authenticated with the switch. If the authentication is successful, the user can use the port normally.

For port-based authentication, both the switch and the end user's PC must support the 802.1x standard, using the Extensible Authentication Protocol over LANs (EAPOL). The 802.1x standard is a cooperative effort between the client and the switch offering network service. If the client PC is configured to use 802.lx but the switch does not support it, the PC abandons the protocol and communicates normally. However, if the switch is configured for 802.1x but the PC does not support it, the switch port remains in the unauthorized state so that it will not forward any traffic to the client PC.

Note: 802.1x EAPOL is a Layer 2 protocol. At the point that a switch detects the presence of a device on a port, the port remains in the unauthorized state. Therefore, the client PC cannot communicate with anything other than the switch by using EAPOL. If the PC does not already have an IP address, it cannot request one. The PC also has no knowledge of the switch or its IP address, so any means other than a Layer 2 protocol is not possible. This is why the PC must also have an 802.1x-capable application or client software.

An 802.1x switch port begins in the unauthorized state so that no data other than the 802.1x protocol itself is allowed through the port. Either the client or the switch can initiate an 802.1x session. The authorized state of the port ends when the user logs out, causing the 802.1x client to inform the switch to revert back to the unauthorized state. The switch can also time out the user's authorized session. If this happens, the client must reauthenticate to continue using the switch port.

802.1x Configuration

Port-based authentication can be handled by one or more external Remote Authentication Dial-In User Service (RADIUS) servers. Although many Cisco switch platforms allow other authentication methods to be configured, only RADIUS is supported for 802.1x.

The actual RADIUS authentication method must be configured first, followed by 802.1x, as shown in the following steps:

Step 1.   Enable AAA on the switch.

By default, AAA is disabled. You can enable AAA for port-based authentication by using the following global configuration command:

```
Switch(config)# aaa new-model
```

The **new-model** keyword refers to the use of method lists, by which authentication methods and sources can be grouped or organized. The new model is much more scalable than the "old model," in which the authentication source was explicitly configured.

Step 2.   Define external RADIUS servers.

First, define each server along with its secret shared password. This string is known only to the switch and the server, and provides a key for encrypting the authentication session. Use the following global configuration command:

```
Switch(config)# radius-server host {hostname | ip-address} [key string]
```

This command can be repeated to define additional RADIUS servers.

Step 3.   Define the authentication method for 802.1x.

Using the following command causes all RADIUS authentication servers that are defined on the switch to be used for 802.1x authentication:

```
Switch(config)# aaa authentication dot1x default group radius
```

Step 4.   Enable 802.1x on the switch:

```
Switch(config)# dot1x system-auth-control
```

Step 5.   Configure each switch port that will use 802.1x:

```
Switch(config)# interface type mod/num
Switch(config-if)# dot1x port-control {force-authorized | force-
  unauthorized | auto}
```

Here, the 802.1x state is one of the following:

force-authorized—The port is forced to always authorize any connected client. No authentication is necessary. This is the default state for all switch ports when 802.1x is enabled.

force-unauthorized—The port is forced to never authorize any connected client. As a result, the port cannot move to the authorized state to pass traffic to a connected client.

auto—The port uses an 802.1x exchange to move from the unauthorized to the authorized state, if successful. This requires an 802.1x-capable application on the client PC.

Tip: After 802.1x is globally enabled on a switch, all switch ports default to the **force-authorized** state. This means that any PC connected to a switch port can immediately start accessing the network. Ideally, you should explicitly configure each port to use the **auto** state so that connected PCs are forced to authenticate through the 802.1x exchange.

Step 6. Allow multiple hosts on a switch port.

It might be obvious that port-based authentication is tailored to controlling access to a single host PC that is connected to a switch port. However, 802.1x also supports cases in which multiple hosts are attached to a single switch port through an Ethernet hub or another access-layer switch.

If the switch should expect to find multiple hosts present on the switch port, use the following interface configuration command:

```
Switch(config-if)# dot1x host-mode multi-host
```

Tip: You can use the **show dot1x all** command to verify the 802.1x operation on each switch port that is configured to use port-based authentication.

802.1x Port-Based Authentication Example

In Example 16-4, two RADIUS servers are located at 10.1.1.1 and 10.1.1.2. Switch ports Fast Ethernet 0/1 through 0/40 will use 802.1x for port-based authentication. When authenticated, the end users will be associated with VLAN 10.

Example 16-4   *Configuring 802.1x Port-Based Authentication*

```
Switch(config)# aaa new-model
Switch(config)# radius-server host 10.1.1.1 key BigSecret
Switch(config)# radius-server host 10.1.1.2 key AnotherBigSecret
Switch(config)# aaa authentication dot1x default group radius
Switch(config)# dot1x system-auth-control
Switch(config)# interface range FastEthernet0/1 - 40
Switch(config-if)# switchport access vlan 10
Switch(config-if)# switchport mode access
Switch(config-if)# dot1x port-control auto
```

Mitigating Spoofing Attacks

Malicious users sometimes can send spoofed information to trick switches or other hosts into using a rogue machine as a gateway. The attacker's goal is to become the man in the middle, with a naive user sending packets to the attacker as if it were a router. The attacker can glean information from the packets sent to it before it forwards them normally. This section describes three Cisco Catalyst features—DHCP snooping, IP Source Guard, and dynamic ARP inspection—that prevent certain types of spoofing attack.

DHCP Snooping

A DHCP server normally provides all the basic information a client PC needs to operate on a network. For example, the client might receive an IP address, a subnet mask, a default gateway address, DNS addresses, and so on.

Suppose that an attacker could bring up a rogue DHCP server on a machine in the same subnet as that same client PC. Now when the client broadcasts its DHCP request, the rogue server could send a carefully crafted DHCP reply with its own IP address substituted as the default gateway.

When the client receives the reply, it begins using the spoofed gateway address. Packets destined for addresses outside the local subnet then go to the attacker's machine first. The attacker can forward the packets to the correct destination, but in the meantime, it can examine every packet that it intercepts. In effect, this becomes a type of man-in-the-middle attack; the attacker is wedged into the path and the client doesn't realize it.

Cisco Catalyst switches can use the DHCP snooping feature to help mitigate this type of attack. When DHCP snooping is enabled, switch ports are categorized as trusted or untrusted. Legitimate DHCP servers can be found on trusted ports, whereas all other hosts sit behind untrusted ports.

Key Topic

A switch intercepts all DHCP requests coming from untrusted ports before flooding them throughout the VLAN. Any DHCP replies coming from an untrusted port are discarded because they must have come from a rogue DHCP server. In addition, the offending switch port automatically is shut down in the Errdisable state.

DHCP snooping also keeps track of the completed DHCP bindings as clients receive legitimate replies. This database contains the client MAC address, IP address offered, lease time, and so on.

You can configure DHCP snooping first by enabling it globally on a switch with the following configuration command:

```
Switch(config)# ip dhcp snooping
```

Next identify the VLANs where DHCP snooping should be implemented with the following command:

```
Switch(config)# ip dhcp snooping vlan vlan-id [vlan-id]
```

You can give a single VLAN number as *vlan-id* or a range of VLAN numbers by giving the start and end VLAN IDs of the range.

By default, all switch ports are assumed to be untrusted so that DHCP replies are not expected or permitted. Only trusted ports are allowed to send DHCP replies. Therefore, you should identify only the ports where known, trusted DHCP servers are located. You can do this with the following interface configuration command:

```
Switch(config)# interface type mod/num
Switch(config-if)# ip dhcp snooping trust
```

For untrusted ports, an unlimited rate of DHCP requests is accepted. If you want to rate-limit DHCP traffic on an untrusted port, use the following interface configuration command:

```
Switch(config)# interface type mod/num
Switch(config-if)# ip dhcp snooping limit rate rate
```

The *rate* can be 1 to 2048 DHCP packets per second.

You also can configure the switch to use DHCP option-82, the DHCP Relay Agent Information option, which is described in RFC 3046. When a DHCP request is intercepted on an untrusted port, the switch adds its own MAC address and the switch port identifier into the option-82 field of the request. The request then is forwarded normally so that it can reach a trusted DHCP server.

Adding option-82 provides more information about the actual client that generated the DHCP request. In addition, the DHCP reply (if any) echoes back the option-82 information. The switch intercepts the reply and compares the option-82 data to confirm that the request came from a valid port on itself. This feature is enabled by default. You can enable or disable option-82 globally with the following configuration command:

```
Switch(config)# [no] ip dhcp snooping information option
```

When DHCP snooping is configured, you can display its status with the following command:

```
Switch# show ip dhcp snooping [binding]
```

You can use the **binding** keyword to display all the known DHCP bindings that have been overheard. The switch maintains these in its own database. Otherwise, only the switch ports that are trusted or that have rate limiting applied are listed. All other ports are considered to be untrusted with an unlimited DHCP request rate.

As an example, interfaces Fast Ethernet 0/35 and 0/36 use access VLAN 104, are considered untrusted, and have DHCP rate limiting applied at three per second. A known DHCP server is located on the Gigabit Ethernet 0/1 uplink. Example 16-5 shows the configuration for this scenario.

Example 16-5 *DHCP Snooping Configuration*

```
Switch(config)# ip dhcp snooping
Switch(config)# ip dhcp snooping vlan 104
Switch(config)# interface range fastethernet 0/35 - 36
Switch(config-if)# ip dhcp snooping limit rate 3
Switch(config-if)# interface gigabitethernet 0/1
Switch(config-if)# ip dhcp snooping trust
```

Example 16-6 shows the resulting DHCP snooping status.

Example 16-6 *DHCP Snooping Status Display*

```
Switch# show ip dhcp snooping
Switch DHCP snooping is enabled
DHCP snooping is configured on following VLANs:
104
Insertion of option 82 is enabled
Interface                    Trusted      Rate limit (pps)
-----------------------      -------      ----------------
FastEthernet0/35             no           3
FastEthernet0/36             no           3
GigabitEthernet0/1           yes          unlimited
Switch#
```

IP Source Guard

Address spoofing is one type of attack that can be difficult to mitigate. Normally, a host is assigned an IP address and is expected to use that address in all the traffic it sends out. IP addresses are effectively used on the honor system, where hosts are trusted to behave themselves and use their own legitimate source addresses.

A rogue or compromised host PC doesn't necessarily play by those rules. It can use its legitimate address, or it can begin to use spoofed addresses—borrowed from other hosts or used at random. Spoofed addresses are often used to disguise the origin of denial-of-service attacks. If the source address doesn't really exist, no return traffic will find its way back to the originator.

Routers or Layer 3 devices can perform some simple tests to detect spoofed source addresses in packets passing through. For example, if the 10.10.0.0 network is known to exist on VLAN 10, packets entering from VLAN 20 should never have source addresses in that subnet.

However, it is difficult to detect spoofed addresses when they are used *inside* the VLAN or subnet where they should already exist. For example, within the 10.10.0.0 network on VLAN 10, as shown in Figure 16-1, a rogue host begins to send packets with a spoofed source address of 10.10.10.10. The 10.10.10.10 address is certainly within the 10.10.0.0/16 subnet, so it doesn't stand out as an obvious spoof. Therefore, the rogue host might be very successful in attacking other hosts in its own subnet or VLAN.

Cisco Catalyst switches can use the IP source guard feature to detect and suppress address spoofing attacks—even if they occur within the same subnet. A Layer 2 switch, and a Layer 2 port in turn, normally learns and stores MAC addresses. The switch must have a way to look up MAC addresses and find out what IP address are associated with them.

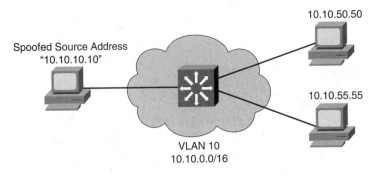

Figure 16-1   *Using a Spoofed Address Within a Subnet*

IP Source Guard does this by making use of the DHCP snooping database and static IP source binding entries. If DHCP snooping is configured and enabled, the switch learns the MAC and IP addresses of hosts that use DHCP. Packets arriving on a switch port can be tested for one of the following conditions:

- The source IP address must be identical to the IP address learned by DHCP snooping or a static entry. A dynamic port ACL is used to filter traffic. The switch automatically creates this ACL, adds the learned source IP address to the ACL, and applies the ACL to the interface where the address is learned.

- The source MAC address must be identical to the MAC address learned on the switch port and by DHCP snooping. Port security is used to filter traffic.

If the address is something other than the one learned or statically configured, the switch drops the packet.

To configure IP Source Guard, first configure and enable DHCP snooping, as presented in the previous section. If you want IP Source Guard to detect spoofed MAC addresses, you also need to configure and enable port security.

For the hosts that do not use DHCP, you can configure a static IP source binding with the following configuration command:

```
Switch(config)# ip source binding mac-address vlan vlan-id ip-address interface
  type mod/num
```

Here, the host's MAC address is bound to a specific VLAN and IP address, and is expected to be found on a specific switch interface.

Next, enable IP source guard on one or more switch interfaces with the following configuration commands:

```
Switch(config)# interface type mod/num
Switch(config-if)# ip verify source [port-security]
```

The **ip verify source** command inspects the source IP address only. You can add the **port-security** keyword to inspect the source MAC address, too.

To verify the IP source guard status, you can use the following EXEC command:

```
Switch# show ip verify source [interface type mod/num]
```

If you need to verify the information contained in the IP source binding database, either learned or statically configured, you can use the following EXEC command:

```
Switch# show ip source bindng [ip-address] [mac-address] [dhcp-snooping | static]
  [interface type mod/num] [vlan vlan-id]
```

Dynamic ARP Inspection

Hosts normally use the Address Resolution Protocol (ARP) to resolve an unknown MAC address when the IP address is known. If a MAC address is needed so that a packet can be forwarded at Layer 2, a host broadcasts an ARP request that contains the IP address of the target in question. If any other host is using that IP address, it responds with an ARP reply containing its MAC address.

The ARP process works well among trusted and well-behaved users. However, suppose that an attacker could send its own crafted ARP reply when it overhears an ARP request being broadcast. The reply could contain its own MAC address, causing the original re-quester to think that it is bound to the IP address in question. The requester would add the bogus ARP entry into its own ARP cache, only to begin forwarding packets to the spoofed MAC address.

In effect, this scheme places the attacker's machine right in the middle of an otherwise le-gitimate path. Packets will be sent to the attacker instead of another host or the default gateway. The attacker can intercept packets and (perhaps) forward them on only after ex-amining the packets' contents.

This attack is known as *ARP poisoning* or *ARP spoofing*, and it is considered to be a type of man-in-the-middle attack. The attacker wedges into the normal forwarding path, transparent to the end users. Cisco Catalyst switches can use the dynamic ARP inspection (DAI) feature to help mitigate this type of attack.

DAI works much like DHCP snooping. All switch ports are classified as trusted or un-trusted. The switch intercepts and inspects all ARP packets that arrive on an untrusted port; no inspection is done on trusted ports.

When an ARP reply is received on an untrusted port, the switch checks the MAC and IP addresses reported in the reply packet against known and trusted values. A switch can gather trusted ARP information from statically configured entries or from dynamic en-tries in the DHCP snooping database. In the latter case, DHCP snooping must be enabled in addition to DAI.

If an ARP reply contains invalid information or values that conflict with entries in the trusted database, it is dropped and a log message is generated. This action prevents invalid or spoofed ARP entries from being sent and added to other machines' ARP caches.

You can configure DAI by first enabling it on one or more client VLANs with the follow-ing configuration command:

```
Switch(config)# ip arp inspection vlan vlan-range
```

The VLAN range can be a single VLAN ID, a range of VLAN IDs separated by a hyphen, or a list of VLAN IDs separated by commas.

By default, all switch ports associated with the VLAN range are considered to be un-trusted. You should identify trusted ports as those that connect to other switches. In other words, the local switch will not inspect ARP packets arriving on trusted ports; it will as-sume that the neighboring switch also is performing DAI on all of its ports in that VLAN. Configure a trusted port with the following interface configuration command:

```
Switch(config)# interface type mod/num
Switch(config-if)# ip arp inspection trust
```

If you have hosts with statically configured IP address information, there will be no DHCP message exchange that can be inspected. Instead, you can configure an ARP access list that defines static MAC-IP address bindings that are permitted. Use the following config-uration commands to define the ARP access list and one or more static entries:

```
Switch(config)# arp access-list acl-name
Switch(config-acl)# permit ip host sender-ip mac host sender-mac [log]
[Repeat the previous command as needed]
Switch(config-acl)# exit
```

Now the ARP access list must be applied to DAI with the following configuration command:

```
Switch(config)# ip arp inspection filter arp-acl-name vlan vlan-range [static]
```

When ARP replies are intercepted, their contents are matched against the access list en-tries first. If no match is found, the DHCP snooping bindings database is checked next. You can give the **static** keyword to prevent the DHCP bindings database from being checked at all. In effect, this creates an implicit deny statement at the end of the ARP ac-cess list; if no match is found in the access list, the ARP reply is considered invalid.

Finally, you can specify further validations on the contents of ARP reply packets. By de-fault, only the MAC and IP addresses contained within the ARP reply are validated. This doesn't take the actual MAC addresses contained in the Ethernet header of the ARP reply.

To validate that an ARP reply packet is really coming from the address listed inside it, you can enable DAI validation with the following configuration command:

```
Switch(config)# ip arp inspection validate {[src-mac] [dst-mac] [ip]}
```

Be sure to specify at least one of the options:

- **src-mac**—Check the source MAC address in the Ethernet header against the sender MAC address in the ARP reply.

- **dst-mac**—Check the destination MAC address in the Ethernet header against the target MAC address in the ARP reply.

- **ip**—Check the sender's IP address in all ARP requests; check the sender's IP address against the target IP address in all ARP replies.

Example 16-7 demonstrates where DAI is enabled for all switch ports associated with VLAN 104 on an access-layer switch. The uplink to a distribution switch is considered to be trusted.

Example 16-7 *Configuring DAI to Validate ARP Replies*

```
Switch(config)# ip arp inspection vlan 104
Switch(config)# arp access-list StaticARP
Switch(config-acl)# permit ip host 192.168.1.10 mac host 0006.5b02.a841
Switch(config-acl)# exit
Switch(config)# ip arp inspection filter StaticARP vlan 104
Switch(config)# interface gigabitethernet 0/1
Switch(config-if)# ip arp inspection trust
```

You can display DAI status information with the **show ip arp inspection** command.

Best Practices for Securing Switches

Although you can configure and use many different features on Cisco Catalyst switches, you should be aware of some common weaknesses that can be exploited. In other words, do not become complacent and assume that everyone connected to your network will be good citizens and play by the rules. Think ahead and try to prevent as many things as possible that might be leveraged to assist an attacker.

This section presents a brief overview of many best-practice suggestions that can help secure your switched network:

■ **Configure secure passwords**—Whenever possible, you should use the **enable secret** command to set the privileged-level password on a switch. This command uses a stronger encryption than the normal **enable password** command.

You also should use external AAA servers to authenticate administrative users whenever possible. The usernames and passwords are maintained externally, so they are not stored or managed directly on the switch. In addition, having a centralized user management is much more scalable than configuring and changing user credentials on many individual switches and routers.

Finally, you always should use the **service password-encryption** configuration command to automatically encrypt password strings that are stored in the switch configuration. Although the encryption is not excessively strong, it can prevent casual observers from seeing passwords in the clear.

■ **Use system banners**—When users successfully access a switch, they should be aware of any specific access or acceptable use policies that are pertinent to your organization. You should configure system banners so that this type of information is displayed when users log in to a switch. The idea is to warn unauthorized users (if they gain access) that their activities could be grounds for prosecution—or that they are unwelcome, at the very least.

You should use the **banner motd** command to define the text that is displayed to authenticated users. Try to avoid using other banner types that display information about your organization or the switch before users actually log in. Never divulge any extra information about your network that malicious users could use.

■ **Secure the web interface**—Decide whether you will use the web interface to manage or monitor a switch. Some network professionals use the command line interface exclusively, so the web interface is not needed in a production environment. In this case, you should disable the web interface with the **no ip http server** global configuration command.

If you do decide to use the web interface, be sure to use the HTTPS interface, if it is supported on the switch platform. The standard HTTP web interface has some glaring weaknesses, mainly because none of the traffic is encrypted or protected. Enable the HTTPS interface with the **ip http secure server** global configuration command instead of the **ip http server** command.

In addition, try to limit the source addresses that can access the HTTPS interface. First, create an access list that permits only approved source addresses; then apply the access list to the HTTPS interface with the **ip http access-class** configuration command. As an example, the following configuration commands permit HTTPS connections that are sourced from the 10.100.50.0/24 network:

```
Switch(config)# ip http secure server
Switch(config)# access-list 1 permit 10.100.50.0 0.0.0.255
Switch(config)# ip http access-class 1
```

■ **Secure the switch console**—In many environments, switches are locked away in wiring closets where physical security is used to keep people from connecting to the switch console. Even so, you always should configure authentication on any switch console. It is usually appropriate to use the same authentication configuration on the console as the virtual terminal (vty) lines.

■ **Secure virtual terminal access**—You always should configure user authentication on *all* the vty lines on a switch. In addition, you should use access lists to limit the source IP addresses of potential administrative users who try to use Telnet or Secure Shell (SSH) to access a switch.

You can use a simple IP access list to permit inbound connections only from known source addresses, as in the following example:

```
Switch(config)# access-list 10 permit 192.168.199.10
Switch(config)# access-list 10 permit 192.168.201.100
Switch(config)# line vty 0 15
Switch(config-line)# access-class 10 in
```

Be sure you apply the access list to all the **line vty** entries in the switch configuration. Many times, the vty lines are separated into groups in the configuration. You can use the **show user all** command to see every possible line that can be used to access a switch.

■ **Use SSH whenever possible**—Although Telnet access is easy to configure and use, Telnet is not secure. Every character you type in a Telnet session is sent to and echoed from a switch in the clear, with no encryption. Therefore, it is very easy to eavesdrop on Telnet sessions to overhear usernames and passwords.

Instead, you should use SSH whenever possible. SSH uses strong encryption to secure session data. Therefore, you need a strong-encryption IOS image running on a switch before SSH can be configured and used. You should use the highest SSH version that is available on a switch. The early SSHv1 and SSHv1.5 have some weaknesses, so you should choose SSHv2 whenever possible.

■ **Secure SNMP access**—To prevent unauthorized users from making changes to a switch configuration, you should disable any read-write SNMP access. These are commands of the form **snmp-server community** *string* **RW**.

Instead, you should have only read-only commands in the configuration. In addition, you should use access lists to limit the source addresses that have read-only access. Don't depend on the SNMP community strings for security because these are passed in the clear in SNMP packets.

■ **Secure unused switch ports**—Every unused switch port should be disabled so that unexpected users can't connect and use them without your knowledge. You can do this with the **shutdown** interface configuration command.

In addition, you should configure every user port as an access port with the **switchport mode access** interface configuration command. Otherwise, a malicious user might connect and attempt to negotiate trunking mode on a port. You also should consider associating every unused access port with a bogus or isolated VLAN. If an unexpected user does gain access to a port, he will have access only to a VLAN that is isolated from every other resource on your network.

Tip: You might consider using the **switchport host** interface configuration command as a quick way to force a port to support only a single PC. This command is actually a macro, as shown in the following example:

```
Switch(config)# interface fastethernet 1/0/1
Switch(config-if)# switchport host
switchport mode will be set to access
spanning-tree portfast will be enabled
channel group will be disabled
Switch(config-if)#
```

■ **Secure STP operation**—A malicious user can inject STP bridge protocol data units (BPDU) into switch ports or VLANs, and can disrupt a stable, loop-free topology. You always should enable the BPDU guard feature so that access switch ports automatically are disabled if unexpected BPDUs are received.

■ **Secure the use of CDP**—By default, CDP advertisements are sent on *every* switch port at 60-second intervals. Although CDP is a very handy tool for discovering neighboring Cisco devices, you shouldn't allow CDP to advertise unnecessary information about your switch to listening attackers.

For example, the following information is sent in a CDP advertisement in the clear. An attacker might use the device ID to physically locate the switch, its IP address to target Telnet or SNMP attacks, or the native VLAN and switch port ID to attempt a VLAN hopping attack.

```
CDP - Cisco Discovery Protocol
   Version:               2
   Time to live:          180    seconds
   Checksum:              0xD0AE
   Device ID:             BldgA-Rm110
Version:                  Cisco Internetwork Operating System Software .IOS
(tm) C3750 Software (C3750-I9-M), Version 12.2(20)SE4, RELEASE SOFTWARE
(fc1).Copyright  1986-2005 by cisco Systems, Inc..Compiled Sun 09-Jan-05
00:09 by antonino
   Platform:              cisco WS-C3750-48P
   IP Address:            192.168.100.85
   Port ID:               FastEthernet1/0/48
   Capabilities:          0x00000028  Switch  IGMP
   VTP Domain:            MyCompany
   Native VLAN:           101
   Duplex:     0x01       Full
```

CDP should be enabled only on switch ports that connect to other trusted Cisco devices. Do not forget that CDP must be enabled on access switch ports where Cisco IP Phones are connected. When the CDP messages reach the IP Phone, they won't be relayed on to a PC connected to the phone's data port. You can disable CDP on a port-by-port basis with the **no cdp enable** interface configuration command.

Exam Preparation Tasks

Review All Key Topics

Review the most important topics in the chapter, noted with the Key Topic icon in the outer margin of the page. Table 16-2 lists a reference of these key topics and the page numbers on which each is found.

Table 16-2 *Key Topics for Chapter 16*

Key Topic Element	Description	Page Number
Paragraph	Discusses port security and MAC address control using sticky MAC addresses	375
List	Explains the actions port security can take when the MAC address limits are violated	376
Paragraph	Discusses port-based authentication using IEEE 802.1x and EAPOL	378
Paragraph	Explains DHCP snooping	381
Paragraph	Describes ARP poisoning, ARP spoofing attacks, and dynamic ARP inspection	385

Complete Tables and Lists from Memory

Print a copy of Appendix C, "Memory Tables" (found on the CD), or at least the section for this chapter, and complete the tables and lists from memory. Appendix D, "Memory Tables Answer Key," also on the CD, includes completed tables and lists to check your work.

Define Key Terms

Define the following key terms from this chapter, and check your answers in the glossary:

sticky MAC address, IEEE 802.1x, DHCP snooping, ARP poisoning (also known as ARP spoofing), dynamic ARP inspection (DAI)

Use Command Reference to Check Your Memory

This section includes the most important configuration and EXEC commands covered in this chapter. It might not be necessary to memorize the complete syntax of every command, but you should remember the basic keywords that are needed.

To test your memory of the STP configuration commands, cover the right side of Tables 16-3 through 16-7 with a piece of paper, read the description on the left side, and then see how much of the command you can remember.

Table 16-3 *Port Security Configuration Commands*

Task	Command Syntax
Enable port security on an interface.	switchport port-security
Set the maximum number of learned addresses.	switchport port-security maximum *max-addr*
Define a static MAC address.	switchport port-security mac-address *mac-addr*
Define an action to take.	switchport port-security violation {shutdown | restrict | protect}

Table 16-4 *Port-Based Authentication Configuration Commands*

Task	Command Syntax
Define a method list for 802.1x.	aaa authentication dot1x default group radius
Globally enable 802.1x.	dot1x system-auth-control
Define the 802.1x behavior on a port.	dot1x port-control {force-authorized | force-unauthorized | auto}
Support more than one host on a port.	dot1x host-mode multi-host

Table 16-5 *DHCP Snooping Configuration Commands*

Task	Command Syntax
Globally enable DHCP snooping.	ip dhcp snooping
Define a trusted interface.	ip dhcp snooping trust
Limit the interface DHCP packet rate.	ip dhcp snooping limit rate *rate*

Table 16-6 *IP Source Guard Configuration Commands*

Task	Command Syntax
Define a static IP source binding entry.	**ip source binding** *mac-address* **vlan** *vlan-id ip-address* **interface** *type mod/num*
Enable IP source guard on an interface.	**ip verify source** [**port-security**]

Table 16-7 *Dynamic ARP Inspection Configuration Commands*

Task	Command Syntax
Enable DAI on a VLAN.	**ip arp inspection vlan** *vlan-range*
Define a trusted interface.	**ip arp inspection trust**
Define a static ARP inspection binding.	**arp access-list** *acl-name* **permit ip host** *sender-ip* **mac host** *sender-mac* [**log**]
Apply static ARP inspection bindings.	**ip arp inspection filter** *arp-acl-name* **vlan** *vlan-range* [**static**]
Validate addresses within ARP replies.	**ip arp inspection validate** {[**src-mac**] [**dst-mac**] [**ip**]}

This chapter covers the following topics that you need to master for the CCNP SWITCH exam:

VLAN Access Lists—This section discusses how traffic can be controlled within a VLAN. You can use VLAN access control lists (ACL) to filter packets even as they are bridged or switched.

Private VLANs—This section explains the mechanisms that you can use to provide isolation within a single VLAN. Private VLANs have a unidirectional nature; several of them can be isolated yet share a common subnet and gateway.

Securing VLAN Trunks—This section covers two types of attacks that can be leveraged against a VLAN trunk link. If a trunk link is extended to or accessible from an attacker, any VLAN carried over the trunk can be compromised in turn.

CHAPTER 17

Securing with VLANs

Traditionally, traffic has been filtered only at router boundaries, where packets naturally are inspected before being forwarded. This is true within Catalyst switches because access lists can be applied as a part of multilayer switching. Catalysts also can filter packets even if they stay within the same VLAN; VLAN access control lists, or VACLs, provide this capability.

Catalyst switches also have the capability to logically divide a single VLAN into multiple partitions. Each partition can be isolated from others, with all of them sharing a common IP subnet and a common gateway address. Private VLANs make it possible to offer up a single VLAN to many disparate customers or organizations without any interaction between them.

VLAN trunks are commonly used on links between switches to carry data from multiple VLANs. If the switches are all under the same administrative control, it is easy to become complacent about the security of the trunks. A few known attacks can be used to gain access to the VLANs that are carried over trunk links. Therefore, network administrators should be aware of the steps that can be taken to prevent any attacks.

"Do I Know This Already?" Quiz

The "Do I Know This Already?" quiz allows you to assess whether you should read this entire chapter thoroughly or jump to the "Exam Preparation Tasks" section. If you are in doubt based on your answers to these questions or your own assessment of your knowledge of the topics, read the entire chapter. Table 17-1 outlines the major headings in this chapter and the "Do I Know This Already?" quiz questions that go with them. You can find the answers in Appendix A, "Answers to the 'Do I Know This Already?' Quizzes."

Table 17-1 *"Do I Know This Already?" Foundation Topics Section-to-Question Mapping*

Foundation Topics Section	Questions Covered in This Section
VLAN Access Lists	1–4
Private VLANs	5–8
Securing VLAN Trunks	9–12

1. Which one of the following can filter packets even if they are not routed to another Layer 3 interface?

   a. IP extended access lists

   b. MAC address access lists

   c. VLAN access lists

   d. Port-based access lists

2. In what part of a Catalyst switch are VLAN ACLs implemented?

   a. NVRAM

   b. CAM

   c. RAM

   d. TCAM

3. Which one of the following commands can implement a VLAN ACL called test?

   a. access-list vlan test

   b. vacl test

   c. switchport vacl test

   d. vlan access-map test

4. After a VACL is configured, where is it applied?

   a. Globally on a VLAN

   b. On the VLAN interface

   c. In the VLAN configuration

   d. On all ports or interfaces mapped to a VLAN

5. Which of the following private VLANs is the most restrictive?

   a. Community VLAN

   b. Isolated VLAN

   c. Restricted VLAN

   d. Promiscuous VLAN

6. The **vlan 100** command has just been entered. What is the next command needed to configure VLAN 100 as a secondary isolated VLAN?

   a. private-vlan isolated

   b. private-vlan isolated 100

   c. pvlan secondary isolated

   d. No further configuration necessary

7. What type of port configuration should you use for private VLAN interfaces that connect to a router?

   a. Host

   b. Gateway

   c. Promiscuous

   d. Transparent

8. Promiscuous ports must be _____ to primary and secondary VLANs, and host ports must be _____.

   a. Mapped, associated

   b. Mapped, mapped

   c. Associated, mapped

   d. Associated, associated

9. In a switch spoofing attack, an attacker makes use of which one of the following?

   a. The switch management IP address

   b. CDP message exchanges

   c. Spanning Tree Protocol

   d. DTP to negotiate a trunk

10. Which one of the following commands can be used to prevent a switch spoofing attack on an end-user port?

   a. switchport mode access

   b. switchport mode trunk

   c. no switchport spoof

   d. spanning-tree spoof-guard

11. Which one of the following represents the spoofed information an attacker sends in a VLAN hopping attack?

   a. 802.1Q tags

   b. DTP information

   c. VTP information

   d. 802.1x information

12. Which one of the following methods can be used to prevent a VLAN hopping attack?

   a. Use VTP throughout the network.

   b. Set the native VLAN to the user access VLAN.

   c. Prune the native VLAN off a trunk link.

   d. Avoid using EtherChannel link bundling.

Foundation Topics

VLAN Access Lists

Access lists can manage or control traffic as it passes through a switch. When normal access lists are configured on a Catalyst switch, they filter traffic through the use of the Ternary content-addressable memory (TCAM). Recall from Chapter 2, "Switch Operation," that access lists (also known as *router access lists*, or RACLs) are merged or compiled into the TCAM. Each ACL is applied to an interface according to the direction of traffic—inbound or outbound. Packets then can be filtered in hardware with no switching performance penalty. However, only packets that pass *between* VLANs can be filtered this way.

Packets that stay in the same VLAN do not cross a VLAN or interface boundary and do not necessarily have a direction in relation to an interface. These packets also might be non-IP, non-IPX, or completely bridged; therefore, they never pass through the multilayer switching mechanism. VLAN access lists (VACL) are filters that directly can affect how packets are handled *within* a VLAN.

VACLs are somewhat different from RACLs or traditional access control lists. Although they, too, are merged into the TCAM, they can permit, deny, or redirect packets as they are matched. VACLs also are configured in a route map fashion, with a series of matching conditions and actions to take.

VACL Configuration

Key Topic

VACLs are configured as a VLAN access map in much the same format as a route map. A VLAN access map consists of one or more statements, each having a common map name. First, you define the VACL with the following global configuration command:

```
Switch(config)# vlan access-map map-name [sequence-number]
```

Access map statements are evaluated in sequence according to the *sequence-number*. Each statement can contain one or more matching conditions, followed by an action.

Next, define the matching conditions that identify the traffic to be filtered. Matching is performed by access lists (IP, IPX, or MAC address ACLs), which you must configure independently. Configure a matching condition with one of the following access map configuration commands:

```
Switch(config-access-map)# match ip address {acl-number | acl-name}
Switch(config-access-map)# match ipx address {acl-number | acl-name}
Switch(config-access-map)# match mac address acl-name
```

You can repeat these commands to define several matching conditions; the first match encountered triggers an action to take. Define the action with the following access map configuration command:

```
Switch(config-access-map)# action {drop | forward [capture] | redirect type
    mod/num}
```

A VACL can either drop a matching packet, forward it, or redirect it to another interface. The TCAM performs the entire VACL match and action as packets are switched or bridged within a VLAN or routed into or out of a VLAN.

Finally, you must apply the VACL to a VLAN using the following global configuration command:

```
Switch(config)# vlan filter map-name vlan-list vlan-list
```

Notice that the VACL is applied globally to one or more VLANs listed and not to a VLAN interface (SVI). Recall that VLANs can be present in a switch as explicit interfaces or as inherent Layer 2 entities. The VLAN interface is the point where packets enter or leave a VLAN, so it does not make sense to apply a VACL there. Instead, the VACL needs to function *within* the VLAN itself, where there is no inbound or outbound direction.

For example, suppose that you need to filter traffic within VLAN 99 so that host 192.168.99.17 is not allowed to contact any other host on its local subnet. Access list local-17 is created to identify traffic between this host and anything else on its local subnet. Then a VLAN access map is defined: If the local-17 access list permits the IP address, the packet is dropped; otherwise, the packet is forwarded. Example 17-1 shows the commands necessary for this example.

Example 17-1   *Filtering Traffic Within the Local Subnet*

```
Switch(config)# ip access-list extended local-17
Switch(config-acl)# permit ip host 192.168.99.17 192.168.99.0  0.0.0.255
Switch(config-acl)# exit
Switch(config)# vlan access-map block-17 10
Switch(config-access-map)# match ip address local-17
Switch(config-access-map)# action drop
Switch(config-access-map)# vlan access-map block-17 20
Switch(config-access-map)# action forward
Switch(config-access-map)# exit
Switch(config)# vlan filter block-17 vlan-list 99
```

Private VLANs

Normally, traffic is allowed to move unrestricted within a VLAN. Packets sent from one host to another normally are heard only by the destination host because of the nature of Layer 2 switching.

However, if one host broadcasts a packet, all hosts on the VLAN must listen. You can use a VACL to filter packets between a source and destination in a VLAN if both connect to the local switch.

Sometimes it would be nice to have the capability to segment traffic within a single VLAN, without having to use multiple VLANs and a router. For example, in a single-VLAN server farm, all servers should be capable of communicating with the router or gateway, but the servers should not have to listen to each other's broadcast traffic. Taking this a step further, suppose that each server belongs to a separate organization. Now each server should be isolated from the others but still be capable of reaching the gateway to find clients not on the local network.

Another application is a service provider network. Here, the provider might want to use a single VLAN to connect to several customer networks. Each customer needs to be able to contact the provider's gateway on the VLAN. Clearly, the customer sites do not need to interact with each other.

Private VLANs (PVLAN) solve this problem on Catalyst switches. In a nutshell, a normal, or *primary*, VLAN can be logically associated with special unidirectional, or secondary, VLANs. Hosts associated with a secondary VLAN can communicate with ports on the primary VLAN (a router, for example), but not with another secondary VLAN. A secondary VLAN is configured as one of the following types:

- **Isolated**—Any switch ports associated with an isolated VLAN can reach the primary VLAN but not any other secondary VLAN. In addition, hosts associated with the same isolated VLAN cannot reach each other. They are, in effect, isolated from everything except the primary VLAN.

- **Community**—Any switch ports associated with a common community VLAN can communicate with each other and with the primary VLAN but not with any other secondary VLAN. This provides the basis for server farms and workgroups within an organization, while giving isolation between organizations.

All secondary VLANs must be associated with one primary VLAN to set up the uni-directional relationship. Private VLANs are configured using special cases of regular VLANs. However, the VLAN Trunking Protocol (VTP) does not pass any information about the private VLAN configuration. Therefore, private VLANs are only locally significant to a switch. Each of the private VLANs must be configured locally on each switch that interconnects them.

You must configure each physical switch port that uses a private VLAN with a VLAN association. You also must define the port with one of the following modes:

- **Promiscuous**—The switch port connects to a router, firewall, or other common gateway device. This port can communicate with anything else connected to the primary or any secondary VLAN. In other words, the port is in promiscuous mode, in which the rules of private VLANs are ignored.

- **Host**—The switch port connects to a regular host that resides on an isolated or community VLAN. The port communicates only with a promiscuous port or ports on the same community VLAN.

Figure 17-1 shows the basic private VLAN operation. Some host PCs connect to a secondary community VLAN. The two community VLANs associate with a primary VLAN, where the router connects. The router connects to a promiscuous port on the primary VLAN. A single host PC connects to a secondary isolated VLAN, so it can communicate only with the router's promiscuous port.

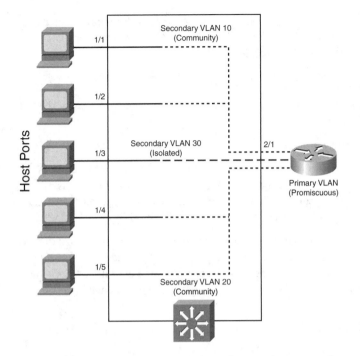

Figure 17-1 *Private VLAN Functionality Within a Switch*

Private VLAN Configuration

Defining a private VLAN involves several configuration steps. These steps are described in the sections that follow so that you can use them.

Configure the Private VLANs

To configure a private VLAN, begin by defining any secondary VLANs that are needed for isolation using the following configuration commands:

```
Switch(config)# vlan vlan-id
Switch(config-vlan)# private-vlan {isolated | community}
```

The secondary VLAN can be an isolated VLAN (no connectivity between isolated ports) or a community VLAN (connectivity between member ports).

Now define the primary VLAN that will provide the underlying private VLAN connectivity using the following configuration commands:

```
Switch(config)# vlan vlan-id
Switch(config-vlan)# private-vlan primary
Switch(config-vlan)# private-vlan association {secondary-vlan-list | add
  secondary-vlan-list | remove secondary-vlan-list}
```

Be sure to associate the primary VLAN with all its component secondary VLANs using the **association** keyword. If the primary VLAN already has been configured, you can add (**add**) or remove (**remove**) secondary VLAN associations individually.

These VLAN configuration commands set up only the mechanisms for unidirectional connectivity from the secondary VLANs to the primary VLAN. You also must associate the individual switch ports with their respective private VLANs.

Associate Ports with Private VLANs

First, define the function of the port that will participate on a private VLAN using the following configuration command:

```
Switch(config-if)# switchport mode private-vlan {host | promiscuous}
```

If the host connected to this port is a router, firewall, or common gateway for the VLAN, use the **promiscuous** keyword. This allows the host to reach all other promiscuous, isolated, or community ports associated with the primary VLAN. Otherwise, any isolated or community port must receive the **host** keyword.

For a nonpromiscuous port (using the **switchport mode private-vlan host** command), you must associate the switch port with the appropriate primary and secondary VLANs. Remember, only the private VLANs themselves have been configured until now. The switch port must know how to interact with the various VLANs using the following interface configuration command:

```
Switch(config-if)# switchport private-vlan host-association primary-vlan-id
    secondary-vlan-id
```

Note: When a switch port is associated with private VLANs, you do not have to configure a static access VLAN. Instead, the port takes on membership in the primary and secondary VLANs simultaneously. This does not mean that the port has a fully functional assignment to multiple VLANs. Instead, it takes on only the unidirectional behavior between the secondary and primary VLANs.

For a promiscuous port (using the **switchport mode private-vlan promiscuous** command), you must map the port to primary and secondary VLANs. Notice that promiscuous mode ports, or ports that can communicate with any other private VLAN device, are mapped, whereas other secondary VLAN ports are associated. One (promiscuous mode port) exhibits bidirectional behavior, whereas the other (secondary VLAN ports) exhibits unidirectional or logical behavior.

Use the following interface configuration command to map promiscuous mode ports to primary and secondary VLANs:

```
Switch(config-if)# switchport private-vlan mapping primary-vlan-id secondary-
    vlan-list | {add secondary-vlan-list} | {remove secondary-vlan-list}
```

As an example, assume that the switch in Figure 17-1 is configured as in Example 17-2. Host PCs on ports Fast Ethernet 1/1 and 1/2 are in community VLAN 10, hosts on ports Fast Ethernet 1/4 and 1/5 are in community VLAN 20, and the host on port Fast Ethernet 1/3 is in isolated VLAN 30. The router on port Fast Ethernet 2/1 is in promiscuous mode on primary VLAN 100. Each VLAN is assigned a role, and the primary VLAN is associated with its secondary VLANs. Then each interface is associated with a primary and secondary VLAN (if a host is attached) or mapped to the primary and secondary VLANs (if a promiscuous host is attached).

Example 17-2   *Configuring Ports with Private VLANs*

```
Switch(config)# vlan 10
Switch(config-vlan)# private-vlan community
Switch(config-vlan)# vlan 20
Switch(config-vlan)# private-vlan community
Switch(config-vlan)# vlan 30
Switch(config-vlan)# private-vlan isolated
Switch(config-vlan)# vlan 100
Switch(config-vlan)# private-vlan primary
Switch(config-vlan)# private-vlan association 10,20,30
Switch(config-vlan)# exit
Switch(config)# interface range fastethernet 1/1 - 1/2
Switch(config-if)# switchport mode private-vlan host
Switch(config-if)# switchport private-vlan host-association 100 10
Switch(config-if)# exit
Switch(config)# interface range fastethernet 1/4 - 1/5
Switch(config-if)# switchport mode private-vlan host
Switch(config-if)# switchport private-vlan host-association 100 20
Switch(config-if)# exit
Switch(config)# interface fastethernet 1/3
Switch(config-if)# switchport mode private-vlan host
Switch(config-if)# switchport private-vlan host-association 100 30
Switch(config-if)# exit
Switch(config)# interface fastethernet 2/1
Switch(config-if)# switchport mode private-vlan promiscuous
Switch(config-if)# switchport private-vlan mapping 100 10,20,30
```

Associate Secondary VLANs to a Primary VLAN SVI

On switched virtual interfaces, or VLAN interfaces configured with Layer 3 addresses, you must configure some additional private VLAN mapping. Consider a different example, where the SVI for the primary VLAN, VLAN 200, has an IP address and participates in routing traffic. Secondary VLANs 40 (an isolated VLAN) and 50 (a community VLAN) are associated at Layer 2 with primary VLAN 200 using the configuration in Example 17-3.

Example 17-3   *Associating Secondary VLANs to a Primary VLAN SVI*

```
Switch(config)# vlan 40
Switch(config-vlan)# private-vlan isolated
Switch(config-vlan)# vlan 50
Switch(config-vlan)# private-vlan community
Switch(config-vlan)# vlan 200
Switch(config-vlan)# private-vlan primary
Switch(config-vlan)# private-vlan association 40,50
```

```
Switch(config-vlan)# exit
Switch(config)# interface vlan 200
Switch(config-if)# ip address 192.168.199.1 255.255.255.0
```

Primary VLAN 200 can forward traffic at Layer 3, but the secondary VLAN associations with it are good at only Layer 2. To allow Layer 3 traffic switching coming from the secondary VLANs as well, you must add a private VLAN mapping to the primary VLAN (SVI) interface, using the following interface configuration command:

```
Switch(config-if)# private-vlan mapping {secondary-vlan-list | add secondary-
    vlan-list | remove secondary-vlan-list}
```

The primary VLAN SVI function is extended to the secondary VLANs instead of requiring SVIs for each of them. If some mapping already has been configured for the primary VLAN SVI, you can add (**add**) or remove (**remove**) secondary VLAN mappings individually.

For Example 17-3, you would map the private VLAN by adding the following commands:

```
Switch(config)# interface vlan 200
Switch(config-if)# private-vlan mapping 40,50
```

Securing VLAN Trunks

Because trunk links usually are bounded between two switches, you might think that they are more or less secure. Each end of the trunk is connected to a device that is under your control, VLANs carried over the trunk remain isolated, and so on.

Some attacks or exploits can be leveraged to gain access to a trunk or to the VLANs carried over a trunk. Therefore, you should become familiar with how the attacks work and what steps you can take to prevent them in the first place.

Switch Spoofing

Recall from Chapter 4, "VLANs and Trunks," that two switches can be connected by a common trunk link that can carry traffic from multiple VLANs. The trunk does not have to exist all the time. The switches dynamically can negotiate its use and its encapsulation mode by exchanging Dynamic Trunking Protocol (DTP) messages.

Although DTP can make switch administration easier, it also can expose switch ports to be compromised. Suppose that a switch port is left to its default configuration, in which the trunking mode is auto. Normally, the switch port would wait to be asked by another switch in the auto or on mode to become a trunk.

Key Topic

Now suppose that an end user's PC is connected to that port. A well-behaved end user would not use DTP at all, so the port would come up in access mode with a single-access VLAN. A malicious user, however, might exploit the use of DTP and attempt to negotiate a trunk with the switch port. This makes the PC appear to be another switch; in effect, the PC is spoofing a switch.

After the trunk is negotiated, the attacker has access to any VLAN that is permitted to pass over the trunk. If the switch port has been left to its default configuration, all VLANs configured on the switch are allowed onto the trunk. This scenario is shown in Figure 17-2. The attacker can receive any traffic being sent over the trunk on any VLAN. In addition, he can send traffic into any VLAN of his choice.

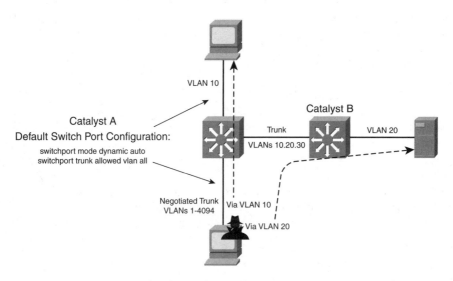

Figure 17-2   *An Example of Switch Spoofing to Gain Access to a Trunk*

To demonstrate this further, consider the output in Example 17-4, which shows the default access switch port configuration. Notice that trunking is possible because the port is set to dynamic auto mode, awaiting DTP negotiation from a connected device. If a trunk is negotiated, all VLANs are permitted to be carried over it.

Example 17-4   *Displaying the Default Switch Port Configuration*

```
Switch# show interfaces fastethernet 1/0/46 switchport
Name: Fa1/0/46
Switchport: Enabled
Administrative Mode: dynamic auto
Operational Mode: trunk
Administrative Trunking Encapsulation: negotiate
Negotiation of Trunking: On
Access Mode VLAN: 1 (default)
Trunking Native Mode VLAN: 1 (default)
Administrative Native VLAN tagging: enabled
Voice VLAN: none
Administrative private-vlan host-association: none
```

```
Administrative private-vlan mapping: none
Administrative private-vlan trunk native VLAN: none
Administrative private-vlan trunk Native VLAN tagging: enabled
Administrative private-vlan trunk encapsulation: dot1q
Administrative private-vlan trunk normal VLANs: none
Administrative private-vlan trunk private VLANs: none
Operational private-vlan: none
Trunking VLANs Enabled: ALL
Pruning VLANs Enabled: 2-1001
Capture Mode Disabled Capture VLANs Allowed: ALL
Protected: false
Unknown unicast blocked: disabled
Unknown multicast blocked: disabled
Appliance trust: none
Switch#
```

The solution to this situation is to configure *every* switch port to have an expected and controlled behavior. For example, instead of leaving an end-user switch port set to use DTP in auto mode, configure it to static access mode with the following commands:

```
Switch(config)# interface type mod/num
Switch(config-if)# switchport access vlan vlan-id
Switch(config-if)# switchport mode access
```

This way, an end user never will be able to send any type of spoofed traffic that will make the switch port begin trunking.

In addition, you might be wise to disable any unused switch ports to prevent someone from discovering a live port that might be exploited.

VLAN Hopping

Key Topic

When securing VLAN trunks, also consider the potential for an exploit called *VLAN hopping*. Here, an attacker positioned on one access VLAN can craft and send frames with spoofed 802.1Q tags so that the packet payloads ultimately appear on a totally different VLAN, all without the use of a router.

For this exploit to work, the following conditions must exist in the network configuration:

■ The attacker is connected to an access switch port.

■ The same switch must have an 802.1Q trunk.

■ The trunk must have the attacker's access VLAN as its native VLAN.

Figure 17-3 shows how VLAN hopping works. The attacker, situated on VLAN 10, sends frames that are doubly tagged as if an 802.1Q trunk were being used. Naturally, the attacker is not connected to a trunk; he is spoofing the trunk encapsulation to trick the switch into making the frames hop over to another VLAN.

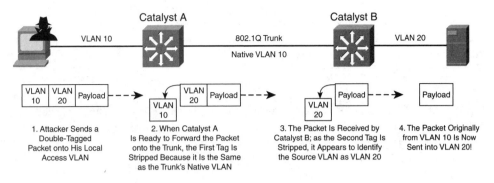

Figure 17-3 *VLAN Hopping Attack Process*

The regular frame—or malicious payload, in this case—is first given an 802.1Q tag with the VLAN ID of the target VLAN. Then a second bogus 802.1Q tag is added with the attacker's access VLAN ID.

When the local switch Catalyst A receives a doubly tagged frame, it decides to forward it out the trunk interface. Because the first (outermost) tag has the same VLAN ID as the trunk's native VLAN, that tag is removed as the frame is sent on the trunk. The switch believes that the native VLAN should be untagged, as it should. Now the second (innermost) tag is exposed on the trunk.

When Catalyst B receives the frame, it examines any 802.1Q tag it finds. The spoofed tag for VLAN 20 is found, so the tag is removed and the frame is forwarded onto VLAN 20. Now the attacker successfully has sent a frame on VLAN 10 and gotten the frame injected onto VLAN 20—all through Layer 2 switching.

Clearly, the key to this type of attack revolves around the use of untagged native VLANs. Therefore, to thwart VLAN hopping, you always should carefully configure trunk links with the following steps:

Step 1.   Set the native VLAN of a trunk to a bogus or unused VLAN ID.

Step 2.   Prune the native VLAN off both ends of the trunk.

For example, suppose that an 802.1Q trunk should carry only VLANs 10 and 20. You should set the native VLAN to an unused value, such as 800. Then you should remove VLAN 800 from the trunk so that it is confined to the trunk link itself. Example 17-5 demonstrates how to accomplish this.

Example 17-5   *Configuring the 802.1Q Trunk to Carry Only VLANs 10 and 20*

```
Switch(config)# vlan 800
Switch(config-vlan)# name bogus_native
Switch(config-vlan)# exit
Switch(config)# interface gigabitethernet 1/1
Switch(config-if)# switchport trunk encapsulation dot1q
```

```
Switch(config-if)# switchport trunk native vlan 800
Switch(config-if)# switchport trunk allowed vlan remove 800
Switch(config-if)# switchport mode trunk
```

Tip: Although maintenance protocols such as CDP, PAgP, and DTP normally are carried over the native VLAN of a trunk, they will not be affected if the native VLAN is pruned from the trunk. They still will be sent and received on the native VLAN as a special case even if the native VLAN ID is not in the list of allowed VLANs.

One alternative is to force all 802.1Q trunks to add tags to frames for the native VLAN, too. The double-tagged VLAN hopping attack won't work because the switch won't remove the first tag with the native VLAN ID (VLAN 10 in the example). Instead, that tag will remain on the spoofed frame as it enters the trunk. At the far end of the trunk, the same tag will be examined, and the frame will stay on the original access VLAN (VLAN 10).

To force a switch to tag the native VLAN on all its 802.1Q trunks, you can use the following command:

```
Switch(config)# vlan dot1q tag native
```

Exam Preparation Tasks

Review All Key Topics

Review the most important topics in the chapter, noted with the Key Topic icon in the outer margin of the page. Table 17-2 lists a reference of these key topics and the page numbers on which each is found.

Key Topic

Table 17-2 *Key Topics for Chapter 17*

Key Topic Element	Description	Page Number
Paragraph	Explains VLAN ACLs and how they are configured	398
Paragraph	Discusses private VLANs, primary and secondary VLANs, and isolated and community VLANs	400
List	Discusses promiscuous and host ports within a private VLAN	404
Paragraph	Explains the switch spoofing attack	
Paragraph	Explains the VLAN hopping attack	406
List	Explains the steps necessary to prevent a VLAN hopping attack	407

Complete Tables and Lists from Memory

Print a copy of Appendix C, "Memory Tables," (found on the CD), or at least the section for this chapter, and complete the tables and lists from memory. Appendix D, "Memory Tables Answer Key," also on the CD, includes completed tables and lists to check your work.

Define Key Terms

Define the following key terms from this chapter, and check your answers in the glossary:

VACL, private VLAN, primary VLAN, secondary VLAN, isolated VLAN, community VLAN, promiscuous port, host port, switch spoofing, VLAN hopping

Use Command Reference to Check Your Memory

This section includes the most important configuration and EXEC commands covered in this chapter. It might not be necessary to memorize the complete syntax of every command, but you should remember the basic keywords that are needed.

To test your memory of the VLAN ACL and private VLAN configuration, cover the right side of Tables 17-3 through 17-4 with a piece of paper, read the description on the left side, and then see how much of the command you can remember.

Table 17-3   *VLAN ACL Configuration Commands*

Task	Command Syntax
Define a VACL.	**vlan access-map** *map-name* [*sequence-number*]
Define a matching condition.	**match** {**ip address** {*acl-number*	*acl-name*}}	{**ipx address** {*acl-number*	*acl-name*}	{**mac address** *acl-name*}}
Define an action.	**action** {**drop**	**forward** [**capture**]	**redirect** *type mod/num*}
Apply the VACL to VLANs.	**vlan filter** *map-name* **vlan-list** *vlan-list*

Table 17-4   *Private VLAN Configuration Commands*

Task	Command Syntax
Define a secondary VLAN.	**vlan** *vlan-id* **private-vlan** {**isolated**	**community**}
Define a primary VLAN; associate it with secondary VLANs.	**vlan** *vlan-id* **private-vlan primary** **private-vlan association** {*secondary-vlan-list*	**add** *secondary-vlan-list*	**remove** *secondary-vlan-list*}
Associate ports with private VLANs.	**switchport mode private-vlan** {**host**	**promiscuous**}
Associate nonpromiscuous ports with private VLANs.	**switchport private-vlan host-association** *primary-vlan-id secondary-vlan-id*
Associate promiscuous ports with private VLANs.	**switchport private-vlan mapping** {*primary-vlan-id*} {*secondary-vlan-list*}	{**add** *secondary-vlan-list*}	{**remove** *secondary-vlan-list*}
Associate secondary VLANs with a primary VLAN Layer 3 SVI.	**private-vlan mapping** {*secondary-vlan-list*	**add** *secondary-vlan-list*	**remove** *secondary-vlan-list*}

Part VI: Final Exam Preparation

Chapter 18: **Final Preparation**

The first 17 chapters of this book cover the technologies, protocols, commands, and features required to be prepared to pass the CCNP SWITCH exam. Although these chapters supply the detailed information, most people need more preparation than just reading the first 17 chapters of this book. This chapter details a set of tools and a study plan to help you complete your preparation for the exam.

This short chapter has two main sections. The first section explains how to install the exam engine and practice exams from the CD that accompanies this book. The second section lists some suggestions for a study plan, now that you have completed all the earlier chapters in this book.

Note: Along with the exam engine and other features, Appendix C, "Memory Tables," and Appendix D, "Memory Tables Answer Key," are included only on the CD that comes with this book. To access those, just insert the CD and make the appropriate selection from the opening interface.

Final Preparation

Exam Engine and Questions on the CD

The CD in the back of this book includes the Boson Exam Environment (BEE). The BEE is the exam-engine software that delivers and grades a set of free practice questions written by Cisco Press. The BEE supports multiple-choice questions, drag-and-drop questions, and many scenario-based questions that require the same level of analysis as the questions on the CCNP SWITCH 642-813 exam. The installation process has two major steps. The first step is installing the BEE software—the CD in the back of this book has a recent copy of the BEE software, supplied by Boson Software (www.boson.com). The second step is activating and downloading the free practice questions. The practice questions written by Cisco Press for the CCNP SWITCH 642-813 exam are not on the CD; instead, the practice questions must be downloaded from www.boson.com.

Note: The CD case in the back of this book includes the CD and a piece of paper. The paper contains the activation key for the practice questions associated with this book. *Do not lose this activation key.*

Install the Exam Engine Software from the CD

The following are the steps you should perform to install the software:

Step 1. Insert the CD into your computer.

Step 2. From the main menu, click the option to install the Boson Exam Environment (BEE). The software that automatically runs is the Cisco Press software needed to access and use all CD-based features, including the BEE, a PDF of this book, and the CD-only appendixes.

Step 3. Respond to the prompt windows as you would with any typical software installation process.

The installation process might give you the option to register the software. This process requires you to establish a login at the www.boson.com website. You need this login to activate the exam; therefore, you should register when prompted.

Activate and Download the Practice Exam

After the Boson Exam Environment (BEE) is installed, activate the exam associated with this book.

Step 1.   Launch the BEE from the Start menu.

Step 2.   The first time you run the software, you should be asked to either log in or register an account. If you do not already have an account with Boson, select the option to register a new account. You must register to download and use the exam.)

Step 3.   After you have registered or logged in, the software might prompt you to download the latest version of the software, which you should do. Note that this process updates the BEE, not the practice exam.

Step 4.   From the Boson Exam Environment main window, click the Exam Wizard button to activate and download the exam associated with this book

Step 5.   From the Exam Wizard dialog box, select Activate a Purchased Exam and click the Next button. Although you did not purchase the exam directly, you purchased it indirectly when you bought the book.

Step 6.   In the EULA Agreement window, click Yes to accept the terms of the license agreement, and then click Next. If you do not accept the terms of the license agreement, you will be unable to install or use the software.

Step 7.   In the Activate Exam Wizard dialog box, enter the activation key from the paper inside the CD holder in the back of the book, and then click Next.

Step 8.   Wait while the activation process downloads the practice questions. When the exam has been downloaded, the main BEE menu should list a new exam. If you do not see the exam, click the My Exams tab on the menu. You might also need to click the plus sign icon (+) to expand the menu and see the exam.

At this point, the software and practice questions are ready to use.

Activating Other Exams

You need to install the exam software and register only once. Then, for each new exam, you will need to complete only a few additional steps. For example, if you bought this book along with another CCNP Official Certification Guide, you would need to perform the following steps:

Step 1.   Launch the BEE (if it is not already open).

Step 2.   Perform Steps 4 through 7 under the section "Activate and Download the Practice Exam," earlier in the chapter.

Step 3.   Repeat Steps 1 and 2 for any exams in other Cisco Press book.

You can also purchase Boson ExSim-Max practice exams that are written and developed by Boson Software's subject-matter experts at www.boson.com. The ExSim-Max practice exams simulate the content on the actual certification exams, enabling you to gauge whether you are ready to pass the real exam. When you purchase an ExSim-Max practice exam, you receive an activation key. You can then activate and download the exam by performing Steps 1 and 2 above.

Study Plan

With plenty of resources at your disposal, you should approach studying for the CCNP SWITCH exam with a plan. Consider the following ideas as you move from reading this book to preparing for the exam.

Recall the Facts

As with most exams, many facts, concepts, and definitions must be recalled to do well on the test. If you do not work with every Cisco LAN switching feature on a daily basis, you might have trouble remembering everything that might appear on the CCNP SWITCH exam.

You can refresh your memory and practice recalling information by reviewing the activities in the "Exam Preparation Tasks" section at the end of each chapter. These sections will help you study key topics, memorize the definitions of important LAN switching terms, and recall the basic command syntax of configuration and verification commands.

Practice Configurations

The latest revision to the CCNP exams includes an emphasis on practical knowledge. You need to be familiar with switch features and the order in which configuration steps should be implemented. You also need to know how to plan a LAN switching project and how to verify your results.

For the first time in the CCNP program, this means that hands-on experience is going to take you over the edge to confidently and accurately build or verify configurations (and pass the exam). If at all possible, you should try to gain access to some Cisco Catalyst switches and spend some time working with various features.

If you have access to a lab provided by your company, take advantage of it. You might also have some Cisco equipment in a personal lab at home. Otherwise, there are a number of sources for lab access, including online rack rentals from trusted Cisco Partners and the Cisco Partner E-Learning Connection (PEC), if you work for a partner. Nothing beats hands-on experience.

In addition, you can review the key topics in each chapter and follow the example configurations in this book. At the least, you will see the command syntax and the sequence the configuration commands should be entered.

Use the Exam Engine

The exam engine on the accompanying CD can also be used as a study tool, presenting a bank of unique exam-realistic questions available only with this book. The exam engine includes two basic modes:

■ **Study mode**—This is most useful when you want to review material or practice recalling information, all without a time constraint. In study mode, you can customize how the questions will be presented, such as randomizing the order of the questions, randomizing the order of the answers, focusing on specific topics, automatically displaying answers as you go, and so on.

■ **Simulation mode**—This mode simulates an actual CCNP SWITCH exam by using a set number of questions and a set time period. These timed exams allow you to study for the actual exam and to hone your time-management skills so that you can complete the full set of questions while under a time constraint.

The Cisco Learning Network

Cisco provides a wide variety of CCNP preparation tools at the Cisco Learning Network website, https://cisco.hosted.jivesoftware.com/index.jspa?ciscoHome=true. The Cisco Learning Network includes Quick Learning Modules, interviews about taking the CCNP exams, documents, discussions, blogs, and access to the CCNP Routing and Switching study group.

You can use the Cisco Learning Network without a registered login, but you can access many more resources by registering for an account or by using your Cisco.com user ID.

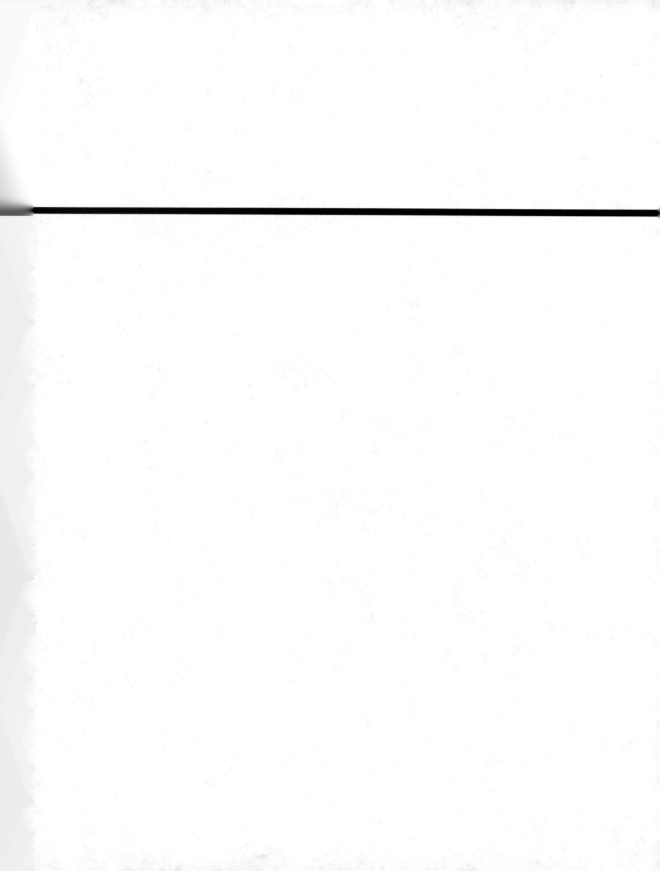

Part VII: Appendixes

Answers to the "Do I Know This Already?" Quizzes

Chapter 2

1. B

2. B

3. B

4. C

5. C

6. B

7. C

8. D

9. B

10. C

11. D

12. B

Chapter 3

1. C

2. B

3. A

4. B

5. B

6. B

7. C

8. C

9. C

10. D

11. E

Chapter 4

1. C

2. B

3. B

4. B

5. B

6. C

7. D

8. C

9. B

10. A

11. C

12. A

13. B and C

14. C

Chapter 5

1. C

2. A

3. C

4. B

5. B

6. B and C

7. A

8. C

9. C

10. B

11. D

12. B

Chapter 6

1. E
2. C
3. C
4. D
5. C
6. C
7. A
8. D
9. B
10. C
11. C
12. C
13. C

Chapter 7

1. C
2. C
3. B
4. B
5. C
6. C
7. A
8. B
9. D
10. B
11. B
12. C

Chapter 8

1. C
2. C
3. D
4. C
5. C
6. C
7. B
8. D
9. C
10. A
11. A
12. D
13. C

Chapter 9

1. B
2. C
3. C
4. B
5. B
6. A
7. B
8. B
9. C
10. C
11. C
12. B
13. B

Chapter 10

1. A
2. C
3. A
4. C
5. A
6. B
7. C
8. D
9. C
10. D
11. B
12. C

Chapter 11

1. D
2. A
3. A
4. B
5. C
6. C
7. C
8. D
9. C
10. C
11. C
12. A

Chapter 12

1. A

2. C

3. B

4. C

5. C

6. C

7. C

8. D

9. C

10. C

11. A and B

12. A and C

13. D

14. A and C

15. C, D, and E

16. B

17. B and C

Chapter 13

1. D

2. D

3. C

4. B

5. B

6. B

7. C

8. C

9. C

10. B

11. B

12. B

Chapter 14

1. B

2. D

3. C

4. B

5. A

6. D

7. E

8. B

9. D

10. C

11. B

12. D

Chapter 15

1. D

2. B

3. B

4. D

5. C

6. A

7. B

8. C

9. B

10. A

11. A

12. D

13. A

14. B

15. C

16. D

Chapter 16

1. C

2. D

3. B

4. B. The trick is in the maximum three keywords. This sets the maximum number of addresses that can be learned on a port. If only one static address is configured, two more addresses can be learned dynamically.

5. C

6. A

7. B

8. C

9. C. Because of the variety of user host platforms, port-based authentication (802.1x) cannot be used. The problem also states that the goal is to restrict access to physical switch ports, so AAA is of no benefit. Port security can do the job by restricting access according to the end users' MAC addresses.

10. B

11. C and D

12. C

13. B and D

14. C

Chapter 17

1. C
2. D
3. D
4. A
5. B
6. A
7. C
8. A
9. D
10. A
11. A
12. C

SWITCH Exam Updates: Version 1.1

> **Note:** Coverage of this topic should be integrated into your study of Chapter 11, "Multilayer Switching," right before the section "Multilayer Switching with CEF."

Controlling the Automatic State of an SVI

Because a Layer 3 SVI is bound to a Layer 2 VLAN on a switch, it normally follows the state of the VLAN on that switch automatically. If the switch has at least one Layer 2 interface that is up and active on the VLAN, the Layer 3 SVI will be brought up, too. If all the Layer 2 interfaces assigned to the VLAN are down, the Layer 3 interface will be brought down.

This is the default "autostate" behavior. The idea is to bring the Layer 3 interface down so that routing protocols will cease advertising a route to the IP subnet if no active switch interfaces exist on the VLAN where the subnet exists.

When the SVI autostate feature is enabled, a Layer 3 SVI can come up only if the following three conditions are met:

- The VLAN bound to the SVI exists and is active in the VLAN database on the switch

- The SVI is not administratively shut down

- At least one Layer 2 interface is assigned to the SVI's VLAN and is in the up state, with STP forwarding

As an example, a switch has VLAN 2 defined and assigned to a variety of Layer 2 interfaces, but none of the interfaces are up. A Layer 3 SVI called interface vlan2 is then defined. Watch what happens to interface vlan2 in the following console output:

```
Switch(config)#interface vlan2
Switch(config-if)#
*Apr 21 10:13:10.949: %LINK-3-UPDOWN: Interface Vlan2, changed state to up
Switch(config-if)#
Switch(config-if)#ip address 192.168.1.1 255.255.255.0
Switch(config-if)#^Z
Switch#
```

```
Switch# show ip interface brief
Interface          IP-Address    OK? Method  Status                    Protocol
Vlan1              unassigned    YES manual  administratively down     down
Vlan2              192.168.1.1   YES manual  up                        down
FastEthernet1/0/1  unassigned    YES unset   down                      down
FastEthernet1/0/2  unassigned    YES unset   down                      down
```

Even before an IP address can be configured on the new SVI, the switch brings its status up but its line protocol stays down. In other words, the SVI now exists and is bound to VLAN 2, but it is unusable until at least one Layer 2 interface becomes active on VLAN 2.

In the following output, notice what happens as a PC is connected to interface FastEthernet1/0/1, which is assigned to VLAN 2:

```
Switch#
*Apr 21 10:21:31.925: %LINK-3-UPDOWN: Interface FastEthernet1/0/1, changed
  state to up
*Apr 21 10:21:32.009: %LINEPROTO-5-UPDOWN: Line protocol on Interface Vlan2,
  changed state to up
*Apr 21 10:21:32.932: %LINEPROTO-5-UPDOWN: Line protocol on Interface
  FastEthernet1/0/1, changed
state to up
Switch#
```

When the Layer 2 interface comes up, so does the line protocol of the SVI. When the PC is disconnected or powered down, the SVI is automatically taken down, as shown in the following output:

```
Switch#
*Apr 21 10:21:45.624: %LINEPROTO-5-UPDOWN: Line protocol on Interface
  FastEthernet1/0/1, changed state to
down
*Apr 21 10:21:45.624: %LINEPROTO-5-UPDOWN: Line protocol on Interface Vlan2,
  changed state to down
*Apr 21 10:21:46.622: %LINK-3-UPDOWN: Interface FastEthernet1/0/1, changed
  state to down
Switch#
```

You can override the default behavior by disabling autostate on a per-interface basis with the following command:

```
Switch(config-if)# switchport autostate exclude
```

When an interface is excluded, any influence that it might have had over the SVI state is removed. This command isn't normally used unless the interface is a special case, such as an interface where a network analyzer is connected. The analyzer would capture traffic without being an active participant in the VLAN that is assigned to the interface.

Note: Coverage of these topics should be integrated into your study of Chapter 13, "Layer 3 High Availability."

Monitoring the Network to Maximize Availability

You can (and should) design and implement a highly available network by leveraging many of the features presented in this book. For example, you can bring up redundant links between switches, redundant gateways between switches, and redundant route processors to provide as much "uptime" as possible for the end users and mission-critical applications. Once configured, these features are all automatic, requiring no further intervention.

But how will you know when some event occurs to trigger a high availability feature? Suppose a redundant link goes down for some reason. If you don't know about it and aren't able to fix it right away, then you no longer have redundant links to mitigate another future failure.

This section covers the following three important ways you can monitor the network to detect failures and gather information about switch activity:

■ Syslog messages

■ SNMP

■ IP SLA

Syslog Messages

Catalyst switches can be configured to generate an audit trail of messages describing important events that have occurred. These system message logs (syslog) can then be collected and analyzed to determine what has happened, when it happened, and how severe the event was.

When system messages are generated, they always appear in a consistent format, as shown in Figure B-1. Each message contains the following fields:

■ **Timestamp**—The date and time from the internal switch clock. By default, the amount of time that the switch has been up is used.

■ **Facility Code**—A system identifier that categorizes the switch function or module that has generated the message; the facility code always begins with a percent sign.

■ **Severity**—A number from 0 to 7 that indicates how important or severe the event is; a lower severity means the event is more critical.

■ **Mnemonic**—A short text string that categorizes the event within the facility code.

■ **Message Text**—A description of the event or condition that triggered the system message.

In Figure B-1, an event in the "System" or SYS facility has triggered the system message. The event is considered to be severity level 5. From the mnemonic CONFIG_I, you can infer that something happened with the switch configuration. Indeed, the text description says that the switch was configured by someone connected to the switch console port.

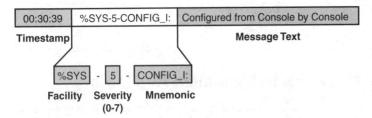

Figure B-1 *Catalyst Switch Syslog Message Format*

Generally, you should configure a switch to generate syslog messages that are occurring at or above a certain level of importance; otherwise, you might collect too much information from a switch that logs absolutely everything or too little information from a switch that logs almost nothing.

You can use the severity level to define that threshold. Figure B-2 shows each of the logging severity levels, along with a general list of the types of messages that are generated. Think of the severity levels as concentric circles. When you configure the severity level threshold on a switch, the switch will only generate logging messages that occur at that level or at any other level that is contained within it.

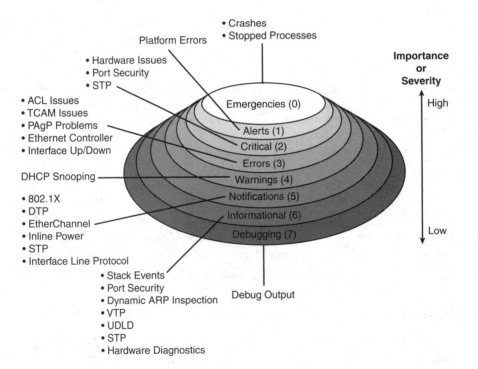

Figure B-2 *Syslog Severity Levels*

For example, if the syslog severity level is set to critical (severity level 2), the switch will generate messages in the Critical, Alerts, and Emergencies levels, but nothing else. Notice that the severity levels are numbered such that the most urgent events are reported at level 0 and the least urgent at level 7.

> **Tip:** You should try to have a good understanding of the severity level names and numbers, as well as their order, in case you need to identify them on the exam.
>
> Remember that the severity numbers are opposite of what you might perceive as the actual message importance. If the exam asks about an event that has a "high" or "greater" severity, that means the severity level number will be lower.

System messages can be sent to the switch console, collected in an internal memory buffer, and sent over the network to be collected by a syslog server. The configuration commands for each of these destinations are covered in the following sections.

Logging to the Switch Console

By default, system messages are sent to the switch console port at the Debugging level. You can change the console severity level with the following command:

```
Switch(config)# logging console severity
```

The *severity* parameter can be either a severity level keyword, such as **informational**, or the corresponding numeric value (0 to 7).

Remember that syslog information can be seen on the console only when you are connected to the console port. Even then, the console isn't a very efficient way to collect and view system messages because of its low throughput. If you are connected to a switch through a Telnet or SSH session, you can redirect the console messages to your remote access session by using the **terminal monitor** command.

Logging to the Internal Buffer

Every Catalyst switch has an internal memory buffer where syslog messages can be collected. The internal buffer is an efficient way to collect messages over time. As long as the switch is powered up, the logging buffer is available.

By default, the internal logging buffer is disabled. To enable it and begin sending system messages into the buffer, you can use the following command:

```
Switch(config)# logging buffered severity
```

The *severity* parameter can be either a severity level keyword, such as **informational**, or the corresponding numeric value (0 to 7).

The logging buffer has a finite size and operates in a circular fashion. If the buffer fills, the oldest messages roll off as new ones arrive. By default, the logging buffer is 4096 bytes or characters long, which is enough space to collect 50 lines of full-length text. If you depend on the logging buffer to keep a running history of logging messages, you might need to increase its size with the following command:

```
Switch(config)# logging buffered size
```

The buffer length is set to *size* (4096 to 2147483647) bytes. Be careful not to set the length too big because the switch reserves the logging buffer space from the memory it might need for other operations.

To review the internal logging buffer at any time, you can use the **show logging** command.

Logging to a Remote Syslog Server

Syslog servers provide the most robust method of logging message collection. Messages are sent from a switch to a syslog server over the network using UDP port 514. This means that a syslog server can be located anywhere, as long as it is reachable by the switch. A syslog server can collect logs from many different devices simultaneously and can archive the logging information for a long period of time.

To identify a syslog server and begin sending logging messages to it, you can use the following commands:

```
Switch(config)# logging host
Switch(config)# logging trap severity
```

The syslog server is located at hostname or IP address *host*. You can enter the **logging** *host* command more than once if you have more than one syslog server collecting logging information. The syslog server severity level can be either a severity level keyword, such as **informational**, or the corresponding numeric value (0 to 7).

Tip: Notice that each of the logging message destinations can have a unique severity level configured. For example, you might collect messages of severity level Debugging into the internal buffer, while collecting severity level Notifications to a syslog server.

Tip: By default, a switch will generate a system message every time it detects an interface going up or down. That sounds like a good thing, until you realize that the syslog server will be receiving news of every user powering their PC on and off each day. Each link state change will generate a message at the Errors (3) severity level, as well as a line protocol state change at Notifications (5) severity level. To prevent this from happening with Access layer interfaces where end users are connected, you can use the following interface configuration command:

```
Switch(config-if)# no logging event link-status
```

Adding Timestamps to Syslog Messages

If you are watching system messages appear in real time, it's obvious what time those events have occurred. However, if you need to review messages that have been collected and archived in the internal logging buffer or on a syslog server, message timestamps become really important.

By default, Catalyst switches add a simple "uptime" timestamp to logging messages. This is a cumulative counter that shows the hours, minutes, and seconds since the switch has been booted up. Suppose you find an important event in the logs and you want to know exactly when it occurred. With the uptime timestamp, you would have to backtrack and compute the time of the event based on how long the switch has been operating.

Even worse, as time goes on, the uptime timestamp becomes more coarse and difficult to interpret. In the following output, an interface went down 20 weeks and 2 days after the switch was booted. Someone made a configuration change 21 weeks and 3 days after the switch booted. At exactly what date and time did that occur? Who knows!

```
20w2d: %LINK-3-UPDOWN: Interface FastEthernet1/0/27, changed state to down
21w3d: %SYS-5-CONFIG_I: Configured from console by vty0 (172.25.15.246)
```

Instead, you can configure the switch to add accurate clock-like timestamps that are easily interpreted. Sometimes you also will need to correlate events in the logs of several network devices. In that case, it's important to synchronize the clocks (and timestamps) across all those devices.

Don't assume that a switch already has its internal clock set to the correct date and time. You can use the **show clock** command to find out, as in the following example:

```
Switch# show clock
*00:54:09.691 UTC Mon Mar 1 1993
Switch#
```

Here the clock has been set to its default value, and it's March 1, 1993! Clearly, that isn't useful at all.

You can use the following commands as a guideline to define the time zone and summer (daylight savings) time, and set the clock:

```
Switch(config)# clock timezone name offset-hours [offset-minutes]
Switch(config)# clock summer-time name date start-month date year hh:mm
  end-month day year hh:mm
[offset-minutes]
-OR-
Switch(config)# clock summer-time name recurring [start-week day month
  hh:mm end-week day month hh:mm [offset-minutes]
Switch(config)# exit
Switch# clock set hh:mm:ss
```

In the following example, the switch is configured for the Eastern time zone in the U.S. and the clock is set for 3:23pm. If no other parameters are given with the **clock summer-time recurring** command, U.S. daylight savings time is assumed.

```
Switch(config)# clock timezone EST -5
Switch(config)# clock summer-time EDT recurring
Switch(config)# exit
Switch# clock set 15:23:00
```

To synchronize the clocks across multiple switches in your network from common, trusted time sources, you should use the Network Time Protocol (NTP). As a simple example, the following commands are used to enable NTP and use the NTP server at 192.43.244.18 (time.nist.gov) as an authoritative source:

```
Switch(config)# ntp server 192.43.244.18
```

After NTP is configured and enabled, you can use the **show ntp status** command to verify that the switch clock is synchronized to the NTP server.

Finally, you can use the following command to begin using the switch clock as an accurate timestamp for syslog messages:

```
Switch(config)# service timestamps log datetime [localtime] [show-timezone]
  [msec] [year]
```

Use the **localtime** keyword to use the local time zone configured on the switch; otherwise, UTC is assumed. Add the **show-timezone** keyword if you want the time zone name added to the timestamps. Use the **msec** keyword to add milliseconds and the **year** keyword to add the year to the timestamps.

In the following example, the local time zone and milliseconds have been added into the timestamps of the logging messages shown:

```
Switch(config)# service timestamps log datetime localtime show-timezone msec
Switch(config)# exit
Switch# show logging
*May  2 02:39:23.871 EDT: %DIAG-SP-6-DIAG_OK: Module 1: Passed Online Diagnostics
*May  2 02:39:27.827 EDT: %HSRP-5-STATECHANGE: Vlan62 Grp 1 state Standby -> Active
*May  2 02:41:40.431 EDT: %OIR-SP-6-INSCARD: Card inserted in slot 9, interfaces
  are now online
*May  3 08:24:13.944 EDT: %IP-4-DUPADDR: Duplicate address 10.1.2.1 on Vlan5,
  sourced by 0025.64eb.216f
*May 13 09:55:57.139 EDT: %SYS-5-CONFIG_I: Configured from console by herring on
  vty0 (10.1.1.7)
```

SNMP

The Simple Network Management Protocol (SNMP) enables a network device to share information about itself and its activities. A complete SNMP system consists of the following parts:

- **SNMP Manager**—A network management system that uses SNMP to poll and receive data from any number of network devices. The SNMP Manager usually is an application that runs in a central location.

- **SNMP Agent**—A process that runs on the network device being monitored. All types of data are gathered by the device itself and stored in a local database. The agent can then respond to SNMP polls and queries with information from the database, and it can send unsolicited alerts or "traps" to an SNMP Manager.

In the case of Catalyst switches in the network, each switch automatically collects data about itself, its resources, and each of its interfaces. This data is stored in a Management Information Base (MIB) database in memory and is updated in real time.

The MIB is organized in a structured, hierarchical fashion, forming a tree structure. In fact, the entire MIB is really a collection of variables that are stored in individual, more granular MIBs that form the branches of the tree. Each MIB is based on the Abstract Syntax Notation 1 (ASN.1) language. Each variable in the MIB is referenced by an object identifier (OID), which is a long string of concatenated indexes that follow the path from the root of the tree all the way to the variable's location.

Fortunately, only the SNMP manager and agent need to be concerned with interpreting the MIBs. As far as the SWITCH exam and course go, you should just be aware that the MIB structure exists and that it contains everything about a switch that can be monitored.

To see any of the MIB data, an SNMP manager must send an SNMP poll or query to the switch. The query contains the OID of the specific variable being requested so that the agent running on the switch knows what information to return. An SNMP manager can use the following mechanisms to communicate with an SNMP agent, all over UDP port 161:

- **Get Request**—The value of one specific MIB variable is needed.

- **Get Next Request**—The next or subsequent value following an initial Get Request is needed.

- **Get Bulk Request**—Whole tables or lists of values in a MIB variable are needed.

- **Set Request**—A specific MIB variable needs to be set to a value.

SNMP polls or requests are usually sent by the SNMP manager at periodic intervals. This makes real-time monitoring difficult because changing variables won't be noticed until the next poll cycle. However, SNMP agents can send unsolicited alerts to notify the SNMP manager of real-time events at any time. Alerts can be sent using the following mechanisms over UDP port 162:

- **SNMP Trap**—News of an event (interface state change, device failure, and so on) is sent without any acknowledgement that the trap has been received.

- **Inform Request**—News of an event is sent to an SNMP manager, and the manager is required to acknowledge receipt by echoing the request back to the agent.

As network management has evolved, SNMP has developed into three distinct versions. The original, SNMP version 1 (SNMPv1), is defined in RFC1157. It uses simple one-variable Get and Set requests, along with simple SNMP traps. SNMP managers can gain access to SNMP agents by matching a simple "community" text string. When a manager wants to read or write a MIB variable on a device, it sends the community string in the clear, as part of the request. The request is granted if that community string matches the agent's community string.

In theory, only managers and agents belonging to the same community should be able to communicate. In practice, any device has the potential to read or write variables to an agent's MIB database by sending the right community string, whether it's a legitimate SNMP manager or not. This creates a huge security hole in SNMPv1.

The second version of SNMP, SNMPv2C (RFC 1901), was developed to address some efficiency and security concerns. For example, SNMPv2c adds 64-bit variable counters, extending the useful range of values over the 32-bit counters used in SNMPv1. In addition, SNMPv2C offers the Bulk Request, making MIB data retrieval more efficient. It also offers Inform Requests, which make real-time alerts more reliable by requiring confirmation of receipt.

Despite the intentions of its developers, SNMPv2C does not address any security concerns over that of SNMPv1. SNMPv2C does offer 64-bit variable counters, which extend the capability to keep track of very large numbers, such as byte counters found on high-speed interfaces. With SNMPv2C, MIB variables can be obtained in a bulk form with a single request. In addition, event notifications sent from an SNMPv2C agent can be in the form of SNMP traps or inform requests. The latter form requires an acknowledgement from the SNMP manager that the inform message was received.

The third generation of SNMP, SNMPv3, is defined in RFCs 3410 through 3415. It addresses the security features that are lacking in the earlier versions. SNMPv3 can authenticate SNMP managers through usernames. When usernames are configured on the SNMP agent of a switch, they can be organized into SNMPv3 group names.

Each SNMPv3 group is defined with a security level that describes the extent to which the SNMP data will be protected. Data packets can be authenticated to preserve their integrity, encrypted to obscure their contents, or both. The following security levels are available. The naming scheme uses "auth" to represent packet authentication and "priv" to represent data privacy or encryption.

- **noAuthNoPriv**—SNMP packets are neither authenticated nor encrypted.

- **authNoPriv**—SNMP packets are authenticated but not encrypted.

- **authPriv**—SNMP packets are authenticated and encrypted.

As a best practice, you should use SNMPv3 to leverage its superior security features whenever possible. If you must use SNMPv1 for a device, you should configure the switch to limit SNMP access to a read-only role. Never permit read-write access because the simple community string authentication can be exploited to make unexpected changes to a switch configuration.

Catalyst switches offer one additional means of limiting SNMP access—an access list can be configured to permit only specific SNMP manager IP addresses. You should configure and apply an access list to your SNMP configurations whenever possible.

Because SNMP is a universal method for monitoring all sorts of network devices, it isn't unique to LAN switches. Therefore, you should understand the basics of how SNMP works, the differences between the different SNMP versions, and how you might apply SNMP to monitor a switched network. You can use Table B-1 as a memory aid for your exam study.

Table B-1 *Comparison of SNMP Versions and Their Features*

Version	Authentication	Data Protection	Unique Features
SNMPv1	Community string	None	32-bit counters
SNMPv2c	Community string	None	Added Bulk Request and Inform Request message types, 64-bit counters
SNMPv3	Username authentication	Hash-based MAC (SHA or MD5) DES, 3DES, AES (128, 192, 256-bit) encryption	Added user authentication, data integrity, and encryption

Configuring SNMPv1 and SNMPv2C

You should be familiar with the basic SNMP configuration. Fortunately, this involves just a few commands, as follows:

```
Switch(config)# access-list access-list-number permit ip-addr
Switch(config)# snmp-server community string [ro | rw] [access-list-number]
!
Switch(config)# snmp-server host host-address community-string [trap-type]
```

First, define a standard IP access list that permits only the IP addresses of your SNMP agent machines. Then apply that access list to the SNMPv1 community string with the **snmp-server community** command. Use the **ro** keyword to allow read-only access by the SNMP manager; otherwise, use the **rw** keyword to allow both read and write access.

Finally, use the **snmp-server host** command to identify the IP address of the SNMP manager where SNMP traps will be sent. By default, all types of traps are sent. You can use the **?** key in place of *trap-type* to see a list of the available trap types.

In Example B-1, the switch is configured to allow SNMP polling from network management stations at 192.168.3.99 and 192.168.100.4. The community string **MonitorIt** is used to authenticate the SNMP requests. All possible SNMP traps are sent to 192.168.3.99.

Example B-1 *Configuring SNMPv1 Access*

```
Switch(config)# access-list 10 permit 192.168.3.99
Switch(config)# access-list 10 permit 192.168.100.4
Switch(config)# snmp-server community MonitorIt ro 10
Switch(config)# snmp-server host 192.168.3.99 MonitorIt
```

Configuring SNMPv2C

Configuring SNMPv2C is similar to configuring SNMPv1. The only difference is with SNMP trap or inform configuration. You can use the following commands to configure basic SNMPv2C operation:

```
Switch(config)# access-list access-list-number permit ip-addr
Switch(config)# snmp-server community string [ro | rw] [access-list-number]
!
Switch(config)# snmp-server host host-address [informs] version 2c community-string
```

In the **snmp-server host** command, use the **version 2c** keywords to identify SNMPv2C operation. By default, regular SNMP traps are sent. To use inform requests instead, add the **informs** keyword.

Configuring SNMPv3

SNMPv3 configuration is a bit more involved than versions 1 or 2C, due mainly to the additional security features.

```
Switch(config)# access-list access-list-number permit ip-addr
!
Switch(config)# snmp-server group group-name v3 {noauth | auth | priv}
Switch(config)# snmp-server user user-name group-name v3 auth {md5 | sha}
  auth-password priv {des | 3des | aes {128 | 192 | 256} priv-password [access-
  list-number]
!
Switch(config)# snmp-server host host-address [informs] version 3 {noauth | auth |
  priv} user-name [trap-type]
```

First, use the **snmp-server group** command to define a *group-name* that will set the security level policies for SNMPv3 users. The security level is defined by the **noauth** (no packet authentication or encryption), **auth** (packets are authenticated but not encrypted), or **priv** (packets are both authenticated and encrypted) keyword. Only the security policy is defined in the group; no passwords or keys are required yet.

> **Tip:** The SNMPv3 **priv** keyword and packet encryption can be used only if the switch is running a cryptographic version of its Cisco IOS software image. The **auth** keyword and packet authentication can be used regardless.

Next, define a username that an SNMP manager will use to communicate with the switch. Use the **snmp-server user** command to define the *user-name* and associate it with the SNMPv3 *group-name*. The **v3** keyword configures the user to use SNMPv3.

The SNMPv3 user must also have some specifics added to its security policy. Use the **auth** keyword to define either MD5 or SHA as the packet authentication method, along with the *auth-password* text string that will be used in the hash computation. The **priv** keyword defines the encryption method (DES, 3DES, or AES 128/192/256-bit) and the *priv-password* text string that will be used in the encryption algorithm.

The same SNMPv3 username, authentication method and password, and encryption method and password must also be defined on the SNMP manager so it can successfully talk to the switch.

Finally, you can use the **snmp-server host** command to identify the SNMP manager that will receive either traps or informs. The switch can use SNMPv3 to send traps and informs, using the security parameters that are defined for the SNMPv3 *user-name*.

In Example B-2, a switch is configured for SNMPv3 operation. Access list 10 permits only stations at 192.168.3.99 and 192.168.100.4 with SNMP access. SNMPv3 access is defined for a group named NetOps using the **priv** (authentication and encryption) security level. One SNMPv3 user named mymonitor is defined; the network management station will use that username when it polls the switch for information. The username will require SHA packet authentication and AES-128 encryption, using the s3cr3tauth and s3cr3tpr1v passwords, respectively.

Finally, SNMPv3 informs will be used to send alerts to station 192.168.3.99 using the **priv** security level and username mymonitor.

Example B-2   *Configuring SNMPv3 Access*

```
Switch(config)# access-list 10 permit 192.168.3.99
Switch(config)# access-list 10 permit 192.168.100.4
Switch(config)# snmp-server group NetOps v3 priv
Switch(config)# snmp-server user mymonitor NetOps v3 auth sha s3cr3tauth priv aes
  128 s3cr3tpr1v 10
Switch(config)# snmp-server host 192.168.3.99 informs version 3 priv mymonitor
```

IP SLA

The Cisco IOS IP Service Level Agreement (IP SLA) feature can be used to gather realistic information about how specific types of traffic are being handled end-to-end across a network. To do this, an IP SLA device runs a preconfigured test and generates traffic that is destined for a far-end device. As the far end responds with packets that are received back at the source, IP SLA gathers data about what happened along the way.

IP SLA can be configured to perform a variety of tests. The simplest test involves ICMP echo packets that are sent toward a target address, as shown in Figure B-3. If the target answers with ICMP echo replies, IP SLA can then assess how well the source and destination were able to communicate. In this case, the echo failures (packet loss) and round trip transit (RTT) times are calculated, as shown in the following example:

```
Switch# show ip sla statistics aggregated
Round Trip Time (RTT) for        Index 1
Type of operation: icmp-echo
Start Time Index: 15:10:17.665 EDT Fri May 21 2010
RTT Values
        Number Of RTT: 24
        RTT Min/Avg/Max: 1/1/4 ms
Number of successes: 24
Number of failures: 0
```

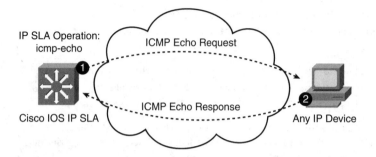

Figure B-3   *IP SLA ICMP Echo Test Operation*

For the ICMP echo test, IP SLA can use any live device at the far end—after all, most networked devices will reply when they are pinged. IP SLA also can test some network protocols, such as DNS, by sending requests to a server at the far end. Cisco IOS is needed only at the source of the IP SLA test because the far end is simply responding to ordinary request packets.

However, IP SLA is capable of running much more sophisticated tests. Table B-2 shows some sample test operations that are available with IP SLA.

Table B-2   *IP SLA Test Operations*

Test Type	Description	IP SLA Required on Target?
icmp-echo	ICMP Echo response time	No
path-echo	Hop-by-hop and end-to-end response times over path discovered from ICMP Echo	No
path-jitter	Hop-by-hop jitter over ICMP Echo path	Yes
dns	DNS query response time	No
dhcp	DHCP IP address request response time	No
ftp	FTP file retrieval response time	No
http	Web page retrieval response time	No
udp-echo	End-to-end response time of UDP echo	No
udp-jitter	Round trip delay, one-way delay, one-way jitter, one-way packet loss, and connectivity using UDP packets	Yes
tcp-connect	Response time to build a TCP connection with a host	No

To leverage its full capabilities, Cisco IOS IP SLA must be available on both the source and the target devices, as shown in Figure B-4. The source device handles the test scheduling and sets up each test over a special IP SLA control connection with the target device. The source generates the traffic involved in a test operation and analyzes the results as packets return from the target. The target end has a simpler role: respond to the incoming test packets. In fact, the target device is called an *IP SLA Responder*.

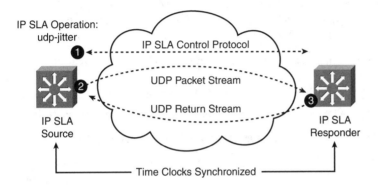

Figure B-4   *IP SLA UDP Jitter Test Operation*

The responder must also add timestamps to the packets it sends, to flag the time a test packet arrived and the time it left the responder. The idea is to account for any latency incurred while the responder is processing the test packets. For this to work accurately, both the source and responder must synchronize their clocks through NTP.

An IP SLA source device can schedule and keep track of multiple test operations. For example, an ICMP echo operation might run against target 10.1.1.1, while UDP jitter operations are running against targets 10.2.2.2, 10.3.3.3, and 10.4.4.4. Each test runs independently, at a configured frequency and duration.

Tip: To set up an IP SLA operation, the Cisco IP SLA source device begins by opening a control connection to the IP SLA responder over UDP port 1967. The source uses the control connection to inform the responder to begin listening on an additional port where the actual IP SLA test operation will take place.

What in the world does this have to do with LAN switching, and why would you want to run IP SLA on a Catalyst switch anyway? Here's a two-fold answer:

- IP SLA will likely appear on your SWITCH exam

- IP SLA is actually a useful tool in a switched campus network

To run live tests and take useful measurements without IP SLA, you would need to place some sort of probe devices at various locations in the network—all managed from a central system. With IP SLA, you don't need probes at all! Wherever you have a Catalyst switch, you already have an IP SLA "probe."

By leveraging IP SLA test operations, you can take advantage of some fancy features:

- Generate SNMP traps when certain test thresholds are exceeded

- Schedule further IP SLA tests automatically when test thresholds are crossed

- Track an IP SLA test to trigger a next-hop gateway redundancy protocol, such as HSRP

- Gather voice quality measurements from all over a network

Configuring IP SLA

You can use the following configuration steps to define and run an IP SLA test operation:

Step 1.   Enable the IP SLA responder on the target switch.

```
Switch(config)# ip sla responder
```

By default, the IP SLA responder is disabled. If the IP SLA operation will involve jitter or time-critical measurements, the responder should be enabled on the target switch.

Step 2.   Define a new IP SLA operation on the source switch.

```
Switch(config)# ip sla operation-number
```

The *operation-number* is an arbitrary index that can range from 1 to a very large number. This number uniquely identifies the test.

Step 3.   Select the type of test operation to perform.

```
Switch(config-ip-sla)# test-type parameters...
```

The *test-type* keyword can be one of the following:

dhcp, dns, ethernet, ftp, http, icmp-echo, mpls, path-echo, path-jitter, slm, tcp-connect, udp-echo, or **udp-jitter**

The list of parameters following the *test-type* varies according to the test operation. As an example, consider the following **icmp-echo** operation syntax:

```
Switch(config-ip-sla)# icmp-echo destination-ip-addr [source-ip-addr]
```

The parameters are simple—a destination address to ping and an optional source address to use. If a switch has several Layer 3 interfaces, you can specify which one of their IP address to use as the source of the test packets.

As another example, the **udp-jitter** command is useful for testing time-critical traffic paths through a switched network. The command syntax is a little more complex, as follows:

```
Switch(config-ip-sla)# udp-jitter destination-ip-addr dest-udp-port
  [source-ip source-ip-addr] [source-port source-udp-port] [num-packets
  number-of-packets] [interval packet-interval]
```

In addition to the source and destination IP addresses, you can define the UDP port numbers that will be used for the packet stream. By default, 10 packets spaced at 20 milliseconds will be sent. You can override that by specifying the **num-packets** and **interval** keywords.

As an alternative, you can configure the **udp-jitter** operation to test Voice over IP (VoIP) call quality. To do this, the **udp-jitter** command must include the **codec** keyword and a codec definition. The IP SLA operation will then simulate a real-time stream of voice traffic using a specific codec. In this way, you can tailor the test to fit the type of calls that are actually being used in the network.

You can define the UDP jitter codec operation by using the following command syntax:

```
Switch(config-ip-sla)# udp-jitter destination-ip-addr dest-udp-port
  codec {g711alaw | g711ulaw | g729a}
```

There are other keywords and parameters you can add to the command, but those are beyond the scope of this book. By default, 1000 packets are sent, 20 milliseconds apart.

Step 4. Schedule the test operation.

```
Switch(config)# ip sla schedule operation-number [life {forever |
  seconds}] [start-time {hh:mm[:ss] [month day | day month] | pending |
  now | after hh:mm:ss}] [ageout seconds] [recurring]
```

In a nutshell, the command tells the switch when to start the test, how long to let it run, and how long to keep the data that is collected.

Set the lifetime with the **life** keyword: **forever** means the operation will keep running forever, until you manually remove it. Otherwise, specify how many seconds it will run. By default, an IP SLA scheduled operation will run for 3600 seconds (one hour).

Set the start time with the **start-time** keyword. You can define the start time as a specific time or date, after a delay with the **after** keyword, or right now with the **now** keyword.

By default, the test statistics are collected and held in memory indefinitely. You can use the **ageout** keyword to specify how many seconds elapse before the data is aged out.

The **recurring** keyword can be used to schedule the test operation to run at the same time each day, as long as you have defined the starting time with *hh:mm:ss*, too.

> **Tip:** Be aware that the IP SLA operation command syntax has changed along the way. In Cisco IOS releases 12.2(33) and later, the syntax is as shown in steps 2 through 4.
>
> Prior to 12.2(33), the commands in steps 2 through 4 included additional keywords, as follows:
>
> **Step 2.** `ip sla monitor` *operation-number*
>
> **Step 3.** `type` *test-type*
>
> **Step 4.** `ip sla monitor schedule` *operation-number*
>
> It isn't clear which version of the IP SLA commands are used in the SWITCH exam; just be prepared to see the syntax in either form.

Using IP SLA

After you have configured an IP SLA operation, you can verify the configuration with the **show ip sla configuration** [*operation-number*] command. As an example, the following configuration commands are used to define IP SLA operation 100—an ICMP echo test that pings target 172.25.226.1 every 5 seconds.

```
Switch(config)# ip sla 100
Switch(config-ip-sla)# icmp-echo 172.25.226.1
Switch(config-ip-sla)# frequency 5
Switch(config-ip-sla)# exit
Switch(config)# ip sla schedule 100 life forever start-time now
```

Example B-3 shows the output of the **show ip sla configuration** command.

Example B-3 *Displaying the Current IP SLA Configuration*

```
Switch# show ip sla configuration
IP SLAs, Infrastructure Engine-II
Entry number: 100
Owner:
Tag:
Type of operation to perform: echo
Target address: 172.25.226.1
Source address: 0.0.0.0
Request size (ARR data portion): 28
Operation timeout (milliseconds): 5000
Type Of Service parameters: 0x0
Verify data: No
Vrf Name:
Schedule:
    Operation frequency (seconds): 5
    Next Scheduled Start Time: Start Time already passed
```

```
        Group Scheduled : FALSE
        Randomly Scheduled : FALSE
        Life (seconds): Forever
        Entry Ageout (seconds): never
        Recurring (Starting Everyday): FALSE
        Status of entry (SNMP RowStatus): Active
Threshold (milliseconds): 5000
Distribution Statistics:
        Number of statistic hours kept: 2
        Number of statistic distribution buckets kept: 1
        Statistic distribution interval (milliseconds): 20
History Statistics:
        Number of history Lives kept: 0
        Number of history Buckets kept: 15
        History Filter Type: None
Enhanced History:
```

You can use the **show ip sla statistics [aggregated]** [*operation-number*] command to display the IP SLA test analysis. By default, the most recent test results are shown. You can add the **aggregated** keyword to show a summary of the data gathered over the life of the operation. Example B-4 shows the statistics gathered for ICMP echo operation 100.

Example B-4 *Displaying IP SLA Statistics*

```
Switch# show ip sla statistics 100
Round Trip Time (RTT) for          Index 100
        Latest RTT: 1 ms
Latest operation start time: 15:52:00.834 EDT Fri May 28 2010
Latest operation return code: OK
Number of successes: 117
Number of failures: 0
Operation time to live: Forever


Switch# show ip sla statistics aggregated 100
Round Trip Time (RTT) for          Index 100
Type of operation: icmp-echo
Start Time Index: 15:43:55.842 EDT Fri May 28 2010
RTT Values
        Number Of RTT: 121
        RTT Min/Avg/Max: 1/1/4 ms
Number of successes: 121
Number of failures: 0
```

It isn't too difficult to configure an IP SLA operation manually and check the results every now and then. But does IP SLA have any greater use? Yes, you can also use an IP SLA operation to make some other switch features change behavior automatically, without any other intervention.

For example, HSRP can track the status of an IP SLA operation to automatically decrement the priority value when the target device stops answering ICMP echo packets. To do this, begin by using the **track** command to define a unique track *object-number* index that will be bound to the IP SLA operation number.

```
Switch(config)# track object-number ip sla operation-number {state | reachability}
```

You can use the **state** keyword to track the return code or state of the IP SLA operation; the state is up if the IP SLA test was successful or down if it wasn't. The **reachability** keyword is slightly different—the result is up if the IP SLA operation is successful or has risen above a threshold; otherwise, the reachability is down.

Next, configure the HSRP standby group to use the tracked object to control the priority decrement value. As long as the tracked object (the IP SLA operation) is up or successful, the HSRP priority stays unchanged. If the tracked object is down, then the HSRP priority is decremented by *decrement-value* (default 10).

```
Switch(config-if)# standby group track object-number decrement decrement-value
```

In Example B-5, SwitchA and SwitchB are configured as an HSRP pair, sharing gateway address 192.168.1.1. SwitchA has a higher priority than SwitchB, so it is normally the active gateway. However, it is configured to ping an upstream router at 192.168.70.1 every five seconds; if that router doesn't respond, SwitchA will decrement its HSRP priority by 50, permitting SwitchB to take over.

Example B-5 *Tracking an IP SLA Operation in an HSRP Group*

```
Switch(config)# ip sla 10
Switch(config-ip-sla)# icmp-echo 192.168.70.1
Switch(config-ip-sla)# frequency 5
Switch(config-ip-sla)# exit
Switch(config)# ip sla schedule 10 life forever start-time now

Switch(config)# track 1 ip sla 10 reachability

Switch(config)# interface vlan10
Switch(config-if)# ip address 192.168.1.3 255.255.255.0
Switch(config-if)# standby 1 priority 200
Switch(config-if)# standby 1 track 1 decrement 50
Switch(config-if)# no shutdown
```

In some cases, you might need many IP SLA operations to take many measurements in a network. For example, you could use UDP jitter operations to measure voice call quality across many different parts of the network. Manually configuring and monitoring more than a few IP SLA operations can become overwhelming and impractical. Instead, you can leverage a network management application that can set up and monitor IP SLA tests automatically. To do this, the network management system needs SNMP read and write access to each switch that will use IP SLA. Tests are configured by writing to the IP SLA MIB, and results are gathered by reading the MIB.

GLOSSARY

20/80 rule Network traffic pattern where 20 percent of traffic stays in a local area, while 80 percent travels to or from a remote resource.

802.1Q A method of passing frames and their VLAN associations over a trunk link, based on the IEEE 802.1Q standard.

access layer The layer of the network where end users are connected.

active virtual forwarder (AVF) A GLBP router that takes on a virtual MAC address and forwards traffic received on that address.

active virtual gateway (AVG) The GLBP router that answers all ARP requests for the virtual router address and assigns virtual MAC addresses to each router in the GLBP group.

adjacency table A table used by CEF to collect the MAC addresses of nodes that can be reached in a single Layer 2 hop.

alternate port In RSTP, a port other than the root port that has an alternative path to the root bridge.

ARP poisoning Also known as ARP spoofing. An attack whereby an attacker sends specially crafted ARP replies so that its own MAC address appears as the gateway or some other targeted host. From that time on, unsuspecting clients unknowingly send traffic to the attacker.

Auto-QoS An automated method to configure complex QoS parameters with a simple IOS macro command.

autonegotiation A mechanism used by a device and a switch port to automatically negotiate the link speed and duplex mode.

autonomous mode AP An access point that operates in a standalone mode, such that it is autonomous and can offer a functioning WLAN cell itself.

BackboneFast An STP feature that can detect an indirect link failure and shorten the STP convergence time to 30 seconds by bypassing the Max Age timeout period.

backup port In RSTP, a port that provides a redundant (but less desirable) connection to a segment where another switch port already connects.

best effort delivery   Packets are forwarded in the order in which they are received, regardless of any policy or the packet contents.

BPDU   Bridge protocol data unit; the data message exchanged by switches participating in the Spanning Tree Protocol.

BPDU filtering   Prevents BPDUs from being sent or processed on a switch port.

BPDU Guard   An STP feature that disables a switch port if any BPDU is received there.

bridging loop   A condition where Ethernet frames are forwarded endlessly around a Layer 2 loop formed between switches.

broadcast domain   The extent of a network where a single broadcast frame or packet will be seen.

CAM   Content-addressable memory; the high-performance table used by a switch to correlate MAC addresses with the switch interfaces where they can be found.

CEF   Cisco Express Forwarding; an efficient topology-based system for forwarding IP packets.

collapsed core   A network design where the core and distribution layers are collapsed or combined into a single layer of switches.

collision domain   The extent within a network that an Ethernet collision will be noticed or experienced.

Common Spanning Tree (CST)   A single instance of STP defined in the IEEE 802.1Q standard.

community VLAN   A type of secondary private VLAN; switch ports associated with a community VLAN can communicate with each other.

Control and Provisioning Wireless Access Point (CAPWAP)   A standards-based tunneling protocol used to transport control messages and data packets between a WLC and an LAP. CAPWAP is defined in RFC 4118.

core layer   The "backbone" layer of the network where all distribution layer switches are aggregated.

CoS marking   A method of marking frames with a QoS value as they cross a trunk link between two switches.

CSMA/CA   Carrier sense multiple access collision avoidance. The mechanism used in 802.11 WLANs by which clients attempt to avoid collisions.

CSMA/CD   Carrier sense multiple access collision detect. A mechanism used on Ethernet networks to detect collisions and cause transmitting devices to back off for a random time.

delay   The amount of time required for a packet to be forwarded across a network.

designated port   One nonroot port selected on a network segment, such that only one switch forwards traffic to and from that segment.

DHCP   Dynamic Host Configuration Protocol; a protocol used to negotiate IP address assignment between a client and a server. The client and server must reside on the same VLAN.

DHCP relay   A multilayer switch that intercepts and relays DHCP negotiation messages between a client and a DHCP server, even if they exist on different VLANs.

DHCP snooping   A security feature that enables a switch to intercept all DHCP requests coming from untrusted switch ports before they are flooded to unsuspecting users.

differentiated services (DiffServ) model   Packet forwarding is handled according to local QoS policies on a per-device or per-hop basis.

discarding state   In RSTP, incoming frames are dropped and no MAC addresses are learned.

distribution layer   The layer of the network where access layer switches are aggregated and routing is performed.

DTP   Dynamic Trunking Protocol; a Cisco-proprietary method of negotiating a trunk link between two switches.

dual core   A network design that has a distinct core layer made up of a redundant pair of switches.

duplex mismatch   A condition where the devices on each end of a link use conflicting duplex modes.

duplex mode   The Ethernet mode that governs how devices can transmit over a connection—half-duplex mode forces only one device to transmit at a time, as all devices share the same media; full-duplex mode is used when only two devices share the media, such that both devices can transmit simultaneously.

Dynamic ARP Inspection (DAI)   A security feature that can mitigate ARP-based attacks. ARP replies received on untrusted switch ports are checked against known, good values contained in the DHCP snooping database.

edge port   In RSTP, a port at the "edge" of the network, where only a single host connects.

end-to-end VLAN   A single VLAN that spans the entire switched network, from one end to the other.

EtherChannel   A logical link made up of bundled or aggregated physical links.

expedited forwarding (EF)   The DSCP value used to mark time-critical packets for premium QoS handling. EF is usually reserved for voice bearer traffic.

FIB   Forwarding Information Base; a CEF database that contains the current routing table.

flooding   An Ethernet frame is replicated and sent out every available switch port.

forward delay   The time interval that a switch spends in the Listening and Learning states; default 15 seconds.

hello time   The time interval between configuration BPDUs sent by the root bridge; defaults to 2 seconds.

hierarchical network design   A campus network that is usually organized into an access layer, a distribution layer, and a core layer.

host port   A switch port mapped to a private VLAN such that a connected device can communicate with only a promiscuous port or ports within the same community VLAN.

HSRP active router   The router in an HSRP group that forwards traffic sent to the virtual gateway IP and MAC address.

HSRP standby router   A router in an HSRP group that waits until the active router fails before taking over that role.

Hybrid Remote Edge Access Point (HREAP)   A special mode where an LAP at a remote site can take on characteristics of a lightweight AP, as long as the LAP can reach the WLC, or an autonomous AP, when the WLC is unreachable.

IEEE 802.1x   The standard that defines port-based authentication between a network device and a client device.

IEEE 802.3   The standard upon which all generations of Ethernet (Ethernet, Fast Ethernet, Gigabit Ethernet, 10 Gigabit Ethernet) are based.

InterVLAN routing   The function performed by a Layer 3 device that connects and forwards packets between multiple VLANs.

ISL   Inter-Switch Link; a Cisco-proprietary method of tagging frames passing over a trunk link.

isolated VLAN   A type of secondary private VLAN; switch ports associated with an isolated VLAN are effectively isolated from each other.

IST instance   Internal spanning-tree instance; used by MST to represent an entire region as a single virtual bridge to a common spanning tree.

jitter   The variation in packet delivery delay times.

LACP   Link Aggregation Control Protocol; a standards-based method for negotiating EtherChannels automatically.

Layer 2 roaming   Movement of a WLAN client from one AP to another, while keeping its same IP address.

Layer 3 roaming   Movement of a WLAN client from one AP to another, where the APs are located across IP subnet boundaries.

lightweight access point (LAP)   An access point that runs a lightweight code image that performs real-time 802.11 operations. An LAP cannot offer a fully functioning WLAN cell by itself; instead, it must coexist with a wireless LAN controller.

Lightweight Access Point Protocol (LWAPP)   The tunneling protocol developed by Cisco that is used to transport control messages and data packets between a WLC and an LAP.

local VLAN   A single VLAN that is bounded by a small area of the network, situated locally with a group of member devices.

Loop Guard   An STP feature that disables a switch port if expected BPDUs suddenly go missing.

max age time   The time interval that a switch stores a BPDU before discarding it or aging it out; the default is 20 seconds.

MST   Multiple Spanning-Tree protocol, used to map one or more VLANs to a single STP instance, reducing the total number of STP instances.

MST instance (MSTI)   A single instance of STP running within an MST region; multiple VLANs can be mapped to the MST instance.

MST region   A group of switches running compatible MST configurations.

native VLAN   On an 802.1Q trunk link, frames associated with the native VLAN are not tagged at all.

Non-Stop Forwarding (NSF)   A redundancy method that quickly rebuilds routing information after a redundant Catalyst switch supervisor takes over.

packet loss   Packets are simply dropped without delivery for some reason.

packet rewrite   Just before forwarding a packet, a multilayer switch has to change several fields in the packet to reflect the Layer 3 forwarding operation.

PAgP   Port Aggregation Protocol; a Cisco-developed method for negotiating EtherChannels automatically.

point-to-point port   In the Cisco implementation of RSTP, a full-duplex port that connects to another switch and becomes a designated port.

PortFast   An STP feature used on a host port, where a single host is connected, that shortens the Listening and Learning states so that the host can gain quick access to the network.

power class   Categories of PoE devices based on the maximum amount of power required; power classes range from 0 to 4.

Power over Ethernet (PoE)   Electrical power supplied to a networked device over the network cabling itself.

primary VLAN   A normal Layer 2 VLAN used as the basis for a private VLAN when it is associated with one or more secondary VLANs.

private VLAN   A special purpose VLAN, designated as either primary or secondary, which can restrict or isolate traffic flow with other private VLANs.

promiscuous port   A switch port mapped to a private VLAN such that a connected device can communicate with any other switch port in the private VLAN.

PVST   Per-VLAN Spanning Tree; a Cisco-proprietary version of STP where one instance of STP runs on each VLAN present in a Layer 2 switch.

PVST+   Per-VLAN Spanning Tree Plus; a Cisco-proprietary version of PVST that enables PVST, PVST+, and CST to interoperate on a switch.

quality of service (QoS)   The overall method used in a network to protect and prioritize time-critical or important traffic.

root bridge   The single STP device that is elected as a common frame of reference for working out a loop-free topology.

Root Guard   An STP feature that controls where candidate root bridges can be found on a switch.

root path cost   The cumulative cost of all the links leading to the root bridge.

root port   Each switch selects one port that has the lowest root path cost leading toward the root bridge.

Route Processor Redundancy (RPR)   A redundancy mode where a redundant supervisor partially boots and waits to become active after the primary supervisor fails.

Route Processor Redundancy Plus (RPR+)   A redundancy mode where a redundant supervisor boots up and waits to begin Layer 2 or Layer 3 functions.

RPVST+   Also known as Rapid PVST+, where RSTP is used on a per-VLAN basis; in effect, RSTP replaces traditional 802.1D STP in the PVST+ operation.

RSTP   The Rapid Spanning-Tree Protocol, based on the IEEE 802.1w standard.

secondary VLAN   A unidirectional VLAN that can pass traffic to and from its associated primary VLAN, but not with any other secondary VLAN.

Spanning Tree Protocol (STP)   A protocol communicated between Layer 2 switches that attempts to detect a loop in the topology before it forms, thus preventing a bridging loop from occurring.

Split-MAC architecture   Normal Media Access Control (MAC) operations are divided into two distinct locations—the LAP and the WLC, such that the two form a completely functioning WLAN cell.

SSID   Service set identifier; a text string that identifies a service set, or a group of WLAN devices, that can communicate with each other.

stateful switchover (SSO)   A redundancy mode where a redundant supervisor fully boots and initializes, allowing configurations and Layer 2 tables to be synchronized between an active supervisor and a redundant one.

sticky MAC address   MAC addresses dynamically learned by the port security feature are remembered and expected to appear on the same switch ports.

superior BPDU   A received BPDU that contains a better bridge ID than the current root bridge.

SVI   Switched virtual interface; a logical interface used to assign a Layer 3 address to an entire VLAN.

switch block   A network module or building block that contains a group of access layer switches, together with the pair of distribution switches that connect them.

switch spoofing   A malicious host uses DTP to masquerade as a switch, with the goal of negotiating a trunk link and gaining access to additional VLANs.

synchronization   In RSTP, the process by which two switches exchange a proposal-agreement handshake to make sure neither will introduce a bridging loop.

TCAM   Ternary content-addressable memory; a switching table found in Catalyst switches that is used to evaluate packet forwarding decisions based on policies or access lists. TCAM evaluation is performed simultaneously with the Layer 2 or Layer 3 forwarding decisions.

TCN   Topology Change Notification; a message sent out the root port of a switch when it detects a port moving into the Forwarding state or back into the Blocking state. The TCN is sent toward the root bridge, where it is reflected and propagated to every other switch in the Layer 2 network.

transparent bridge   A network device that isolates two physical LANs but forwards Ethernet frames between them.

trust boundary   A perimeter in a network, formed by switches and routers, where QoS decisions take place. QoS information found inside incoming traffic is evaluated at the trust boundary; either it is trusted or it is not trusted. In the latter case, the QoS information can be altered or overridden. All devices inside the trust boundary can assume that QoS information is correct and trusted, such that the QoS information already conforms to enterprise policies.

UDLD   Unidirectional Link Detection; a feature that enables a switch to confirm that a link is operating bidirectionally. If not, the port can be disabled automatically.

unknown unicast flooding   The action taken by a switch when the destination MAC address cannot be found; the frame is flooded or replicated out all switch ports except the receiving port.

UplinkFast   An STP feature that enables access layer switches to unblock a redundant uplink when the primary root port fails.

VACL   VLAN access control list; a filter that can control traffic passing within a VLAN.

VLAN   Virtual LAN; a logical network existing on one or more Layer 2 switches, forming a single broadcast domain.

VLAN hopping   A malicious host sends specially crafted frames that contain extra, spoofed 802.1Q trunking tags into an access port, while the packet payloads appear on a totally different VLAN.

VLAN number   A unique index number given to a VLAN on a switch, differentiating it from other VLANs on the switch.

VLAN trunk   A physical link that can carry traffic on more than one VLAN through logical tagging.

voice VLAN   The VLAN used between a Cisco IP Phone and a Catalyst switch to carry voice traffic.

VRRP backup router   A router in a VRRP group that waits until the master router fails before taking over that role.

VRRP master router   The router in a VRRP group that forwards traffic sent to the virtual gateway IP and MAC address.

VTP   VLAN Trunking Protocol; used to communicate VLAN configuration information among a group of switches.

VTP configuration revision number   An index that indicates the current version of VLAN information used in the VTP domain; a higher number is more preferable.

VTP domain   A logical grouping of switches that share a common set of VLAN requirements.

VTP pruning   VTP reduces unnecessary flooded traffic by pruning or removing VLANs from a trunk link, only when there are no active hosts associated with the VLANs.

VTP synchronization problem   An unexpected VTP advertisement with a higher configuration revision number is received, overriding valid information in a VTP domain.

wireless LAN controller (WLC)   A Cisco device that provides management functions to lightweight access points and aggregates all traffic to and from the LAPs.

Index

N

P

Q

R

T

Tag Control Information (TCI) field, 76

Tag Protocol Identifier (TPID), 76

tagging. *See* frame identification

TCAM (ternary content-addressable memory), 30–34

example of, 32–33

Layer 2 switching, 25

monitoring, 37

port operations in, 33–34

structure of, 30–32

TCI (Tag Control Information) field, 76

TCN BPDU, 143–148

telephony. *See* IP telephony

Telnet, SSH versus, 388–389

ternary content-addressable memory. *See* TCAM (ternary content-addressable memory)

throttling adjacency, 230

tie-breaking process in STP (Spanning Tree Protocol), 137

timers in STP (Spanning Tree Protocol), 141–143, 166–168

Token Ring, VTP support for, 98

topology changes

in RSTP (Rapid Spanning Tree Protocol), 203–204

in STP (Spanning Tree Protocol), 143–148

topology-based MLS, 26–27

TPID (Tag Protocol Identifier), 76

track interface command, 298

traditional WLAN architecture, 346–348

traffic patterns in Cisco Unified Wireless Networks, 354–356

transparent bridging, 22–24, 128–129

transparent mode (VTP), 90–91, 96–97

troubleshooting

EtherChannel, 118–121

port connectivity, 57–58

STP protection, 189

VLAN trunks, 81–83

VLANs (virtual LANs), 81–83

VTP (VLAN Trunking Protocol), 102–103

trunk links. *See* VLAN trunks

trust boundary, configuring, 321–323

tuning. *See also* configuring

convergence (STP), 166–168

port IDs, 165–166

root path cost, 163–164

STP timers, 166–168

U

UDLD (Unidirectional Link Detection) feature (STP), 186–188

udld command, 192

udld reset command, 189, 192

unexpected BPDUs, protecting against, 182–184

Unidirectional Link Detection (UDLD) feature (STP), 186–188

unidirectional links, 56, 186

unknown unicast flooding, 24, 99–101, 129

unrecognized Type-Length-Value, VTP support for, 98

unused switch ports, securing, 389

UplinkFast feature (STP), 170–172

V

VACL (VLAN access lists), 398–399

values (TCAM), 31

W

CISCO

ciscopress.com: Your Cisco Certification and Networking Learning Resource

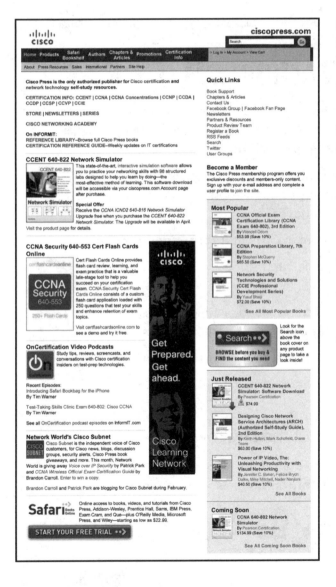

Subscribe to the monthly Cisco Press newsletter to be the first to learn about new releases and special promotions.

Visit **ciscopress.com/newsletters**.

While you are visiting, check out the offerings available at your finger tips.

–Free Podcasts from experts:
  • OnNetworking
  • OnCertification
  • OnSecurity

Podcasts

View them at **ciscopress.com/podcasts**.

–Read the latest author **articles** and **sample chapters** at **ciscopress.com/articles**.

–Bookmark the Certification Reference Guide available through our partner site at **informit.com/certguide**.

Connect with Cisco Press authors and editors via Facebook and Twitter, visit **informit.com/socialconnect**.

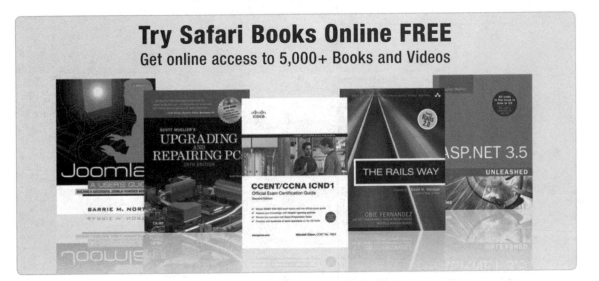

CCNP SWITCH 642-813
Official Certification Guide

✔ Master the **CCNP SWITCH 642-813** exam with this official study guide
✔ Assess your knowledge with **chapter-opening quizzes**
✔ Review key concepts with **Exam Preparation Tasks**
✔ Practice with **realistic exam questions** on the CD-ROM

ciscopress.com   David Hucaby, CCIE® No. 4594

FREE Online Edition

Your purchase of **CCNP SWITCH 642-813 Official Certification Guide** includes access to a free online edition for 45 days through the Safari Books Online subscription service. Nearly every Cisco Press book is available online through Safari Books Online, along with more than 5,000 other technical books and videos from publishers such as Addison-Wesley Professional, Exam Cram, IBM Press, O'Reilly, Prentice Hall, Que, and Sams.

SAFARI BOOKS ONLINE allows you to search for a specific answer, cut and paste code, download chapters, and stay current with emerging technologies.

Activate your FREE Online Edition at
www.informit.com/safarifree

> **STEP 1:** Enter the coupon code: UZYFQGA.

> **STEP 2:** New Safari users, complete the brief registration form.
> Safari subscribers, just log in.

If you have difficulty registering on Safari or accessing the online edition, please e-mail customer-service@safaribooksonline.com